D1604732

Introduction to Machine and Assembly Language Programming

PHILIP J. GUST
Hewlett-Packard Co.

PRENTICE-HALL, INC., Englewood Cliffs, New Jersey 07632

Library of Congress Cataloging in Publication Data

Gust, Philip.
Introduction to machine and assembly language programming.

Includes index.
1. Assembler language (Computer program language)
2. Electronic digital computers—Programming.
I. Title.
QA76.73.A8G88 1985 001.64′24 84-26406
ISBN 0-13-486416-6

Editorial/production supervision: *Raeia Maes*
Cover design: *Diane Saxe*
Manufacturing buyer: *Gordon Osbourne*

Prentice-Hall Software Series
Brian W. Kernighan, Advisor

Printed in the United States of America

10 9 8 7 6 5 4 3 2 1

ISBN 0-13-486416-6 01

Prentice-Hall International, Inc., *London*
Prentice-Hall of Australia Pty. Limited, *Sydney*
Editora Prentice-Hall do Brasil, Ltda., *Rio de Janeiro*
Prentice-Hall Canada Inc., *Toronto*
Prentice-Hall Hispanoamericana, S.A., *Mexico*
Prentice-Hall of India Private Limited, *New Delhi*
Prentice-Hall of Japan, Inc., *Tokyo*
Prentice-Hall of Southeast Asia Pte. Ltd., *Singapore*
Whitehall Books Limited, *Wellington, New Zealand*

Contents

3

Elementary Programming Techniques 43

4

Program Development 70

5

Arrays 85

6

Procedures 102

7

A More Complex Computer 139

Preface

This is a book about machine and assembly language programming, although it is not a "how to" book about a particular machine. Instead, the material concentrates on the more fundamental concepts that are important no matter what machine is used.

To clear the way for this kind of presentation, two relatively simple computers are used. The first has a single accumulator and a one-address instruction format. The second provides eight general-purpose registers and uses a two-address instruction format. Many computer science texts that a student is likely to encounter in later course work use similar machines to illustrate key concepts, from compilers and systems programming to analysis of algorithms.

A feature of this work is that complete assemblers and emulators for the two machines are provided so that programs for both machines can actually be assembled and run. The assemblers and emulators are "portable" versions, written in **Pascal,** and should run on most systems without modification. The programs were written in such a way that local modifications are easy to make, if necessary, to improve execution efficiency for a particular environment.

The material is divided into two halves. The one-address machine is used for the first half of the text. Covered in this first half are

Basic machine architecture, including the components of the CPU, arithmetic unit, and memory.

The nature of instructions, including the instruction cycle, address modes, and effective address computation.

The assembly process, including the use of both absolute and symbolic addresses, instruction formats, and pseudo-instructions.

Elementary programming techniques, including storage allocation, evaluation of arithmetic expressions, branching on logical conditions, and looping.

Array manipulation, including both one- and two-dimensional arrays and a discussion of both indices and pointers for array referencing.

Procedures, including the various forms of parameter passing commonly used and the trade-offs involved.

Examples are kept short, usually less than half a page. They are used to illustrate specific concepts and can easily be understood with only a few moments' effort. The use of longer examples more often than not leads the reader to skip over them rather than treat them as part of the discussion. In the few cases where a longer example is given, it is taken apart and presented in smaller pieces during the discussion. A summary of the key ideas is presented at the end of each chapter, along with numerous problems.

This first half of the book would make a good introductory text for a lower-division assembler course. It could be presented comfortably in a single quarter. It would also be a good launching point for the presentation of another machine of the instructor's choice.

The second half of the book presents a simple two-address machine. After a presentation of the architecture and instruction set, more advanced concepts are presented, including

Use of stacks, including parameter stacks, return stacks, and recursive programming.

Bit manipulation, including the use of both logical and shift operations to manipulate individual bits or fields of bits.

Floating-point numbers, including the construction of a floating-point format and algorithms to perform arithmetic with such numbers and formats.

Character manipulation, including character codes and string representation and manipulation.

Input and output programming, including simple bus architecture and the roles played by device controllers and the CPU.

Examples presented in this half of the text are a bit more complicated. They usually take the form of complete procedures that could be combined into a useful library of routines. Many of the basic procedures are used in later examples to code other procedures. In addition to a summary at the end of each chapter, problems are presented that take somewhat longer to solve. They may, for example, point up a shortcoming in an algorithm presented in the chapter and call for an improvement to be made.

Together with a briefer treatment of the first half of the book, this second half would be a good text for an assembly programming course that lasts either a single semester or three quarters.

This text is also a good starting point for several other courses in the computer science curriculum. The two machines could, for example, be used as target machines for a compiler project. Having two similar computers would provide an opportunity to study such aspects as register management and optimization techniques. A systems programming course could make significant extensions to the assembler, including macroprocessing and conditional assembly. Because of its I/O facilities, the second machine could be used as the host for a version of the one- or two-address assemblers written to run on this machine.

The material presented was developed by the author for a course on machine and assembly programming at the University of Arizona. A manuscript of this book (in various stages of completion) was used for several years as the text for the course. A special note of gratitude goes to the many students who offered their encouragement and constructive criticism during its development. Thanks also go to the Department of Computer Science, especially to Dr. Ralph Griswold, Dr. David Hanson, and Dr. Christopher Fraser for their support and advice.

The bulk of this manuscript was prepared or edited using the WORD/80 document preparation system on a Hewlett-Packard HP–87 personal computer. The package was developed by the author and Keith Taylor at the Portable Computer Division of Hewlett-Packard Co., where the author is presently a member of the technical staff.

Philip Gust

1

A Simple Computer

In this first part of the book, we will study a simple computer that is similar to many existing machines. Because more complicated features have been eliminated, we will be able to examine in some depth how the machine actually operates.

1.1 HARDWARE AND PHYSICAL CHARACTERISTICS

The first question that may come to mind is, why worry about the hardware? In most programming languages, the physical machine makes almost no difference. A program written to run on one computer will run on any other computer that supports that language, with few if any changes. That is as it should be. These languages were defined with the express purpose of hiding the details of a particular machine's design. However, at the machine level, the task of programming is accomplished by issuing commands directly to the hardware. It is no longer possible to ignore the physical machine.

Our simple computer comes in two pieces. The first is a *central processing unit (CPU)*, which actually executes the instructions. The other is a *memory unit (MU)*, from which the CPU retrieves both instructions and data. Information on its way between the CPU and the MU travels over a set of lines interconnecting the two. Figure 1-1 shows a block diagram of these components.

1.1.1 The Memory Unit (MU)

The memory provides storage for information needed by the central processor. The smallest unit of storage in the memory is a *bit*, which can be in one of two possible

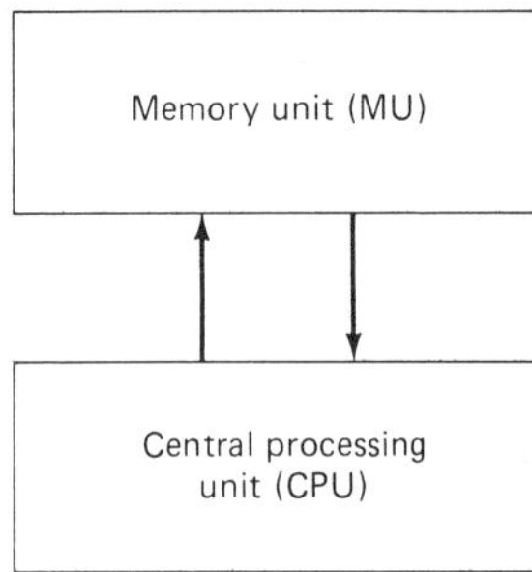

Figure 1-1 Block diagram of our simple computer

states. For notational convenience, we represent the two states by the digits 0 and 1.*

Most memory units are not built to allow access to each bit directly. Instead, the basic unit of storage is a *word.* A word is a fixed group of bits that are treated as a single unit within the machine. Each word of memory can be referenced by a unique number, called an *address.* The first location is traditionally assigned address 0, the second address 1, and so forth. In general, the *n*th location in memory is at address $(n - 1)$.

The number of bits per word is called the *word size.* The choice of a word size depends on many factors, including cost and intended application. Typical word sizes range from 8 bits to as large as 64 bits. Our machine has a word size of 16 bits. This is typical of machines that are moderate in cost and intended for small, general applications.

Figure 1-2 shows a block diagram of the MU and its components. It will be useful to refer to during the following discussion.

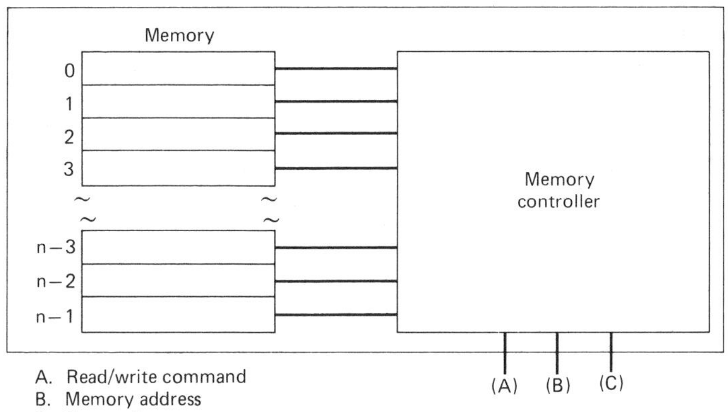

Figure 1-2 The memory unit (MU)

*In fact, *bit* comes from the words *b*inary dig*it*. In the binary, or base-2, number system, the only two numbers are 0 and 1. Appendix A offers a good review of the binary number system. It may be useful to turn back to it from time to time.

A processor within the memory unit called a *memory controller* performs the actual storage and retrieval of data. The controller has three input lines, one of which also serves as an output line. The first line signals the controller to perform one of two operations:

1. Write data into a location in memory
2. Read data from a location in memory

The second line carries the address, A, of a memory location. Together, these two lines carry the message "Read from/Write to the memory location whose address is A."

If the operation is a memory write, the controller resets the specified memory location to the value being sent in over the data line. The write operation is called *destructive* because the old contents of the memory location being written to are lost when replaced by the new value.

In the case of a memory read, the controller fetches the value stored at the location indicated and transmits it over the data line. The read operation is called *nondestructive* because the contents of the memory location being read are not changed.*

The memory unit, then, consists of a group of memory locations, each referred to by an address, and a memory controller, which manages read/write requests sent in over its input lines. The behavior of the memory unit can be summarized by Table 1-1.

TABLE 1-1 SUMMARY OF MEMORY UNIT OPERATIONS

Operation	Input	Output
Memory read	Read command, memory address	Contents of the memory address
Memory write	Write command, memory address, data to write	None

1.1.2 The Central Processing Unit (CPU)

The central processing unit (CPU) is the main part of the computer. It is responsible for executing programs and issuing commands to other components. The CPU and the other parts of the machine are in what is known as a *master-slave* relationship. For example, the MU operates only when commanded by the CPU.

*Many of the earlier memory storage devices did not have this property. To read the contents of a memory location, its content had to be destroyed! One of the purposes of a memory controller in such memory units was to "refresh" the location being read.

Our CPU contains two processors and a small number of high-speed storage locations called *registers*. The first processor is the *sequencer.* Its function is to direct the flow of instruction execution. The second processor is an *arithmetic unit*. It serves the same purpose as a calculator, performing arithmetic operations on demand from the sequencer. We will examine each of the three parts separately, then look at how they work together.

Figure 1-3 is a block diagram of the CPU that shows how the registers, arithmetic unit, and sequencer are connected.

Registers. The CPU has a small amount of memory built into it. This memory is used by the sequencer to maintain information about its own state and about the instruction currently being executed. These storage locations are constructed of special components and are called *registers*.

It takes a finite amount of time to place a value into a memory location or register and a finite amount of time to recover a value. Because the registers are built of special, high-speed components and are contained within the CPU, the *access time* of a register is a good deal less than that of a memory location. For this reason, registers are often referred to as "high-speed memory."

Our CPU has six registers. All six are under direct control of the sequencer, although executing instructions written by the programmer may alter their contents. Each register has a special purpose. Although we will discuss each later in more detail, here is a brief description of how the registers are used. It may be helpful later to glance back at this summary.

Program counter (PC): This register holds the address of a memory location where the next instruction to be executed by the sequencer can be found.

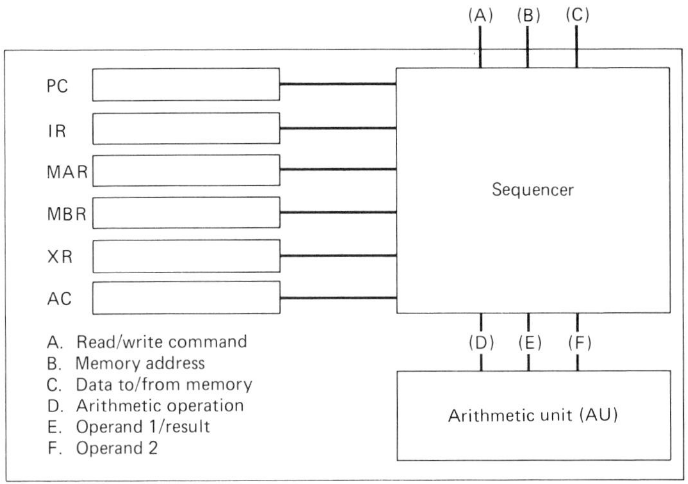

Figure 1-3 Layout of the central processing unit

Instruction register (IR): The instruction currently being executed by the sequencer was transferred from memory into this register prior to its execution.

Memory address register (MAR): If the programmer needs to read or write a memory location, the address of that location is stored in this register by the sequencer.

Memory buffer register (MBR): The contents of the memory location indicated by the MAR can be read from memory into this register during a memory read. In the case of a memory write, the sequencer places the value destined for memory here.

Index register (XR): The programmer can have the contents of this register added to the MAR before issuing a memory read or write command. This is often useful when referencing successive memory locations in some order.

Accumulator (AC): This register is used by the sequencer to hold intermediate results of calculations. All arithmetic operations take one of their operands from this register, and the result is saved here when the operation is complete. The name accumulator was chosen because if, for example, a chain of additions is done, this register accumulates the results of the calculations.

Arithmetic unit. The arithmetic unit (AU) on our machine is nothing more than a four-function calculator under control of the sequencer. It has three input lines, one of which also serves as an output line. The first input line indicates which of the four functions (addition, subtraction, multiplication, or division) is to be performed. The other two input lines carry in the operands. The result is sent out over the line that carried in the first operand. Although arithmetic units on many machines perform more than the four basic functions, this simple version is sufficient for our purpose.

Sequencer. The sequencer acts as a general manager, taking an instruction from memory and issuing commands to the other processors. Instructions in a program may require the MU to retrieve data from memory or the AU to perform arithmetic. The sequencer also does the work of fetching the next instruction and any data it may need to operate.

1.1.3 The CPU–MU Connection

The CPU and MU are connected by three lines, which transmit commands, addresses, and data between the two units. Both instructions and data flow between the CPU and MU as a program is executed. Figure 1-4 is a block diagram of the CPU and MU that shows how they are connected.

The memory address register (MAR) in the CPU is connected to the address line of the memory controller in the MU. Similarly, the memory buffer register (MBR) is connected to the data line in the MU. If the sequencer sends a write memory command on the command line, both the address in the MAR and the data in the MBR are sent at the same time, as shown in Figure 1-5.

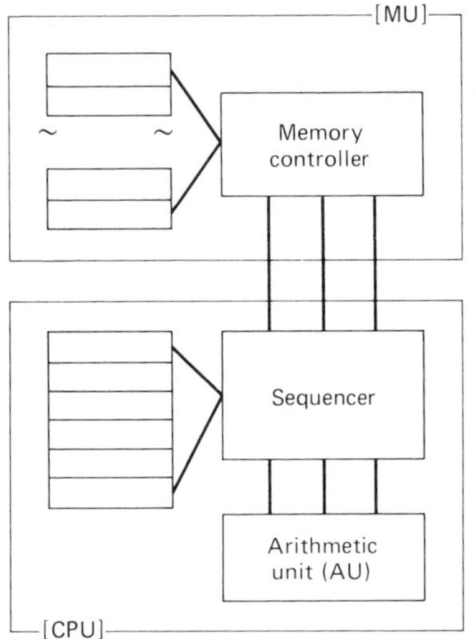

Figure 1-4 Layout of the entire computer

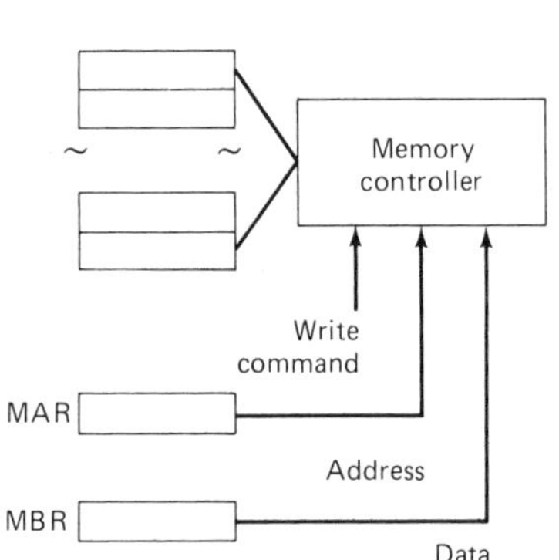

Figure 1-5 Write command and data sent to the memory controller

If the sequencer sends a read memory command on the command line, the address in the MAR is sent on the address line as shown in Figure 1-6. The memory controller on the other end responds by returning the contents of that memory location on the data line to the MBR, as shown in Figure 1-7.

If the sequencer sends a write memory command on the command line, both the address in the MAR and the data in the MBR are sent at the same time, as shown in Figure 1-5.

A special feature of the machine is worth noting at this point. Read and write commands to memory locations 0 or 1 are treated in a special way. If the address in the MAR is 0, no memory command is sent to the MU. Instead, the operation takes

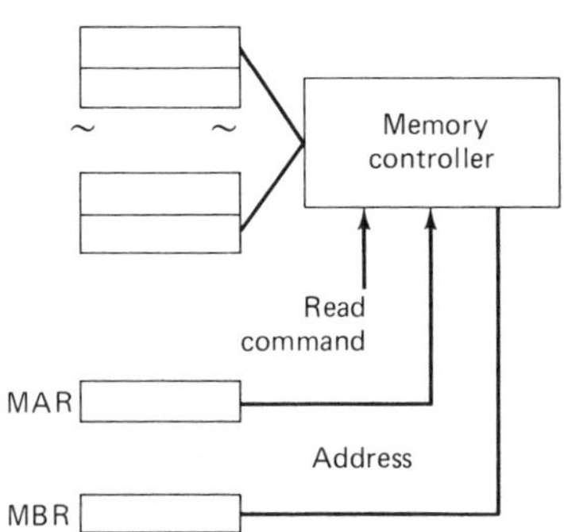

Figure 1-6 Read command sent to the memory controller

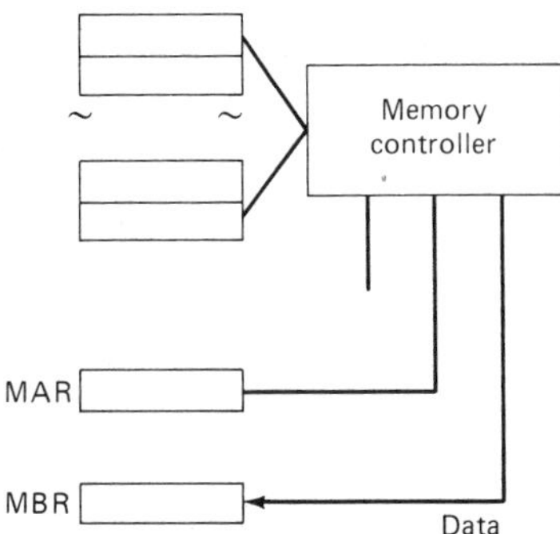

Figure 1-7 Data returned from the memory controller

place using the accumulator (AC) as though it were memory location 0. If the address in the MAR is 1, the index register (XR) is used instead of location 1 in memory.

Both the AC and the XR are referred to as *memory-mapped* registers because they can be accessed using memory read and write operations, even though they are actually registers within the CPU. Although the purpose of this arrangement is not immediately apparent, we will discover later how it can simplify programs written for our machine.

1.2 INSTRUCTIONS

Unlike the MU and AU, the sequencer does not have a separate set of input lines. Instead, it takes as its input instructions that are stored in memory. An instruction has three separate *fields*. Each field serves the same purpose as one of the lines between the CPU and the MU.

1.2.1 Instruction Fields

The three fields of an instruction tell the sequencer what operation to perform and where to find any data required. The next several sections describe how each field is used.

Operation field. The first field is known as the *operation field*. Our sequencer was designed to perform any of 12 operations. The contents of the operation field determine which operation to perform. The operations fit into three categories:

Memory operations allow a program to fetch data from memory or store data in memory for later use. Memory commands initiate memory read and write operations between the MU and the accumulator in the CPU.

Test/branch operations change the order in which the instructions of a program are executed. The sequencer "branches" to a new location in the program, depending on the result of "testing" the contents of the accumulator. This gives a programmer the opportunity to make decisions while the program is executing.

Arithmetic operations perform arithmetic between data in the accumulator and whatever data are indicated in the rest of the instruction.

Mode and address fields. The second and third fields together indicate what data to use in executing a command. The third field is called the *address field*. Normally it represents an address in memory where the actual data are stored. The second field is called the *address mode*. The address mode tells the sequencer how to interpret the number in the address field.

Sometimes it is impossible to give the address directly when writing an instruction. For example, the address to use may be computed by a previous step and stored in memory. The actual address is known only indirectly, by where it was stored. Two of the address modes allow the sequencer to use a number in memory or a register as an address.

We will return to the subject of address modes shortly. For now, here is a summary of the four address modes available on our machine. It may be helpful later to glance back at this summary.

Direct mode: Use the number in the address field as a memory address in executing the command.

Indirect mode: The number in the address field is a memory address. Stored at that location in memory is another number. Use that second number as a memory address in executing the command.

Indexed mode: Use the sum of the index register and the number in the address field as a memory address in executing the command.

The final address, arrived at by considering the mode and address fields together, is called the *effective address* because it is the one to be used in executing the instruction. The fourth address mode does not really specify an address. Instead, it signals that the number in the address field is the actual information needed by the instruction:

Immediate mode: Use the number in the address field as a constant.

In this case, the information is placed directly in the address field of the instruction that uses it, and the effective address is not defined.

1.2.2 Instruction Format

Instructions are stored as words in memory. Each word on our machine contains 16 bits. The bits must be divided into three groups, one for each of the three instruction fields. In this section, we look at the instruction format and how the bits are divided among the three fields.

To decide how many bits go to each field, we need to consider how many distinct values each field must represent. The number of values that can be encoded in a field is related to its size by a very simple formula. The number of distinct states that can be represented using a field of bits must be some power of 2. For example, if the size of the field is 2 bits, it can take on four states. If it is 3 bits wide, eight states are possible. The number of states that can be represented by n bits is just 2 raised to the nth power.

The minimum number of bits needed for a given field is easily calculated using logarithms. Recall that for any number n, if

$$N = 2^n$$

then given N, we can determine n by taking the base-2 logarithm of N.* That is,

$$\log_2 N = n$$

If the field can take on any of N possible values, the number of bits needed is the smallest integer greater than or equal to the base-2 logarithm of N. The "smallest integer greater than or equal to" some number x is known as the *ceiling* of x. For example, the ceiling of 5.2 is 6, whereas the ceiling of 5.0 is 5.

There are 12 sequencer commands, so the operation field must be at least

$$\begin{aligned} &\text{ceiling}(\log_2 12) \\ &= \text{ceiling}(3.58496) \\ &= 4 \end{aligned}$$

bits wide. Four bits is sufficient to represent up to 16 values, although we are using only 12 of them.

The number of bits for the address mode field is easy to calculate. There are four address modes, which require

$$\begin{aligned} &\text{ceiling}(\log_2 4) \\ &= \text{ceiling}(2.0) \\ &= 2 \end{aligned}$$

bits to represent.

So far, the operation and address mode fields have taken up 6 of the 16 bits in a memory word. This leaves 10 bits to represent the address field. Ten bits is sufficient to represent up to

$$\begin{aligned} &2^{10} \\ &= 1{,}024_{10} \end{aligned}$$

words. Existing machines have address fields of between 8 and 32 bits, with 16 as an average. Although our machine can address only 1,024 words directly, this amount of memory will be sufficient for our purposes. There are several methods used on similar machines to get around this limitation.

Figure 1-8 shows how the three fields of an instruction fit into a 16-bit memory word. This arrangement of fields is typical of those found on similar machines.

Bit positions in the word are designated by the corresponding power of 2. For example, bit 0, the least significant bit position, corresponds to the 0th power of 2, the 1's place.

*For readers with calculators or slide rules,

$$\log_2 N = \frac{\log_{10} N}{\log_{10} 2}$$

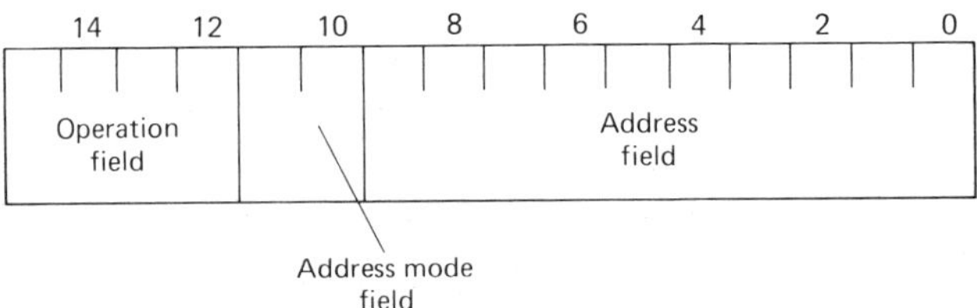

Figure 1-8 The instruction format

1.2.3 Symbolic Notation

Before looking at the instruction set, it is worth mentioning that no matter how the instruction set is encoded, it will be a very tedious job to write programs. Instructions must be presented to the machine in terms of bits. Programmers, however, prefer to think at a more conceptual level.

Early programmers solved this problem by developing their own notations to represent the fields. Programs were written using these notations, then translated by hand into the corresponding bit fields. As commercial production increased, the manufacturer's notations eventually became more or less standardized for a given machine. The advent of "assemblers," which automatically translate the symbolic notation into internal binary form, firmly established symbolic notations as the method of choice in writing machine-level programs. The subject of assemblers and their development is discussed in the next chapter.

Instructions are shown in their symbolic form throughout most of the text. Keep in mind, however, that the symbolic form is only a convenient shorthand and must be translated into bits before being entered into the machine.

1.2.4 The Instruction Set

Table 1-2 lists both operations and address modes in both internal and symbolic forms.

The instruction set nicely divides into the three groups discussed earlier. The memory group contains two instructions. LOAD moves data from memory into the CPU. STORE moves data from the CPU back into memory. Instructions in the arithmetic group correspond to the four functions built into the arithmetic unit. The test/branch group contains an unconditional branch and three conditional branches. Together, these are sufficient to perform *all six* possible conditional branches. There is also an instruction, CALL, for branching to the machine-level equivalent of a procedure. The HALT instruction causes the machine to stop executing instructions. It is executed as the last step in a program.

Most instructions are written using the direct mode of addressing. Letting the *absence* of an address mode symbol represent direct mode is a reasonable choice.

TABLE 1-2 COMMAND AND ADDRESS MODE CODES AND MNEMONICS

Operation Field (Commands)		
Code	Mnemonic	Meaning
0000	HALT	halt execution
0001	LOAD	load from memory
0010	STORE	store to memory
0011	CALL	branch to procedure
0100	BR	unconditional branch
0101	BREQ	branch if ac $=$ 0
0110	BRGE	branch if ac $\geq$ 0
0111	BRLT	branch if ac $<$ 0
1000	ADD	integer addition
1001	SUB	integer subtraction
1010	MUL	integer multiplication
1011	DIV	integer division

Address Mode Field		
Code	Mnemonic	Meaning
00	*(none)*	direct mode
01	=	immediate mode
10	$	indexed mode
11	@	indirect mode

1.2.5 Comparison of Binary and Symbolic Forms

There is an exact correspondence between fields in the binary form and "fields" in the symbolic form. This makes it especially easy to translate between the mnemonics and their binary encoding. In using the symbolic form, it is customary to offset the operation field by a space for ease of viewing. All three fields in the binary representation are separated by spaces as well.

Unless otherwise noted, we will interpret the value in the address field as a *decimal* number. However, certain kinds of values are clearer if not expressed in base 10. A convenient shorthand for binary is the base 8 or octal number system.*

If we want the number to be interpreted as an octal number, we will follow it with a *B*, which looks enough like an 8 to remind us without being taken for a digit itself. This is a useful feature, since addresses are often expressed in octal form and constants in decimal form.

*Appendix A offers a short review of octal numbers and how to convert between base 2 and base 8.

The following examples should help to point out the similarities. The mnemonic form is shown directly below the corresponding internal binary representation. In the second example, no explicit address mode is shown in the mnemonic form, indicating the direct mode.

```
1000   01       0000010111
   ADD          =23

0001   00       0000001101
   LOAD          15B

0110   10       0011101000
   BRGE         $1350B

0010   11       0100111111
   STORE        @477B
```

As we write larger and larger programs using mnemonic instructions, we will find that even these can become confusing. While the function of an individual instruction may be clear, its purpose in the overall solution of the problem is easily forgotten. A good practice is to make a note to the side of an instruction about its *logical* purpose in the program. An example of a useful comment might be

```
ADD   =1    add 1 to #days in Feb. if a leap year
```

Here is an example of a useless comment:

```
ADD   =1    add 1 to the accumulator
```

The first example describes what role this instruction plays in the solution. The second example only states the obvious and gives no additional information.

Comments are shown in lowercase throughout the text. Mnemonic instructions are printed in uppercase. When writing them out longhand, it is convenient to use block letters for mnemonics and script letters for the comments.

1.3 OUR SIMPLE COMPUTER IN OPERATION

In the two preceding sections, we studied the design of our simple computer. In this section, we will take a look at the machine in operation.

We saw earlier that our machine can perform any of 12 operations. To perform an operation, the sequencer may have to read information from memory, move data from one register to another, and perhaps even perform some arithmetic. The sequencer carries out an instruction by breaking it down into a number of smaller steps.

Many of the steps are the same, no matter what the operation. Other steps are unique to a particular operation.

1.3.1 Register Transfer Expressions

A simple notation called a *register transfer expression* describes the individual steps performed within the computer while carrying out an instruction. This notation is very concise and makes the machine's operation easier to understand. We will use it often in the course of our discussion. Although we will make no formal definitions, several examples should be sufficient to give the general idea.

Register-to-register transfer: If we want to copy the contents of the MBR into the AC, we denote it by the expression

```
AC ← MBR
```

The arrow shows the direction of transfer.

Register-to-register arithmetic: To indicate the addition of the two registers, we write

```
AC ← AC + MBR
```

Register-to-memory transfer: Writing the contents of the MBR to the memory location whose address is in the MAR is denoted by

```
M[ MAR ] ← MBR
```

Memory-to-register transfer: Reading a word from memory into the MBR uses the contents of the MAR for the address. This is written as

```
MBR ← M[ MAR ]
```

Bit fields within words: A specific field of bits within a word can be indicated by placing the bit range within angle brackets to the right of the word. The leftmost (upper) 4 bits of the IR are referenced by

```
IR<15:12>
```

Since this field is well known to represent the operation code of an instruction, we could also specify it by writing

```
IR<operation field>
```

TABLE 1-3 OPERATIONS PERFORMED BY THE SEQUENCER

Sequencer/Memory Controller			
MBR	⟵	M[MAR]	memory read
M[MAR]	⟵	MBR	memory write
Sequencer			
MAR	⟵	MBR⟨address field⟩	for indirect addressing
MBR	⟵	MAR	for immediate addressing
IR	⟵	MBR	used to fetch instruction
AC	⟵	MBR	for LOAD instruction
MBR	⟵	AC	for STORE instruction
MAR	⟵	IR⟨address field⟩	first step in effective address calculation
MBR	⟵	PC	for CALL instruction
MAR	⟵	PC	used to fetch instruction
PC	⟵	MAR	for BR instructions
(AC = 0)	=>	PC ⟵ MAR	for BREQ instruction
(AC ≥ 0)	=>	PC ⟵ MAR	for BRGE instruction
(AC < 0)	=>	PC ⟵ MAR	for BRLT instruction
Sequencer/Arithmetic Unit			
AC	⟵	AC + MBR	for ADD instruction
AC	⟵	AC − MBR	for SUB instruction
AC	⟵	AC * MBR	for MUL instruction
AC	⟵	AC / MBR	for DIV instruction
MAR	⟵	MAR + XR	for indexed addressing
PC	⟵	PC + 1	for referencing next instruction to execute

Of course, if no field is given, the entire word is assumed. Thus, "IR" is equivalent to "IR⟨15:0⟩" on our 16-bit machine.

Table 1-3 shows the operations that are built into the sequencer.

1.3.2 The Instruction Cycle

There are a number of extra steps that the sequencer must perform to execute an instruction. Included is the overhead of bringing the instruction from memory into the instruction register (IR) and computing the effective address based on the address and address mode fields. Since this extra overhead is the same for all instructions, the sequencer has a routine built into it that performs these extra steps automatically. This fixed set of steps carried out by the sequencer is called the *instruction cycle*. The instruction cycle is repeated for each instruction executed.

The instruction cycle consists of four steps. Only the last one is concerned with executing a particular command:

1. Read the next instruction into the IR.
2. Perform effective addressing.
3. Update the PC.
4. Perform the operation.

As an example, we will follow the execution of the instruction

```
LOAD  170B
```

The instruction is represented internally by the following bit pattern:

```
0001   00   0001111000
```

and can be characterized by its register transfer expression:

```
AC ← M[ 170B ]
```

Assume that the instruction is stored in memory location 605B and that the number 1 is stored in memory location 170B. We start off with the address 605B in the PC. How it got there, at this point, is not important.

Read the next instruction. The first thing to do is bring the instruction into the IR. The address of the instruction is copied from the PC into the MAR. This operation is denoted by

```
MAR ← PC
```

The read request to the MU brings the instruction into the MBR:

```
MBR ← M[ MAR ]
```

Since the address, 605B, was copied from the PC to the MAR, the expression can be rewritten as

```
MBR ← M[ 605B ]
```

Once in the MBR, the instruction is copied into the IR for use by the sequencer:

```
IR ← MBR
```

The IR now contains the instruction "LOAD 170B" in the form of the word

```
0001   00   0001111000
```

Here are the contents of our registers so far:

```
PC    =  605B
IR    =  "LOAD 170B"

MAR   =  605B
MBR   =  "LOAD 170B"

AC    =  ?
```

The content of the AC is unknown at this point.

Perform effective addressing. The next step is to put the effective address into the MAR. Because the address mode is *direct*, the effective address is just that number stored in the address field. This operation is denoted by

```
MAR  ←—  IR <address field>
```

The address field contains the address 170B, so this expression is equivalent to

```
MAR  ←—  170B
```

Update the program counter. Now we update the PC. Unless the instruction in the IR is one of the branches, the next instruction executed will be taken from the memory location following the one where this instruction was stored. Updating the PC involves nothing more than adding 1 to it:

```
PC  ←—  PC + 1
```

The PC held the address 605B, so this step has the effect of

```
PC  ←—  606B
```

The next pass through the instruction cycle will begin with the PC set to this address.

We pause again to review the contents of our registers:

```
PC    =  606B
IR    =  "LOAD 170B"

MAR   =  170B
MBR   =  "LOAD 170B"

AC    =  ?
```

The content of MBR has not changed since the last time, and the content of the AC is still unknown.

Execute the command. Remember that our goal is to bring the contents of M[170B] into the AC. Since the MAR now contains the address 170B, we can use the contents of the MAR to read memory. The operation

```
MBR ⟵ M[ MAR ]
```

brings the contents of M[170B] into the MBR from memory. That is,

```
MBR ⟵ M[ 170B ]
```

The only thing left to do is copy the contents of the MBR into the AC:

```
AC ⟵ MBR
```

This completes the job by causing the data transfer

```
AC ⟵ 1
```

Here are the registers at the end of the instruction cycle:

```
PC   =  606B
IR   =  "LOAD 170B"

MAR  =  170B
MBR  =  1

AC   =  1
```

Review of the instruction cycle. To review, the operations performed by the sequencer were:

```
MAR ⟵ PC                      instruction address to MAR
MBR ⟵ M[ MAR ]                fetch instruction
IR  ⟵ MBR                     instruction to IR
MAR ⟵ IR<address field>       effective address to MAR
PC  ⟵ PC + 1                  update PC

MBR ⟵ M[ MAR ]                data to MBR
AC  ⟵ MBR                     ... copied to AC
```

Most of the work done by the sequencer to execute "LOAD 170B" would be the same for *any* instruction. Only the last two steps are the result of performing the LOAD operation as the fourth step of the instruction cycle.

At the outset, we mentioned that the effect of executing the instruction

```
LOAD    170B
```

could be characterized by the expression

```
AC  ←—  M[ 170B ]
```

The net effect of an instruction is derived by looking at the instruction cycle. The steps involved with pure overhead are not considered. Those directly involved with the operation itself are reduced to a single register transfer expression that summarizes the instruction. Since the effective address 170B was placed in the MAR before performing the operation, the two steps associated with the LOAD command are written as

```
MBR  ←—  M[ 170B ]

AC   ←—  MBR
```

The two expressions can be simplified by replacing "MBR" in the second with the description of its contents from the first. The result is a single expression that describes this LOAD instruction:

```
AC  ←—  M[ 170B ]
```

1.3.3 Effective Address Calculation

The example of "LOAD 170B" illustrates the *direct* mode of addressing. That is, the address shown in the address field is the address actually used in executing the instruction. The other three addressing modes are handled in a similar way. The next few sections show how the effective address is computed for each of the four address modes.

Direct addressing. Only one step is needed for direct addressing. The address field of the instruction is simply copied into the MAR:

Direct mode of addressing

```
MAR  ←—  IR<address field>
```

Immediate addressing. With the immediate address mode, the number in the address portion of the instruction represents the actual data used by the instruction. For example, the instruction

```
LOAD =170B
```

brings the number 170B into the AC. The extra step performed for immediate mode is transferring the contents of the MAR into the MBR, where it will be available for use by the instruction. The two steps for immediate address mode are:

Immediate mode of addressing

```
MAR ⟵ IR<address field>
MBR ⟵ MAR
```

Indexed addressing. The effective address for indexed address mode is the sum of the index register (XR) and the number in the address field of the instruction. We will use this address mode later in working with arrays. After transferring the address portion of the instruction from the IR to the MAR, the number in XR is added to the MAR. The step

```
MAR ⟵ MAR + XR
```

has the effect of "indexing" the contents of the address field by the contents of the XR. The steps for indexed address mode are:

Indexed mode of addressing

```
MAR ⟵ IR<address field>
MAR ⟵ MAR + XR
```

Indirect addressing. With indirect addressing, the sequencer treats the number in the address field as a memory address. Stored at that location in memory is the effective address to use with the instruction. Some thought will show that the steps needed to bring the effective address into the MAR are:

Indirect mode of addressing

```
MAR ⟵ IR<address field>
MBR ⟵ M[ MAR ]
MAR ⟵ MBR<address field>
```

Summary of address modes. Table 1-4 is a summary of the steps carried out by the sequencer in performing the effective address calculation. This table will be useful while learning what the address modes do.

TABLE 1-4 SUMMARY OF ADDRESS MODES

Direct mode of addressing		
MAR	⟵	IR⟨address field⟩
Immediate mode of addressing		
MAR	⟵	IR⟨address field⟩
MBR	⟵	MAR
Indexed mode of addressing		
MAR	⟵	IR⟨address field⟩
MAR	⟵	MAR + XR
Indirect mode of addressing		
MAR	⟵	IR⟨address field⟩
MBR	⟵	M[MAR]
MAR	⟵	MBR⟨address field⟩

1.3.4 Instruction Operations

At this stage in the instruction cycle, the registers are in one of two states. Either the effective address is in the MAR (for direct, indexed, or indirect mode), or the data themselves are already in the MBR (for immediate mode). With any of the instructions that transfer data from memory, the first case requires a memory read operation. The second case requires no action at all, because the data to use are already in the MBR.

The only steps specific to the LOAD instruction are

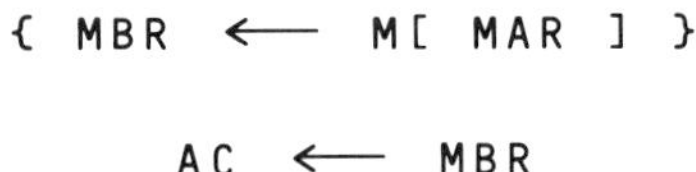

```
{ MBR ⟵ M[ MAR ] }

      AC ⟵ MBR
```

The brackets around the first of the two steps indicate that it should not be performed if the address mode of the instruction is immediate.

Table 1-5 shows the steps performed for each of the 12 operations.

1.4 PERSPECTIVE

The machine presented in this chapter is typical of many simple computers that can be found in laboratory and industrial use. Most have a limited amount of memory and a CPU with only a few registers available to the programmer.

One of the most successful and enduring commercial computers of this type was the PDP-8. Introduced by Digital Equipment Corporation in 1965, the PDP-8 was one of the early *minicomputers*. It was compact enough to set on a cart or benchtop and inexpensive enough to be found in many laboratory and industrial settings.

TABLE 1-5 STEPS PERFORMED IN EXECUTING AN INSTRUCTION

Instruction	Steps
LOAD	{ MBR ⟵ M[MAR] } AC ⟵ MBR
ADD	{ MBR ⟵ M[MAR] } AC ⟵ AC + MBR
SUB	{ MBR ⟵ M[MAR] } AC ⟵ AC − MBR
MUL	{ MBR ⟵ M[MAR] } AC ⟵ AC * MBR
DIV	{ MBR ⟵ M[MAR] } AC ⟵ AC / MBR
STORE	MBR ⟵ AC M[MAR] ⟵ MBR
BR	PC ⟵ MAR
BREQ	(AC = 0) => PC ⟵ MAR
BRGE	(AC ≥ = 0) => PC ⟵ MAR
BRLT	(AC < 0) => PC ⟵ MAR
CALL	MBR ⟵ PC M[MAR] ⟵ MBR PC ⟵ MAR PC ⟵ PC + 1

The PDP-8 had a 12-bit word. The CPU included a program counter, a memory address register, a memory data register, and an accumulator. Three bits were reserved in an instruction for the operation field, 2 bits for the address mode, and 7 bits for the address field. Using a combination of address modes, up to 4,096 words were addressable by an instruction. A curious feature was the lack of a LOAD instruction. Instead, the STORE instruction zeroed the accumulator, and the ADD instruction was used both to add and to load.

Another minicomputer of this type was the HP-2100 series, first introduced in 1967 by Hewlett-Packard Company. This machine had a 16-bit word. In addition to the usual internal registers, the HP-2100 provided two general-purpose registers, labeled *A* and *B*. Each register had its own set of operations, which were not always duplicated for both. The two registers could be used separately or could be combined for certain operations to produce a 32-bit result. As with our machine, the *A* and *B* registers were also accessible via memory references to locations 0 and 1, respectively.

Four bits of the 16-bit instruction were reserved for the operation, 2 more bits specified the address mode, and the remaining 10 bits were used for the address. The HP-2100 was able to address up to 32,767 words of memory.

More recently, *microprocessors* are commonly found in laboratory instruments and home appliances, often replacing more expensive special-purpose components. These processors are very small and inexpensive. Although a relatively recent development, their size and low cost will make them even more ubiquitous in the future.

One of the most popular microprocessors of the recent past was the Intel 8080. The 8080 used a smaller, 8-bit word size. An instruction required one to three 8-bit words of storage in memory. The first word held the operation field. After reading this word, the sequencer could determine how many more words to fetch. Certain operations took no additional words. Operations with a literal or constant operand occupied one more word. An operation that required an address used the following two words to specify a 16-bit address. The sequencer had to add the correct number to the PC, depending on the length of the instruction. The 8080 had an accumulator and several other registers that could be used individually or combined by certain operations to produce 16-bit results.

1.5 SUMMARY

This chapter introduced a simple computer. Starting with the most elementary level, we looked at the machine in progressively more detail, beginning with the central processing unit (CPU) and the memory unit (MU). As we saw, the MU contains not only storage but also a processor called a memory controller. The memory controller is responsible for responding to commands sent to it over the three lines that connect to the MU.

The CPU also contains a small amount of memory in the form of registers. The registers are used by the CPU to maintain state information while executing an instruction. The memory address register (MAR) and memory buffer register (MBR) are connected to the address and data lines leading to memory. The address in the MAR is used for all memory read and write operations. The MBR is read from or written to as data are transferred between the CPU and the MU. Two other registers, the accumulator (AC) and the index register (XR), are memory-mapped. Although they are part of the CPU, they can also be referred to as though they were the first two locations in memory.

The processor in the CPU is called the sequencer. The sequencer is responsible for executing instructions that are stored in memory. It does this by going through a fixed set of operations called the instruction cycle.

During the instruction cycle, the next instruction is fetched from memory into the instruction register (IR). Next, the effective address of the operand is computed and placed in the MAR. Then, the program counter (PC) register is updated to address the next instruction in memory. Finally, the instruction in the IR is executed, using the effective address in the MAR and any data in the AC and MBR. These four steps are repeated for each instruction in the program.

We followed the execution of a single instruction through this cycle and looked at how these internal operations are combined by the sequencer. Register transfer expressions were introduced as a convenient way to describe the internal operation of the machine. They are also useful for describing the net effect of an instruction.

The machine presented in this chapter is typical of many simple computers that can be found in both laboratory and industrial use. Most have a limited amount of memory and a CPU with a few registers available to the programmer. In the final section, we looked briefly at several commercially available machines. Included were two early minicomputers, the PDP-8 and the HP-2100. We concluded with a discussion of a more recent development, the microprocessor. One of the first microprocessors, the Intel 8080, was used as an example.

This chapter is only an introduction to the organization or architecture of our simple machine. We still do not know how instructions are entered into memory. Even more important, we have not yet considered the principles of programming at the machine level. The rest of the chapters devoted to this machine explore these two topics in more detail.

PROBLEMS

1-1. Name the two main components of our simple machine.

1-2. What is the smallest unit of storage in memory? Are memories usually built to allow direct access to this unit of storage?

1-3. How are words in memory "labeled"? What is the "label" of the *first* word of memory?

1-4. What three pieces of information are sent to the memory controller over its lines when writing a value into a word of memory?

1-5. What two pieces of information are sent to the memory controller over its lines when reading a value from a word of memory? What does the memory controller send back?

1-6. Why is reading *from* a word of memory called *nondestructive*? Is writing *to* a word of memory destructive or nondestructive? Why?

1-7. Why are the CPU and MU said to be in a *master-slave* relationship?

1-8. Name the components of the CPU.

1-9. How do registers differ from words of storage in memory?

1-10. What three things would be sent to the arithmetic unit to cause it to add the numbers 44 and 36? Over which of the three lines would the result be returned?

1-11. In what way does the sequencer act as the "manager" of the computer?

1-12. To which registers are the address and data lines leading to the MU connected?

1-13. What is meant by a *memory-mapped* register? Which registers in the CPU are memory-mapped? To which memory address is each mapped?

1-14. The sequencer has no control lines. How is it commanded?

1-15. What is meant in saying that the sequencer has three "conceptual input lines"?

1-16. Describe the similarities between a sequencer instruction and an "instruction" to either the AU or the MU.

1-17. Explain what information a complete "instruction" to the AU would contain.

1-18. What three types of operations can be performed by instructions to the sequencer? Which kind would be used to fetch a number from memory? Which kind would be used to add two numbers?

1-19. What is the difference between the address in the address field of an instruction and the *effective address*? In which address mode are they the same? In which address mode is the effective address undefined (not meaningful)?

1-20. What is the derivation of the word *bit*?

1-21. When examining the contents of memory, it is impossible in most cases to tell the difference between instructions and ordinary numbers. Explain why this is so.

1-22. How many *distinct values* can be stored in a field of (a) 1 bit? (b) 2 bits? (c) 5 bits? (d) 10 bits? (e) 16 bits?

1-23. What is the *biggest number* that could be stored in a field of (a) 1 bit? (b) 2 bits? (c) 5 bits? (d) 10 bits? (e) 16 bits?

1-24. At least how many bits would it take to represent the number (a) 1? (b) 2? (c) 5? (d) 75? (e) 511?

1-25. How many bits wide must the operation field of an instruction be to represent 12 instructions? How many more could be represented in the same number of bits?

1-26. How many bits wide must the address mode field of an instruction be to represent four address modes? How many more could be represented in the same number of bits?

1-27. How many bits wide is a word in the memory of our machine?

1-28. Given that an instruction must fit into a single word of memory, at most how many bits can we make the address field of an instruction?

1-29. What is the maximum number of memory locations that we can address directly with an instruction? What is the address of the highest location in memory that can be directly addressed in this way?

1-30. If we wanted to perform the following operations, which instructions would we use to do it? Show only the mnemonic operation (e.g., DIV).

(a) Read a number from memory.
(b) Add that number to another number.
(c) Write the result back to memory.
(d) Execute some other sequence of instructions if the sum was exactly 0.
(e) Stop the machine.

1-31. Here are instructions written in internal binary form. Rewrite them using the mnemonics discussed in this chapter.

(a) 1010 01 0000100110
(b) 0110 00 1100100111
(c) 0010 10 0000000000
(d) 0101 11 0001010011
(e) 0000 00 0000000000

1-32. Here are instructions written in mnemonic form. Rewrite them in their internal binary form.

```
(a) LOAD  $100B
(b) DIV   =9
(c) BR    @14B
(d) HALT
(e) BRGE  1277B
```

1-33. What is wrong with annotating an instruction in the following way?

```
BREQ  500B      if AC is zero, branch to 500B
```

1-34. Write a single register transfer expression for each of the following. Place a star beside those that can be performed directly by the sequencer.

(a) moving data from the AC to the MBR
(b) fetching the contents of the memory location whose address is the sum of the value in the XR and the value in the MAR
(c) placing the number 5 in memory location 46B
(d) copying the MAR into the PC if the value in the AC is nonnegative
(e) copying into the MAR the address field of the IR

1-35. What is in the accumulator after performing the operations indicated by the following register transfer expressions? Assume that memory locations 1 through 5 contain these values at the beginning of each:

```
M[1]: -1
M[2]:  7
M[3]:  5
M[4]:  3
M[5]:  4
```

(*Hint:* What is special about M[0] and M[1]?)

(a) AC ⟵ M[5]
(b) AC ⟵ M[M[4]]
(c) AC ⟵ M[3]
AC ⟵ AC * M[3]
(d) AC ⟵ M[XR + 3]
(e) AC ⟵ M[M[5]]
AC ⟵ AC + M[0]

1-36. Name the four steps performed by the sequencer in executing the instruction cycle.

1-37. Assume that the PC contains the address 350B. Show the register transfer expressions *actually performed* by the sequencer in executing the following instructions:

(a) LOAD 50B
(b) SUB $3
(c) BR 147B
(d) STORE @37B
(e) MUL =14

1-38. Show the contents of all of the registers after executing the following sequence of instructions. Assume that the PC is initially set to the address 345B.

```
345B:  0001000011101001
346B:  0010000000000001
347B:  0001100000000011
350B:  0000000000000000
351B:  0000000011100101
```

1-39. Write a short program, starting at memory location 100B, that counts down from 20 to 0, then stops.

1-40. Write a short program, starting at memory location 100B, that computes the sum of the first N integers, then stops. This sum is given by the formula

$$(N + 1)*N/2$$

Assume that the value of N is stored in M[77B].

1-41. Write a short program, starting at memory location 100B, that tests the value in the accumulator. If the value is negative, the program replaces it by 0. Otherwise, the value is unchanged. The program then stops.

1-42. Write a short program, starting at memory location 100B, that brings into the accumulator the *negative* of the value stored in memory location 50B, then stops. If, for example, M[50B] contained -1, it would leave a $+1$ in the AC. If M[50B] contained a $+1$, it would leave a -1 in the AC. Do not use the MUL instruction.

2

Running a Program

Chapter 1 described the physical components of our computer and how they work together. In this chapter, we will learn how to enter a program into memory and run it. This chapter also describes a program called an *assembler*, which automatically translates mnemonic instructions and data into binary form, suitable for direct execution. An assembler/emulator provided with this text allows programs written for the machine to be assembled and run on most other computers.

2.1 GETTING INSTRUCTIONS INTO THE MEMORY

Before we can run a program on our computer, we must store the instructions and data in its memory. Computers like the one described here come with a very simple input/output device, which is mounted on the front panel of the machine. It is called a *front panel display*. Figure 2-1 shows the front panel on our machine.

Along the top of the panel is a row of 16 illuminated push-button switches. The switches are placed on the panel in groups of three, from right to left. Switch 15 stands alone. This row of lights is called the *switch register*.

Below these switches and in the center is a rotary switch with six positions. Each position is labeled with the name of one of the six registers. The switch register displays the contents of whichever register is indicated by the rotary switch.

Modifying the switch register also modifies the contents of that register. For example, if bit 6 is lit, indicating a 1 in that bit position, and that bit should be a 0, pushing the corresponding button will turn bit 6 off. If bit 12 is off when it should be on, pushing the button for bit 12 will put a 1 in the corresponding position.

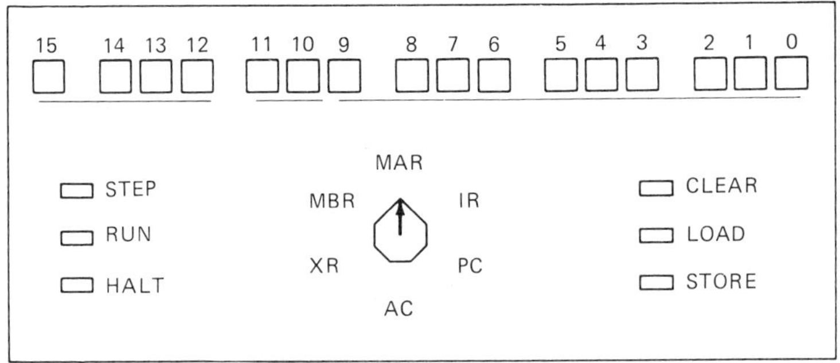

Figure 2-1 The front panel of our simple machine

The set of three push buttons to the right of the rotary switch provides a way to transfer data between the CPU and the MU. The button marked CLEAR sets all of the bits in the switch register (and the selected register) to 0. The button marked LOAD causes the sequencer to perform the operations

```
MBR ← M[ MAR ]
MAR ← MAR + 1
```

The contents of whatever memory address is in the MAR will be transferred into the MBR. The STORE button causes the sequencer to perform the operations

```
M[ MAR ] ← MBR
MAR ← MAR + 1
```

Incrementing the MAR after loading or storing is especially handy when entering programs into memory because programs are usually entered into consecutively increasing memory locations.

To illustrate how a program is stored into memory, we will store the instruction

```
SUB    =570B
```

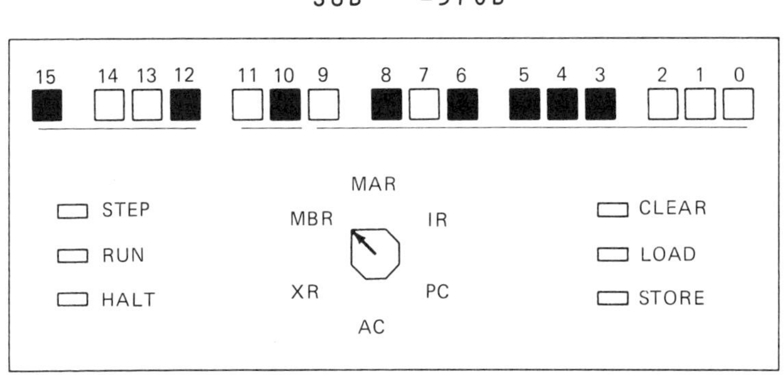

Figure 2-2 Instruction placed into the MBR

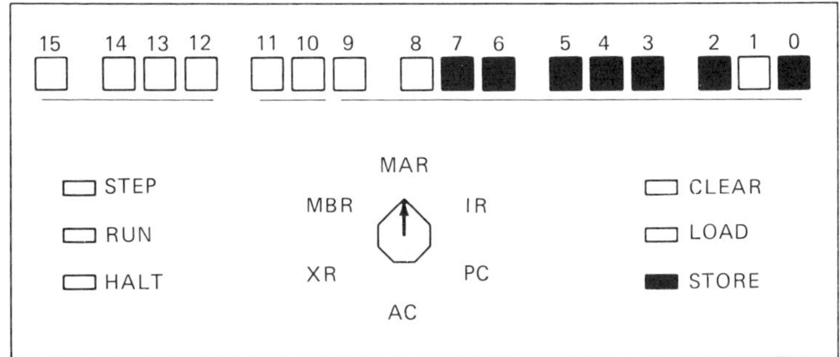

Figure 2-3 Instruction stored at the address placed in the MAR

at memory location 375B. The numbers used for this example are given in octal to avoid the complication of converting from decimal. The instruction is represented internally by the bit pattern

1001 01 0101111000

First we turn the rotary switch to select the MBR and set the lights of the switch register to the bit pattern for the instruction (Figure 2-2). The MBR is now set to the value shown in the switch register. Depending on what was previously in the MBR, it might be faster to press the CLEAR button first, then turn on the required bits.

Next, we select the MAR and set the switch register to the address 375B (Figure 2-3).

With the instruction "SUB =570B" in the MBR and the address 375B in the MAR, we can store the instruction in memory by pressing the button marked STORE. Memory location 375B now contains the instruction "SUB =570B", and the MAR is incremented to 376B.

Reviewing instructions already in memory is just as easy. For example, we can quickly verify the fact that the instruction "LOAD 201B" is at memory location 765B. Select the MAR, set the switch register to the address 765B, and press the button marked LOAD (Figure 2-4). Next, switch over to the MBR. It has been set to the

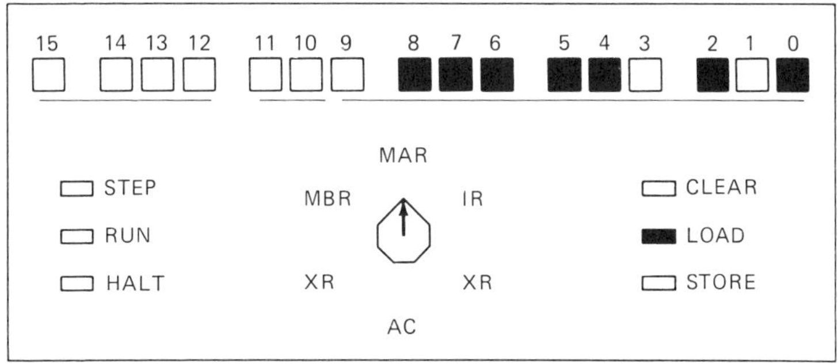

Figure 2-4 Instruction loaded from the address placed in the MAR

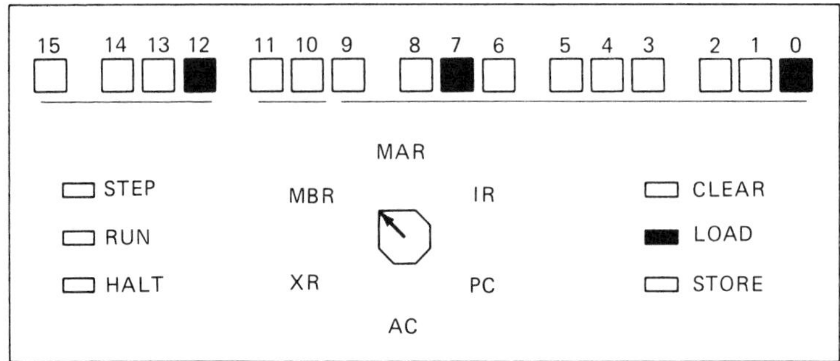

Figure 2-5 View of instruction just loaded into the MBR

contents of memory location 375B. As shown in Figure 2-5, this is the binary representation of "LOAD 201B". The LOAD button also increments the MAR. This is convenient for reviewing entire programs. Switching back to the MAR shows that it has been incremented to 766B.

With this basic tool, we are able to examine and modify any of the registers or memory locations. Data, as well as instructions, can be entered into the memory by selecting the appropriate register and using the STORE button on the front panel display.

2.2 EXECUTING INSTRUCTIONS FROM THE FRONT PANEL

Three illuminated buttons to the left of the rotary switch allow instructions in memory to be executed via the normal instruction cycle of the sequencer. There are two modes of execution. In the first, the entire program is run from beginning to end. The other automatically halts after executing each instruction. This mode is useful in debugging a program.

2.2.1 Run Mode Execution

Programs are normally executed in *run mode*. First we enter the program and data into memory and set the PC to the address of the first instruction to be executed. When we push the RUN button, program execution begins. The sequencer stops processing only after executing a HALT instruction. There is no opportunity to examine the contents of memory or the registers during execution in run mode.

If the program fails to halt after an unreasonably long period of time, there is no alternative but to stop it forcibly by pressing the button labeled HALT on the front panel. The sequencer will halt *after* fetching the next instruction but *before* computing its effective address. This is just after step 1 but just before step 2 of the instruction cycle.

When the sequencer executes the HALT instruction, the RUN light goes out and the HALT light comes on to indicate the end of execution. There is no opportunity to bring the next instruction into the IR, because the HALT instruction physically stops the sequencer. Of course, the PC has already been incremented to the address beyond the one from which the HALT instruction was read.

2.2.2 Single-Step Mode Execution

If there is an error in a program, *single-step mode* can help to find it. One instruction is executed each time the STEP button is pressed. After the instruction executes, the contents of registers and memory can be examined to find the nature and location of the problem. Often, simply observing the program counter is sufficient to show where the problem lies.

The cycle begins by bringing the current instruction into the IR and ends after going completely through the cycle and bringing the next instruction into the IR. This means that some extra work is done in fetching the same instruction twice, but it allows us to examine the next instruction before it is actually executed.

Single-step mode can be used together with run mode to help debug a program. We could HALT an errant program executing under run mode and begin single-stepping through it without having to update any of the registers. It is also easy to go from single-step to run mode because run mode ignores the fact that the next instruction is already in the IR and begins at step 1 of the instruction cycle. Since the PC has not yet been updated, performing step 1 of the cycle once again certainly does no harm.

Single-step mode is a useful debugging aid for operators who have direct access to the front panel display of their computer. On large-scale machines with many users, this technique is seldom permitted to any but the systems programmers. Instead, many computing systems include a debugging package that provides the same facilities as the switch register. The user can easily examine and change the contents of both registers and memory and single-step through the program for debugging purposes.

2.3 THE ASSEMBLER

Translating instructions from mnemonic to binary form can be hazardous because there is so great a chance for error. This fact was realized very early in the development of computers. The solution is a program known as an *assembler*, which "assembles" the correct bit patterns from mnemonic instructions written by the programmer. For each line of the program that contains an instruction written in mnemonic form, the assembler outputs the bit pattern corresponding to that instruction.

2.3.1 Object Format

The output of the assembler includes all the information needed to load the program into memory and run it. Along with the actual instructions, there must be some indication of where to load them into memory and where to begin execution. This additional information must be supplied to the assembler by the programmer. The output of the assembler is traditionally known as *object* because that is the "object" of the assembly process.

When we loaded programs through the switch register, we set the MAR to an address and entered a block of instructions and data. Then we changed the MAR to a new address and entered another block of instructions and data. Our assembler's object format reflects this process. The first piece of information is the address to place in the PC, the starting address. This is followed by the blocks of instructions and data themselves. Here is a diagram of our object format:

```
start address of program

[block 1]
[block 2]
  ...
[block N]
```

Each block output by the assembler begins with the address where the block is to be placed in memory. The next item is the number of words in the block. Finally comes the instructions and data themselves. Here is a diagram of a typical block:

```
load address of block
number of words in block

<word 1>
<word 2>
  ...
<word n>
```

2.3.2 Pseudo-operations

Just as there are machine instructions, there are also assembler instructions. Assembler instructions are commands to the assembler program but not instructions to the machine itself. Although they look like machine instructions, they are only acted on by the assembler. For this reason, they are known as *pseudo-operations*, or "pseudo-ops" for short.

One use of pseudo-ops is to give the programmer control over how the program is loaded into memory. Using pseudo-ops, instructions and data can be placed anywhere in memory by allowing the programmer to specify a new loading address at any time. The programmer can also indicate the starting address to place into the PC before running.

The next several sections describe some of the pseudo-ops for the assembler provided with this text. Several other pseudo-ops are discussed later in the chapter. One other pseudo-op is not needed yet and will be described in a later chapter.

ORG. The ORG pseudo-op allows the programmer to control the placement of instructions and data in memory by changing the *ORiGin of assembly.* The assembler instruction to establish a new origin of assembly is

```
ORG      n
```

The instructions that follow the ORG assembler instruction will be placed in memory starting at memory location *n*. For example, the instruction sequence

```
ORG      100B
LOAD     106B
ADD      105B
STORE    104B
```

specifies that the LOAD instruction should be placed at memory location 100B, the ADD instruction at memory location 101B, and the STORE instruction at memory location 102B.

The ORG pseudo-op causes the assembler to begin a new block in the object output. The value in the address field of the ORG pseudo-op will be used as the load address of the block. Here is the output of the assembler for the instructions just shown:

```
0001000000           - origin
0000000011           - # words
0001000001000110   ┐
1000000001000101   │  instructions
0010000001000100   ┘
```

Since ORG is only an instruction to the assembler, the address in the address field is not subject to the effective address calculation that a machine instruction would be. For example,

```
ORG      @350B
```

does not set the origin according to the contents of location 350B. The contents of location 350B cannot in general be determined until the program actually executes. Instead, the assembler program will simply report an error.

DATA. The DATA pseudo-op provides a way of entering data into memory by initializing one or more memory locations when the program is loaded into memory. It has the form

```
DATA    n1,n2,...,nk
```

Values are placed in successive words of storage. A full 16 bits is used for each data item. Each item in the list can be expressed in either decimal or octal. For example, the sequence

```
ORG     150B
DATA    42,947,155412B,0,128
```

causes the assembler to output the following:

```
0001101000          - origin
0000000101          - # words
0000000000101010   ┐
0000001110110011   │
1101101100001010   │ data
0000000000000000   │
0000000010000000   ┘
```

BSS. It is often useful to skip over one or more locations that are used for storage once the program is running. For example,

```
ORG     100B
LOAD    106B
ADD     105B
STORE   104B
HALT

ORG     105B
DATA    39,183
```

Here, the origin of assembly is simply reset to avoid placing anything into location 104B.

Rather than reset the origin explicitly, another pseudo-op tells the assembler to skip over a block of memory locations that may be used as storage. The pseudo-op has the form

```
BSS    n
```

BSS stands for *block storage statement*. The preceding example could be rewritten using BSS as

```
ORG       100B
LOAD      106B
ADD       105B
STORE     104B
HALT
BSS       1
DATA      39,183
```

In either case, the output of the assembler would be the same:

```
0001000000                 - origin
0000000100                 - # words
0001000001000110          ┐
1000000001000101          │
0010000001000100          │ instructions
0000000000000000          ┘
0001000101                 - origin
0000000010                 - # words
0000000000100111          ┐
0000000010110111          ┘ data
```

By convention, BSS is used to reserve storage space and ORG is used to reset the origin when there is no intent to reserve storage. It is a good idea to comment any storage reserved to document how it will be used. If we want to reserve space for three different values, using three separate BSS instructions is better than using a single BSS because it allows us to comment each one individually.

END. The last physical line in the program is the END pseudo-op. END has this form:

```
END       starting address
```

The PC is set to the starting address given in the END pseudo-op before execution begins. The instruction at the address indicated by the END pseudo-op is treated as the logical beginning of the program. The starting address is the first line output by the assembler.

Here is a complete program ready to be assembled and run:

```
ORG       100B
LOAD      106B
ADD       105B
STORE     104B
HALT
BSS       1
DATA      39,183
END       100B
```

The assembler outputs the following result:

```
0001000000            - start address
0001000000            - origin
0000000100            - # words
0001000001000110    ┐
1000000001000101    │
0010000001000100    │  instructions
0000000000000000    ┘
0001000101            - origin
0000000010            - # words
0000000000100111    ]
0000000010110111    ]  data
```

2.3.3 *The Assembler Listing*

The assembler program also produces a listing of the program. For each instruction or data item the listing shows

- the memory address
- the assembled instruction or data
- the source line
- the listing line number

Here is the listing for the program given earlier:

```
0100                  ORG     100B        1
0100  010106          LOAD    106B        2
0101  100105          ADD     105B        3
0102  020104          STORE   104B        4
0103  000000          HALT                5
0104    0001          BSS     1           6
0105  000047          DATA    39,183      7
0106  000267                              7
                      END     100B        8
```

The memory locations, assembled instructions, and data are printed in octal to save space in the listing. The numbers shown for the BSS pseudo-op represent the number of locations reserved. The line number in the listing is given in decimal and reflects the source line number. Notice, for example, that both lines produced from the DATA pseudo-op have the line number 7.

Several pseudo-operations are provided to help control the listing. Normally, the assembler produces a listing of the entire program. To help reduce the size of longer programs, two pseudo-ops selectively turn the listing on and off. The pseudo-op

```
NOLIST
```

turns the listing feature off, and

```
LIST
```

turns it back on again.

The other pseudo-op that controls the listing is

```
PAGE
```

The printer will eject the current page and begin listing on a new page, starting with the current line. This is useful for placing different parts of a large program on their own pages to improve readability.

2.3.4 Preparing Assembler Input

A few miscellaneous notes on preparing a program for the assembler provided with this text are in order. First, blank lines are ignored. That means it is easy to make a program more readable by separating logically related sequences of instructions by a blank line to set them off visually.

A comment can be placed to the side of an instruction, separated by at least one blank. The assembler treats the entire line as a comment if it has an asterisk (*) in column 1. Good comments make a program more readable. Here is another version of the program, with comments and blank lines added to improve readability.

```
** This is a very simple assembly language program that
*  adds together two numbers. Five instructions are placed
*  in memory, along with two pieces of data.

          ORG     100B
          LOAD    106B         add two numbers together
          ADD     105B
          STORE   104B         ... and save the sum
          HALT

          BSS     1            for the sum
          DATA    39,183       two numbers
          END     100B
```

Do not begin instructions in column 1. In fact, it is fairly common practice to place the operation field starting in about column 11. The operation field must be separated from the address mode field by at least a single blank. The address mode and address field must have no spaces between them, since a space is used to mark the beginning of a comment. Thus,

```
LOAD     @ 125B     this is wrong
```

will not be interpreted correctly. In fact, the 125B will be taken as part of the comment and ignored. The instruction is correctly written as

```
LOAD     @125B     this is right!
```

2.4 THE MACHINE EMULATOR

This text also includes an emulator for our machine so that programs can actually be written, assembled, and run. The emulator includes a phase that loads the output of the assembler into memory. When the program halts, the emulator will print the contents of the registers and memory. All values are printed in octal to save space in the listing.

```
Program halted at PC= 0105       AC= 000336       XR= 000000

Memory:
 0100: 010106 100105 020104 000000 000336 000047 000267
```

Recall that the sequencer increments the PC before executing the HALT instruction. The PC shown is at 105B, although the HALT instruction is at location 104B in memory.

To give the effect of executing a program a step at a time, two other pseudo-ops are provided. They control a feature of the emulator that prints a record of what instructions have executed and what was in the registers at the time. This can be done selectively for ranges of instructions. The pseudo-op

```
TRACE
```

turns on the feature, and the pseudo-op

```
NOTRACE
```

turns it off again. In the absence of either of these, none of the instructions is traced. In the previous program, for example,

```
** This is a very simple assembly language program that
*  adds together two numbers. Five instructions are placed
*  in memory, along with two pieces of data.

          ORG    100B
          LOAD   106B          add two numbers together
         TRACE                 turn trace mode on
```

```
 ADD    105B
 STORE  104B          ... and save the sum
NOTRACE               turn trace mode off again
 HALT

 BSS    1             for the sum
 DATA   39,183        two numbers
 END    100B
```

only the ADD and STORE instructions are traced on output, although all of the instructions are executed:

```
Trace of program execution:

PC: 0101  AC: 000047  XR: 000000  IR: 100105 ADD   105B
PC: 0102  AC: 000336  XR: 000000  IR: 020104 STORE 104B
```

The IR is shown both in octal and symbolically, the same way it was given in the program. The content of the AC is shown as it was *before* executing the instruction.

Turning on TRACE causes the assembler to insert an image of the traced instructions directly in its output:

```
0001000000
0001000000
0000000100
0001000001000110
1000000001000101    ADD   105B
0010000001000100    STORE 104B
0000000000000000
0001000101
0000000010
0000000000100111
0000000010110111
```

The emulator stores the symbolic form when it loads the program and prints it in the trace whenever the instruction is executed. If the program overwrites the instruction with some other information, the symbolic form is lost, and that location will no longer be traced.

2.5 PERSPECTIVE

Although the idea of using an assembler to convert symbolic instructions into their internal representation seems obvious to us today, this was not always the case. For a number of years, there were people who felt that the programmer should work as close to the machine level as possible. Fortunately, those who supported the use of assembler programs have prevailed.

Perhaps the most influential program in the history of assemblers was the Symbolic Assembly Program (SAP), written for the IBM 704 computer. Developed in the latter part of the 1950s, SAP introduced the external form that has remained almost unchanged to this day. Even some of its mnemonics are still in use.

SAP also introduced the idea of pseudo-ops. In fact, the BSS pseudo-op was first introduced by that assembler. Mnemonics are by no means standard among assemblers, however. For example, many assemblers use BLK or BLOCK rather than BSS. Where the original SAP assembler used LOC, we use ORG, while some other assemblers use ORIG. No matter how the operation is spelled, however, all assemblers owe a debt to the ideas contributed by that early program.

We will learn about some more advanced assembler features after exploring the elementary programming techniques discussed in the next chapter. The assembler described here is by no means "state of the art." It is, however, a great improvement over having to hand-translate programs written with mnemonics into the actual bits that they represent.

Before leaving the subject, we should consider one final question. What is the difference between "machine language" and "assembly language"? The two terms are used interchangeably by many people, although there is a distinct difference between them.

Machine language programs are made up of the binary instructions and data that can be entered into memory via the switch register and executed immediately. Assembly language programs are written in terms of mnemonics, in a form that can be easily read by the programmer. Many instructions in an assembly language program, such as "LOAD", are also present in the corresponding machine language program. However, some assembler instructions, such as "EJECT" or "BSS", have no counterpart at the machine level. These instructions play their part by directing either the assembly or the loading process and have no role during execution.

2.6 SUMMARY

In this chapter, we looked at how a program can be entered into our machine and executed. The front panel of our machine includes a switch register. Using the switch register, we can examine or modify the content of any register in the machine. A rotary switch determines which register is displayed at any time. By using the LOAD and STORE switches, we can also examine and modify the content of any memory location.

A program in memory can be executed from the front panel by setting the PC to its starting address and pressing the RUN switch on the front panel. The program will run either until a HALT instruction is executed or until we press the HALT switch on the front panel. The machine also provides a way to single-step through the program to discover any problems during execution. Each time we press the STEP switch, the sequencer executes the next instruction. We can change from single-step to run mode at any time by pressing the RUN switch. We can also single-step after pressing the HALT switch if we suspect that there is a problem.

In the second part of the chapter, we looked at a program called an assembler. An assembler automatically translates the symbolic form of instructions into its internal binary form, ready to be loaded and run. The object format output by the assembler consists of the starting address for execution, followed by blocks of instructions and data. Each block is begun by the address where the block is to be loaded and the number of words in the block.

Pseudo-operations allow the programmer to provide this additional information to the assembler. A pseudo-operation is a command to the assembler but not to the machine itself. For example, the END pseudo-op marks the end of the assembly language program for the assembler and specifies the start address to place in the PC before execution.

An emulator program provided with this book allows assembled programs to be executed. To simulate access to the front panel, two pseudo-ops allow selected portions of the machine language program to be single-stepped. Once the program halts, the emulator reports the final register contents as well as the contents of any nonzero portions of memory.

The final section provided a brief historical perspective on assemblers, including the early controversy surrounding their use. It also discussed the difference between assembly language and machine language.

PROBLEMS

2-1. What is the purpose of the front panel display on our simple machine?

2-2. Describe how to change the AC to hold the bit configuration equivalent to the octal number 103251B. The switch is currently set to the MBR. Are any other registers affected by making this change?

2-3. Describe *in detail* how to deposit the instruction "LOAD @315B" at memory location 517B via the front panel display. What is in the MAR and MBR *after* this is done?

2-4. What must be placed into the PC before a program in memory can be executed?

2-5. Suppose that the HALT button was pushed while a program was running in run mode. Describe what is in the PC and IR. (Do these correspond to the instruction just executed?)

2-6. Describe the purpose of an assembler program. Include in your description what is input to the program as well as what the program does with the input.

2-7. How does a pseudo-operation differ from a machine instruction?

2-8. What assembler instruction directs that a word of data instead of a machine instruction should be deposited in memory?

2-9. What assembler instruction directs that the next instructions should be placed in memory starting some number of words from the *current* position?

2-10. What assembler instruction directs that the next group of instructions should be placed in memory starting at a certain address in memory?

2-11. What assembler instruction must be physically the last one in the program?

2-12. Describe how to cause the next two executable instructions read by the assembler to be traced as they are executed.

2-13. How does the programmer indicate which instruction is the first one to be executed when the program is run?

2-14. Show the contents of memory prior to execution of the following program. Assume that any uninitialized locations are set to 0.

```
** This program adds two numbers.
*
        ORG     100B
        LOAD    105B        add two numbers
        ADD     106B
        STORE   104B        ... and save the sum
        HALT

        BSS     1           for sum
        DATA    14,35B      two numbers
        END     100B
```

2-15. Try running the programs suggested in the problems section of Chapter 1 on the assembler/emulator at your installation.

3

Elementary Programming Techniques

Now that we are familiar with how instructions are entered into our machine, we can explore how to combine instructions in useful ways. The examples shown in this chapter are fairly simple. We will discuss more sophisticated techniques in the following chapters.

This chapter draws its examples from features commonly found in most high-level programming languages. To run on a computer, a program written in a high-level language must be translated into instructions that the machine can execute. This is done either by hand or by a sophisticated program called a *compiler*. Although we would rather let a compiler do the work in most cases, there are some valuable lessons to be learned through hand translation.

The coded examples shown in this chapter are small fragments that illustrate specific points. The location of an instruction in memory is often an important part of the example. For convenience, the location of each instruction is shown to the left of the code itself, as it might appear in the assembler listing. To actually run an example, these locations should not be entered as part of the instructions. Assembler pseudo-ops must also be inserted to cause the instructions to be loaded at the locations shown.

3.1 EVALUATING ARITHMETIC EXPRESSIONS

High-level languages allow storage locations to be represented in a program as symbolic names. Historically, this was a result of attempts to carry out numeric calculations by encoding algebraic formulas in machine-readable form. Rather than write the Greek letter alpha, for example, the intent was to allow it to be written symbolically as "ALPHA." These symbolic names are called *identifiers*.

The programmer can express complicated arithmetic expressions in much the same form as they appear in algebraic formulas. An identifier takes on a new value by *assigning* to it the result of such an expression. The syntax of an *assignment statement* resembles that of an algebraic equality. Consider the assignment statement

```
Y:= (X - Y) / Z;
```

This statement takes the difference of the values represented by the identifiers X and Y and divides into it the value represented by the identifier Z. The final value is assigned to the identifier Y. We will translate this assignment statement into an equivalent set of machine instructions for our computer.

First, we must reserve space in memory for the value represented by each identifier. To help us remember, we will make a table of identifiers and their storage addresses. This is called a *symbol table*. There are only three identifiers used in the assignment statement above. A symbol table for the assignment statement might look like this:

Symbolic identifier	Memory address
X	50B
Y	52B
Z	54B

The choice of memory addresses is pretty much arbitrary. The only important thing is that once a location is chosen, it should be used consistently for that purpose until it is no longer needed.

Now that we have reserved memory for the identifiers X, Y, and Z, we are ready to translate the assignment statement. The first step is to bring the value stored at the location represented by the identifier X into the accumulator. This is accomplished by the instruction:

```
LOAD  50B
```

The difference $X - Y$ can now be formed by subtracting the contents of the location represented by the identifier Y from the value in the accumulator:

```
SUB   52B
```

Next, the difference is divided by the value stored in the location represented by the identifier Z:

```
DIV   54B
```

Finally, the result is stored back at the location represented by the identifier *Y*, replacing the previous value:

```
STORE   52B
```

This assignment statement is fairly easy to translate. Once storage has been allocated for the identifiers, the computation is broken down into a series of instructions that evaluate the arithmetic expression. The result is assigned to *Y* by storing it at the location reserved for the identifier.

Not all arithmetic expressions are quite as easy to generate code for. Suppose that the assignment statement had instead been given as

```
Y: =  Z / (X - Y);
```

Although it looks no more complicated than the first statement, the machine-level translation requires not only more instructions but a temporary storage location as well. There is simply no way to avoid using a temporary location in many cases. Our first example happened to be one that did not require it.

The first operation still forms the difference $X - Y$. The two instructions for this are the same as before:

```
LOAD    50B     fetch X
SUB     52B     difference X - Y
```

Next, we divide the value represented by *Z* by this difference. It should now be clear why we need a temporary memory location. The difference in the accumulator must be saved in memory temporarily to make room for the contents of the location represented by *Z*. We will use location 56B temporarily to save the difference now in the accumulator:

```
STORE   56B     save temporarily
LOAD    54B     fetch Z
```

Finally, the difference that we saved temporarily at location 56B can be divided into the value in the accumulator, and the result stored at the location represented by *Y*:

```
DIV     56B     Z / (X - Y)
STORE   52B     assign to Y
```

Compare the number of instructions needed to perform these two assignment statements of seemingly equal complexity. The second one requires a third again as many instructions as the first. It is difficult to judge the complexity of a statement written in a high-level language without considering its translation into instructions for a particular machine.

When writing code to evaluate an arithmetic expression, it is sometimes helpful first to rewrite the expression in fully parenthesized form. For example, a fully parenthesized version of the expression

```
Y / (X - 6) - (Z + 4) * (X - Y)
```

would be written as

```
((Y / (X - 6)) - ((Z + 4) * (X - Y)))
```

The sequence of instructions to evaluate this expression follows the same pattern required to solve it by hand. We begin with the innermost set of parentheses and evaluate outward, simplifying as we go along. As a rule, it is best to evaluate the second argument of an operator first if it is not a simple identifier or constant. The result is saved in a temporary location. Then, after evaluating the first operand in the AC, the second operand will be ready to use.

The maximum number of temporary locations required to evaluate an expression is one less than the maximum depth of the fully parenthesized expression. We saw that the expression $(Z/(X - Y))$ has a depth of two and required one temporary location. The maximum depth of the expression shown is three, so we would expect to use up to two temporary locations.

Here is a translation of the expression. The identifiers X, Y, and Z again represent locations 50B, 52B, and 54B, respectively. We will use locations 56B and 60B as temporary locations.

```
100B    LOAD    50B        (X-Y)
101B    SUB     52B
102B    STORE   56B        save as T1

103B    LOAD    54B        (Z+4)
104B    ADD     =4
105B    MUL     56B        (Z+4)*T1
106B    STORE   56B        save as T1

107B    LOAD    50B        (X-6)
110B    SUB     =6
111B    STORE   60B        save as T2
112B    LOAD    52B        Y/T2
113B    DIV     60B
114B    SUB     56B        T2 - T1
```

3.2 CONDITIONAL BRANCHES

It may seem that few of the possible conditional branches can be written using only the three available on this machine. Although some may be easier to express than others, any conditional branch imaginable can be built out of our unconditional and three conditional branch instructions.

3.2.1 Tests Against Zero

The three conditional branches available on this machine compare the contents of the accumulator against zero and branch if the comparison is true:

```
BREQ  -  branch if AC =  0

BRGE  -  branch if AC ≥  0

BRLT  -  branch if AC <  0
```

The other three conditional branches that are tests against zero can be built using pairs of the three branches shown, along with the unconditional branch, BR.

```
          What We Want              How to Do It

          "branch if Not Equal to zero"
150B      BRNE    100B       150B    BREQ    152B ──┐
                             151B    BR      100B   │
                                                 <──┘

          "branch if Greater than zero"
150B      BRGT    100B       150B    BREQ    152B ──┐
                             151B    BRGE    100B   │
                                                 <──┘

          "branch if Less than or Equal to zero"
150B      BRLE    100B       150B    BRLT    100B
                             151B    BREQ    100B
```

As an example, we will look at how to translate the traditional IF–THEN statement found in many languages. Suppose that we want to translate

```
IF Y > 0 THEN
  Z := X/Y;
END IF
```

If the value of the identifier Y is greater than zero, this statement assigns the result of dividing X by Y to Z.

A straightforward way to translate this is to evaluate the logical condition and branch to the code for the THEN clause if it is true. Otherwise, we fall through to an unconditional branch that skips past the code for the THEN clause. Assume that the code begins at memory location 100B and that the identifiers *X*, *Y*, and *Z* once again represent locations 50B, 52B, and 54B, respectively. Here is how our IF–THEN statement might be translated:

```
100B   LOAD   52B      fetch value of Y
101B   BREQ   103B     IF Y>0
102B   BRGE   104B     ...branch to THEN code
103B   BR     107B     otherwise branch around

104B   LOAD   50B         THEN Z := X/Y
105B   DIV    52B
106B   STORE  54B
```

While this method is easy to apply, it does require the use of an extra instruction to branch around the THEN code if the condition is false.

Another method is to test the *opposite condition* and branch around the assignment statement if it is true. The opposite of a logical condition is called its *logical negation*. Here is a table of logical conditions and their logical negations:

Logical condition	Logical negation
equal	not equal
greater than	less than or equal
greater than or equal	less than

From this table we see that the logical negation of "greater than" is "less than or equal."

Here is how our IF–THEN statement might be translated using logical negation. Assume again that the code begins at memory location 100B and that the identifiers *X*, *Y*, and *Z* once again represent locations 50B, 52B, and 54B, respectively.

```
100B      LOAD   52B      fetch value of Y
101B      BRLT   106B     if Y<=0
102B      BREQ   106B     ...branch around THEN code

103B      LOAD   50B         THEN Z := X/Y
104B      DIV    52B
105B      STORE  54B
```

The main drawback to this second method is having to compute the logical negation of the condition. For simple conditions this is easy. However, it is sometimes more trouble than it is worth for more complicated logical conditions. In such cases it may be easier to use the first method presented. Even though it may take a few extra instructions, the first method does not require computing the logical negation of an expression.

If we want to assign a different value when the value of the identifier *Y* is less than or equal to zero, we could add an ELSE part to the statement:

```
IF Y > 0  THEN
   Z := X/Y
ELSE
   Z := 0;
END IF
```

The first method really has an empty ELSE clause anyway. We simply insert the code for the ELSE part immediately before the unconditional branch around the THEN part:

```
100B    LOAD     52B     fetch value of Y
101B    BREQ     105B    If Y>0
102B    BRGE     106B    ...branch to THEN code

103B    LOAD     =0          ELSE Z := 0
104B    STORE    54B

105B    BR       111B    otherwise branch around

106B    LOAD     50B         THEN Z := X/Y
107B    DIV      52B
110B    STORE    54B
```

The second method simply adds the instructions for the ELSE part at the end, preceded by a branch around them to terminate the THEN part:

```
100B    LOAD     52B     fetch value of Y
101B    BRLT     107B    if Y<=0
102B    BREQ     107B    ...branch to ELSE code

103B    LOAD     50B        THEN Z := X/Y
104B    DIV      52B
105B    STORE    54B

106B    BR       111B    branch around ELSE code

107B    LOAD     =0         ELSE Z := 0
110B    STORE    54B
```

This IF statement is a very special case, because the identifier Z is assigned a new value whether the condition is true or false. Some languages recognize this fact and allow IF in an expression. If the condition is true, the IF expression has the value computed by the THEN clause. Otherwise, it takes on the value computed by the ELSE clause:

```
Z := IF Y > 0 THEN X/Y ELSE 0 END IF;
```

Here is a version based on this form. Both parts join at the end and execute the same STORE instruction to assign a result to Z:

```
100B    LOAD   52B     fetch value of Y
101B    BRLT   106B    if Y<=0
102B    BREQ   106B    ...branch to ELSE code

103B    LOAD   50B     THEN X/Y
104B    DIV    52B
105B    BR     107B    branch around ELSE code

106B    LOAD   =0        ELSE 0
107B    STORE  54B     Z:=
```

3.2.2 Transforming Nonzero Tests

Constructing tests against values other than zero requires a little more effort. Suppose that we want to encode the statement

```
IF X  > Z  THEN
   Y:= 7;
END IF
```

We already know how to deal with the statement

```
IF X  > 0  THEN
   Y:= 7;
END IF
```

Assume that the instructions begin at location 100B and that X and Y represent locations 50B and 52B, as before. The instructions would be

```
100B        LOAD    50B         fetch value of X
101B        BRLT    105B        if X<=0
102B        BREQ    105B        ...branch around THEN code

103B        LOAD    =7             THEN Y:= 7
104B        STORE   52B
```

The only difference between this and the earlier version is that instead of comparing X to Z, we are comparing X to zero. The first IF statement can be made to look like the second one by subtracting Z from both sides of the $>$ operator:

```
IF   X-Z  > 0   THEN
     Y:= 7;
END IF
```

This is a comparison against zero that we know how to do:

```
100B        LOAD    50B         compute X-Z
101B        SUB     54B
102B        BRLT    106B        if X-Z <= 0
103B        BREQ    106B        ...branch around THEN code

104B        LOAD    =7             THEN Y:= 7
105B        STORE   52B
```

This simple example can be shortened by doing a little algebra first. We will multiply the logical condition by -1. This is called the *arithmetic negation* of the condition. Whereas logical negation reverses the condition, arithmetic negation leaves its meaning unchanged. The arithmetic negation of

```
X-Z > 0
```

is the condition

```
Z-X < 0
```

Here is a table of logical conditions and their arithmetic negations:

Logical condition	Arithmetic negation
equal	equal
not equal	not equal
greater than	less than
greater than or equal	less than or equal

Notice that equality is preserved under arithmetic negation; it is not preserved under logical negation. By performing some algebra first, we can work with a relation whose logical negation requires one less instruction on our machine than the previous version:

```
100B     LOAD    54B        if Z-X >=0
101B     SUB     50B
102B     BRGE    105B       ...branch around THEN code

103B     LOAD    =7            THEN Y:= 7
104B     STORE   52B
```

3.2.3 Testing Compound Logical Conditions

A *compound condition* involves two or more logical conditions joined together by either AND or OR. For example, the compound OR condition in the IF statement

```
IF  X<Y OR Y>Z  THEN
    Z:=6;
END IF
```

is true if either of the simple conditions is true.

The principle here is to evaluate each condition except the last one and jump to the code for the THEN clause if it is true. We evaluate the logical negation of the last condition and branch around the THEN code if the negated condition is true. Here is how the IF statement shown above would be evaluated:

```
100B     LOAD    50B        if X<Y is true
101B     SUB     52B
102B     BRLT    106B       ...jump to THEN code

103B     LOAD    54B        if Y>Z is false,
104B     SUB     52B
105B     BRGE    110B       ...jump around THEN code

106B     LOAD    =6            THEN Z:= 6
107B     STORE   54B
```

The compound AND condition in the IF statement

```
IF   X<Y AND Y>Z   THEN
   Z:=6;
END IF
```

is true only if both simple conditions are true.

For AND, the principle is to branch around the THEN code if any negated condition is true. Here is how the IF statement shown above would be evaluated:

```
100B      LOAD   50B          if X<Y is false
101B      SUB    52B
102B      BRGE   110B         ...jump around THEN code

103B      LOAD   54B          if Y>Z is false,
104B      SUB    52B
105B      BRGE   110B         ...jump around THEN code

106B      LOAD   =6              THEN Z:= 6
107B      STORE  54B
```

If the compound condition contains both AND and OR relations, AND takes precedence. The compound condition in the IF statement

```
IF   X<Y AND Y>Z    OR    X>Y AND Y<Z   THEN
   Z:=6;
END IF
```

has the fully parenthesized form

```
(((X<Y) AND (Y>Z))   OR   ((X>Y) AND (Y<Z)))
```

This expression can be evaluated simply by evaluating the two compound conditions connected by OR. The expression is true if either of these two compound AND conditions is true. Here is how this statement would be translated:

```
100B      LOAD   50B          if X<Y is false
101B      SUB    52B
102B      BRGE   106B         ...try second AND clause
```

```
103B     LOAD    54B        if Y>Z is true,
104B     SUB     52B
105B     BRLT    114B       ...branch to THEN code

106B     LOAD    52B        if X>Y is false
107B     SUB     50B
110B     BRGE    116B       ...jump around THEN code

111B     LOAD    52B        if Y<Z is false,
112B     SUB     54B
113B     BRGE    116B       ...jump around THEN code

114B     LOAD    =6       THEN Z:= 6
115B     STORE   54B
```

The last test in the first AND clause has been optimized. If we had followed the pattern, it would have looked something like this:

```
103B    LOAD    54B      if Y>Z is false,
104B    SUB     52B
105B    BRGE    106B     ... try second AND clause

????    BR      114B     else true -- branch to THEN
```

The two instructions are easily combined as shown earlier. This optimization can be applied for any number of AND clauses connected by OR conditions. Only the last AND clause in the sequence is unchanged.

3.3 USING BRANCHES TO FORM LOOPS

Almost every high-level language provides some way of repeatedly executing a section of code and some way of deciding during execution when to stop repeating. Some idea of what these high-level control structures look like and how they are expressed at the machine level will lead to a coding style that is clearer, more systematic, and easier to debug later on.

3.3.1 Loops That Count

The Pascal FOR loop and the FORTRAN DO loop are two examples of a type of loop that is said to "count." The body of the loop is executed a fixed number of times that can easily be determined before the loop is ever executed. Many algorithms can be expressed very naturally in terms of counting loops.

Indexed counting loops. An indexed counting loop is based on the concept of summation found in algebra. The summation

$$\sum_{i=1}^{5} i$$

means "the sum of the first five integers." The Greek letter sigma represents the summation operation. Its first letter, *s*, is the same as the first letter of the word *sum*.

The symbol *i* is the *index of summation*. It first takes on the value 1, then 2, and so on through 5. This index can be used in the summation itself, as shown. The numbers on the top and bottom dictate how many terms are in the sum.

Most high-level languages have a similar notation. In our discussion, we will adopt the following form:

```
FOR   I:= J   TO   K   BY   L   DO
               ...
      <loop body>
               ...
END FOR
```

The identifier *I* is called the *loop index* and corresponds to the index of summation. On the first time through the loop, the loop index takes on the *initial value J*. At the end of the loop, the value of the *increment*, *L*, is added to the index. In the case of a positive increment, if the new value of the index is no larger than the value of the *final value*, *K*, the loop is repeated with the new loop index. Otherwise, the loop is finished, and execution proceeds to the statement past the end of the loop. Similarly, if the increment is negative, the loop is repeated only if the new index value is no less than the final value.

There are several ways to implement an indexed counting loop at the machine level. Each has an advantage for a range of applications.

The trip count method. The trip count is the number of times the loop executes. It can easily be determined before the loop is entered for the first time by considering the initial and final values and the value of the increment. The formula for the trip count is

$$\text{Maximum (floor ((final } - \text{ initial } + \text{ increment)/increment), 0)}$$

For example, the loop

```
FOR   I:=   1   TO   10   BY   2   DO
```

would execute

```
    maximum(floor((10 - 1 + 2) / 2),0)
=   maximum(floor(11/2),0)
=   maximum(5,0)
=   5 times
```

The index takes on the values 1, 3, 5, 7, and 9. Similarly, the loop

```
FOR  I:=  10  TO  1  BY  -2  DO
```

would execute

```
    maximum(floor((1 - 10 + ( -2)) / (-2)), 0)
=   maximum(floor((-11) / (-2)), 0)
=   max (5, 0)
=   5 times
```

This time, the index takes on the values 10, 8, 6, 4, and 2. Finally, the loop

```
FOR  I:=  10  TO  1  BY  2  DO
```

executes

```
    maximum(floor((1 - 10 + 2) / 2), 0)
=   maximum(floor((-7) / 2), 0)
=   max (-4, 0)
=   0 times
```

This method requires us to keep two values throughout the execution of the loop:

1. the current trip count
2. the current loop index

To illustrate the implementation of an indexed counting loop, we will use the following locations and assume that the initial, final, and index values are correctly set:

Location	Use	
30B	trip count	
40B	loop index	(I)
50B	initial value	(J)
60B	final value	(K)
70B	increment	(L)

The loop begins at location 100B:

```
100B    LOAD     50B       initialize loop index
101B    STORE    40B
```

```
102B    LOAD    60B     compute trip count
103B    SUB     50B
104B    ADD     70B
105B    DIV     70B

106B    BRLT    126B    terminate if count expired
107B    BREQ    126B
110B    STORE   30B
        ...             execute body of loop

120B    LOAD    40B     increment loop index
121B    ADD     70B
122B    STORE   40B
123B    LOAD    30B     decrement trip count
124B    SUB     =1
125B    BR      106B    ... and repeat
```

The loop has four distinct parts:

1. *Initialization:* The values of the loop index and trip count are established.
2. *Test:* The condition for loop termination is tested.
3. *Loop body:* Explains what the loop is supposed to do.
4. *Reinitialization:* The values of the loop index and trip count are updated in preparation for the next iteration.

Of the four, only the initialization phase is done just once, outside the loop. Most of our effort at writing shorter code ought to be focused on the portions actually inside the loop—even at the expense of a few extra instructions during the initialization phase.

Notice that there is quite a bit of overhead associated with the trip count, mostly in the initialization phase. More important is the number of instructions inside the loop that are needed to branch out of the loop if the trip count is less than or equal to zero. Could something be done about this?

Suppose that instead of testing the trip count for less than or equal to zero, we arrange things so that the loop terminates if the trip count is greater than or equal to zero. This can be done by using the negative of the trip count and stepping it toward zero.

How can the trip count formula be changed to yield a negative number? The trip count formula, remember was

$$\text{Maximum}\ (\text{floor}\ ((\text{final} - \text{initial} + \text{increment})/\text{increment}),\ 0)$$

A negative trip count can be formed by exchanging additions and subtractions in the numerator and taking the minimum instead of the maximum:

Minimum (floor ((initial − final − increment)/increment), 0)

Instead of subtracting 1 from the trip count each time, we must now add 1. Here is the revised section of code, which uses a negative trip count:

```
100B    LOAD    60B     initialize loop index
101B    STORE   40B

102B    SUB     50B     compute negative
103B    SUB     70B     ... trip count
104B    DIV     70B

105B    BRGE    125B    terminate if count expired
106B    STORE   30B
        ...             execute body of loop

117B    LOAD    40B     update loop index
120B    ADD     70B
121B    STORE   40B
122B    LOAD    30B     increment trip count
123B    ADD     =1
124B    BR      105B    ... and repeat loop
```

We can do one more thing to reduce the number of instructions executed in the loop. After incrementing the trip count at location 123B, the loop will repeat only if the count is still negative. Otherwise, the BRGE instruction at location 105B would transfer control out of the loop. Therefore, we can shorten the loop a little by replacing the BR instruction at location 124B by a BRLT instruction and moving the BRGE instruction out of the loop:

```
100B    LOAD    60B     initialize loop index
101B    STORE   40B

102B    SUB     50B     compute negative
103B    SUB     70B     ... trip count
104B    DIV     70B
105B    BRGE    125B    skip loop if count expired

106B    STORE   30B
        ...             execute body of loop

117B    LOAD    40B     update loop index
120B    ADD     70B
121B    STORE   40B
122B    LOAD    30B     increment trip count
123B    ADD      =1
124B    BRLT     106B   repeat if count not expired
```

The total overhead is reduced from 15 to 13 instructions. A LOAD instruction was eliminated from the initialization clause, and two branches were eliminated from within the loop itself. This second fact is more important because these instructions are executed once for each iteration.

The trip count method is the most general way to implement an indexed count loop. A disadvantage is that there is double the overhead, since two values must be updated with each iteration. We will take another look at this method shortly.

The loop index method. The other commonly used technique for controlling an indexed counting loop is to do away with the trip count and test the loop index directly. The problem is that the terminating test is different for a loop that steps upward and one that steps downward. In the first case, the loop terminates when the loop index becomes *greater than* the final value. In the second, the loop terminates when the loop index becomes *less than* the final value. This method, then, is practical only when the step direction is fixed. It must be known at the time the program is written whether the increment is positive or negative so that the correct terminating condition can be coded.*

Suppose we limit ourselves to positive increments. Consider how the FOR loop

```
FOR    I:= J   TO   K   BY   L   DO
         ...
<loop body>
         ...
END   FOR
```

could be written, using the loop index to control the number of times the loop executes. Here are the memory locations we will use for storage:

```
Location              Use
   40B          loop index      (I)
   50B          initial value   (J)
   60B          final value     (K)
   70B          increment       (L)
```

Assume again that the loop begins at location 100B:

```
100B      LOAD      50B       get initial value
```

*The 1966 FORTRAN standard permitted only positive increments to take advantage of the space and time efficiency possible with this method. Another approach, taken by the Pascal language, was to use a different syntax for loops that step upward—

```
FOR    I:= J TO K   DO
```

—than for loops that step downward—

```
FOR    I:= J   DOWNTO K    DO
```

```
101B    STORE   40B     save new index
102B    SUB     60B     if index >  final value
103B    BREQ    105B
104B    BRGE    123B    ... terminate loop
                ...     execute loop body
120B    LOAD    40B     increment index
121B    ADD     70B
122B    BR      101B    ... and repeat loop
```

Using the loop index to control the number of iterations performed results in substantially fewer instructions, compared to the trip count method. Since only one value must be initialized and updated, all phases of the loop are shorter. Only 8 instructions are required for the index-controlled version. The trip count-controlled version uses at least 13. The index-controlled version also has one instruction fewer within the loop than the trip count-controlled version.

On the other hand, the index-controlled version is more limited than the trip count-controlled version. The step direction is built right in to the termination test. If the initial value were greater than the final value, the loop would execute zero times.

Although the index-controlled method imposes some restrictions, in a sufficient number of cases these restrictions can easily be met to give a decided advantage over the trip count-controlled method.

Unindexed counting loops. There are cases in which we want the loop to execute a certain number of times but have no use for a loop index within the body of the loop. Such a loop requires less overhead than an indexed counting loop because it is no longer necessary to maintain a separate loop index. The only requirement is that the loop execute a certain number of times.

The trip count method discussed earlier is really an extension of this. The trip count is, after all, the number of times the loop will execute. The only difference in this case is that a separate loop index is not maintained.

To illustrate this method, consider the problem of computing the *n*th Fibonacci number. The Fibonacci sequence is defined as follows:

$$f(1) = 1$$
$$f(2) = 1$$
$$f(n) = f(n - 1) + f(n - 2) \qquad n > 2$$

The first several values are 1, 1, 2, 3, 5, 8, 13, and so forth. Each new value is the sum of the preceding two.

Here is a FOR loop that solves the problem: The *n*th Fibonacci number is left in the variable FIB:

```
LSTFIB:= 1;
FIB:= 1;
```

```
FOR   I:= 3 TO N  DO

   TEMP:=   FIB;
   FIB:=    FIB + LSTFIB;
   LSTFIB:= TEMP;

END FOR
```

Consider first a translation of this loop using the index to control the loop. Here are the storage locations used:

Location	Use	
300B	for current f(n-1)	(LSTFIB)
302B	for current f(n)	(FIB)
304B	for updating f(n) and f(n-1)	(TEMP)
306B	loop index	(I)
310B	position in Fibonacci sequence	(N)

The code begins at location 100B:

```
100B    LOAD     =1       initialize f(0)
101B    STORE    300B

102B    STORE    302B     initialize f(1)

+------------------------------------------------------+
| 103B  LOAD     =3       initialize loop index        |
|                                                      |
| 104B  STORE    306B                                  |
| 105B  SUB      310B     if index > final value       |
| 106B  BREQ     110B                                  |
| 107B  BRGE     121B     ... terminate loop           |
+------------------------------------------------------+

110B    LOAD     302B     save previous f(n)
111B    STORE    304B

112B    ADD      300B     compute new f(n)
113B    STORE    302B

114B    LOAD     304B     use previous f(n) as
115B    STORE    300B     ... new f(n-1)

+------------------------------------------------------+
| 116B  LOAD     306B     increment loop index         |
| 117B  ADD      =1                                    |
| 120B  BR       104B     ... and repeat               |
+------------------------------------------------------+
```

The eight instructions enclosed in boxes can be counted as overhead in controlling the loop. Seven of these are actually inside the loop.

Now, consider how the problem would be solved using a trip count. From the trip count formula, the loop must execute

$$\begin{aligned} &\text{Maximum } ((N - 3 + 1), 0) \\ = &\text{ maximum } ((N - 2), 0) \end{aligned}$$

times, since the implied increment is 1. This time, though, there is no need to keep a separate index.

We will use a negative trip count again to terminate the loop with a single conditional branch instruction. An additional memory location is used for the trip count. Here are the storage locations used:

```
Location                 Use
  300B        for current f(n-1)                (LSTFIB)
  302B        for current f(n)                  (FIB)
  304B        for updating f(n) and f(n-1)      (TEMP)
  306B        trip count
  310B        position in Fibonacci sequence    (N)
```

The instructions begin at location 100B:

```
      100B    LOAD     =1      initialize f(0)
      101B    STORE    300B

      102B    STORE    302B    initialize f(1)
   ---------------------------------------------------
   |  103B    LOAD     =2      initialize trip count |
   |  104B    SUB      310B    ... to 2-N            |
   |  105B    BRGE     120B    skip if count expired |
   |                                                 |
   |  106B    STORE    306B    save new count        |
   ---------------------------------------------------
      107B    LOAD     302B    save previous f(n)
      110B    STORE    304B

      111B    ADD      300B    compute new f(n)
      112B    STORE    302B

      113B    LOAD     304B    use previous f(n) as
      114B    STORE    300B    ... new f(n-1)
   ---------------------------------------------------
   |  115B    LOAD     306B    increment count       |
   |  116B    ADD      =1                            |
   |  117B    BRLT     105B    repeat if in range    |
   ---------------------------------------------------
```

There are only seven instructions of overhead in this count-controlled version, compared to eight in the index-controlled version. What is more significant is the fact that only four of the instructions are actually inside the loop. The index-controlled version had seven instructions inside the loop.

For applications where a trip count can be precomputed outside the loop, the trip count method uses fewer instructions, both overall and within the loop itself. Although the trip count method was more expensive when implementing indexed count loops, it is superior when implementing unindexed count loops.

3.3.2 Loops That Terminate by Condition

There is a second major type of loop. Unlike a counting loop, the number of iterations made depends entirely on the result of executing the body of the loop. It is either more difficult or not at all possible to compute that number ahead of time. This second type is known as a *conditional loop*. A typical form is the WHILE–DO statement:

```
WHILE condition DO
        ...
     <loop body>
        ...
 END WHILE
```

Any kind of condition is possible. There is no formal initialization to perform. However, the cost of evaluating the terminal condition can be expensive, depending on the complexity of the condition.

As a simple example, consider writing a WHILE–DO loop that finds the greatest Fibonacci number less than 1,000:

```
LSTFIB:= 1;
FIB:= 1;

WHILE FIB < 1000 DO

    ANSW:= FIB;
    FIB:= FIB + LSTFIB;
    LSTFIB:= ANSW;

END WHILE
```

Here is how this might be written at the machine level. As we did before, we will use the following memory locations for storage:

```
Location          Use
  300B        for current f(n-1)     (LSTFIB)
  302B        for current f(n)       (FIB)
  304B        for final result       (ANSW)
```

The code begins at location 100B:

```
100B   LOAD    =1
101B   STORE   302B     initialize f(1)

102B   STORE   300B     save new f(n-1)
103B   LOAD    302B     if f(n) >= 1000
104B   SUB     =1000
105B   BRGE    114B     ... terminate loop

106B   LOAD    302B     save previous f(n)
107B   STORE   304B
110B   ADD     300B     compute new f(n)
111B   STORE   302B
112B   LOAD    304B     recover previous f(n)
113B   BR      102B     ... and repeat
```

3.3.3 Some Variations on the Theme

The two major types of loops discussed in the preceding sections appear to cover the entire spectrum of possible loops. After all, what else is there beyond counting loops and loops that terminate on condition? Even so, these are only broad categories within which a number of variations are possible. There are many ways to write conditional and counting loops other than those shown here.

For example, it may be useful to have a conditionally controlled loop that checks its condition at the end rather than at the beginning of the loop. This type of conditional loop is known as a REPEAT–UNTIL loop and has the following form:

```
REPEAT
     ...
  <loop body>
     ...
UNTIL  condition
```

What new problems does this form of conditional loop pose?

Another kind of loop is a hybrid of the counting loop and the conditional loop. Its syntax has the form

```
FOR I:= J TO K BY L WHILE C DO
    ...
```

```
<loop body>
    ...
END FOR
```

where I, J, K, and L serve the usual function in a count-controlled loop and C is an arbitrary condition (i.e., $X \leq Y$). This kind of loop could be used, for example, to search an array for some value. The loop would terminate when either the value is found or the array has been totally searched. How does the implementation of this hybrid loop compare to the implementation of the count-controlled and conditional loops discussed in the chapter?

3.4 SUMMARY

The theme of this chapter has been to study how algorithms written in terms of higher-level languages can be expressed at the machine level. Concepts such as the assignment statement, the conditional statement, and the various forms of loops all carry over and apply equally well to machine language programming.

The techniques described so far should help us gain experience at machine-level programming. However, the only road to proficiency is practice. Do as many of the exercises at the end of this chapter as possible (preferably all of them) before going on to the more sophisticated techniques described in the following chapters.

PROBLEMS

3-1. What is a symbol table? How is it used while writing a program?

3-2. Explain why it is sometimes necessary to use temporary storage locations while evaluating an arithmetic expression. How can we predict the maximum number of temporary locations needed?

3-3. Write a sequence of instructions, each beginning at location 100B, that perform the following arithmetic calculations. Assume the following locations for I, J, and K:

Location	Use
50B	I
52B	J
54B	K
56B	temporary

(a) `K:= (3 + I)*(J + K);`
(b) `J:= (I*K + J/2) + (I/3)`
(c) `K:= J / (3*I + 2*J + K);`
(d) `I:= J*K/(I-4) - K*J*(I-7);`
(e) `I:= (((J - 2*K)/ K + J)/K - 3*I)/K;`

3-4. Write a sequence of code beginning at location 100B that branches to location 200B if

(a) M[250B] >= 0
(b) M[M[27B]] > 0
(c) M[AC + 42] < 0
(d) M[455B] <> 0
(e) M[AC] <= 0

3-5. For each of the following conditions, write a sequence of code starting at location 100B that branches to location 200B if the condition is true. Since there are several ways of encoding a condition, you should choose the way that produces the smallest amount of code. Also show exactly how you reexpressed the condition.

(a) M[250B] < 5
(b) (-7) > M[250B]
(c) M[250B] < M[20B]
(d) M[M[355B]] > M[M[370B]]
(e) M[M[220B]] < 12

3-6. Write a sequence of code beginning at location 100B that translates each of the following IF statements. Assume the following locations for *I*, *J*, and *K*:

Location	Use
50B	I
52B	J
54B	K
56B	temporary

(a)
```
IF I < 7 THEN
     J:= 3;
END IF
```
(b)
```
IF J<= 5*I THEN
     J:= 5*I;
END IF
```
(c)
```
IF K >= 0 THEN
     J:= K
ELSE
     J:= -K;
END IF
```
(d)
```
IF I <> 0 THEN
     K:= K+1;
     I:= 2*I + K;
END IF
```
(e)
```
IF I*J < K THEN
     K:= K+I*J
     J:= J+1
ELSE
     K:= 0;
     J:= J+1;
END IF
```

3-7. Write the logical negation of the following conditions:

(a) `I < 3`
(b) `J >= K*I`
(c) `K = J`
(d) `J <= I*(3-K)`
(e) `K > I/J`

3-8. Write the arithmetic negation of the conditions shown in Problem 3-7.

3-9. Explain the difference between logical negation and arithmetic negation of a condition. Which one preserves the original condition? Which one negates the original condition? Under which is equality preserved?

3-10. Name the two ways of implementing an indexed counting loop.

3-11. Using the formula for the trip count, how many iterations would be made by a loop with the following *initial value, final value,* and *increment*?

(a) `1, 5, 1` (b) `-5, -5, -1`
(c) `5, 1, -1` (d) `-5, 5, -2`
(e) `10, 2, -2` (f) `0, 99, 3`
(g) `4, 1, 1` (h) `99, 0, -3`
(i) `-5, -5, 1` (j) `1, 10, 10`

3-12. Write a trip count–controlled indexed counting loop beginning at location 100B that forms the sum of all even numbers between 2 and *N*. Use the following locations:

Location	Use	
30B	initial value	(M)
40B	final value	(N)
50B	loop index	
51B	trip count	
60B	sum	

3-14. Repeat Problem 3-12 with an index-controlled implementation, using the following locations:

Location	Use	
40B	final value	(N)
50B	loop index	
60B	sum	

3-15. Repeat Problem 3-13 with an index-controlled implementation, using the following locations:

Location	Use	
30B	initial value	(M)
40B	final value	(N)
50B	loop index	
60B	sum	

3-16. Why is the trip count implementation of the indexed counting loop considered more general than the index-controlled implementation. Give an example in which the first is superior to the second. Give an example in which the second is superior to the first.

3-17. Explain the difference between an indexed and an unindexed count loop.

3-18. Write an unindexed counting loop starting at location 100B that evaluates the following function:

```
g(0) = 3
g(i) = g(i-1)**2 - g(i-1)  i>0
```

Use the following locations

Location	Use	
50B	number to evaluate function	(N)
60B	function evaluated at N	(g(N))

3-19. How does a conditional loop differ from a counting loop? Can the number of iterations made by a conditionally controlled loop always be determined ahead of time?

3-20. Write a WHILE–DO loop that finds the largest value of $g(i)$ less than M. Use the following locations:

Location	Use	
40B	upper limit	(M)
60B	function evaluated at N	(g(i))
70B	temporary location	

3-21. The form of conditional loop

```
REPEAT
        ...
     <loop body>
        ...
UNTIL   condition
```

is similar to the WHILE–DO form, except that it tests its terminal condition at the end instead of the beginning. If the condition is false, the loop repeats; if the condition is true, it terminates. Suppose that we want a REPEAT–UNTIL loop to iterate as long as $g(i)$ is less than M. What terminal condition would be used to stop the loop correctly? Rewrite the loop from Problem 3-19 in its REPEAT–UNTIL form.

3-22. Many languages include a structure that transfers control to one of several places, depending on the value of a variable or expression. For example, the CASE statement

```
CASE V OF
   5:
      <statements>
   1..3:
      <statements>
   7,9,11:
      <statements>
   ELSE
      <statements>
END CASE
```

executes the first group of statements if the value of V is 5, the second group of statements if the value of V is between 1 and 3, the third group of statements if the value of V is either 7, 9, or 11, and the fourth group of statements if none of the other conditions is true. Show how this CASE statement would be translated for our machine.

4

Program Development

Now that we have written some simple pieces of code, it is clear that programming at this level poses some new problems. First, machine language programs are very difficult to understand. Assembly language programs are somewhat easier because they allow mnemonic operations and comments. Even so, how easy a program is to understand depends heavily on the quality of its documentation. It is especially difficult to determine what memory locations are used to hold given values just by reading the code. Though good-quality documentation goes a long way toward solving this problem, that alone is often not enough.

The second problem is that once a program is written, it is very difficult to modify. As we saw in Chapter 3, inserting or deleting a sequence of instructions may require extensive changes in the address fields of other instructions and data. The problem is most evident during program development, when the program may change from run to run.

Several solutions to these problems have been developed over the years. We will address the second issue first. The technique presented evolved very early in the development of machine-level programming techniques. Although the technique leaves much to be desired, it is still used under some circumstances today.

4.1 "PATCHING" A BROKEN PROGRAM

Suppose that we had just entered a new program into our machine through the switch register, set the PC to the starting address, and pushed the RUN button. After waiting several minutes for the program to finish, we reluctantly push the HALT button and begin to single-step through the program.

As we suspected, the culprit is an error in the terminating condition of a loop. We meant to write a REPEAT–UNTIL loop with the terminating condition

```
UNTIL  (N*N >= MAX)
```

Our code, however, corresponds to the terminating condition

```
UNTIL  (N >= MAX)
```

The problem is that *N* itself was used, instead of the square of *N*. Here are the actual instructions. Assume that MAX represents memory location 65B and *N* represents location 70B.

```
220B    LOAD    70B     if N*N >= MAX
221B    SUB     65B
222B    BRGE    224B    ... break out of loop
223B    BR      147B    else repeat again
```

It seems as though it should be a simple matter to insert the instruction "MUL 70B" just after location 220B. Unfortunately, correcting the error is more difficult than that. Here is what the code would look like if we simply moved the instructions starting at location 221B upward in memory to make room for the new one:

```
220B    LOAD    70B     if N*N >= MAX
221B    MUL     70B     <-- added instruction
222B    SUB     65B
223B    BRGE    224B    ... break out of loop
224B    BR      147B    else repeat again
```

Simply moving all the instructions upward is not enough. Some instructions in the program may no longer refer to the correct memory locations after they are moved. For example, the instruction "BRGE 224B" should be changed to "BRGE 225B". The purpose of the instruction is to branch past the instruction "BR 147B". Once this second branch is moved to location 224B, the instruction "BRGE 224B" no longer does the right thing.

However, it is not as simple as adding a constant to each of the address fields. Some are unaffected by the insertion. The address field of the instruction "BR 147B" is still correct because it refers to a memory location not involved in the change. The difficulty is in deciding which to change and which not to change. Each must be considered separately. It is painfully clear that moving even a small program around in memory can be quite a bit of work.

We would prefer a technique that spares us most of this trouble. Ideally, it would require little more work than entering the instruction that was left out. The method known as *patching* is just such a technique. The idea behind patching is to branch to a sequence of instructions somewhere else in memory that does what the omitted instruction(s) would do, then branch back and resume normal execution.

To illustrate the technique, we will patch the preceding section of code. Assume that a group of memory locations starting at location 600B are presently unused. First, we replace the LOAD instruction at 220B with a branch to location 600B:

```
220B    BR      600B        patch computes N*N

221B    SUB     65B         if N*N >= MAX
222B    BRGE    224B        ... break out of loop
223B    BR      147B        else repeat again
```

Then, starting at location 600B, we enter a sequence of code that leaves $N*N$ in the accumulator:

```
600B    LOAD    70B         compute N*N
601B    MUL     70B
602B    BR      221B        return to main code
```

The LOAD instruction at location 220B has been replaced by a branch to a patch at location 600B. The LOAD instruction is now the first instruction in the patch. It is followed by the previously omitted MUL instruction. The last instruction causes execution to continue at the instruction following the branch to the patch, in the main sequence of code, as shown in Figure 4-1.

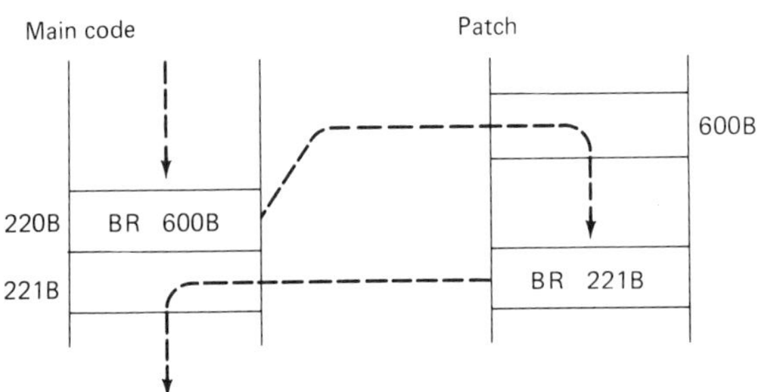

Figure 4-1 Path taken in executing a patch

This technique works regardless of the size of the patch. It would have been just as easy to patch in the code for the sixth power of N. The disadvantage is that if there are too many patches, the code becomes a rat's nest of branches all over memory. The situation can become unworkable after a while.

Patches are useful under two conditions. The first is when an error is discovered in a program already in memory. A patch can be carefully inserted and the program restarted with a minimum of delay. In this case, the patch must be noted in a program listing. The error should be corrected in some other way before reloading the program.

The second use of a patch is during development. An error may take some time to track down and correct. This may require inserting or deleting instructions in the process. It is easy to introduce even more errors while adjusting address fields and data to reflect the changes. Patches help limit errors by isolating the changes to a small section of code. Of course, once the problem is found and corrected, the changes should be made by inserting or deleting instructions and adjusting address fields and data accordingly. It is a bad idea to leave patches in a finished program.

4.2 SYMBOLIC LABELS

The technique of patching is not a very satisfactory long-term development technique. The resulting code is quite unreadable and very difficult to document. It is even more prone to error if patches are themselves patched.

It would be much better to discourage the use of patching and encourage the programmer to insert the sequence of code where it belongs in the program. While this requires extra effort on the part of the programmer, the resulting code is much easier to read and maintain.

The best solution would be to make the assembler program clever enough to change all of the addresses to account for the new instructions. Although there are several ways of doing this, the best way is simply to refrain from referring to fixed addresses.

Instead, the assembler should provide the programmer with some way of "marking" an instruction so that, for example, rather than writing a branch to a particular address, the programmer can write a branch to a particular instruction, regardless of where it is located in memory:

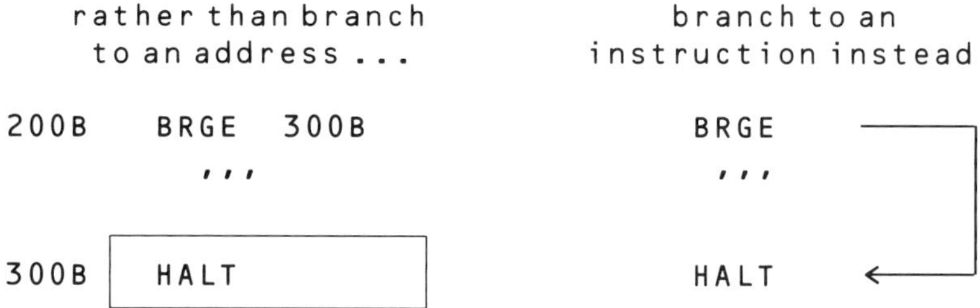

In most assemblers, this is accomplished by allowing instructions to be marked with a *symbolic label*. For example:

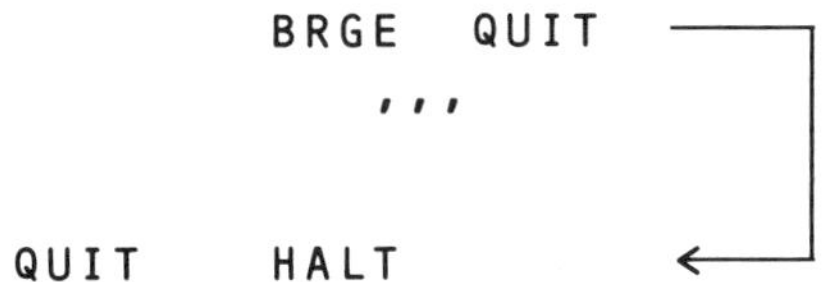

It is up to the assembler to determine at which address the instruction labeled QUIT is stored. The assembler then inserts the correct address into the address field of the BRGE instruction.

This solves two problems at once. First, the programmer is free to insert or delete any number of instructions between the BRGE instruction and the HALT instruction. The assembler will account for this and adjust all addresses accordingly. Second, symbolic labels can be used further to document the purpose of a given branch. It is much clearer that the instruction

```
BRGE    QUIT
```

causes the program to terminate than if it is written as

```
BRGE    300B
```

To illustrate how symbolic labels can aid program development, we will reconsider the trip count implementation of a loop that computes the *n*th Fibonacci number. We discussed this problem in Chapter 3. Here is how symbolic labels can be applied to the example. It is shown here exactly as it would be presented to the assembler provided with this text:

```
          ORG       100B
**   This program calculates the n-th Fibonacci number.
*    given the value of n stored at the location whose
*    label is N. Notice how symbolic labels are used
*    instead of physical addresses.

START     LOAD      =1        initialize f(0)
          STORE     LSTFIB
          STORE     FIB       initialize f(1)
          LOAD      =2        initialize trip count
          SUB       N         ... to 2-N
          BRGE      DONE      skip count expired

LOOP      STORE     I         save new count
          LOAD      FIB       save previous f(n)
```

```
              STORE     TEMP
              ADD       LSTFIB      compute new f(n)
              STORE     FIB
              LOAD      TEMP        use previous f(n) as
              STORE     LSTFIB      ... new f(n-1)

              LOAD      I           increment count
              ADD       =1
              BRLT      LOOP        repeat if in range

DONE          HALT

LSTFIB        BSS       1           for current f(n-1)
FIB           BSS       1           for current f(n)
TEMP          BSS       1           for updating f(n) and f(n-1)
I             BSS       1           for trip count
N             DATA      3           typical value for n

              END       START       post starting address
```

Compare this version with the one written in terms of physical addresses. Notice especially that *all* physical addresses have been replaced with references to labels. The code is much easier to read because the labels have mnemonic value. The code is easier to modify because the programmer is no longer directly concerned with physical addresses. Instead, that job is left to the assembler.

Notice also that storage locations as well as instructions can be labeled. This makes memory allocation much easier, because it is easy to change the physical location of a word without changing any of the instructions that refer to it. Again, the assembler determines the physical address associated with each label and assembles the instruction with the correct address in the address field.

An assembler that allows symbolic labels is quite a bit more complicated than one that expects physical addresses. There are two issues involved:

1. how symbolic labels are defined
2. how symbolic references are resolved

4.2.1 Defining Symbolic Labels

As we saw in the example just given, the assembler is alerted to a new definition whenever it encounters a string of nonspace characters immediately preceding the operation field of the instruction.

Assemblers often place certain restrictions on the formation of labels. For example, it is common to find a length restriction of about 8 characters. Although the assembler provided with the text makes no such restriction, it does impose a limit on the total number of characters in all of the labels. In practice, labels longer than about 8 characters make the program more difficult to read. We will have more to say about restrictions on labels in the next section.

How the label is distinguished from the operation field depends on the assembler. Some assemblers require that the label be followed by some unique symbol that is not otherwise allowed in the label; for example,

```
NEXT:     LOAD     N     load contents of location N
```

The symbol : is not part of the label itself. The assembler uses the colon as an indication that the preceding characters define a new label. The label can begin in any column. It cannot be confused with the operation field because of the trailing colon. However, if the colon were accidentally omitted, the assembler would interpret the label as the operation, the operation as the address, and the address as a part of a comment:

How the assembler would misinterpret this:

Other assemblers require that the label begin in a fixed column, usually column 1. The label is distinguished by the fact that it begins in column 1 and is separated from the operation field by one or more blanks. If an instruction had no label and accidentally began in column 1, the assembler would incorrectly interpret the operation field as the label, the address field as the operation, and the first word of the comment as the address field:

How the assembler would misinterpret this:

```
  ┌ label                 ┌ address
 /                       /
LOAD      /N          load contents of location N
         /               /
        └ operation     └ comment
```

The assembler provided with this text uses this second form. Labels *must* begin in column 1. If any nonspace character (except *, of course) is in column 1, it is interpreted as the first character of a label.

When the assembler encounters a new symbolic label, it enters it into a symbol table, which it maintains throughout the assembly process. We first encountered the symbol table in Chapter 3. There we used it to keep track of how particular locations were used. The assembler uses a symbol table for the same purpose.

The assembler's symbol table has at least two fields. The first is the symbolic label, and the second is its definition. The definition is usually the address at which the corresponding instruction or data will be placed into memory. Table 4-1 is the symbol table information for the Fibonacci program shown earlier.

TABLE 4-1 THE ASSEMBLER'S SYMBOL TABLE

Symbol	Definition
START	100B
LOOP	105B
DONE	120B
LSTFIB	121B
FIB	122B
TEMP	123B
I	124B
N	125B

A symbol can have only one definition. What does the assembler do if the same symbol appears in the label field of more than one instruction or data item? The usual thing is to issue an error message and ignore the new definition. This is how a duplicate label is treated in the assembler provided with this text.

4.2.2 Resolving Symbolic References

When a symbol is encountered in the address field of an instruction, the assembler must substitute the correct definition to assemble the instruction. For instance, when the assembler encounters the instruction

```
BR        LOOP
```

it must go to the symbol table and search for the symbolic label LOOP. The instruction is assembled after substituting the defined address 105B. The effect is the same as if the programmer had written

```
BR        105B
```

directly.

The assembler must be prepared for the case where a symbolic label is undefined. Most assemblers issue an error message and assemble something. The assembler provided with the text assembles a HALT instruction. Although this seems peculiar, the alternative is worse. The assembler *could* assemble the address 0B instead. By assembling a HALT, the programmer is assured that if the program is run anyway, it will stop running if the instruction is ever executed, rather than using the address 0B and producing the wrong answer. Both methods are actually in use by production assemblers.

Although the assembler provided with this text imposes no restrictions on what symbols are allowed in a label (except space, of course), there are certain practical restrictions. Consider the effect of the following instruction:

```
@LABEL    BR    @LABEL
```

It does *not* send the machine into an infinite loop. In fact, it causes an assembly error.

The assembler will happily enter "@LABEL" into the symbol table. However, in decoding the address field, the @ will be interpreted as the indirect address mode character. The assembler will then look up the definition of the symbolic label "LABEL", which is probably not defined. An undefined label message is issued, and the assembler will assemble a HALT instruction.

As a practical matter, the programmer should avoid any symbolic label that could be misinterpreted if it appeared in the address field of an instruction.

4.2.3 The Look-Ahead Problem

As the assembler scans the program, it enters new definitions into the symbol table and substitutes definitions for references to symbolic labels. Consider the instruction

```
LOAD    FIB         save previous f(n)
```

from the preceding example. When the assembler encounters this instruction, it looks in the symbol table for the definition of FIB . . . and *does not find it*! Why? The assembler has not yet encountered the line

```
FIB           BSS     1             for current f(n)
```

which comes much later in the program.

This dilemma is resolved by scanning the program more than once. Each scan is called a *pass*. An assembler that allows symbolic labels is almost always a *multipass assembler.*

Pass 1 is devoted to building the symbol table. During this pass, some preliminary work might also be done toward assembling instructions as far as possible. Instructions that do not make forward references to labels can be completely assembled on this pass.

Pass 2 is devoted to substituting definitions for references to symbolic labels. If pass 1 also assembles some instructions, pass 2 can ignore instructions that were completely assembled.

The listing can be made either on a third pass or during pass 2. Error messages also appear in the listing. They usually refer to the line numbers that appear in the margin of the listing.

4.2.4 Address Arithmetic

Many assemblers allow a limited form of arithmetic on references to symbolic labels. For example, the instruction

```
              ORG     100B
HERE          BR      HERE+1
```

does absolutely nothing! The label HERE is defined as 100B. In assembling the BR instruction, the assembler looks up the definition of HERE in the symbol table and adds 1 to it. Thus, the instruction is assembled as if the programmer had written

```
ORG     100B
BR      101B
```

This branch instruction simply branches to the following instruction.

The assembler provided with this text performs only addition (+) and subtraction (−). Any number of terms can be added and subtracted. Since the assembler detects the end of the address field at the first space, *no spaces can be embedded within the expression.*

4.2.5 The Special Symbol "Here"

The assembler recognizes a special symbol, read as "here," that always refers to the address of the current instruction. The assembler provided with this text uses the asterisk (*) for this purpose. Some other assemblers use the period (.) instead. "Here" finds its greatest use in composing compound branches. This is how "here" can be used to branch on not equal to zero or greater than zero:

```
What we want                  How to do it

        "branch if Not Equal to zero"
BRNE    100B                  BREQ    *+2   ──┐
                              BR      100B    │
                                            <─┘

"branch if Greater than zero"
BRGT    100B                  BREQ    *+2   ──┐
                              BRGE    100B    │
                                            <─┘
```

The symbol "here" is also used for very short branches forward or backward in loops. It is good practice to label the branch target explicitly if it is more than about five instructions away. Any further, and the program is likely to suffer from miscounted instructions or later additions and deletions between the branch and its target.

4.2.6 Another Way to Define a Symbol

Many high-level languages provide a way to define certain constants with symbolic names that describe their purpose. This would be an important feature to include in an assembler, too. All it requires is a way for the programmer to make arbitrary entries into the symbol table. Definitions in the symbol table are not necessarily restricted to addresses.

The pseudo-operation EQU allows the programmer to enter definitions of constants into the symbol table. For example,

```
N        EQU    20
```

enters the value 20 as the definition of the symbol label *N*. The symbol can then be referenced as if the constant 20 were actually written:

```
BSS    N      reserve N locations
ORG    N      set origin to N
SUB    =N     subtract N from AC
BR     N      branch to location N
```

Notice in the third case that immediate mode must be used to subtract the *number* 20 from the accumulator. Had we instead written

```
SUB    N      AC ⟵ AC - M[N]
```

it would subtract the *contents* of memory location 20 from the accumulator.

We will see many applications of the EQU pseudo-op throughout the text. It is especially useful in isolating *magic constants* within the program. A magic constant is a parameter of the program that is fixed at the time of assembly but may change from one assembly to the next. An example is the number of locations reserved by a BSS statement for a block of storage.

One good application for EQU is to define symbolic constants for the accumulator and index register:

```
AC      EQU    0       memory mapped address of AC
XR      EQU    1       memory mapped address of XR
```

Rather than writing

```
LOAD    @0
```

we could instead write the instruction in a more meaningful form as

```
LOAD    @AC
```

The assembler provided with this text has these two symbols predefined as shown. There is no need to make these definitions again before using them.

4.3 SUMMARY

The techniques presented in this chapter can significantly reduce the amount of time and effort required to write and debug a program. People who have programmed strictly in terms of physical addresses appreciate the fact that even a small change in a program may require a good deal of work.

Of the two techniques, patching is the less powerful. When it was first developed, symbolic assemblers were still a dream instead of a reality. In fact, the amount of effort required in writing *any* assembler was substantial. Today, patching is used mainly by systems programmers to correct errors in large systems already in memory. The correction will also be made in the assembly language program so that it will be correct the next time it is reassembled and loaded into memory.

Symbolic addresses are the rule in most programming environments. In fact, very few programmers today can even imagine what it would be like to program in terms of physical addresses, let alone survive the experience for any but the most trivial of programs.

However, learning without this feature has benefits. Beginning programmers find that starting out with physical addresses aids in understanding how the machine processes a program. Symbolic labels hide this to some extent.

Another benefit is that the programmer quickly learns to check a program carefully before actually running it. The consequence of not doing this is having to retype a number of statements to correct even a minor error. Hand-checking a program can reduce the overall development time by catching errors before the program is entered, rather than wasting a number of runs to find the problem.

PROBLEMS

4-1. Why is it so difficult to insert the missing instruction "DIV 70B" in the following example? Describe what would have to be done to make the insertion correctly.

...

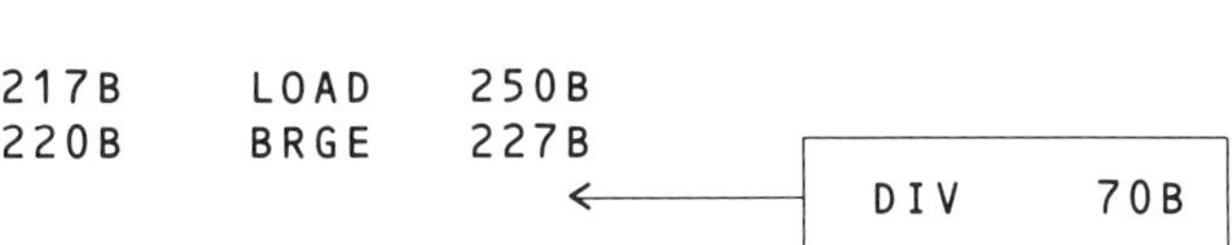

```
221B    ADD     =2
222B    STORE   250B
223B    LOAD    50B
224B    ADD     =1
225B    STORE   50B
226B    BR      217B
                 ...
```

4-2. How does the technique of patching make the job of inserting instructions easier?

4-3. Assume that a block of storage starting at location 300B is presently unused. Patch in the missing instruction.

4-4. Describe the problem with patching in terms of the long-term development of a program.

4-5. Why is it advantageous to write a branch to an *instruction* rather than to a fixed location in memory?

4-6. What is the marker called by which the programmer can indicate a given instruction rather than a fixed location in memory?

4-7. Rewrite the following instructions in terms of physical memory addresses:

```
                ORG     200B
                LOAD    N
                BRGE    NOT.NEG
                MUL     MINUS.ONE
NOT.NEG         HALT
MINUS.ONE       DATA    -1
N               DATA    -15
```

4-8. A label is delimited by a colon in some assemblers. Why is it unnecessary to start a label in a particular column with such an assembler?

4-9. What happens if the programmer accidentally leaves off the colon?

4-10. A label is delimited by a blank in other assemblers. Why are labels required to begin in some fixed column with these assemblers?

4-11. Which method does the assembler supplied with this text use?

4-12. What happens if the programmer accidentally begins an unlabeled instruction in column 1 with this assembler?

4-13. Describe the purpose of a symbol table in an assembler.

4-14. Name the fields in the assembler's symbol table and describe their purpose.

4-15. Construct the symbol table for the program in Problem 4-7.

4-16. Why does it not make sense to allow the same label to mark two different instructions?

4-17. Can two labels mark the *same* instruction? (*Hint:* What is the effect of the pseudo-op "BSS 0"? An experiment might be in order.)

4-18. How does our assembler handle the case of a duplicate label?

4-19. What does the assembler do on encountering a symbol in the address field of an instruction?

4-20. Describe two alternative actions of an assembler upon encountering an undefined symbol in the address field of an instruction. Which alternative does our assembler choose? Why?

4-21. Some of these labels are illegal, some are legal but can never be used in the address field of an instruction, and others are perfectly all right. Decide which is the case for each. Briefly state the reason for each.

(a) `LABEL` **(b)** `%_CHANGE`
(c) `MY.LABEL` **(d)** `*LITE*BRITE`
(e) `FIRST ONE` **(f)** `$AMOUNT`
(g) `X<Y?` **(h)** `ITEM#`
(i) `#_CORRECT` **(j)** `@HOME`

4-22. Explain why referring to a label before the assembler encounters the definition is a problem.

4-23. How do most assemblers get around this problem?

4-24. Describe the purpose of each pass.

4-25. Under what circumstances can an instruction be completely assembled during pass 1?

4-26. What arithmetic operations does our assembler perform between addresses and numbers during assembly? Why does this make the use of parentheses unnecessary?

4-27. Here is a small symbol table. Evaluate the following expressions.

Symbol	Definition
L	500B
M	123B
N	2B

(a) `L+3` **(b)** `-M+L`
(c) `M-N+2` **(d)** `L+M-N`
(e) `-2+N`

4-28. Describe the purpose of the special symbol "here." What two characters are often chosen for this symbol? Which does our assembler use?

4-29. What is the value of the address field in each of the lines marked by a letter? What is stored at location 106B after the HALT instruction executes?

```
    ORG     100B
(a) LOAD    *+4
(b) ADD     *+4
(c) STORE   *+4
    HALT
(d) DATA    *
(e) DATA    *
    BSS     1
```

4-30. Why is it a good idea to label the branch target explicitly if it is more than about five instructions away, rather than use the symbol "here"?

4-31. Create a symbol table for the following program.

```
N.TIMES     EQU     20
```

```
                ORG      100
BLOCK           BSS      N.TIMES
START           LOAD     =NTIMES-1
AGAIN           BRGE     *+2
                HALT
                STORE    $BLOCK
                SUB      =1
                BR       AGAIN
                END      START
```

4-32. Assemble the program into binary machine code, ready to be entered through the switch register.

4-33. What would have been loaded had we instead written

```
START           LOAD     NTIMES-1
```

in Problem 4-31?

4-34. What are the predefined values of the symbols AC and XR?

5

Arrays

The techniques presented in the preceding chapters allow us to write programs of moderate complexity. We saw how to write assignment and arithmetic statements, achieve the effect of any conditional branch, and compose an arbitrarily complex loop. However, the number of "interesting" programs that can be written using only these simple tools is quite small. To get the most out of our machine, more advanced techniques are called for.

In this chapter, we will look at how arrays of data are stored in memory. We will also consider several ways to *access* this data efficiently. In the process, several myths about the cost of using arrays will be dispelled.

5.1 WHY DO WE NEED ARRAYS?

Arrays provide a means of processing a large amount of related data in a very simple and uniform way. Most programs process arrays of data, rather than running the program once for each datum in the set. Many problems, such as sorting, require that the entire array be present to work correctly.

The simplest way to represent an array is as a contiguous block of storage in memory. Why contiguous? Having the next piece of data at the next location in memory makes *referencing* successive array elements very easy. If we knew the address of an array element and wanted to move to the next one, we could simply add 1 to the address we had. This is just what occurs when the PC is incremented during program execution. Memory itself can be viewed as a large array that holds both programs and data. The PC serves as a pointer into that array.

Loops and arrays are very much interrelated. On one hand, not much can be done to arrays without using loops. On the other, the most interesting examples of using loops involve arrays. With this in mind, we will take another look at loops, this time focusing on loop bodies that involve arrays.

5.2 TWO MODELS OF AN ARRAY

Most high-level programming languages tell us that an array is a contiguous block of storage that can be referenced by means of an *array index*. This is a convenient way to think about arrays in many cases. However, there is another model, seldom supported in higher-level languages. It is just as useful and is often less expensive to implement at the machine level. We will examine each of these to discover their relative merit.

5.2.1 The Base-Offset Model

Consider the way most high-level languages encourage us to think about arrays. A particular location within the array can be referenced as a fixed *offset* from a starting or *base address*. Suppose that an array five items long begins at memory location 100B. The address of the first item, 100B, is the base address of this array. The first item in the array is referenced by the base address 100B, plus an offset of 0 from the base address. The second item is referenced by the base address 100B, plus an offset of 1 from the base address.

In some cases, it is convenient to think of the first item as having an offset other than 0. For instance, a table of the number of days in each month of the year is more naturally referenced with an offset of 1 for January through 12 for December. This gives rise to the notion of a *lower bound* for the array. The lower bound on the array of months is 1. The address of the *k*th item in the array is given by the formula

$$\text{Address} = \text{base address} - \text{lower bound} + k$$

As an example, suppose that we want to form the average of a number of test scores held in the array SCORE. The number of scores to average is given by the variable *N*. Assume that the lower bound of SCORE is 1. Here is a simple loop that does the job:

```
SUM:= 0;
FOR I:=  1 TO N DO
        SUM:= SUM + SCORE[I];
END FOR
AVG:= SUM/N;
```

Here is a direct translation of this loop into instructions written for our simple machine. The locations used by the program are

Use	Label
Number of scores	(N)
Sum of scores	(SUM)
Average of scores	(AVG)
Base address of the array	(SCORE)

Assume that these locations are established and initialized elsewhere in the program.

```
            LOAD    =0          initialize sum
            STORE   SUM

LOOP        ADD     =1          increment loop index
            STORE   XR          save index in index reg.
            SUB     N           if index > no. to sum,
            BREQ    *+2
            BRGE    DONE        ... terminate loop

            LOAD    $SCORE-1    fetch next score
            ADD     SUM         add score to old sum
            STORE   SUM         save new sum

            LOAD    XR          fetch loop index
            BR      LOOP        ... and repeat again

DONE        LOAD    SUM         compute average
            DIV     N
            STORE   AVG
```

The index was used here directly to control the loop. We noted earlier that this method is often shorter than the trip count method in cases where the step direction is known. If the order of summation is not important, we could make the loop somewhat shorter by running a descending rather than an ascending loop index.

The loop index in this example was used not only to control the loop itself but also as the array index. To use the indexed address mode to reference the array, it is important that we use the index register (XR) to hold the loop index. Recall from Chapter 1 that the index register is memory-mapped to memory address 1. Our assembler predefines the symbol XR as 1.

Now for the body of the loop itself. The indexed address mode is ideal for manipulating arrays. For example, the register transfer expression for an indexed load,

$$\text{AC} \longleftarrow \text{M[XR + k]}$$

is just the form needed for an array reference. In this example, XR holds the array index, while the constant k represents the difference

$$\text{Base address} - \text{lower bound}$$

There is no need to perform this subtraction during execution. Since the lower bound is a fixed constant, the difference is also a fixed constant that can be computed by the programmer and placed directly in the code. Here, the instruction

```
LOAD  $SCORE-1
```

serves this purpose.*

A rather interesting result came out of this exercise that bears closer examination. We noticed that referencing an array element A[I], according to the formula A + M[I] − 1 could be made cheaper by precomputing the difference A − 1 at the time the code is written, rather than adding instructions to do it while the program is running.

The question now arises as to whether certain other arithmetic operations can be eliminated from array references. For example, how cheaply can the array reference A[I + 6] be written? The formula for this reference is

$$(A-1) + M[I] + 6$$

Clearly, if the 6 is also added to the address A at the same time that the lower bound is subtracted, the addition of the constant during execution need never be performed. That is, rather than write

```
LOAD      =A-1          the address A-1
ADD       I             ...plus the index value
ADD       =6               ...plus a constant, 6
```

to compute the address A[I + 6], we can instead write

```
LOAD      =A-1+6        the address (A-1)+6
ADD       I             ...plus the index value
```

This means that the addition or subtraction of constants in array references generally costs nothing extra. They can all be done when the reference is assembled, instead of adding extra instructions to do it while the program is running. This result is quite surprising at first.

Even more surprising is the fact that array references involving *strictly* constant values cost no more than simple memory references. For example, bringing the contents of A[6] into the accumulator is as simple as

```
LOAD      A-1+6
```

since A − 1 + 6 is the address of the sixth memory location of the array with a lower bound of 1, beginning at location A.

Another case where the base-offset model works well is when there are several array references within the loop, each related to the same index. Consider the prob-

*This is why most languages that allow the programmer to choose a lower bound require that it be given as a fixed constant instead of a variable. If the lower bound is given as a fixed constant, the compiler can compute this difference and generate a single instruction, as was done in the present case.

lem of adding two arrays, A and B, storing the sum in array C. Assuming a lower bound of 0, we might express the algorithm like this:

```
FOR I:= 0 TO N-1 DO
  C[I]:= A[I] + B[I];
END FOR
```

Once again, we use an indexed controlled loop, with the index in XR. Here is how memory is used:

Use	Label
Size of arrays	(N)
Base address of first array	(A)
Base address of second array	(B)
Base address of sum array	(C)

Assume that these locations are established and initialized elsewhere in the program.

```
             LOAD    =0          initialize loop index

LOOP         STORE   XR          save index in index reg.
             SUB     N           if index >= array size
             BRGE    DONE        ... terminate loop

             LOAD    $A          fetch next value from A
             ADD     $B          add in next value from B
             STORE   $C          save in next loc. in C

             LOAD    XR          increment index
             ADD     =1
             BR      LOOP        ... and repeat again

DONE         BSS     0           exit point from loop
```

Although we are dealing with three different arrays in the same loop, all references are controlled by the same index. If order is not important, we could also shorten this loop a little by running a descending rather than an ascending loop index.

As a final example of the base-offset method, suppose that we want a table of the first *N* Fibonacci numbers. Assuming that the array FIB is defined with a lower bound of 0, this loop will compute the table values:

```
FIB[0]:= 1;
FIB[1]:= 1;
  FOR i:= 2 TO N-1 DO
```

```
        FIB[I]:= FIB[I-1] + FIB[I-2];

    END FOR
```

Once again, we use an index-controlled loop, with the index in XR. Here is how memory is used:

Use	Label
Number of values to compute	(N)
Base address of array	(FIB)

Assume that these locations are established and initialized elsewhere in the program.

```
            LOAD    =1
            STORE   FIB         initialize FIB[0]
            STORE   FIB+1       initialize FIB[1]

LOOP        ADD     =1          increment loop index
            STORE   XR          save index in index reg.
            SUB     N           if index >= array size
            BRGE    DONE        ... terminate loop

            LOAD    $FIB-1      fetch FIB[I-1]
            ADD     $FIB-2      add in FIB[I-1]
            STORE   $FIB        save in FIB[I]

            LOAD    XR          fetch loop index
            BR      LOOP        ... and repeat again

DONE        BSS     0           exit point from loop
```

Here we referenced FIB[I – 1] and FIB[I – 2] by subtracting constants from the base address FIB rather than from the index.

5.2.2 The Pointer Model

Consider again the problem, presented at the beginning of the last section, of averaging the *N* scores in the array SCORE. The reason for having an index in this example

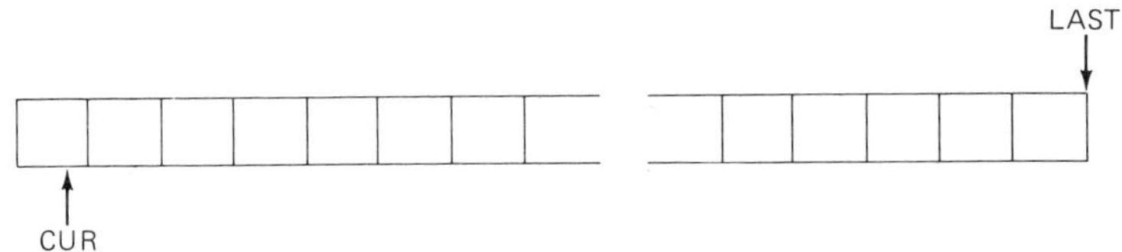

Figure 5-1 CUR and LAST point to the beginning and end of the array

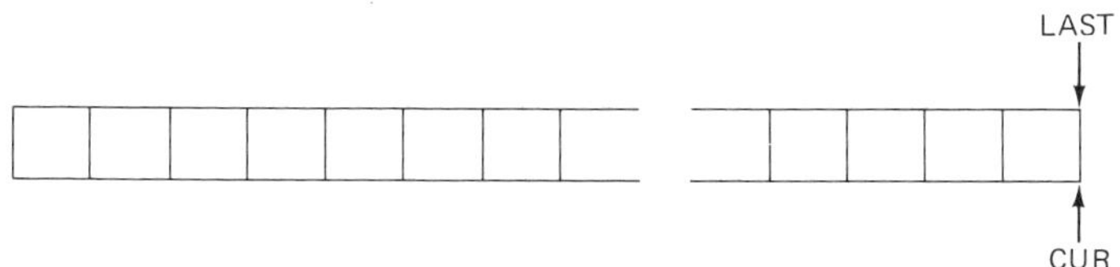

Figure 5-2 Loop terminates when CUR pointer meets LAST pointer

was to control the loop and references to successive scores in the array. In this section, we will take another approach.

Instead of an index relative to the base address of the array, we will use an index that is the absolute memory address of an item in the array. Accessing the content of a word is done using indirect addressing. An index used in this way is known as a *pointer*, because it "points" to a location within the array.

To form the sum of the scores in SCORE, we must use two pointers, as shown in Figure 5-1. One serves the same role as the index in the previous version. It is initialized to the base address of the array. The other points to the end of the array. It is used to check the terminating condition each time through the loop. This pointer plays the same role as the array size in the base-offset version. As the first pointer steps along the array, it is compared to the second one. The loop terminates when the first pointer meets the second one (Figure 5-2).

Here is how this program would be written using the pointer rather than the base-offset model. The locations used by the program are

Use	Label
Pointer to current element	(CUR^)
Pointer past last element	(LAST^)
Sum of scores	(SUM)
Average of scores	(AVG)
Size of array	(N)
Base address of the array	(SCORE)

Assume that these locations are established and initialized elsewhere in the program.

```
          LOAD    =0         initialize sum
          STORE   SUM
          LOAD    =SCORE     initialize ending ptr.
          ADD     N
          STORE   LAST^
          LOAD    =SCORE     initialize current ptr.

LOOP      STORE   CUR^       save current ptr.
          SUB     LAST^      if ptr. off end of array,
          BRGE    DONE       ... terminate loop
```

```
          LOAD      @CUR^          fetch next score
          ADD       SUM            add score to old sum
          STORE     SUM            save new sum

          LOAD      CUR^           advance pointer
          ADD       =1             ... to next score
          BR        LOOP           ... and repeat again

DONE      LOAD      SUM            compute average
          DIV       N
          STORE     AVG
```

Although there are a few more instructions during initialization and an extra storage location, this version clearly illustrates how the pointer model works. Notice that if the order of summation is unimportant, we could save a few instructions by running CUR^ backwards from the end of the array to the beginning. Since the base address SCORE is constant, this would also eliminate the need for the second pointer, LAST^.

A final example of using pointers shows their advantage over the base-offset model. Consider the problem of reversing the contents of an array. For example, given the array in Figure 5-3, its reverse would be as shown in Figure 5-4.

An easy way to reverse an array is to establish pointers to the first and last location in the array (Figure 5-5). For each iteration, exchange the two values indicated by the pointers (Figure 5-6). Then increment the lower pointer and decrement the upper pointer (Figure 5-7). The exchange is complete when the two pointers cross (Figure 5-8). Here is a list of the storage used.

Use	Label
Pointer to first array location	(FIRST^)
Pointer to last array location	(LAST^)
Temporary for exchange	(TEMP)
Size of array	(N)
Base address of array	(A)

1	2	3	4	5	6	7	8

Figure 5-3 Array before being reversed

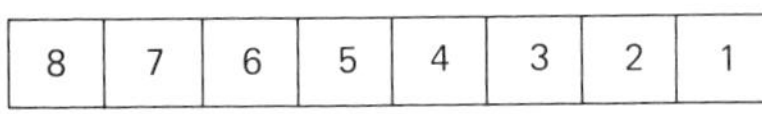

Figure 5-4 Array after being reversed

LAST (points to 8)

1	2	3	4	5	6	7	8

FIRST (points to 1)

Figure 5-5 Pointers initialized to the beginning and end of the array

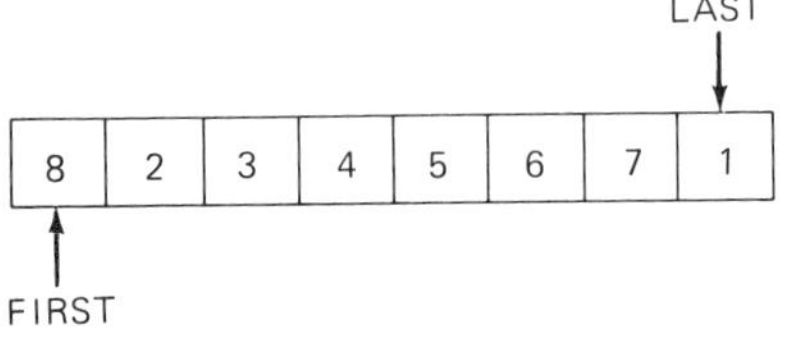

Figure 5-6 First and last array values exchanged

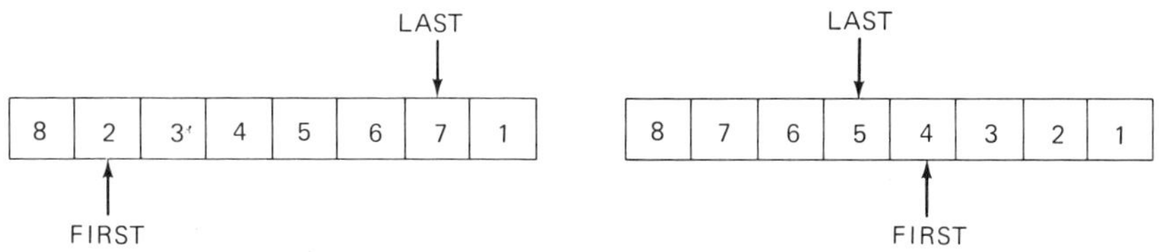

Figure 5-7 Pointers stepped to next values to be exchanged

Figure 5-8 Array is reversed when the two pointers cross

Assume again that these locations were reserved and initialized elsewhere in the program.

```
            LOAD    =A         initialize FIRST^
            STORE   FIRST^
            ADD     N          initialize LAST^

LOOP        SUB     =1         decr. LAST^ to prev. item
            STORE   LAST^      save new LAST^
            SUB     FIRST^     if pointers have crossed
            BRLT    DONE       ... terminate loop

            LOAD    @FIRST^    exchange values pointed to
            STORE   TEMP       ... by FIRST^ and LAST^
            LOAD    @LAST^
            STORE   @FIRST^
            LOAD    TEMP
            STORE   @LAST^

            LOAD    FIRST^     advance FIRST^ to next item
            ADD     =1
            STORE   FIRST^
            LOAD    LAST^      fetch current LAST^
            BR      LOOP       ... and repeat

END.LOOP    BSS     0          exit from loop
```

Using the pointer model for this example provides the most natural way to express the algorithm. Trying to use the base-offset model leads to code that is not only larger but also more difficult to understand.

5.3 TWO-DIMENSIONAL ARRAYS

A two-dimensional array is one that has both height and width. An item in such an array is referenced by a row number and a column number. The *i*th row and the *j*th column of the array A is referenced as

```
A[I,J]
```

The easiest way to represent a two-dimensional array is to store it sequentially in memory one row or column at a time. For example, a three-by-three array

$$\begin{bmatrix} a_{11} & a_{12} & a_{13} \\ a_{21} & a_{22} & a_{23} \\ a_{31} & a_{32} & a_{33} \end{bmatrix}$$

could be stored starting at memory location 100B by column as follows:

```
100B    a11
101B    a21
102B    a31
103B    a12
104B    a22
105B    a32
106B    a13
107B    a23
110B    a33
```

A two-dimensional array that is stored linearly in memory by column is said to be stored in *column-major order*. Similarly, one that is stored by row is said to be stored in *row-major order*. The FORTRAN language stores arrays in column-major order; practically all other languages use row-major order. We will assume column-major storage in the examples that follow. The changes required for row-major storage are not difficult and are left as exercises.

Our first problem at the machine level is being able to reference the correct memory location given a row and column number. The formula is really not difficult to derive. Three other pieces of information must be known about the array to make this determination:

1. the base address B of the array
2. the number of rows, N_r, in the array
3. the lower bound of each dimension, LB_r and LB_c

Given these, the address of the *i*th row and *j*th column is

$$B + (j - LB_c) * N_r + (i - LB_r)$$

The first term gives the position of the array in memory. The second term accounts for the number of whole columns that must be skipped over to get to column *j*. The last term accounts for the position of row *i* in the *j*th column.

To illustrate the technique, suppose we want to form the sum of the items stored in a two-dimensional array A, which has *NROWS* rows and *NCOLS* columns. A loop that accomplishes this is

```
SUM:= 0;
FOR I:= 1 TO NROWS DO
   FOR J:= 1 TO NCOLS DO

      SUM:= SUM + A[I,J];

   END FOR
END FOR
```

Two indexed counting loops are called for, one nested within the other. We will again choose the index-controlled method. Here is how storage is used:

Use	Label
Sum of array elements	(SUM)
Index of outer loop	(I)
Index of inner loop	(J)
Number of rows	(NROWS)
Number of columns	(NCOLS)
Base address of array	(A)

Assume that these locations were reserved and initialized elsewhere in the program.

```
           LOAD     =0          initialize sum
           STORE    SUM
           LOAD     =1          set outer loop index

LOOP.ROW   STORE    I           save new outer loop index
           SUB      NROWS       if index exceeds # of rows
           BREQ     *+2
           BRGE     END.ROW     ... terminate outer loop
           LOAD     =1          set inner loop index

LOOP.COL   STORE    J           save new inner loop index
           SUB      NCOLS       if index exceeds # of columns
           BREQ     *+2
           BRGE     END.COL     ... terminate inner loop
           LOAD     J           calculate offset [i,j]
           SUB      =1          ... as (j-1)*NROWS + i
           MUL      NROWS
           ADD      I
```

```
         ADD       =A-1        add A - lower row bound of 1
         LOAD      @AC         fetch value using addr. in AC
         ADD       SUM         ... and add to sum
         STORE     SUM
         LOAD      J           increment inner loop index
         ADD       =1
         BR        LOOP.COL    ... and repeat inner loop
END.COL  BSS       0           exit point for inner loop

         LOAD      I           increment outer loop index
         ADD       =1
         BR        LOOP.ROW    ... and repeat outer loop
END.ROW  BSS       0           exit point for outer loop
```

Notice how the array reference formula was integrated into the inner loop. The constant lower-row bound of 1 was subtracted at the same time that the base address A was added in. Since the AC is memory-mapped to address 0, the address in the AC was used to fetch the array element by loading indirectly through address 0. The constant *AC* is predefined by our assembler to be 0.

This code is a literal translation of the FOR loop shown earlier. There are a number of improvements we could make. For example, we could run both the inner and outer loop indices from 0 instead of 1. This would eliminate both

```
BREQ      *+2
```

instructions from the termination test of the inner and outer loops. It would also shorten the reference calculation in the inner loop to

```
LOAD      J          calculate offset [i,j]
MUL       NROWS
ADD       I
ADD       =A         add base address
LOAD      @AC        fetch A[i,j]
```

We can also take advantage of the pattern of successive array references. We are stepping through a column-major array in row-major order. Here, for example, is the reference pattern for the three-by-three column-major array shown earlier:

100B	a_{11}	(1)
101B	a_{21}	(4)
102B	a_{31}	(7)
103B	a_{12}	(2)
104B	a_{22}	(5)
105B	a_{32}	(8)

106B	a_{13}	(3)
107B	a_{23}	(6)
110B	a_{33}	(9)

Columns within each row are spaced NROWS elements apart in the column-major array. To reference the next column in the row, we simply add NROWS to the current index. We can tell when the index is past the last column in the row, because it will also be past the end of the array. Subtracting the array size and adding 1 at this point will "wrap" the index around to the first column in the next row. The loop terminates when the index is past the last row in the array. Here is how storage is used:

Use	Label
Sum of array elements	(SUM)
Number of rows	(NROWS)
Number of columns	(NCOLS)
Total size of array	(ASIZE)
Base address of array	(A)

Assume that these locations were reserved and initialized elsewhere in the program.

```
          LOAD    NROWS      size of array
          MUL     NCOLS
          STORE   ASIZE
          LOAD    =0
          STORE   SUM        initial sum

LOOP.ROW  STORE   XR         save index to next row
          SUB     NROWS      if past last row in array,
          BRGE    END.ROW    ... terminate outer loop
          LOAD    XR

LOOP.COL  SUB     ASIZE      if past last column in row,
          BRGE    END.COL    ... terminate inner loop
          LOAD    $A         sum next array element
          ADD     SUM
          STORE   SUM
          LOAD    XR         advance index
          ADD     NROWS      ... to next column in row
          STORE   XR
          BR      LOOP.COL   repeat for next column

END.COL   ADD     =1         advance index to new row
          BR      LOOP.ROW   repeat for next row
END.ROW   BSS     0
```

If the exact order of summation is unimportant, we can do even better. When scanning a column-major array, it is easier to scan along the columns than along the rows. In effect, we can treat the two-dimensional array as an *NR*-by-*NC*-long singly dimensioned array. Here is how memory is used:

Use	Label
Sum of array elements	(SUM)
Number of rows	(NROWS)
Number of columns	(NCOLS)
Base address of array	(A)

Assume again that these locations have been reserved and initialized elsewhere in the program.

```
            LOAD     =0        initial sum
            STORE    SUM
            LOAD     NROWS     initial loop index
            MUL      NCOLS

LOOP        SUB      =1        decrement loop index
            BRLT     DONE      exit if out of range
            STORE    XR        save new index
            LOAD     $A        get next item from array
            ADD      SUM       ... and add it into sum
            STORE    SUM
            LOAD     XR        fetch loop index
            BR       LOOP      ... and repeat
END.LOOP    BSS      0
```

There are many cases where, by analyzing the problem carefully first, two-dimensional array referencing can be deferred in favor of an equivalent problem with a one-dimensional array.

5.4 SUMMARY

This chapter introduced the concept of an array from the machine-level perspective. It was shown that there are really two ways to reference a location within an array:

1. as an offset from a fixed base
2. as a pointer directly to the location

Which way we think about an array depends on the nature of the particular problem.

We also explored a way to reference two-dimensional arrays. As we saw, the most important thing about them is to try to avoid them by changing the problem slightly. Armed with our knowledge of arrays, we will begin applying it in the next chapter.

PROBLEMS

5-1. What is an array? Why can memory itself be thought of as an array?

5-2. An array begins at location 345B. We want to reference the item stored at location 350B. What is the base of the array? What is the offset to location 350B?

5-3. What is the purpose of a lower bound on an array? How are the lower bound and index different from the base and offset?

5-4. The array A begins at location 100B in memory. Given is a lower bound and a reference to an item in that array. Compute the address being referenced.

(a) A[2], lower bound: 0
(b) A[5], lower bound: 1
(c) A[−3], lower bound: −7
(d) A[10], lower bound: 10
(e) A[6], lower bound: −22

5-5. Under what condition are instructions for the subtraction

Base address − lower bound

not actually written in computing an array reference? How then is this difference formed?

5-6. Explain why the cost of computing the array reference A[I + 6] is no more than that for the reference A[I]. Assume that A is an array with a base address of 100B and a lower bound of 5. I is stored at location 50B. Write a sequence of instructions that brings the contents of A[I + 6] into the accumulator.

5-7. Explain why the cost of referencing A[6] is no greater than the cost of referencing a simple variable. Assume that A is an array with a base address of 350B and a lower bound of −4. Write a single instruction that brings the contents of A[9] into the accumulator.

5-8. Write an index-controlled, indexed counting loop that does the same thing as the following FOR loop:

```
N:= 0;
FOR I:= 1 TO K DO
    N:= N + A[I]/K
END FOR
```

Assume that the following locations have been reserved and that location K and the array A contain the correct values. The index register is used for the loop index.

Use	Label
Number of terms to add	(K)
Loop index	(XR)
Sum of terms	(N)
Base address of array	(A)

Use *indexed addressing* for this problem.

5-9. Write the register transfer expression for the assignment A[I]: = J;.

5-10. What is a pointer? How does its use in stepping through an array in a loop simplify the code?

5-11. Rewrite the loop from Problem 5-8 using the pointer method. Use the pointer to control the loop. Assume that the following memory locations have already been reserved and that location K and array A contain the correct values.

Use	Label
Number of terms to add	(K)
Current pointer	(CUR^)
Final pointer	(LST^)
Sum of terms	(N)
Base address of array	(A)

5-12. How would the items in the three-by-two array A be stored in column-major order? In row-major order?

5-13. In which form does FORTRAN store two-dimensional arrays? In which form do most other languages store two-dimensional arrays?

5-14. Assume that the two-dimensional array A has three rows and four columns. The array is stored in column-major order. Given are the lower bounds for the row and column dimensions and an array reference. At what address would that item be found?

(a) A[2,2], LB_r : 1, LB_c : 1
(b) A[2,4], LB_r : 0, LB_c : 2
(c) A[-2,5], LB_r : -3, LB_c : 3
(d) A[2,1], LB_r : 0, LB_c : 0
(e) A[2,1], LB_r : 2, LB_c : 1

5-15. There is a formula for referencing a row-major array that is similar to the one for a column-major array. Write the formula.

5-16. Redo Problem 5-14 assuming that the array is stored in row-major order.

5-17. Write a sequence of code that places the sum of matrices A and B into matrix C. Both A and B are *NR* rows high and *NC* columns wide. Matrix C is large enough to hold the sum. Assume that the following locations have already been reserved and that locations NR, NC, and the arrays A and B contain the correct values.

Use	Label
Temporary for address	(A^)
Temporary for address	(B^)
Temporary for address	(C^)
Number of rows	(NR)
Number of columns	(NC)
Base address of A	(A.LOC)
Base address of B	(B.LOC)
Base address of C	(C.LOC)

(*Hint:* The lower bounds are not given in the problem, nor are they needed. Why?)

6

Procedures

One of the oldest and most important programming concepts is that of a *procedure*. In this chapter we will look at the basic procedure mechanism and how to express it at the machine level. We will also consider the idea of a parameter and the trade-offs between many of the same parameter-passing methods found in higher-level languages.

We have already discussed a concept that is very much related to procedures. As we will see, procedures can be thought of as an extension of the idea of patching.

6.1 THE PROCEDURE AS AN EXTENSION OF PATCHING

Procedures have quite a bit in common with patches. The difference is that procedures are planned ahead of time, while patches are made after the fact. Why would someone write a program that incorporates a patch from the start? A patch by itself would not be very useful in general. However, a procedure has properties that make it more useful than a patch. Procedures serve three purposes:

1. They save space, because they can be used wherever there is an often-repeated section of code. A single copy of the instructions can be shared, rather than duplicating them each time they are needed.
2. They save programming effort, because once a useful procedure is written, it can be applied in almost the same way as a new machine instruction. There is no need to redesign a long sequence of code each time it is needed.
3. They form building blocks in structured programs. By modularizing with pro-

cedures, a structured approach is one way to assist the programmer in arriving at a correct program. This is independent of how many times the procedure is used within a program.

A procedure is used almost like a patch. A sequence of code is replaced by a branch to a procedure that does what the omitted code would do. Once those instructions have been executed, control transfers back to the main sequence of code at the instruction following the branch.

Writing a procedure requires a bit more effort than does a simple patch. A patch is branched to from a fixed location in memory and returns control to the location following that branch once its instructions are executed. A procedure, on the other hand, can be branched to from any location in memory. Some means must be provided so that control is returned to the correct location once its instructions have executed.

Suppose that in the course of writing a program, we find ourselves taking the absolute value of *N* quite often:

```
          ...
        LOAD    N         if N is positive
        BRGE    *+3       ... do nothing
        LOAD    =0        else
        SUB     N         ... form its negative
          ...
```

If this sequence were written as a simple patch, here is how it would look:

```
                  ...
        BR      PATCH     find abs. value of N
NEXT    BSS     0         resume processing here
                  ...

* TAKES ABSOLUTE VALUE OF N
*
PATCH   LOAD    N         if N is positive
        BRGE    NEXT      ... return to main code
        LOAD    =0        else
        SUB     N         ... form negative
        BR      NEXT      return to main code
```

The problem, of course, is that it can be used only at location NEXT-1 because control always returns to location NEXT. It would take very little effort to generalize this patch into a simple procedure that could be used anywhere. The only thing holding us back at this point is how to return control to the correct location in the main sequence of code once the absolute value of *N* has been found.

As a first attempt (and there will be several), suppose that before branching to the procedure, we load the *return address* into the accumulator. We must also add an instruction at the beginning of the patch to save this address in a temporary location.

Once the absolute value of N is found, control returns to the main sequence of code by branching *indirectly* through this temporary location.

We must be very careful to reserve a memory location for the return address. Lest we forget, we will reserve the location just before the procedure for this purpose. For reasons that we will soon discover, this location is given the procedure label:

```
                 ...
        LOAD    =*+2              put return address in AC
        BR      ABS.N+1           ... and branch to proc.
                 ...

** ABS. N - TAKES ABSOLUTE VALUE OF N
*
*       OUTPUT:
*             ABSOLUTE VALUE IN THE AC
*
ABS.N         BSS     1           for return address
              STORE   ABS.N       save return address
              LOAD    N           if N is positive
              BRGE    @ABS.N      ... return to main code
              LOAD    =0          else
              SUB     N           ... form negative
              BR      @ABS.N      return to main code
```

The advantage of a procedure over a patch should be clear at this point. Our absolute value procedure can be *called* wherever the absolute value of N is needed. The term refers not only to the transfer of control (i.e., the branch) itself but also to any other overhead required in transferring control to the procedure. This includes both saving the return address and branching to the procedure. We have thus reduced the cost of taking the absolute value of N from four to only two instructions, a savings of 50 percent.

In all honesty, this is not quite an accurate assessment because it does not include the cost of the 7 words occupied by the procedure itself. Before going on, we should look at the cost of using a procedure in terms of both time and space. Are procedures really less expensive than keeping duplicate copies of their code? We shall see.

First, consider whether a procedure really saves space. We saw that calling a procedure required two instructions, one to bring the return address into the accumulator and another to branch to the procedure. The cost of the procedure itself can be uniformly shared by each call. The cost of the procedure itself is 7 words of storage. Each call requires 2 words of storage. Thus, a procedure called in k places requires $2k + 7$ words.

In how many different places must a procedure be used to begin saving space? Since the cost of duplicating the code k times is $4k$ instructions, the relation can be expressed as

$$2k + 7 < 4k$$

Solving for k shows that the procedure method would be more space-efficient if it were called from as few as four different places in the program. The more places we use it instead of writing the code "in-line," the more space is saved. As the size of the procedure increases, it can be called from fewer places and still remain cost-effective. Procedures can actually save space.

Can a procedure ever make our program run faster than if the code were duplicated in each place it was needed? Unfortunately not. No matter what the length of the procedure, it will always take some number of instructions to call it and some number of instructions to return to the correct place in the main sequence of code. In-line code is always more time-efficient than a procedure. Procedures are more space-efficient but less time-efficient than using in-line code.

Are there other factors that make procedures more attractive? Consider the second point made about procedures earlier. Once a useful function, such as taking the absolute value of N, has been written as a procedure and thoroughly tested, the problem need never be considered again.

It would be unthinkable, for example, if everywhere an array of numbers had to be sorted, we rewrote code to do it. Not only is it a waste of space, but it is also too easy to make a mistake. The best approach is to write a sorting procedure, which can then be used almost as if it were a new instruction on our machine.

The final point, however, is the most important one. The use of procedures allows the program to be divided into modules. Each module performs a well-defined function whose purpose can be easily understood. A sort procedure, for example, performs the sorting function. The behavior of this procedure can be understood and tested without knowing anything else about the program in which it is used. This is helpful, even if the procedure is used only once in the program.

6.2 TOWARD A MORE FLEXIBLE PROCEDURE

The concept of a simple procedure, as we understand it, still has some shortcomings. Consider the problem of absolute values again. The simple procedure from the preceding section takes the absolute value of the location N. Suppose that in the same program we also need the absolute value of location M. Should we write another procedure for this?

If we did, most of the code would be the same as the procedure we already have. In fact, the only difference would be whether the address N or the address M was used. Clearly, it would be better to have a single procedure that can take the absolute value of *any* number. The only problem is how to tell the procedure which number to use.

There are quite a few approaches we could take in solving this problem. We will try the simplest one first. We will transmit the number to the procedure through the accumulator. The procedure takes the absolute value of whatever number is in the accumulator and leaves the result in the accumulator.

This decision will cause us some difficulty, because the accumulator is currently being used to transmit the return address. Before going on, we must find some other way to handle the return address that does not tie up the accumulator.

Look again at the procedure from the preceding section. The first thing it does is store the return address in the location reserved for that purpose. If this were done before branching to the procedure, the accumulator would then be free for us to use to transmit the number. Here is a version of our absolute value procedure that can take the absolute value of any number, along with a typical *calling sequence*:

```
                      ...
            LOAD    =RTN.ADR      save return address in
            STORE   ABS           ... first word of proc.
            LOAD    N             fetch N
            BR      ABS+1         ... and take abs. value
RTN.ADR     BSS     0             returns here
                      ...


** ABS - TAKES ABSOLUTE VALUE OF A NUMBER
*
*       INPUT:
*           NUMBER IN THE AC
*
*       OUTPUT:
*           ABSOLUTE VALUE IN THE AC
*
ABS         BSS     1             for return address
            BRGE    @ABS          return if positive
            STORE   N.SAVE        else save number
            LOAD    =0            ... and form negative
            SUB     N.SAVE
            BR      @ABS          return to main code
N.SAVE      BSS     1             for working value
```

The number of instructions in the calling sequence has doubled. The first two instructions save the return address in the first word of the procedure. The third instruction brings the value from location N into the accumulator. Control is then transferred to the procedure by the fourth instruction.

Instead of fetching from memory, the procedure tests the number already in the accumulator. If it is nonnegative, it returns with the number unchanged. Otherwise, the negative number is made positive by subtracting it from 0. To do this, it must be stored temporarily, in order to bring a 0 into the accumulator. It was unnecessary to store the number temporarily in the previous version because the procedure always operated on the same memory location.

6.3 A NEW INSTRUCTION TO CALL PROCEDURES

Procedures are sufficiently useful that most machines provide an instruction that makes them easier to call. The instruction must

1. Save the return address
2. Branch to the procedure

Although we have been doing these two things for ourselves, the special instruction is worth having. The instruction has the mnemonic *CALL*. The easiest way to understand how it works is to see it in use:

```
                    ...
        ORG    200B
        LOAD   N            fetch N
        CALL   ABS          ... and take abs. value
                    ...
** ABS - TAKES ABSOLUTE VALUE OF A NUMBER
*
*      INPUT:
*         NUMBER IN THE AC
*
*      OUTPUT:
*         ABSOLUTE VALUE IN THE AC
*
ABS     BSS    1            for return address
        BRGE   @ABS         return if positive
        STORE  N.SAVE       else save number
        LOAD   =0           ... and form negative
        SUB    N.SAVE
        BR     @ABS         return to main code
N.SAVE  BSS    1            for working value
```

The effect of "CALL ABS" is to store the return address 202B at location ABS, then branch to location ABS + 1. It took three separate instructions to do this in the previous example. CALL has no effect on the accumulator. The procedure itself remains the same as the one in the previous example.

The internal register transfer expressions for the CALL instruction were given in Chapter 1. They are

```
MBR      ←   PC
M[ MAR ]   ←   MBR
PC    ←   MAR
PC    ←   PC + 1
```

Recall that the PC was incremented at step 3 of the instruction cycle. By the time the instruction actually executes at step 4, the PC already points to the instruction following the CALL. This happens to be the return address for the procedure. Thus the return address can be gotten from the PC and stored in the first word of the procedure.

After setting the PC to the address of the procedure, it is incremented again, because the first word of the procedure is not an instruction but storage for the return address. The overall behavior of the instruction can be more clearly seen by combining the first two and last two register transfer expressions:

```
M[ MAR ]  ←—  PC
PC  ←—  MAR + 1
```

Various address modes can be used with CALL, as they can with any of the instructions. Although branching to a procedure indirectly seems somewhat strange, there is no reason why it could not be done if necessary. As with the other branch instructions, using immediate mode does not make sense.

6.4 SOME TERMINOLOGY

Before continuing, we should define some terms related to procedures. These terms are fairly standard in the vocabulary of programming languages. The definitions presented here are on a more intuitive level and are often little more than an example of the concept being applied.

The important feature of a *procedure* is that its code can be *called* from anywhere in the program and will transfer control to the correct location when finished. The terms *subprogram* or *subroutine* are sometimes used instead of *procedure*.

When a procedure is called, control transfers to the first executable instruction in the procedure. This location is known as its *entry point*. The location to which a procedure transfers control when it is done executing is called the *return point* or *return address*. Transferring control out of a procedure to the return point is known as *returning* from a procedure.

The values sent to a procedure, such as the number our absolute value procedure operates on, are called *parameters*. Parameters are said to be *transmitted* or *passed* to the procedure. We will have more to say about parameters in the next section.

The value produced by our absolute value procedure is called the *result* of the procedure. This result is said to be *returned* by the procedure. Not all procedures return a result. A procedure that returns a result is often referred to as a *function* or *function subprogram*. The returned result is usually left in a register rather than being stored in memory. The register to which the result is returned is called the *result register*. On our machine, the accumulator serves this purpose.

6.5 PARAMETERS

The two main issues involved with parameters are

1. their form
2. their means of transmission

We will look at each of these separately, then see how they are related.

6.5.1 The Form of a Parameter

Our absolute value procedure expected a single value as its parameter. A value transmitted to a procedure is called a *value* parameter and is said to be transmitted "by value." Transmission by value is conceptually the easiest to understand.

Transmission by value is not the only form parameters can take. Numbers are usually kept in memory until needed. A memory location can be characterized by either its value or its address. If the address were transmitted to a procedure, the value could easily be recovered. A parameter transmitted as an address rather than a value is called a *reference* parameter and is said to be transmitted "by reference" or "by address."

How would transmitting a reference parameter to our absolute value procedure change things? As far as the calling sequence is concerned, there is almost no difference. Most of the changes occur in the way the procedure uses the parameter. Here is a version that expects an address instead of a value:

```
                 ...
        LOAD    =N          set the address of N
        CALL    ABS         ... and take abs. value
                 ...

** ABS - TAKES ABSOLUTE VALUE OF A NUMBER
*
*       INPUT: (IN AC, BY REFERENCE)
*          A NUMBER
*
*       OUTPUT:
*          ABSOLUTE VALUE OF NUMBER
*
ABS     BSS     1           for return address
        LOAD    @AC         fetch value at address
        BRGE    @ABS        return if positive
        STORE   N.SAVE      save param. value
        LOAD    =0          ... to form negative
        SUB     N.SAVE
        BR      @ABS        return to main code
N.SAVE  BSS     1           for working value
```

Although no other use was made of the address in this example, there are cases in which the address itself is also a useful piece of information. We will look at some such cases later in this chapter. It is interesting to note that transmitting a parameter by reference is really the same as transmitting a *pointer* to the parameter *by value*. This view is actually taken by several high-level programming languages.

Transmission by value and by reference are the two major forms commonly used at the machine level. Some high-level languages provide several others that are much more involved. They are not often used at the machine level and are not covered in this text.

6.5.2 How Parameters Are Transmitted

The other issue is how parameters are transmitted to the procedure. When we wrote our first procedure, we decided to take the simplest route by transmitting its parameter through the accumulator. Unfortunately, this works only for a single parameter. How would we handle a procedure that needs ten parameters, for example? We will examine and compare a number of methods designed to solve this problem and get a sense of which are best suited for a given application.

Register transmission. The simplest means of parameter transmission is *by register*. This is a fairly straightforward and efficient method. The major drawback to transmission by register on our simple machine is that we have only one general-purpose register available to us: the accumulator. What would happen if a procedure required more than one parameter? Even machines with several general-purpose registers have this problem. If there are k registers available for parameter transmission, how can $k + 1$ parameters be transmitted by register? Clearly, we must come up with more flexible means of transmitting parameters for these cases.

A more general approach. Just as we did with return addresses, we could use locations in memory to transmit parameters. There are a number of methods available. To illustrate these methods, we will use a procedure that requires two parameters. This eliminates transmission by register as an option.

Our simple machine can only represent integer values. The exact result of a dividing two integers N and M can only be expressed as an integer quotient and an integer remainder. The remainder is, of course, undefined if M is 0. As an example, the remainder of 7/4 is 3. If M is a factor of N, then their remainder is 0. The remainder of 12/4, for instance, is 0. The remainder is computed by the formula

$$N - \text{floor}\ (N/M) \quad * \quad M$$

Integer division automatically gives the floor of the quotient.

To start, we will first encode this formula as a simple sequence of in-line instructions.

```
        LOAD    M       if M is zero,
        BREQ    DONE    ... answer is zero

        LOAD    =0      form negative of
        SUB     N       ... greatest multiple
        DIV     M       ... of M <= N
        MUL     M
        ADD     N       remainder is N + this result
DONE    BSS     0
```

It is important that some action be taken if *M* is 0. We define the remainder to be 0 if *M* is 0. Another alternative would be simply to halt the machine. Since the effect of dividing by 0 varies from machine to machine, it pays to avoid it by checking the dividend before dividing.

If we needed the remainder often, it would be reasonable to write the sequence of code as a procedure with two parameters representing the dividend and divisor, *N* and *M*. The procedure returns the remainder as its result.

Transmission through global locations. A simple extention of transmission by register is to reserve a group of memory locations and use them to transmit parameters. Any procedure that requires parameters would expect the first parameter in the first of these locations, the second one in the second location, and so forth.

The word *global* implies that these locations can be used by any procedure that requires them. Conversely, locations reserved solely for use by a single procedure are called *local*.

Suppose that a group of words labeled GBL are reserved for global parameters. Procedures expect the first parameter in location GBL, the second in location GBL + 1, and so forth. Here is a section of code that calls a procedure, transmitting two value parameters through the first two global locations:

```
LOAD    =3      copy params. for procedure.
STORE   GBL     ... into global locations
LOAD    =2
STORE   GBL+1
CALL    PROC    branch to procedure
```

There are disadvantages to transmitting parameters through global locations. First, the parameters must be copied into those locations, if they are not already there. Second, the values stored in these locations must be saved by the procedure if it in turn calls another procedure with different parameters. If this were not done, the first procedure would be using the wrong parameters after the second procedure returns.

Transmission through global locations is used primarily as a substitute for transmission by register on machines that have a limited number of registers available.

Copy-in transmission. An improvement over using a single set of global locations is to reserve a separate group of parameter locations for each procedure. The parameters are copied directly into these before branching to the procedure. If one procedure then calls another, the parameters for the first procedure will be left intact.

Here is how we would rewrite the remainder procedure. Two words immediately preceding the one for the return address will be reserved for parameters. Before calling the procedure, we copy the values of *N* and *M* into these two locations. The result is still returned in the accumulator. Here is a typical calling sequence:

```
    ...

LOAD      M            copy in value of M
STORE     RMDR-2       ... as the 1st param.
LOAD      N            copy in value of N
STORE     RMDR-1       ... as the 2nd param.
CALL      RMDR
    ...
```

The code for the procedure is almost identical to the instruction sequence written earlier:

```
** RMDR  -  RETURNS WHOLE REMAINDER OF A QUOTIENT
*           (DEFINED AS 0 IF DIVISOR IS 0)
*
*        INPUT: (VALUE, COPY IN)
*            RMDR-2  -  DIVISOR  (MVAL)
*            RMDR-1  -  DIVIDEND (NVAL)
*
*        OUTPUT:
*            WHOLE REMAINDER OF QUOTIENT IN AC
*
MVAL         BSS    1        for value of N
NVAL         BSS    1        for value of M
RMDR         BSS    1        for return address
             LOAD   MVAL     if MVAL is zero,
             BREQ   @RMDR    ... return with zero

             LOAD   =0       form negative of
             SUB    NVAL     ... greatest multiple
             DIV    MVAL     ... of MVAL <= NVAL
             MUL    MVAL
             ADD    NVAL     remainder is NVAL + this result
             BR     @RMDR    return remainder
```

The technique presented here is known as *copy-in*, because the parameters are copied directly into storage locations reserved for them in the procedure. As far as the procedure itself is concerned, no special treatment of parameters is necessary. The values of N and M are always found at the same two locations.

However, the ease of recovering parameters must be balanced against the cost of copying the parameters into the locations reserved for them. The cost of using the copy-in technique is related both to the number of parameters copied and the number of different places that the procedure is used.

In-line transmission. Another way of transmitting parameters is known as the *in-line* method, because storage for the parameters is reserved "in line," immediately following the CALL instruction. This method takes advantage of the fact that the address where the parameters are stored is exactly the address saved by the CALL instruction.

Here is how our remainder procedure would be called, transmitting the parameters in line by value:

```
                  . . .
          LOAD     M
          STORE    PARAM
          LOAD     N
          STORE    PARAM+1
          CALL     RMDR
PARAM     BSS      2              for parameters
                  . . .
```

A moment's thought should tell us that this method is doomed to failure, even if the procedure itself executes correctly. Control would transfer back to the first word following the CALL instruction and cause the sequencer to execute the first parameter as an instruction! Clearly, this was not our intent.

There are two ways of dealing with this situation. The first is to modify the return address in the procedure before using it in an indirect branch. Since the procedure knows how many parameters were sent, it is a simple matter to offset the return address by that amount. The second way is to place a branch between the CALL instruction and the first parameter:

```
                  . . .
          LOAD     M
          STORE    PARAM
          LOAD     N
          STORE    PARAM+1
          CALL     RMDR
          BR       *+3          branch around parameters
PARAM     BSS      2            for parameters
                  . . .
```

This is the approach we will take. The development of the first method as well as a comparison of the two is left as an exercise.

We must rewrite the procedure itself to recover its parameters correctly. Here is our remainder procedure, modified to recover value parameters transmitted in line:

```
** RMDR  - RETURNS WHOLE REMAINDER OF A QUOTIENT
*          (DEFINED AS 0 IF DIVISOR IS 0)
*
*        INPUT: (VALUE, IN LINE)
*            <RETURN>+1 - DIVISOR  (MVAL)
*            <RETURN>+2 - DIVIDEND (NVAL)
*
*        OUTPUT:
*          WHOLE REMAINDER OF QUOTIENT IN AC
*
NVAL       BSS     1        for value of N
MVAL       BSS     1        for value of M

RMDR       BSS     1        for return address
           LOAD    RMDR     get address of params.
           STORE   XR       ... and use as index
           LOAD    $2       recover value of N
           STORE   NVAL     save value of N
           LOAD    $1
           BREQ    @RMDR    return 0 if M is 0

           STORE   MVAL     save value of M
           LOAD    =0       form negative of
           SUB     NVAL     ... greatest multiple of M <= N
           DIV     MVAL
           MUL     MVAL
           ADD     NVAL     remainder is N + this result
           BR      @RMDR    return remainder.
```

Notice how indexed addressing was used to recover the two parameters at the beginning of the procedure. The first parameter's address is one past the address stored at location RMDR. With the return address in the index register, fetching the value of the first parameter requires indexed LOAD with an offset of 1. Fetching the value of the second parameter requires an indexed LOAD with an offset of 2.

We can convince ourselves that this is correct, using the sample calling sequence shown earlier. The register transfer expressions for the first two instructions have the effect of

```
XR  ←—  M[ RMDR ]
```

since the index register is memory-mapped to memory location 1.

The register transfer expression for the next instruction is

```
AC  ⟵  M[ 2 + XR ]
```

With M[RMDR] in XR, this reduces to

```
AC  ⟵  M[ 2 + M[ RMDR ] ]
```

The CALL instruction stored the address PARAM-1 at location RMDR, so the term "M[RMDR]" can be replaced by its content. The resulting register transfer expression

```
AC  ⟵  M[ 1 + PARAM ]
```

brings the value of the second parameter into the accumulator.

In-line parameter transmission is sometimes preferable to the copy-in method. If the parameters being transmitted are constants, they can be assembled and loaded into memory with the program rather than copied during execution. The overhead of the calling sequence no longer grows as the number of parameters but only as the number of different places it is called in program. If there are more than a few parameters or if the procedure is called at quite a few points, the savings can be worth the extra effort.

Although calling our remainder function with constant-value parameters might not be very useful, calling it with constant-reference parameters would be. Here is the procedure modified to recover in-line reference parameters, along with a sample calling sequence:

```
            . . .
         CALL     RMDR
         BR       *+3        branch around parameters
         DATA     M,N        addresses M and N
            . . .

** RMDR  -  RETURNS WHOLE REMAINDER OF A QUOTIENT
*             (DEFINED AS 0 IF DIVIDEND IS 0)
*
*        INPUT: (REFERENCE, COPY IN)
*           <RETURN>+1  -  DIVISOR  (MVAL)
*           <RETURN>+2  -  DIVIDEND (NVAL)
*
*        OUTPUT:
*           WHOLE REMAINDER OF QUOTIENT IN AC
*
NVAL     BSS      1         for value of N
MVAL     BSS      1         for value of M

RMDR     BSS      1         for return address
```

```
LOAD    RMDR    get address of params.
STORE   XR      ... use it as index
LOAD    $2      get address of N
LOAD    @AC     ... recover its value
STORE   NVAL    save value of N
LOAD    $1      get address of M
LOAD    @AC     ... recover its value
BREQ    @RMDR   if M = 0, remainder is 0

STORE   MVAL    save value of M
LOAD    =0      form negative of
SUB     NVAL    ... greatest multiple of M <= N
DIV     MVAL
MUL     MVAL
ADD     NVAL    ... N - this result
BR      @RMDR   ... and return
```

It is interesting to compare this method of implementing in-line parameter transmission with the one that modifies the return address to avoid executing the parameter list. The details of implementation as well as the comparison are left as exercises.

Parameter list transmission. The problem with the in-line method is that something must be done to avoid executing the parameters upon return from a procedure. The attractive feature is that the overhead of passing the parameters can be reduced significantly for constant-reference parameters. We would like a method that still has this feature yet eliminates the need to avoid executing the parameters.

The solution is to put the parameters somewhere other than immediately following the CALL instruction. Then, we place the address where they are stored into the accumulator before branching to the procedure. This address is a pointer to the array or list of parameters. This is known as the *parameter list* method.

Here is our remainder procedure from the previous example, modified to accept reference parameters transmitted via a parameter list:

```
          ...

        LOAD    =PLIST      param list address
        CALL    RMDR

          ...

PLIST   DATA  M,N         pointers to M and N
          ...

** RMDR - RETURNS WHOLE REMAINDER OF A QUOTIENT
*         (DEFINED AS 0 IF DIVIDEND IS 0)
*
```

```
*       INPUT: (REFERENCE, PARAMETER LIST THROUGH AC)
*           <PARAM>+0  - DIVISOR  (MVAL)
*           <PARAM>+1  - DIVIDEND (NVAL)
*
*       OUTPUT:
*           WHOLE REMAINDER OF QUOTIENT IN AC
*
NVAL        BSS     1           for value of N
MVAL        BSS     1           for value of M
RMDR        BSS     1           for return address
            STORE   XR          use param list addr as index
            LOAD    $1          get address of N
            LOAD    @AC         ... recover its value
            STORE   NVAL        save value of N
            LOAD    MVAL        get value of M
            LOAD    $0          get address of M
            LOAD    @AC         ... recover its value
            BREQ    @RMDR       remainder is 0 if M = 0

            STORE   MVAL        save value of M
            LOAD    =0          form negative of
            SUB     NVAL        ... greatest multiple of M <= N
            DIV     MVAL
            MUL     MVAL
            ADD     NVAL        ... N - this result
            BR      @RMDR       ... and return
```

This is only slightly different from the in-line version. The address we had before was 1 less than the address of the first parameter. Here, the address is exactly the one where the first parameter is stored.

One advantage of the parameter list method over the in-line method is that the same parameter list can be used for any number of calls, as long as the parameters are the same. In effect, two calls of our remainder procedure with the same N and M share the storage cost of the parameter list between them. That was not true of the in-line method. There, separate storage was reserved for each set of parameters directly after its own CALL instruction.

Some similarities. Here is a brief summary of the parameter transmission methods just described:

> **Transmission by register:** Only one parameter can be transmitted because there is only one general-purpose register available on our simple machine.
>
> **Transmission by global locations:** A single group of locations is reserved for transmitting parameters to any number of procedures. These locations are used almost like extra accumulators would be in register transmission.

Copy-in transmission: A separate group of locations is reserved for each procedure body.

In-line transmission: A separate group of locations is reserved for each procedure call.

Parameter list transmission: The amount of space reserved depends on how many different parameter lists are needed.

The goal behind all of these methods is to gather a group of unrelated parameters together for easier transmission. Value parameters are gathered together by placing copies of them into an array. Reference parameters are gathered by placing pointers to the values into the array, instead of the values themselves. Recovering the parameters involves no more effort than fetching values from an array. In effect, all of the methods described here use a parameter list in one form or another. The difference is how the procedure gains access to that list.

6.5.3 Arrays as Parameters

Many useful procedures operate on arrays rather than individual values. In this section, we will look at the problem of transmitting an array as a parameter to a procedure. We will discover that if we choose wisely among the methods presented, transmitting an array as a parameter is surprisingly easy.

Consider a procedure that searches an array for a value and returns to its position in the array. Rather than finding what value is stored at a given position, this procedure allows us to find the position given the value. An array used in this way is called a *table*. Finding the position of a value in the table is called *table lookup*.

The first thing to consider in writing such a procedure is how to transmit the table to the procedure. This question has two parts. The first is in what form to transmit the table; the second is by what means.

Transmitting an array by value requires copying the array into another group of locations. This can be a very expensive proposition, because it makes the cost of transmission proportional to the array size. There are cases in which this is desirable. If the procedure modifies the array, we may want to be sure those changes are not reflected outside of that procedure. In that case, transmitting the array by value is the natural thing to do.

Here, however, there is no need to copy the array. The procedure only reads from the array and never modifies it. Reference transmission saves not only the time required to make the copy but also the space required for it.

Since the array can be characterized by its starting address, transmitting an array by reference is no more costly than transmitting a simple value by reference. In either case, the parameter is represented by a single pointer. We will write our procedure to expect the table itself as a reference parameter.

The value sought must also be transmitted as a parameter. Is there anything else the procedure needs? If the value being sought is always in the table, the answer is no.

Suppose, however, that the value may not be in the table. How does the procedure decide when to stop looking? This is a more realistic problem. To solve it, we must also transmit a parameter that gives the size of the table. Once all the values in the table have been checked, the procedure can stop looking and report that the value was not found.

Our procedure, then, requires three parameters:

1. The value being sought
2. The table
3. The size of the table

For this example we will transmit the value being sought and the table size by value and the table itself by reference. The parameters are transmitted using the copy-in technique.

Several other decisions must be made before actually writing the procedure. The first is how to indicate that the value being sought was not found. The easiest way is to return a value that is not a valid table position and is easy to check for upon return. The choice here is to return a negative number if the item was not found in the table. If the value is found in the first position, the procedure returns the number 0. If it is found in the second position, the procedure returns the number 1, and so forth.

The other decision concerns the order in which the table is searched. If there were two occurences of a value in the table, which position should be returned, the first or the second? We will assume in writing this procedure that there are no duplicates, so the order of search does not matter. We can code the loop to search in the most efficient way.

Having made these decisions, we are now able to write the actual procedure. Here is our table lookup procedure, along with a typical calling sequence and some sample data:

```
                LOAD      =47           value sought
                STORE     LOOKUP-3
                LOAD      =MYTABLE      table address
                STORE     LOOKUP-2
                LOAD      =5            table size
                STORE     LOOKUP-1
                CALL      LOOKUP
                      ...

** table of numbers
*
MYTABLE     DATA      22,-2,47,133,-18
                      ...

** LOOKUP  -  RETURNS POSITION OF ITEM IN TABLE
*             (NEGATIVE IF ITEM NOT IN TABLE)
```

```
*
*       INPUT: (COPY IN)
*            LOOKUP-1  -  TABLE SIZE       (VALUE)
*            LOOKUP-2  -  TABLE            (REFERENCE)
*            LOOKUP-3  -  VALUE SOUGHT     (VALUE)
*
*       OUTPUT:
*            POSITION IN TABLE
*
KEY          BSS      1           for value sought
TBL          BSS      1           for table address
SIZE         BSS      1           for table size

LOOKUP       BSS      1           for return address
LK.NXT       LOAD     SIZE        index of next value
             SUB      =1          ... in the table
             BRLT     @LOOKUP     return if end of tbl

             STORE    SIZE        save new index
             ADD      TBL         fetch next value
             LOAD     @AC         ... in the table
             SUB      KEY         if it matches,
             BREQ     *+2         ... break out
             BR       LK.NXT      else next value

             LOAD     SIZE        get table position
             BR       @LOOKUP     ... and return
```

The table size parameter is used as an index into the table. The index is decremented first because the index of the last item in the table is 1 less than the table size. A negative value means that the table size is less than or equal to 0. The procedure returns with the negative value in the accumulator in this case, indicating that the value sought was not in the (empty) table.

Each item in the table is compared with the value sought. If the value does not match, control transfers to the top of the loop for the next pass. If the value matches the one sought, its index is brought into the accumulator and returned as the result.

6.5.4 Procedures as Parameters

It is sometimes necessary to pass another procedure as a parameter. The procedure passed may take the form of a function that makes some decision whose criteria change from call to call. Procedures passed as parameters are almost always passed by reference (what would it mean to pass the procedure by value?).

Consider a procedure AVG that computes the average of a list of numbers. This version of AVG averages only the number in the list that meet some criteria specified by the user. For example, we may wish to average a list of ages only for ages less than 18 or greater than 65 years old.

In addition to the array size and the array itself, AVG expects a procedure as its third parameter. This procedure decides for each item in the array whether that item meets the criteria. The function should expect an item from the array by value through the AC and return true (1) if the item should be included in the average and false (0) if the item should not be averaged in. The caller is responsible for writing a procedure that conforms to these conditions.

Here is a typical call using the example just given, with a user-defined routine (not shown) that selects only certain ages. We will pass all three values to AVG by reference, using a parameter list. The parameter to the user-define function is passed to the function by value through the AC.

```
            LOAD    =PARLIST
            CALL    AVG
                ...

PARLIST     DATA    AGES            list of ages
            DATA    NAGES           number of ages in list
            DATA    AGEFN           function to select ages
                                    (not shown)
                ...

AGES      DATA    45,17,33,2,75,66,97,12,53,24
                ...

NAGES     DATA    10
                ...
```

```
** AVG - COMPUTES THE AVERAGE OF SELECTED ITEMS IN AN ARRAY
*
*          INPUT (REFERENCE, PARAMETER LIST)
*              <param+0> - ARRAY
*              <param+1> - ARRAY SIZE
*              <param+2> - USER-SPECIFIED FUNCTION:
*                          INPUT (VALUE, THROUGH AC)
*                              NUMBER
*                          OUTPUT (THROUGH AC)
*                              TRUE (1) IF NUMBER IS IN RANGE,
*                              OR FALSE (0) IF NUMBER IS NOT
*                              IN RANGE.
*          OUTPUT (THROUGH AC)
*              AVERAGE OF SELECTED ITEMS FROM ARRAY
*
ARRAY      BSS     1               ptr. to array
AINDEX     BSS     1               current index into array
USERFN     BSS     1               ptr. to user function
```

```
NSAVE      BSS      1          to save current array item
NAVG       BSS      1          number of items in average
SAVG       BSS      1          sum of items in average

AVG        BSS      1          for return address
           STORE    XR         use param list ptr as index
           LOAD     $0         address of array
           STORE    ARRAY
           LOAD     $1         array size
           LOAD     @AC
           STORE    AINDEX
           LOAD     $2         address of user fn.
           STORE    USERFN

           LOAD     =0
           STORE    NAVG       init. avg count
           STORE    SAVG       init. avg sum
AVG.NXT    LOAD     AINDEX     decrement array index
           SUB      =1
           BRLT     AVG.OUT    done if no more in array
           STORE    AINDEX
           ADD      ARRAY      fetch next item
           LOAD     @AC
           STORE    NSAVE      save it for sum
           CALL     @USERFN    see if item ok
           BREQ     AVG.NXT    skip if not ok
           LOAD     NSAVE      else include in average
           ADD      SAVG
           STORE    SAVG
           LOAD     NAVG
           ADD      =1
           STORE    NAVG
           BR       AVG.NXT    repeat for next item

AVG.OUT    LOAD     NAVG       return 0 if none averaged
           BREQ     @AVG
           LOAD     SAVG       else return average
           DIV      NAVG
           BR       @AVG
```

The procedure uses the array size both as an index and to control the loop. For each value in the array, AVG calls the user function *indirectly*, using the function address from the parameter list. The user function decides whether the value meets its criteria and returns the appropriate code.

A procedure parameter is really no more difficult to deal with than a simple parameter. The important thing in this example is to use the indirect address mode for the call instruction.

6.5.5 Transmitting a Variable Number of Arguments

All the procedures we have written so far expect a fixed number of arguments. If more or fewer arguments were actually transmitted, they would not work correctly. There are times, however, when the number of arguments being transmitted varies from one call to the next. In this section, we will look at how to deal with this situation.

Count-delimited parameter list. The most common way to tell how many parameters are in a list is to transmit that number along with the parameters. This parameter count is usually transmitted at the beginning of the list.

Suppose that if too few parameters are transmitted to a procedure, it should assume the value 0 for any missing parameters. This technique is used sometimes to fill in "defaults" for parameters left out. Of course, it will only handle the case where parameters are left out at the end of the list.

Here is a sample calling sequence, along with a section of the procedure. This section recovers the value of the fifth parameter. The rest of the procedure is of no interest here. The parameters are transmitted by value, through a parameter list. The parameter count is included at the beginning of the list and records how many *other* parameters there are.

```
                LOAD       =PLIST
                CALL       PROC
                    ...

PLIST           DATA       4                no. of items in list
                DATA       31,-92,31,724    list of
items
                    ...

** PROC --  DEMONSTRATES RECOVERY OF PARAMETER FROM A
*           COUNT-DELIMITED PARAMETER LIST
*
*        INPUT (VALUE, PARAM LIST THROUGH AC)
*           LIST OF NUMBERS
*
PSAVE   BSS     1         for param. list addr.
PROC    BSS     1         for return address
        STORE   PSAVE     save param. list addr.
            ...

        LOAD    PSAVE     use base of param list
        STORE   XR        ... as index
        LOAD    $0        get no. of params
        SUB     =5        if 5th param exists
        BRGE    *+3       ... go fetch it
```

```
        LOAD    =0      else default to 0
        BR      *+2
        LOAD    $5      fetch 5th param.
             ...
```

This section of code could have been made more efficient if we had saved the parameter list address in XR upon entry and could assume that it remained unchanged.

Sentinel-delimited parameter list. Some procedures access their parameters sequentially, starting with the first one and ending with the last. Once a parameter has been recovered and processed, it is not needed again. The extra overhead of running a count-controlled loop is unnecessary in these cases.

Instead of a parameter count, a special marker called a *sentinel* is placed at the end of the list. This sentinel value is one that, if detected, can readily be distinguished from a valid parameter. When the procedure encounters the sentinel value, it can be sure that there are no more parameters in the list.

A sentinel-delimited parameter list would not have been very useful in the previous example for two reasons. First, the parameters are not recovered in order. Fetching the value of the fifth parameter would require stepping past the other four to make sure the fifth one is present.

The second reason is that the parameters are passed by value. Unless there is some restriction placed on the range of values, we cannot choose a sentinel value that could be distinguished from a valid parameter. In general, the sentinel technique cannot be used when transmitting value parameters unless some restriction is placed on the values transmitted.

Reference parameters are restricted in just this way, since they can only be positive numbers. We will use 0 as the sentinel value. The reason is that if something goes wrong, our procedure is more likely to find a 0 at a given memory location than any other value. Zero is the value most often chosen as a sentinel.

As an example, here is a procedure that computes the sum of its parameters. A pointer to the parameter list is sent through the accumulator. We must be careful to append the sentinel at the end of the list, for it is the only way the procedure has to stop processing!

```
        LOAD    =PLIST
        CALL    SUM
             ...

PLIST   DATA    PAR1    1st param. addr
        DATA    PAR2    2nd param. addr
        DATA    PAR3    3rd param. addr
        DATA    PAR4    4th param. addr
        DATA    PAR5    5th param. addr
        DATA    0       sentinel value
             ...
```

```
** SUM - COMPUTES THE SUM OF ITS PARAMETERS
*
*       INPUT
*          AC - PTR TO SENTINEL-DELIMITED LIST OF
*               REFERENCE PARAMETERS
*
*       OUTPUT
*          SUM OF PARAMETERS
*
PSAVE       BSS      1         for param list ptr
TSUM        BSS      1         for sum of params
SUM         BSS      1         for return addr
            STORE    PSAVE     save param list ptr
            LOAD     =0        init. sum to 0
            STORE    TSUM
            LOAD     PSAVE     restore param list ptr

SUM.NXT     LOAD     @AC       fetch next param in list
            BREQ     SUM.OUT   break out if sentinel found
            LOAD     @AC       fetch value of param
            ADD      TSUM      ... and add into sum
            STORE    TSUM
            LOAD     PSAVE     increment ptr to next param
            ADD      =1
            STORE    PSAVE
            BR       SUM.NXT   repeat for next param

SUM.OUT     LOAD     TSUM      fetch sum
            BR       @SUM
```

6.6 RETURNING RESULTS FROM A PROCEDURE

So far, if the procedure produces a result, it has been returned through the accumulator. As we will discover, there are a number of ways to transmit results back from a procedure, just as there are a number of ways to transmit parameters to a procedure. Although the register technique is the simplest, there are cases in which it cannot be used.

6.6.1 Modifying Reference Parameters

Another way to return a result is to modify a reference parameter. We noted earlier that reference parameters give more information than value parameters. They supply not only a value but also the location in memory where the value is stored. Here we will make use of that additional information. We will retain the address of the parameter and change the contents of that location at the appropriate time.

Modifying a simple reference parameter. Here is a version of the absolute value procedure that accepts a single reference parameter transmitted by register. This version is not a function. Instead, the number stored at the referenced location is replaced by its absolute value directly:

```
            LOAD        =N          address of param
            CALL        ABS
                 ...
N           DATA        -5          current contents
                 ...

** ABS - TAKES ABSOLUTE VALUE OF NUMBER
*
*         INPUT (REFERENCE, THROUGH AC)
*           NUMBER
*
*         OUTPUT
*           ABSOLUTE VALUE OF NUMBER REPLACES
*           NUMBER AT REFERENCED LOCATION
*
PSAVE     BSS       1          for param address
ABS       BSS       1          for return addr
          STORE     PSAVE      save param address
          LOAD      @AC        fetch param value
          BRGE      @ABS       ... if pos., return
          LOAD      =0         else form neg.
          SUB       @PSAVE
          STORE     @PSAVE     replace param val.
          BR        @ABS
```

In this example, the content of location N is changed to +5. The value in the accumulator upon return from the procedure can be disregarded. Modifying the parameter within the procedure was probably not very useful in this example, since the result could be returned more simply through the accumulator. There are, however, cases in which the accumulator cannot be used.

Modifying an array passed by reference. Consider the problem of sorting an array of numbers into ascending order. The parameters of such a procedure are the array and the array size. The sorted array replaces the unsorted one in memory. This is known as "sorting in place" because no additional storage is used for a copy of the sorted array.

The sorting technique we will use is not very efficient, but it is one of the easiest to understand. On each pass through the array, we compare adjacent values. If a pair are found to be out of order, we simply exchange them in memory. Assuming that we start scanning at the beginning of the array, the largest value will be in the last location of the array after the first pass. The sorting technique is known as "bubble sort" because it brings to mind a bubble that tends to float to the surface.

Once this last location contains the correct value, it can never be changed by subsequent passes through the array. We can stop short of this location on the next pass. In effect, the next pass sorts an array that is one location shorter than on the previous pass. When the size of the array reaches 1, we are done, because a single-element array is in order by definition.

We will transmit both parameters by reference, using a parameter list technique. Here is a typical calling sequence:

```
                LOAD     =P.LIST          param. list addr.
                CALL     BSORT
                     ...

** parameter list
*
P.LIST          DATA     A                pointer to array
                DATA     ASIZE            pointer to array size
                     ...

ASIZE           DATA     5                array size
                     ...

** array to be sorted
*
A               DATA     12,-3,147,-26,28
                     ....

** BSORT - BUBBLE SORTS AN ARRAY
*
*               INPUT (REFERENCE, PARAM LIST THROUGH AC)
*                   <PARAM>+0         ARRAY
*                   <PARAM>+1         SIZE OF ARRAY
*
*               OUTPUT
*                   ORIGINAL ARRAY IS SORTED IN PLACE
*
PSAVE           BSS       1               param. list ptr
NELMTS          BSS       1               no. elements in array
NPAIRS          BSS       1               inner loop count
CUR^            BSS       1               ptr to current element
NEXT^           BSS       1               ptr to next element
TEMP            BSS       1               exchange temp

BSORT           BSS       1               for return addr.
                STORE     PSAVE           save param. list addr.
                ADD       =1              point to 2nd param
```

```
                LOAD     @AC          get address of array size
                LOAD     @AC          ... recover array size
                SUB      =2           offset for loop control

*        make next pass through array
NXT.PASS        BRLT     @BSORT       done if new array size < 2
                STORE    NELMTS       save new array size
                STORE    NPAIRS       init. inner loop count
                LOAD     @PSAVE       init. next ptr. to
                STORE    NEXT^        ... first array addr.

*        compare next pair of items
NXT.PAIR        LOAD     NEXT^        advance current ptr
                STORE    CUR^         ... using next ptr value
                ADD      =1           advance next ptr.
                STORE    NEXT^
                LOAD     @NEXT^       if pair are in order
                SUB      @CUR^
                BRGE     END.PAIR     ... loop for next pair

                LOAD     @NEXT^       else exchange pair
                STORE    TEMP
                LOAD     @CUR^
                STORE    @NEXT^
                LOAD     TEMP
                STORE    @CUR^

END.PAIR        LOAD     NPAIRS       decr inner loop count
                SUB      =1
                STORE    NPAIRS
                BRGE     NXT.PAIR     repeat if more pairs

                LOAD     NELMTS       else decr array size
                SUB      =1
                BR       NXT.PASS     repeat for next pass
```

This procedure is somewhat more complicated than the ones presented so far. It would be a good idea to look at it again in smaller sections. Notice how the concepts we have studied come together here.

The sorting algorithm uses two loops, one nested within the other. The outer loop controls the number of passes through the array. The inner loop controls the number of comparisons made on a single pass. Both of these loops are count-controlled. The number of passes through the outer loop depends on the size of the original array. The inner loop depends on the current array size as it gets shorter and shorter with each pass through the array.

The original array size is not quite the value needed to control the outer loop. If there were only two elements, one pass through the array would leave them sorted.

Three elements could be sorted in two passes. We will use 2 less than the original array size as the outer loop counter. This allows the use of a BRLT instruction on the loop index as a means of terminating the loop.

Here again are the instructions that control the outer loop, along with the ones that recover the parameters:

```
BSORT       BSS     1           for return addr.
            STORE   PSAVE       save param. list addr.
            ADD     =1          point to 2nd param
            LOAD    @AC         get address of array size
            LOAD    @AC         ... recover array size
            SUB     =2          offset for loop control

*       make next pass through array
NXT.PASS    BRLT    @BSORT      done if new array size < 2
            STORE   NELMTS      save new array size
             ...

            LOAD    NELMTS      else decr array size
            SUB     =1
            BR      NXT.PASS    repeat for next pass
```

We can easily verify for a two-element array that the outer loop executes exactly once. Furthermore, if the original array size was less than 2, the outer loop would not be executed at all. Instead, the procedure would simply return.

The inner loop follows a similar pattern. It is controlled by a loop count that is initialized to the outer loop count. The number of locations that must be compared on each pass decreases by 1 each time through the array. The inner loop count is not involved in recovering pairs of values from the array. Instead, two pointers are set to the pair of array locations whose values are being compared. These pointers are updated to the next pair of locations each time through the loop.

Here again are the sections of code that control the inner loop and maintain the pointers to the pair of locations being compared within the loop:

```
            STORE   NPAIRS      init. inner loop count
            LOAD    @PSAVE      init. next ptr. to
            STORE   NEXT^       ... first array addr.

*       compare next pair of items
NXT.PAIR    LOAD    NEXT^       advance current ptr
            STORE   CUR^        ... using next ptr value
            ADD     =1          advance next ptr.
            STORE   NEXT^
             ...

END.PAIR    LOAD    NPAIRS      decr inner loop count
            SUB     =1
```

```
        STORE    NPAIRS
        BRGE     NXT.PAIR     repeat if more pairs
```

The first three instructions set up the loop initially. The outer loop counter is already in the accumulator, so a copy is stored as the initial value of the inner loop counter. The pointers must also be initialized. This is done by setting only the next pointer outside of the loop and taking advantage of the code within the loop that advances the pointers.

Recall that location PSAVE was used to save the address of the parameter list. The first location in the parameter list is the starting address of the array. Thus the instruction

```
LOAD     @PSAVE
```

brings the array starting address into the accumulator. This address serves as the initial value of the pointer to the next array element.

Once inside the inner loop, the pointers are updated immediately. The current element pointer is advanced by setting it to the next element pointer, and the next element pointer is advanced by incrementing its value. This method saves a few instructions within the loop by not having to reload the current pointer. It also explains why we only had to initialize the next element pointer just outside the loop.

It is easy to verify that the inner loop terminates correctly by looking at the behavior of the inner loop count. There is also no need to check that the initial value of the inner loop count is in range. It is the same as the current value of the outer loop index, which was checked just a few instructions earlier. We can also verify that the pointers are correctly set to the first two locations in the array upon entering the loop for the first time.

The body of the inner loop does the actual work of making sure that the two locations pointed to are in ascending order and, if not, exchanging them:

```
LOAD     @NEXT^       if pair are in order,
SUB      @CUR^
BRGE     END.PAIR     ... loop for next pair

LOAD     @NEXT^       else exchange pair
STORE    TEMP
LOAD     @CUR^
STORE    @NEXT^
LOAD     TEMP
STORE    @CUR^
```

The pair are exchanged only if the number stored at the higher of the two array address is smaller than the number stored at the lower one. This is the job done by the first three instructions shown here. To actually exchange the contents of the two words we need a temporary location. The following instructions, for example, would not do the job:

```
LOAD    @NEXT^     else exchange pair
STORE   @CUR^
LOAD    @CUR^
STORE   @NEXT^
```

An examination of the register transfer expressions for this sequence quickly reveals the problem. (Try it with a few sample values.)

Although this procedure appears a bit complicated at first, it is nothing more than an application of principles we have already learned. Perhaps the most difficult decision was to use pointers that are independent of the loop count to fetch array values. After that, setting up the pointers and the two nested count loops is fairly straightforward.

6.6.2 Result Parameters

Another way to return results is to reserve extra locations in the parameter list where they can be left by the procedure. On returning from the procedure, these results are copied into whichever locations were meant to receive them. The extra locations in the parameter list are used in much the same way as the accumulator is for returning a single value.

The result method is sometimes combined with transmission of a parameter by value. The combination is referred to as *value-result*. In most cases, the effect is equivalent to reference. Here is a version of the absolute value procedure, which uses the value-result method. Parameter transmission is by means of copy-in.

```
          LOAD    N        copy original value
          STORE   ABS-1    ... into param. loc.
          CALL    ABS      take its abs. value
          LOAD    ABS-1    overwrite original
          STORE   N        ... value with result
           ...
N         DATA    -5       content before call
           ...

** ABS - COMPUTES THE ABSOLUTE VALUE OF A NUMBER
*
*        INPUT (VALUE, COPY IN)
*           NUMBER
*
*        OUTPUT (VALUE, COPY OUT)
```

```
*              COPY IN LOCATION GETS ABSOLUTE
*              VALUE OF NUMBER.
*
N.VAL     BSS       1          for parameter
ABS       BSS       1          for return address
          LOAD      N.VAL      if value already positive
          BRGE      @ABS       ... do nothing - return
          LOAD      =0         else form negative
          SUB       N.VAL
          STORE     N.VAL      replace as param. value
          BR        @ABS       ... and return
```

The value stored at location N is not modified until after the procedure returns. The version that used reference transmission changed the content of location N from within the procedure itself. This difference can sometimes produce unexpected results if care is not taken. FORTRAN compilers, for example, may generate machine language code equivalent to either the reference or value-result method. A programmer writing in FORTRAN does not know which. The rules of the language were designed specifically to eliminate the possibility of writing a program that depends on the method.

6.6.3 Global Results

Sometimes a result produced by a procedure is of more global interest. In such cases it is better to post the result in a location global to all procedures. This is similar to transmitting parameters through global locations.

One use for global results is in signaling errors. Earlier we discussed handling division by zero. The effect of requesting the arithmetic unit to perform this division varies from machine to machine. It might simply cause the machine to halt. On the other hand, some value might be assigned by the arithmetic unit as the result of the division. The error in this case would simply go undetected as processing continued. There are cases in which neither of these is very attractive.

On many machines, either special registers are provided or certain words of memory are reserved for the AU to signal an error but continue processing. For example, a result might be assigned as the quotient, but a special location in memory would be set to indicate an error. If it was important to halt in this case, the location could be tested immediately after the division to determine whether an error occurred. If it was not important, no special action would be necessary.

Even though our machine does not have such a feature, we can achieve the same effect by writing a special division procedure to check for a zero denominator before trying to perform the division. We will also reserve a memory location in which the procedure can deposit a signal to indicate a zero-valued dividend. If the dividend was zero, the location will be set to the value zero. Otherwise, the location is set to a nonzero value. We will reserve a memory location for this purpose and give it the name DIVERR.

The value stored in this location is called a *flag*, because it signals some condition in the same way a mailbox flag signals that a letter is inside. If we detect a zero dividend, we must "raise the flag" to indicate that fact. On this machine, using the value zero to indicate a raised flag makes sense because branching to a special piece of code if the flag is raised requires only one instruction. Another choice might have been to let a nonnegative value represent a raised flag. However, lowering the flag would require setting the location to a negative value. Forming a negative value requires an extra instruction, so this choice would not have been as convenient.

Here is the procedure itself. Three value parameters are expected, transmitted by means of the copy-in technique. The first two are the dividend and divisor. The third parameter allows the user to define a quotient if the divisor is zero. The procedure assumes that the flag was originally down (i.e., set to the value 1).

```
** DIVIDE  -  FORM A QUOTIENT; SET ERROR FLAG IF
*             DENOMINATOR IS ZERO.
*
*             INPUT (VALUE, COPY-IN)
*                DIVIDE-3  - DIVIDEND
*                DIVIDE-2  - DIVISOR
*                DIVIDE-1  - ERROR QUOTIENT
*
*             OUTPUT
*                AC         - QUOTIENT OR DEFAULT VALUE
*                DIVERR     - ERROR FLAG (0=ERROR)
*
FLAG.UP       EQU      0            raised flag signal
DVND          BSS      1            for dividend
DVSR          BSS      1            for divisor
DEFLT         BSS      1            for default quotient

DIVIDE        BSS      1            for return address
              LOAD     DVSR         if divisor is zero
              BREQ     FLAG.IT      ... signal error
              LOAD     DVND         else perform division
              DIV      DVSR
              BR       @DIVIDE

FLAG.IT       LOAD     =FLAG.UP     raise flag
              STORE    DIVERR       ... and post it
              LOAD     DEFLT        return default quotient
              BR       @DIVIDE
```

This procedure does not lower the flag each time. The flag really indicates whether a division by zero was attempted at any time since it was last lowered. This is often useful, especially if the default quotient allows the computation to continue normally.

It might also be useful to have a procedure that lowers the flag and returns its previous value. This procedure could then be called at the beginning of a program to lower the flag initially. It also provides a convenient way to test the flag for division by zero and reset it in very few steps.

```
** RESET  -  reset division error flag and return
*            previous flag.
*
*            INPUT (GLOBAL)
*               DIVERR  -  DIVISION ERROR FLAG
*
*            OUTPUT
*               AC         -  PREVIOUS VALUE OF FLAG
*               DIVERR     -  FLAG RESET
*
FLG.DN       EQU        1              lowered flag signal
TEMP         BSS        1              for previous flag

RESET        BSS        1              for return address
             LOAD       DIVERR         save previous flag
             STORE      TEMP
             LOAD       =FLG.DN        lower flag
             STORE      DOVERR
             LOAD       TEMP           return previous flag
             BR         RESET
```

Since DIVERR is a global location, it can be set by our special division procedure and reset by our reset procedure. The information does not have to be passed between the procedures. The flag is also accessible from anywhere else in the program.

6.7 SUMMARY

This chapter began by presenting procedures as an extension of the idea of patching. Although we have certainly come a long way from that point, the basic idea behind a procedure is not far removed from that of the patch. Control transfers to some remote section of code and returns once that code has finished executing.

The main difference is that procedures can be parameterized, both in where they return and what data they use. A new instruction, CALL, provided a convenient way of setting up and calling a procedure. The rest of the chapter was devoted to looking at various ways of getting data into and back from a procedure. There are two issues here: the form of the parameter and the means of transmitting it. Sometimes the choice of one influences the other, but they are by and large independent decisions.

There are still some techniques that we have not explored. We will come back to the subject of procedures again as we look at another machine in the next part of the book. On that machine, certain features give us another level of flexibility in writing procedures.

PROBLEMS

6-1. In what way are patches and procedures related?

6-2. What two purposes do procedures serve?

6-3. The following section of code calculates $x^2 + 2x + 1$.

```
ORG     100B
LOAD    X       square X
MUL     X
ADD     X       add in 2X
ADD     X
ADD     1       add in 1
```

Change this code into a simple procedure called POLY. Place the return address in the AC, before branching to the procedure. Reserve location POLY for the procedure to save the return address. Place the first executable instruction at POLY+1.

6-4. In how many different places would this procedure have to be used in order to begin saving space? Briefly explain your reasoning.

6-5. A procedure usually saves space. Can it ever speed up execution time? Why or why not?

6-6. Rewrite the procedure from Problem 6-3 so that the value of x is sent to it through the accumulator. Assume that the return address is already stored at location POLY when execution of the procedure begins.

6-7. Show how the version of POLY from Problem 6-6 is called. Do not use the CALL instruction. Instead, STORE the return address at location POLY, bringing the contents of location X into the accumulator, then branch to POLY + 1.

6-8. Show how to call the version of POLY from Problem 6-6. This time use the CALL instruction.

6-9. What advantages are there to having a procedure branching instruction? How many instructions are saved by using CALL instead of a sequence of instructions that do the same thing?

6-10. Define the following terms:

(a) procedure
(b) parameter transmission
(c) entry point
(d) procedure result
(e) return point
(f) function
(g) return address
(h) result register
(i) parameter
(j) procedure call

6-11. What are the two issues involved with parameters?

6-12. Explain the difference between a value parameter and a reference parameter.

6-13. Rewrite the procedure from Problem 6-6 to expect a reference parameter instead.

6-14. Explain what is meant by saying that a reference parameter is really just a pointer passed by value.

6-15. What does a language that supports only value parameters have to include in order to achieve the effect of supporting reference parameters?

6-16. Why is the use of transmission by register so restricted on our simple machine?

6-17. Write a procedure COMB that computes the number of combinations of N things taken K at a time. The formula is

$$\binom{N}{K} = \frac{N!}{K!\ (N - K)!}$$

This procedure in turn makes use of another procedure, NFACT, to compute $X!$, the *factorial* of X. It is defined as

$$0! = 1$$
$$X! = X * (X - 1) * (X - 2) * \ldots * 3 * 2 * 1 \quad X > 0$$

Transmit the values N and K to COMB through a group of global locations reserved for this purpose:

```
.GBL   BSS   2   for global parameter transmission
```

Transmit the value X to NFACT through the same group of global locations. In each case, place the first parameter at .GBL, the second at .GBL + 1, and so forth.

6-18. Implement COMB using copy-in transmission. Implement NFACT using register transmission.

6-19. Show how the version of procedure COMB, as described in Problem 6-18, would be called to compute the number of combinations of 7 things taken 4 at a time.

6-20. With in-line parameter transmission, what is the problem with putting the parameters immediately following the CALL instruction? Briefly describe two methods of solving this problem.

6-21. Under what conditions does the cost of calling a procedure with in-line parameters no longer depend on the number of parameters transmitted? With which form of parameter is the restriction more realistic?

6-22. Reimplement COMB using in-line value parameters. Employ the method of inserting a branch instruction immediately following the CALL instruction to branch around the parameter list. Use register transmission again in implementing NFACT.

6-23. Show how to call the version of COMB described in Problem 6-22 to compute the number of combinations of 5 things taken 3 at a time.

6-24. Redo Problem 6-22 using the method of fixing up the return address from within the procedure.

6-25. Redo Problem 6-23 to invoke the procedure as implemented in Problem 6-24.

6-26. Why is parameter list transmission good if there are a number of procedures that use the same arguments?

6-27. Reimplement COMB from Problem 6-22 to use reference parameters, transmitted via a parameter list. Change FACT so that it expects parameters transmitted in the same way.

6-28. Show how to invoke COMB from Problem 6-27 to compute the number of combinations of N things taken M at a time. Also, show the parameter list involved.

6-29. Why are arrays more easily passed by reference than by value?

6-30. On what factor does the cost of passing an array by value depend?

6-31. An array is sorted if its values are in either ascending or descending order. Write a procedure ORDERED that scans an array and returns the value 1 if it is sorted in ascending order, -1 if it is in descending order, and 0 if it is not in sorted order. The procedure has two parameters, passed by reference by means of a parameter list. The parameters are the array and the size of the array.

6-32. If SORT makes a complete pass through the array and makes no changes, the array must be in order. Modify SORT to keep track of exchanges made during each pass and to return early if no exchanges were made.

6-33. Modify procedure SORT to sort an array into *descending* rather than ascending order. (This should require only a minor change to the existing code.)

6-34. Modify procedure SORT to accept a procedure as a third parameter. The procedure expects a pair of numbers by value transmitted by the copy-in method. The procedure returns true (1) if the pair are in order and false (0) otherwise. SORT uses this procedure to decide whether or not each pair of number must be exchanged. Test this new version of sort by writing two user-defined routines. ASCEND ensures that the array is sorted in ascending order, and DESCEND results in an array sorted in descending order.

6-35. Describe the difference between a count-delimited parameter list and a sentinel-delimited parameter list.

6-36. Why is it important to transmit the count in some fixed position in the parameter list? What is the most usual position?

6-37. Write a procedure MAX that returns the maximum value from among its input parameters. The parameters are transmitted by reference by means of a count-delimited parameter list.

6-38. What is the difficulty with transmitting *value* parameters by means of a sentinel-delimited parameter list? Why does the difficulty not arise when transmitting *reference* parameters?

6-39. Why is it difficult to recover an arbitrary parameter from a sentinel-delimited parameter list? Why is this easy with a count-delimited parameter list?

6-40. Statistically speaking, zero is the most likely value to be encountered if we sample locations in memory randomly. Why would this be a consideration in choosing zero as the sentinel value, rather than some negative number?

6-41. Modify MAX from Problem 6-37 to accept a sentinel-delimited parameter list.

6-42. Compare the cost of the two versions of MAX (Problems 6-37 and 6-41). The comparison should include two factors. The first is the relative size of the two versions. The other is the execution efficiency of each version. How much of each procedure is a fixed overhead (independent of the number of items in the list)? What is the execution cost of the loop as a function of the number of items in the list? Which version is more space-efficient? Which one is more time-efficient?

6-43. Write a procedure SWAP that expects two reference parameters in line. The purpose of SWAP is to exchange the contents of the two referenced locations.

6-44. Write a procedure REVERSE that reverses the order of values within an array. The first is swapped with the last, the second with the second from last, and so forth. The array and its size are passed to REVERSE by reference through a parameter list.

6-45. Write a procedure ACOPY that copies an array from a source to a destination. The procedure has three parameters, passed by reference by means of a parameter list. The parameters are the source array, the destination array, and the number of words to copy.

6-46. What is the term introduced in this chapter that describes the role played by the destination array in Problem 6-45?

6-47. Rewrite procedure SWAP from Problem 6-43 to use the value-result.

6-48. The last section in this chapter suggested a way to signal an error condition within a procedure by setting a global flag, which could be tested at any time after returning from the procedure. Another way to signal an error within a procedure is by using an *alternate return point*. If there was an error in the procedure, it returns to an alternate return point, and any results are ignored. Otherwise, it returns to a normal return point with any results generated. A call to DIVIDE might look like this:

```
LOAD     N            numerator
STORE    DIVIDE-3
LOAD     M            denominator
STORE    DIVIDE-2

CALL     DIVIDE       perform division (no default)
BR       ERR          ←    return here if error
STORE    RESULT       ←    return here if no error
```

Although the version of DIVIDE shown in the chapter had a third parameter, an error default value, there is no need to transmit it now because the returned value will be ignored in case of an error. Modify DIVIDE to return to the error return point in case of an error condition and to the normal return point otherwise.

7

A More Complex Computer

In this next part of the book, we will study another, more complex computer. Although its architecture resembles the one presented earlier, some significant changes have also been made. As we did earlier, we begin by looking at the architecture.

7.1 ARCHITECTURE

In the first part of the book, we worked on a machine with a single general-purpose accumulator and a second special-purpose index register. Modifying branching based on the index register required that it first be copied into the accumulator. Some machines provide additional instructions for the index register. The number of instructions range from a few limited ones to adding an extra index register instruction for almost every accumulator instruction, nearly doubling the size of the instruction set.

This second machine takes the idea a step further by providing eight identical registers, numbered 0 through 7. Each can act as either an accumulator or an index register, depending on how it is used. No one register is distinguished as *the* accumulator. When fetching a value from memory, for example, the programmer must designate into which register the value is copied.

Multiple registers also allow the programmer to keep often-used values in registers at all times for faster access. This is an important savings in execution time, because access to registers is several orders of magnitude faster than access to memory locations. However, it also means that the programmer must keep track of what is in the registers at any given time.

Figure 7-1 shows how the CPU of the machine is laid out. R0 through R7 are *memory-mapped* registers, as were the AC and XR on the previous machine. Recall that a memory-mapped register can be addressed as though it were a location in memory. Like the AC, the eight registers on this machine can also be addressed as registers as well. R0 is mapped to address 0, R1 to address 1, and so forth.

A new register on this machine is the *compare* (*CMPR*) *register*. On the previous machine, the only way to compare two values was to subtract one from the other and to branch conditionally, according to whether the difference was positive, negative, or zero. The number originally in the accumulator had to be destroyed in the process.

The CMPR register changes this. The sequencer still subtracts the number in one of R0 through R7 from the value in the MBR. However, the sequencer uses the result to set the bits of the CMPR register and discards the difference. The other registers are unchanged.

There are only three possible outcomes of comparing two values, *A* and *B*. Either *A* and *B* are equal, *A* is less than *B*, or *A* is greater than *B*. These three conditions can be represented using only two bits. The CMPR register represents these three conditions in the following way:

```
00      Ri and MBR are equal
01      Ri is greater than MBR
10      Ri is less than MBR
11      unused
```

We will see later how this register is controlled by the programmer.

The arithmetic unit has also changed with this machine. Only the four arithmetic operations were provided by the previous version. The new version provides a number of other operations. Included are some that make it easier to manipulate individual bits and fields of bits within a word. Others perform operations between two values that are based on logical operations, including AND, OR, and NOT. This new version of the old arithmetic unit is called the *arithmetic/logic unit* (*ALU*) in recognition of these improvements.

Also added is the ability to take input and output results in a more human-compatible way than the front panel and switch register. The CPU communicates with various input/output devices over an *I/O bus*. This is a communication line that carries commands and messages to I/O equipment like printers, keyboards, displays, and mass storage. The I/O bus is connected to the CPU through the *input/output unit* (*IOU*). The IOU handles communication between the CPU and the I/O devices.

As we will see, printing the result in human-readable form, such as

```
Your monthly balance for June is $514.43
```

is much more complicated than one would first imagine. The way a printer expects a number and its representation inside the machine are usually quite different. One of the problems we face is translating from one form to the other.

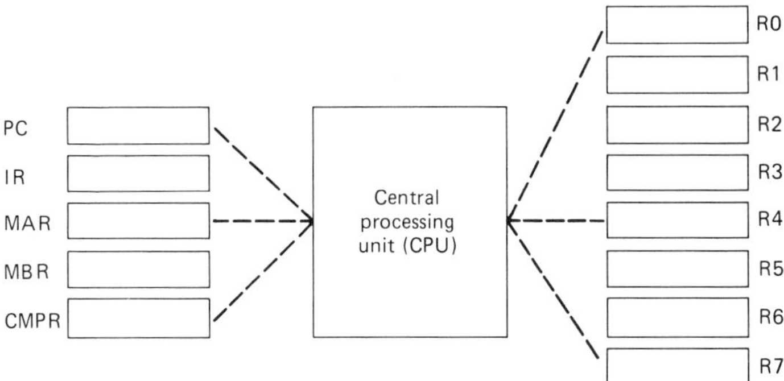

Figure 7-1 The CPU layout of our new machine

We will discuss how programs are written to use this hardware in Chapter 12. In the same chapter, we will write a number of useful I/O procedures. These routines will make the job of getting information into and out of our new machine much easier. New instructions to manage the IOU are presented in the next section.

7.2 INSTRUCTION FORMAT

In this section, we look at the instruction format and review changes to the individual fields. As we noted earlier, this machine is really an extension of the one presented in the first part of the text. Although there have been some changes and extensions in both instruction format and field layout, most of the material about to be presented should seem familiar.

The size of a word on this new machine has been increased to 32 bits, twice the size of a word on the previous machine. This not only increases the range of values that can be represented but also makes room for a larger instruction format.

An instruction on the previous machine had three fields: operation, address mode, and address. There was no need to specify registers because there was only one accumulator. On this machine the programmer must specify a data register as well as an address. This arrangement is called a *two-address* instruction format. The programmer may also specify an index register to use. It need not be (in fact, it seldom is) the same as the data register.

The instruction, then, is made up of the following fields:

- Operation field
- Data register field
- Index register field
- Address mode field
- Address field

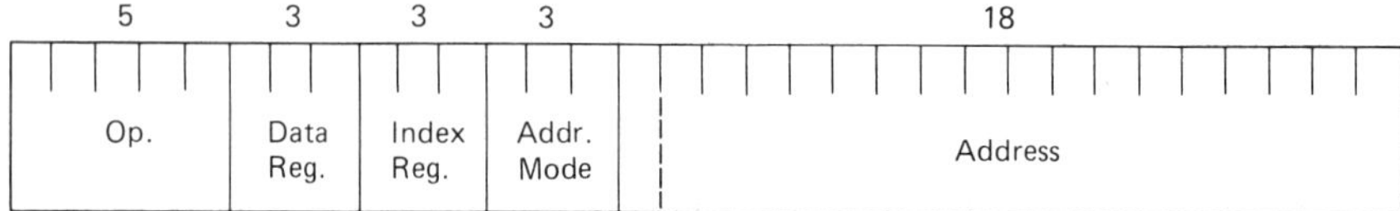

Figure 7-2 Layout of fields within a word

Figure 7-2 shows how the fields are laid out within a word. The address field is now 18 bits wide. The most significant bit of the address field is treated as a sign bit. Although we cannot refer to negative addresses, we *can* use negative numbers to form positive addresses (e.g., fixed negative offset from an address in the index register). They can also be used as fixed constants in the immediate address mode (e.g., load the constant −2).

The number of address modes has also been expanded. We had four modes on the previous machine: direct, immediate, indexed, and indirect. Several new address modes have been added to this new machine that are combinations of those four.

Each bit position of the address mode field indicates a particular address mode computation. If a bit is turned on, the corresponding computation is made on the current value of the effective address in the MAR. If more than one bit is turned on, each computation selected is carried out in a fixed order. Here is what the three bit positions indicate:

Indexed	Indirect	Immediate
0 = no	0 = no	0 = no
1 = yes	1 = yes	1 = yes

The index register field specifies which register to use as an index register. Any of the eight registers can be used as either an accumulator, as an index register, *or both* within an instruction.

7.3 INSTRUCTION CYCLE

The instruction cycle is almost the same as it was for the first machine. The four steps are

1. Fetch the instruction into the IR.
2. Compute the effective address and leave the result in the MAR.
3. Increment the PC.
4. Execute the instruction.

The effective address computation is a little more complicated because a richer set of address modes is available. Here is the algorithm used by the sequencer for computing the effective address of an instruction:

1. Copy the address field of the instruction into the MAR (MAR ← IR⟨17:0⟩).
2. If the *indexed* bit is set, add the contents of the indicated register to the MAR (MAR ← MAR + Rindex).
3. If the *indirect* bit is set, fetch the contents of the memory location whose address is in the MAR and put this value back into the MAR (MBR ← M[MAR], MAR ← MBR⟨17:0⟩).
4. If the *immediate* bit is set, copy the contents of the MAR into the MBR for use by the instruction (MBR ← MAR).

Each of these steps should be familiar from the earlier machine. The important thing here is that they can be applied one after another in the *same* effective address calculation.

Mode	Name	Example
000	direct	R2 ⟵ M[addr]
001	immediate	R2 ⟵ addr<17:0>
010	indirect	R2 ⟵ M[M[addr]]
100	indexed	R2 ⟵ M[addr + R3]
101	indexed immediate	R2 ⟵ (addr + R3)<17:0>
110	indexed indirect	R2 ⟵ M[M[addr + R3]]

Indexed immediate mode is a bit deceptive at first glance. The MAR, like the address field of an instruction, is only 18 bits long. Step 1 of the effective address calculation brings the 18-bit address field into the MAR. Step 2 adds the contents of the selected index register to this value and places the lower 18 bits of the sum back into the MAR. Step 3 does not apply because the indirect bit is not set. Finally, step 4 copies the correct 32-bit version of the 18-bit signed number from the MAR into the MBR.

The value copied into the MBR is correct as long as the sum of the address field and the index register can be correctly represented as a signed 18-bit number. For example, this mode can be used to compute the address of an array element A[I] and place the address into a register. The address field might contain the base address of A and the index register might contain the offset I.

7.4 INSTRUCTION SET

We now look at the set of instructions available. Many of them will be familiar from the first machine. Some, of course, have been added to support the extra hardware added to this machine.

Table 7-1 is a summary of the operation codes and mnemonics for the instruction set. The operations marked with an asterisk are the same or similar to those on the first machine.

TABLE 7-1 OPERATION CODES AND MNEMONICS FOR THE INSTRUCTION SET

Opcode	Mnemonic	Opcode	Mnemonic	Opcode	Mnemonic
* 00000	HALT	01011	PUSH	10110	NOT
* 00001	LOAD	01100	POP	10111	ASH
* 00010	STORE	* 01101	CALL	11000	CSH
* 00011	BR	01110	RTN	11001	LSH
* 00100	CMPR	* 01111	ADD	11010	INCHR
* 00101	BREQ	* 10000	SUB	11011	OUTCHR
* 00110	BRNE	* 10001	MUL	11100	IOSTAT
* 00111	BRGT	* 10010	DIV	11101	IOCMD
* 01000	BRLT	10011	AND		
* 01001	BRGE	10100	OR		
* 01010	BRLE	10101	XOR		

All six conditional branches are provided. These branches test the condition of the CMPR register and transfer control if the given condition is true. Table 7-2 gives the six conditional branches and the CMPR register values that make them true. Three of the conditions are satisfied by either of two values.

TABLE 7-2 CMPR REGISTER TRUTH VALUES

Branch	Value
BREQ	00
BRNE	10 or 01
BRGT	01
BRLT	10
BRGE	00 or 01
BRLE	00 or 10

The CMPR register is set by the sequencer whenever the result of an instruction modifies its data register. For example, the instruction

```
LOAD      3,N
```

sets the CMPR register depending on whether the contents of M[N] is negative, zero, or positive:

```
{MBR   <--  M[MAR]}
Ri     <--  MBR
CMPR   <--  Ri ? 0
```

The last expression sets the CMPR register based on a comparison of Ri with 0. Recall that the first action is performed only if immediate addressing is not part of the address mode. In this case, the second value is brought into the MBR from memory. If immediate addressing was selected, the correct value is already in the MBR from step 2 of the instruction cycle.

It is often useful to compare the contents of a register to some other value without modifying any of the registers. CMPR is a special instruction that does nothing but set the CMPR register. It does this by comparing the contents of some register Ri to the contents of the MBR. CMPR causes the sequencer to take the following actions:

```
{MBR   <--  M[MAR]}
CMPR   <--  Ri ? MBR
```

The arithmetic instructions also operate on the contents of a register and the MBR. For example, the actions taken by the SUB instruction are

```
{MBR   <--  M[MAR]}
Ri     <--  Ri - MBR
CMPR   <--  Ri ? 0
```

The CMPR register is set based on the results of the subtraction.

Rather than look at the other instructions now, we will wait to introduce them in the context of specific examples in which they are used. Instead, we will turn our attention to how the assembler notation must change to handle the somewhat different instruction format.

7.5 ASSEMBLER

The assembler for this machine closely follows the design of the previous one. The instruction is divided into four fields, separated from one another by one or more spaces. This is the same format that we adopted for the previous assembler:

```
LABEL     OPERATION     ADDRESS        COMMENT
-----     ---------     -------        -------
```

We examined a number of ways to detect an optional label earlier. If the label always begins in the first column and the operation field never does, it is very easy to detect a label. This is also the rule we adopted for the previous assembler. As a matter of practice, it is usually easier to read a program whose fields all line up under one another. All of the examples in this book follow this style.

The real difference between the two assemblers is in how the address field is interpreted. The address field must now contain the following information:

- Data register number
- Address mode
- Address
- Index register number

In the previous assembler, the address field contained only two of these, the address mode and the address. We will adopt a notation that fits in nicely with this. Here is a simple case:

```
LOAD    3,LOC
```

The data register is R3, and the address is simply LOC. The effect of this instruction is

```
R3   ←—   M[LOC]
```

Address modes fit into this notation equally well. For example, the instruction

```
LOAD    3,@LOC
```

specifies the action

```
R3   ←—   M[ M[LOC] ]
```

This is nothing more than the familiar indirect address mode. Immediate addressing is denoted in much the same way:

```
LOAD    3,=849
```

Since the address field is treated as a *signed* 18-bit field, we can also place a negative number in the address field. Thus

```
LOAD    3,=-849
```

brings the number −849 into R3. The 18-bit number is extended to a full 32-bit signed representation when it is copied from the MAR into the MBR during the effective address calculation.

Indexed address mode is specified somewhat differently than before. Since indexing is so often associated with arrays, we will use a notation based on this idea.

The effective address of the instruction

```
LOAD    3,A(5)
```

is

```
R3  ←—  M[A + R5]
```

If the address A is the base address of an array and R5 holds the array index, this instruction brings the *R5*th element of A into R3. For example,

```
LOAD    5,=2
LOAD    3,A(5)
```

brings the third element of A (i.e., M[A + 2]) into R3.

The two other useful address modes are combinations of the ones already illustrated. The instruction

```
LOAD    3,=A(5)
```

uses indexed immediate addressing to bring not the contents but the *address* into R3:

```
R3  ←—  (A + R5)<17:0>
```

Immediate addressing inhibits the memory reference normally caused by LOAD.

Finally, the instruction

```
LOAD    3,@A(5)
```

represents indexed indirect addressing. The effect of this instruction is

```
R3  ←—  M[ M[A + R5] ]
```

This address mode may seem a bit complicated, but it does have some good uses. We will see one of them when we take another look later at parameter passing.

Table 7-3 summarizes the address modes and gives examples of each. As we saw earlier, the eight general-purpose registers are memory-mapped to the first eight memory locations. The address modes have special interpretations in this case. To copy the contents of R5 into R3, for example, we simply issue the instruction

```
LOAD    3,5
```

This instruction can be viewed in two ways. The first is

```
R3  ←—  M[5]
```

TABLE 7-3 ADDRESS MODES

Mode	Examples				
immediate	LOAD	3,=A	R3	←	A<17:0>
direct	LOAD	3,A	R3	←	M[A]
indirect	LOAD	3,@A	R3	←	M[M[A]]
indexed	LOAD	3,A(5)	R3	←	M[A + R5]
indexed immediate	LOAD	3,=A(5)	R3	←	(A +R5)<17:0>
indexed indirect	LOAD	3,@A(5)	R3	←	M[M[A + R5]]

But because R5 is memory-mapped to memory address 5, it also denotes

```
R3 ← R5
```

This is called a *register* address mode because the result is a simple transfer from one register to another.

By setting their address fields to zero, we can put indexed and indexed indirect address modes to a new use. In the case of indexed address mode, the effect of the instruction

```
LOAD    3,0(5)
```

is just

```
R3 ← M[0 + R5]
```

or simply

```
R3 ← M[R5]
```

Our assembler recognizes either this form or the more abbreviated form

```
LOAD    3,(5)
```

The assembler recognizes this form and fills in the address field with the value 0.

Because the registers are memory-mapped, another way to achieve the same effect is to use the indirect address mode:

```
LOAD    3,@5
```

The register transfer expression

```
R3 ← M[ M[5] ]
```

reduces to the one shown previously by noting that M[5] and R5 are the same.

Either form achieves the effect of *register direct* addressing. The content of R5 serves the same purpose as the address field for normal direct addressing. The second form has more mnemonic value when the register contains a pointer, and it is used in future examples in such cases.

In the same way, the instruction

```
LOAD    3,@(5)
```

is just a special case of the indexed indirect address mode. The assembler will detect the missing address field and supply the value 0, just as though we had written

```
LOAD    3,@0(5)
```

instead. This special case is called *register indirect*. The effect of this LOAD instruction is

```
R3  <--  M[ M[0 + R5] ]
```

or simply

```
R3  <--  M[ M[R5] ]
```

We will use this abbreviated form whenever we specifically mean register indirect address mode.

Table 7-4 summarizes the special address modes just discussed.

TABLE 7-4 SPECIAL ADDRESS MODES

Mode	Example	Action
register	LOAD 3,5	R3 ← R5
register direct	LOAD 3,(5)	
	or LOAD 3,@5	
register indirect	LOAD 3,@(5)	R3 ← M[M[R5]]

Before going on, we should look at how the assembler notation corresponds to the actual machine instruction. The instruction

```
LOAD    3,@A(5)
```

is translated by the assembler into the machine instruction in Figure 7-3. Assume that the symbol A corresponds to the address 567B.

Figure 7-3 Use of bits in the address mode field

The assembler does not require the programmer to specify every field explicitly in each instruction. As we just saw, if the address field is left out, the assembler detects this and fills in the default value of 0.

This assembler will fill in the default value 0 for almost any of the fields in the corresponding machine instruction. In fact, the only field the programmer is required to fill in is the operation field. As an example, the instruction

```
LOAD    5,A
```

is assembled into

```
00001    101    000    000    0 00000000101110111
```

The absence of an address mode symbol preceding the address A signifies that neither indirect nor immediate addressing was chosen. Thus the upper two bits of the address mode field were set to 0. Similarly, the absence of parentheses following the address tells the assembler that indexed address mode was not chosen. The assembler sets the lower bit of the address mode field and the unused index register field to 0.

If a data register number is not needed for an instruction, it can also be omitted. For example, the BR instruction does not use the address register. To branch to location THERE, we simply write

```
BR      THERE
```

If the assembler does not find a comma, it assumes data register 0 and continues translating the instruction. If THERE is defined as 1516B, this instruction would be assembled into

```
00011    000    000    000    0 00000001101001110
```

The address field also has the default value 0. This is especially useful when using one of the "register" address modes mentioned earlier. The instructions

```
LOAD    3,0(6)
```

and

```
LOAD    3,(6)
```

are both assembled into

```
00001   011   110   100   0 00000000000000000
```

While it is true that the assembler provides the default value 0 for most of the instruction fields, there are times when it is better to state the value explicitly. The field should be given explicitly instead of by default whenever the field plays an important part in the instruction. For example, although the instructions

```
LOAD    0,@A
```

and

```
LOAD    @A
```

both assemble into the same instruction, the first form is preferred because it is important that the value being loaded goes into R0. In the same way, the form

```
LOAD    3,A(0)
```

makes it clear that R0 is being used as the index register. It would look very strange to write

```
LOAD    3,A()
```

instead.

Finally, when loading from R0, the address 0 should appear explicitly in the address field:

```
LOAD    3,0
```

It would have been less clear to write

```
LOAD    3,
```

even though the assembler correctly assumes the default 0.

The assembler also supports all of the pseudo-operations described in connection with the previous machine. These include:

	BSS	n	Reset the origin of assembly; forward n words of memory (i.e., "reserve" n memory locations).
	ORIG	n	Reset the origin of assembly to memory location n.
lbl	EQU	n	Enter the symbol lbl into the symbol table with n as its definition (i.e., define the symbolic constant lbl as n).
	DATA	n1,...,nk	Assemble the values n1 through nk into the next k consecutive locations in memory.
	END	n	Marks the physical end of program; start address of program is memory location n.

Also included are the three pseudo-ops that control the program listing during assembly:

PAGE	Begin next line of listing on a new printer page.
LIST	Turn on listing at this point.
NOLIST	Turn off listing at this point.

Two pseudo-operations that provide a trace execution have also been included in this new assembler:

TRACE	Trace the execution of all instructions that lie between this pseudo-op and either the end of program or the next NOTRACE pseudo-operation.
NOTRACE	Marks the last instruction to be traced during execution.

As with the previous machine, more than one TRACE/NOTRACE pair can occur within a program.

Symbolic constants defined with the EQU pseudo-op can appear in any of the fields of an assembler instruction. This includes not only the address field but also the data and index register fields. The assembler provided with this text has the following definitions built in:

```
R0      EQU    0
R1      EQU    1
R2      EQU    2
R3      EQU    3
R4      EQU    4
R5      EQU    5
R6      EQU    6
R7      EQU    7
```

The instruction

```
LOAD    3,5
```

is somewhat easier to read if it is written as

```
LOAD    R3,R5
```

Unless otherwise noted, the examples in the text will use these definitions instead of referring directly to register numbers.

7.6 PROGRAMMING WITH MULTIPLE REGISTERS

We now turn to the problem of actually programming this new machine. In this section, we discuss ways to use the eight registers.

One of the problems with the single-accumulator machine was that intermediate results had to be stored in memory temporarily to make room for the next calculation. This was inefficient for two reasons:

1. Having to recover intermediate results from memory slows down program execution. Accessing memory is much slower than accessing the contents of a register.
2. Because values must be moved to memory, several extra instructions are needed to move them to and from memory, perhaps each time that they are used.

With several identical registers available, intermediate results can often be left in a register until they are needed. As a simple example, consider once again the problem of generating code for the assignment

```
J = K / (I - J)
```

When we looked at this example in chapter three, we generated the following sequence of instructions for the previous machine:

```
LOAD    I
SUB     J
STORE   temp
LOAD    K
DIV     temp
STORE   J
```

The sequence required a temporary memory location and an extra instruction to store the difference I − J. While we cannot get around using a temporary for I − J, there is no longer a need for a temporary memory location. We simply leave the difference in one register while the content of location K is brought into another register:

```
LOAD    R0,I
SUB     R0,J
LOAD    R1,K
DIV     R1,R0
STORE   R1,J
```

As another example, consider the problem of exchanging the contents of two memory locations X and Y. On the previous machine, the solution was something like this:

```
LOAD    X
STORE   temp
LOAD    Y
STORE   X
LOAD    temp
STORE   Y
```

With an extra register, the solution can be written as

```
LOAD    R0,X
LOAD    R1,Y
STORE   R0,Y
STORE   R1,X
```

The presence of extra registers also plays an important part in writing efficient code for loops. Since the body of the loop is executed repeatedly, it is important not only to cut down on the number of instructions within the loop but also to reduce the number of memory references made by those instructions. One way to do this is to keep the most frequently used values in registers throughout the execution of the loop.

Consider once again the problem of computing the *n*th Fibonacci number. The Fibonacci sequence is defined as follows:

$$f(1) = 1$$
$$f(2) = 1$$
$$f(n) = f(n-1) + f(n-1) \qquad n>2$$

The values are 1, 1, 2, 3, 5, 8, 13, and so forth. Each new value is the sum of the preceding two. We looked at a solution to this problem based on a simple counting loop:

```
LSTFIB:= 1;
FIB:= 1;

FOR:= 3 to N DO
    TEMP:= FIB;
    FIB:= FIB + LSTFIB;
    LSTFIB:= TEMP;
END FOR
```

Four values are used in this loop. TEMP, FIB, and LSTFIB are used in computing the next Fibonacci number from the previous two. The fourth value is the loop index I, whose only role is as a trip count. Here is the code that implements the Fibonacci algorithm. R0 through R3 are used to hold the four values throughout the execution of the loop.

Register	Value
R0	FIB
R1	LSTFIB
R2	TEMP
R3	I

```
        LOAD    R0,=1       init. FIB
        LOAD    R1,=1       init. LSTFIB
        LOAD    R3,N        init. trip count

NEXT    CMPR    R3,=3       if trip count expired,
        BRLT    OUT         ... then exit

        LOAD    R2,R0       save previous FIB
        ADD     R0,R1       compute new FIB
        LOAD    R1,R2       new LSTFIB is old FIB
```

```
        SUB     R3,=1       decrement trip count,
        BR      NEXT        ... and repeat

OUT             ...
```

We step the trip count downward to the lower bound because the lower bound is a constant while the upper bound is stored in memory. Otherwise, we would either have to load the value of *N* for each iteration of the loop or keep it in a register for the duration.

The first attempt can be improved upon. Notice that at the end of the loop, the trip count is decremented, and control transfers to the CMPR instruction labeled NEXT. We can take advantage of the fact that the SUB instruction also sets the CMPR register:

```
        LOAD    R0,=1       init. FIB
        LOAD    R1,=1       init. LSTFIB
        LOAD    R3,N        init. trip count
        SUB     R3,=3
        BRLT    OUT         exit if trip count expired

NEXT    LOAD    R2,R0       save previous FIB
        ADD     R0,R1       compute new FIB
        LOAD    R1,R2       new LSTFIB is old FIB

        SUB     R3,=1       decrement trip count,
        BRGE    NEXT        ... and repeat
OUT             ...
```

While the total number of instructions remained the same, the number of instructions executed during each iteration of the loop decreased from seven to five. Since the SUB instruction in the reinitialization code sets the CMPR register with respect to 0, we can shorten the loop by making the trip count expire when it passes 0 instead of 3. The branch to NEXT can now be made conditional. To make everything come out if the initial value of *N* is less than 3, we add a conditional branch to the initialization code.

Extra registers also make array operations easier to implement. Consider, for example, the problem of squaring the content of each element in the array A. We might write a solution to this problem using either the pointer or the indexed model of an array.

The pointer model allows us to control the loop by testing the pointer to see if it has gone beyond the end of the array. The advantage is that the overhead of controlling the loop is consolidated with the overhead of updating the pointer. We begin by computing the addresses of the first and last array elements to be squared. Assume that the array size is stored at a memory location whose symbolic name is N.

```
        LOAD    R0,=A          address of first element
        LOAD    R1,=A-1        address of last element
        ADD     R1,N

NEXT    CMPR    R0,R1          if pointers have crossed,
        BRGT    OUT            ... exit loop

        LOAD    R2,@R0         fetch next element
        MUL     R2,R2          ... and square it
        STORE   R2,@R0

        ADD     R0,=1          increment pointer
        BR      NEXT           ... and repeat
OUT             ...
```

In this version, the pointer initially set to the first array element is used to point to each successive location. The upper-bound pointer remains fixed. When the pointer to the current location is incremented past the pointer to the last location, the loop terminates with all elements squared. If the number of elements indicated by N happened to be zero or negative, the loop behaves reasonably by not executing at all.

Notice that in computing the address of the last array element, we used the address A − 1 rather than A. The value at location N represents the *number* of elements to square. If the number is 1, then the last address is

```
(A - 1) + 1
```

or simply A.

In actually squaring each array element, we have taken advantage of the "register" address modes mentioned earlier. First, we fetch the value of the array element into R2 using register direct addressing. Then the MUL instruction multiplies the contents of R2 by itself using register immediate addressing. We could just as well have used register direct addressing and written

```
MUL     R2,@R0
```

However, this version requires an extra memory reference to bring another copy of the array element into the MBR. By using the copy already in R2, we avoided an unnecessary reference to memory. This savings is increased by the number of iterations required to square the entire array.

In certain cases the indexed model is superior to the pointer model. Suppose we want to copy the content of array A into array B. If we used the pointer model, we would have to compute lower bounds for both and upper bounds for at least one of the arrays. We would also have to update both pointers each time through the loop.

The indexed array model allows us to maintain a single array index, which can be used to index either array as well as to control the loop. Once again, assume that the number of elements to copy is stored in memory at location N.

```
          LOAD   R0,N           number of elements to copy
          BRLT   OUT            exit if count exhausted

NEXT      LOAD   R1,A-1(R0)     fetch next element of A
          STORE  R1,B-1(R0)     store into B
          SUB    R0,=1          decrement number to copy,
          BRGT   NEXT           ... and repeat needed

OUT              ...
```

Since the order in which the loop executes does not matter in this case, we run it backward to take advantage of the fixed lower bound. Notice also how the addresses A-1 and B-1 were used. Using an index from 1 to N assumes a lower bound on the arrays of 1. Thus, we use one less than each address to make things work out.

7.7 PERSPECTIVE

This machine is typical of the architecture found on many *mainframe* computers. These are generally larger machines that are mounted in tall racks or "frames." In addition to size, however, the term has come to indicate their capacity and functionality as well. Most are able to address a large amount of memory, some in the millions of words. The CPUs have a number of general- and special-purpose registers that can be used by the programmer.

Perhaps the most successful computers in this class are the IBM 360/370 family from the International Business Machines Corporation. The IBM 360 was introduced in the mid-1960s. In 1970, IBM brought out the IBM 370 with a superset of the 360 instruction set. The IBM 370 took advantage of more advanced hardware technology that became available after the IBM 360 was designed.

Although the word size of the IBM 360/370 is 32 bits, its memory is addressable in 8-bit multiples called *bytes*. The address of a full word of data must be evenly divisible by 4, since a full word is made up of four 8-bit bytes. Addresses are 24 bits wide, giving a total memory capacity of over 16 million bytes, or 4 million words.

The CPU included sixteen 32-bit general-purpose registers and a special register called the *program status word (PSW)*. The PSW contained fields that served the same purpose as our program counter and compare register. The 360/370 ALU provided floating-point as well as integer arithmetic. Four 64-bit floating-point registers in the CPU were included to hold the results of floating-point operations.

The length of an instruction was either 2 or 4 bytes. The opcode in the first byte implied one of four instruction formats and hence the length of the instruction. The formats included fields for an opcode, data register, index register, address field, and base register field. The 360/370 had only immediate, direct, and indexed addressing.

Direct or immediate was determined by the opcode. If the value in the index register field was zero, no indexing was performed. Thus general register zero (G0) could not be used as an index register. The instruction set included instructions that operated on bytes, half words, full words, and multiple words.

Since the address field of the instruction was only 12 bits long, a method for allowing 24-bit addresses was needed. The use of a *base register* provided the solution. As one of the steps in the effective address calculation, the *base address* in the specified base register was added to the *offset* in the address field. If the value in the base register field was zero, the offset in the address field was used directly. To avoid the inconvenience of having to specify the base register for each instruction, the IBM 360/370 assembler provided an assembler pseudo-op called USING. This pseudo-op told the assembler to assemble all instructions using the specified register as the base register, unless another one was given explicitly. Certain conventions on the use of base registers meant several general registers were always tied up holding base addresses for various parts of memory.

Another very successful mainframe computer was the Digital Equipment Corporation PDP-10. This machine was also introduced in the mid-1960s and had much in common with the design of our computer. In the early 1970s, Digital upgraded the processor technology and reintroduced the machine as the DEC System 10. Whereas the IBM 360/370 computers gained their greatest popularity in the business market, the PDP-10 became best known for its use in scientific and research applications.

The PDP-10 had a word size of 36 bits. Addresses were 18 bits wide, giving a memory capacity of over 200,000 words. An extended address on later models added 4 bits for a capacity of over 4 million words.

The CPU provided 16 general-purpose registers, each 36 bits long. These 16 registers were memory-mapped, with R0 mapped to memory location 0, R1 to memory location 1, and so forth. The ALU included floating-point arithmetic, whose results were returned to one of the general-purpose registers. A condition register recorded the results of comparisons for use by the conditional branch instructions.

Instructions were always one word long. The 7-bit opcode allowed for up to 128 instructions. Although the effective address calculation was nearly the same as in our machine, the address mode was scattered among the opcode, address type, and index register fields.

If the index register field was nonzero, the content of the specified register was added to the value in the address field. Thus R0 could never be used as an index register. The indirect bit specified whether to perform indirection or not. If the bit was on, the word fetched was treated as another address, including its own index register, indirect bit, and address fields. The algorithm repeated until an address was fetched whose indirect bit was not set. Finally, immediate addressing was indicated by the type of the opcode.

A novel feature of this machine was the ability to define new instructions. Many of the possible 128 commands were unused. If the sequencer tried to execute one of these, the instruction was trapped and could be interpreted by a routine included for that purpose by the programmer. This in effect provided a user-extensible instruction set that could customize the machine for a particular purpose.

7.8 SUMMARY

Our new machine has a number of features not found on the previous one. These include

- Extended instruction format
- Multiple accumulators
- Extended modes of addressing
- Boolean and bit manipulation operations
- Input/output operations

Although we have not explored all of them, this chapter has given us some idea of the machine's capabilities. The addition of multiple accumulators along with the extended instruction format can significantly reduce the number of references made to memory. By keeping several values at a time in CPU registers, we also reduce the number of instructions otherwise needed to shuffle data between the CPU and memory. The result is that our programs promise to be more concise, easier to write, and, equally important, easier to read.

On the other hand, each instruction takes up twice as much storage as did an instruction on the previous machine. Furthermore, managing data in both memory and registers at the same time can take some getting used to.

From the programmer's point of view, the two machines are distinguished by their respective instruction formats. The first one, the "one-address" machine, has a comparatively simple instruction format. The destination of a LOAD operation is implicit in the instruction. The address space is fairly limited, as are the number of address modes available.

The second, "two-address" machine allows the programmer to specify both the source and the destination of an operation. The instruction format needed to accommodate this is somewhat more complicated. The address space available is usually somewhat larger, and a number of new address modes are added.

Now that we have been introduced to this new machine, we will go on in the next chapter to take a look at some new ways to implement procedures.

PROBLEMS

7-1. In the previous machine, the AC served as both an accumulator and an index register. Why does this make operations such as indexed STOREs impossible to perform? How do some one-address machines solve this problem?

7-2. How many general-purpose registers are available on this second machine? Why is this a better solution to the problem of an index register?

7-3. What is meant by the term *memory-mapped*? To what addresses are the registers mapped?

7-4. What is the purpose of the CMPR register on this machine? Why was there no such register on our previous machine?

7-5. How is the ALU on this machine different from the AU on the previous machine? What does the *L* in *ALU* stand for?

7-6. What is the purpose of the I/O bus? How is it connected to the CPU?

7-7. What does *IOU* stand for? What is the purpose of the IOU?

7-8. Why is it difficult to print a number on this machine?

7-9. How many operations can be represented in the operation field of an instruction on this new machine? How many different address modes are possible?

7-10. In what two ways is the address field of an instruction different on this machine from an address field on the previous one?

7-11. How many of the registers can be used as index registers? Can a register be used both as a data register and an index register in the same instruction?

7-12. In what order are the address modes carried out during the effective address computation?

7-13. Under what conditions does the execution of an instruction modify the CMPR register? What is the purpose of the CMPR instruction?

7-14. What four pieces of information must be contained in the address field of an assembler instruction on this machine? Which two of these were contained in the address field of the previous machine?

7-15. Write a single register transfer expression for each of the following instructions:

(a) `STORE`	`5,N`	**(b)** `ADD`	`7,@N`
(c) `LOAD`	`0,=N`	**(d)** `BR`	`N`
(e) `MUL`	`4,N(2)`	**(f)** `LOAD`	`2,=N(1)`
(g) `ADD`	`1,@N(6)`	**(h)** `BR`	`@N(3)`

7-16. What is meant by *register address mode*? Instead of the address field of the instruction, where is the address stored?

7-17. Give an example of an instruction using each of these register address modes:
(a) Register immediate
(b) Register direct
(c) Register indirect

7-18. Another combination of address modes has the same register transfer expression as register direct. Write an instruction equivalent to the one from (b) in Problem 7-17 that illustrates this address mode.

7-19. Translate the assembler instructions from Problem 7-15 into binary machine-level instructions. Assume that the symbol N is defined as 567B.

7-20. Write a problem that forms the sum of corresponding elements of two arrays A and B and places the sum in the corresponding location of array C. Initialize the arrays A and B using DATA pseudo-instructions. Initialize a location N to the size of each of the arrays. Use the pointer model to reference the three arrays.

7-21. Repeat Problem 7-20, this time using the indexed array model.

7-22. What advantage is there to using the indexed array model rather than the pointer model when copying from one array to another?

8

Procedures Revisited

We turn once again to the subject of procedures. In this chapter we will look at some techniques that would not have been obvious on the previous machine. We will also review a few of the issues from Chapter 6. The architectural changes made to this new machine offer some opportunities not available on the previous one.

8.1 THE CALL INSTRUCTION

On our first machine, the CALL instruction placed the return address at the location specified by the effective address, then transferred control to the location following that address.

```
M[MAR]  ←  PC
PC  ←  MAR+1
```

For programs with a large number of procedures, some amount of space is wasted by this method. While the number of levels of nested calls is usually fairly small, space must be reserved in each procedure for a return address.

The CALL instruction on our new machine is based on an interesting data structure known as a *stack*. The name suggests a stack of plates at a cafeteria, sitting on top of a spring-loaded tray. A plate placed on top of the stack pushes the other plates down. When a plate is removed, the others pop up. The top plate on the stack was the last one placed there and is the next one to be removed.

In a similar way, the *push* operation enters data onto a stack, and the *pop* operation removes data from the stack. The pop operation is defined in such a way that the

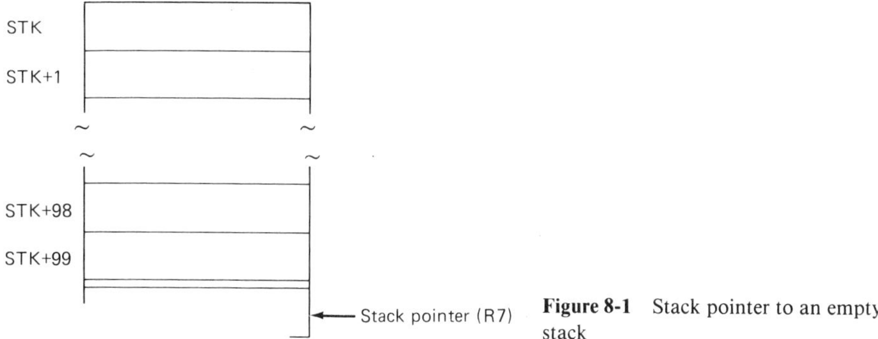

Figure 8-1 Stack pointer to an empty stack

item most recently pushed onto the stack is the next to be popped. This item is said to be the *top of stack*. Of course, if there are no items on the stack, it is said to be *empty*.

A stack can be implemented as an array of memory locations, along with a pointer, called the *stack pointer,* that indicates which location is the next to be popped. The stack pointer points to the current top of stack. Here is a sequence of instructions that establishes a stack STK and initializes a stack pointer in R7:

```
STK         BSS      100
             ....
            LOAD     R7,=STK+100      init stack pointer
```

The stack pointer initially points to one location past the end of the stack space (Figure 8-1). The CALL instruction pushes the return address onto a stack, then transfers control to the procedure indicated. The stack pointer is in the data register, and the procedure is at the effective address. Here are the register transfer expressions for this:

```
CALL      Ri    ←   Ri - 1
          M[Ri]  ←   PC
          PC    ←   MAR
```

Assume that a stack was set up as in Figure 8-1, with the stack pointer in R7. Executing the CALL instruction

```
HERE      CALL    R7,PROC
```

pushes the address HERE + 1 onto the stack and transfers control to memory location PROC:

```
R7    ←   R7 - 1
M[R7]   ←   (HERE+1)
PC    ←   PROC
```

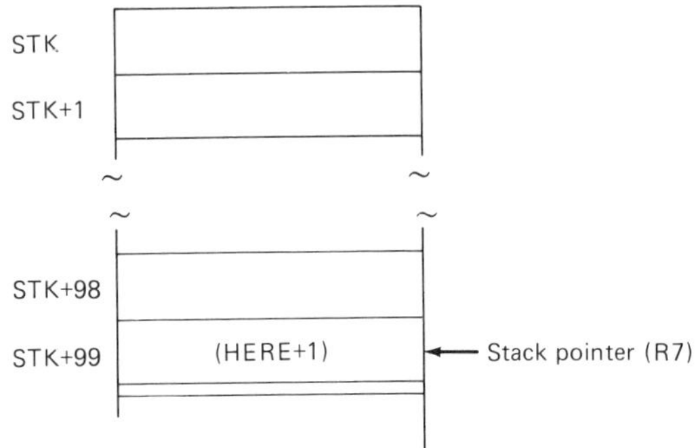

Figure 8-2 Return address pushed onto the return stack

Figure 8-2 shows how the stack looks just after executing the CALL instruction.

A stack that is used to hold return addresses is called a *return stack*. The one shown in the figures is a *decreasing stack* because its stack pointer moves toward lower memory each time a return address is pushed.

8.2 THE RTN INSTRUCTION

Once control has transferred to the procedure, we are faced with the problem of returning. Since calling pushed the return address onto the stack, returning must pop the return off the stack and transfer control to that location. A new instruction, RTN, accomplishes this. The register transfer expressions for the RTN instruction are

```
RTN        PC  ←—  M[Ri]
           Ri  ←—  Ri+1
```

When we are ready to return from procedure PROC, executing the instruction

```
RTN     R7,
```

has the effect

```
PC  ←—  (HERE+1)
R7  ←—  R7+1
```

The stack is empty once again, and execution continues at location HERE + 1 (Figure 8-3). Notice how the RTN instruction was written. Only the data register field is used, and the address field is left unspecified. If we had instead written

```
RTN     R7
```

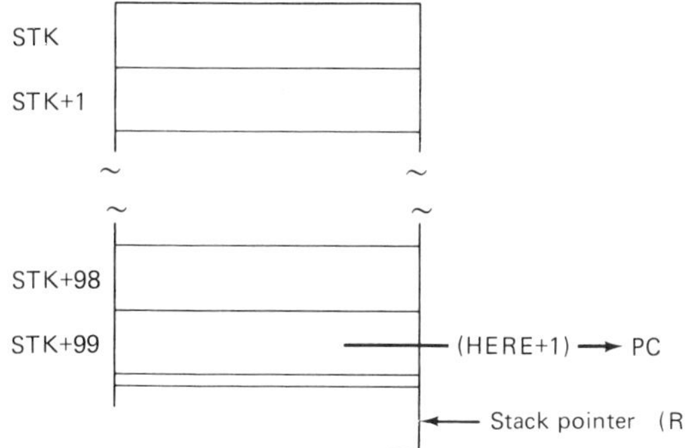

Figure 8-3 Return address popped from the return stack

the assembler would have assembled it to the instruction

```
RTN     R0,R7
```

8.3 REVIEW OF PARAMETER PASSING METHODS

In this section we will review some of the parameter passing methods discussed in Chapter 6 and become more familiar with the use of the CALL and RTN instructions just presented. For these examples, we will assume that storage for a return stack has been reserved and that R7 is a stack pointer into that storage.

We will again use the RMDR procedure presented in Chapter 6 as an example for this discussion. RMDR computes the whole remainder of dividing N into M. The formula for this is

$$N - \text{floor}\ (N/M)\ *\ M$$

If the value of M is 0, we defined the remainder to be 0 as well. We will continue to return the result of the procedure in a register. R0 is used as the result register for these examples.

8.3.1 Register Transmission

In Chapter 6 we transmitted the two parameters to RMDR by several methods. One method that we did not use was *transmission by register.* Since we had only one register and two parameters, the method simply did not apply. On our new machine we have eight registers, so register transmission is an option for most procedures.

```
    ...
LOAD   R0,M
LOAD   R1,N
CALL   R7,RMDR            pushes rtn addr on R7 stk
    ...
```

```
** RMDR   -  RETURNS THE WHOLE REMAINDER OF A QUOTIENT
*            (DEFINED AS 0 IF DIVISOR IS 0)
*
*           INPUT (VALUE, REGISTER)
*              R0 - DIVISOR     (M)
*              R1 - DIVIDEND    (N)
*
*           OUTPUT
*              R0 - WHOLE REMAINDER OF QUOTIENT
*
RMDR        LOAD    R2,R0          save copy of M
            BREQ    RMD.OUT        if M=0, return 0 in R0

            LOAD    R0,R1          copy of N for subtraction
            DIV     R1,R2          compute greatest multiple
            MUL     R1,R2          ... of M <= N
            SUB     R0,R1          remainder is N - this result
RMD.OUT     RTN     R7,            return with remainder in R0
```

First, notice that an extra word at the beginning of the procedure has not been reserved for a return address. The return address was pushed onto the stack pointed to by R7. The label RMDR indicates the first executable instruction in the procedure.

Some consideration was given to the order of the parameters in the registers, as we shall see. R0 contains the value of M upon entry, but the same register is also needed for the result. The first step is to free up R0 by copying the value of M into R2. Doing this step has the added benefit that it sets the CMPR register based on the value of M. Since the result is defined as 0 when the value of M is 0, the procedure simply returns if that is the case. Since the formula calls for two copies of N, we make an extra copy in R2 and leave the copy in R0 for the final subtraction. The rest is straightforward.

The situation differs little if M and N are passed by reference:

```
        ...
    LOAD   R0,=M
    LOAD   R1,=N
    CALL   R7,RMDR            pushes rtn addr on R7 stk
        ...

** RMDR   -  RETURNS THE WHOLE REMAINDER OF A QUOTIENT
*            (DEFINED AS 0 IF DIVISOR IS 0)
*
*           INPUT (REFERENCE, REGISTER)
*              R0  -  DIVISOR
*              R1  -  DIVIDEND
*
*           OUTPUT
*              R0  -  WHOLE REMAINDER OF QUOTIENT
```

```
*
RMDR       LOAD    R1,@R1        fetch value of N
           LOAD    R0,@R0        fetch value of M
           BREQ    RMD.OUT       if M=0, return 0 in R0

           LOAD    R2,R0         copy M to free R0
           LOAD    R0,R1         copy N for subtraction
           DIV     R1,R2         compute greatest multiple
           MUL     R1,R2         ... of M <= N
           SUB     R0,R1         remainder is N - this result
RMD.OUT    RTN     R7,           return rmdr in R0
```

There is a little more register juggling in this version because dereferencing the parameters takes a couple of extra steps. The LOAD operation that fetches the value of M now serves to set the CMPR register.

8.3.2 Copy-in Transmission

The copy-in method is much the same as it was on our first machine. The only improvement here is the use of additional registers to eliminate a number of memory references. This version of the RMDR procedure is written to expect two value parameters by copy-in:

```
        ...
    LOAD    R0,M          store M into procedure
    STORE   RMDR-2
    LOAD    R0,N
    STORE   RMDR-1        store N into procedure
    CALL    RMDR          pushes rtn addr on R7 stk
        ...
```

```
** RMDR   -   RETURNS THE WHOLE REMAINDER OF A QUOTIENT
*             (DEFINED AS 0 IF DIVISOR IS 0)
*
*          INPUT (VALUE, COPY-IN)
*             RMDR-2   -   DIVISOR (MVAL)
*             RMDR-1   -   DIVIDEND (NVAL)
*
*          OUTPUT
*             R0   -   WHOLE REMAINDER OF QUOTIENT
*
MVAL       BSS     1          for value of M
NVAL       BSS     1          for value of N
RMDR       LOAD    R1,NVAL    fetch value of N
           LOAD    R0,MVAL    fetch value of M
           BREQ    RMD.OUT
```

```
          LOAD    R2,R0       copy M to free R0
          LOAD    R0,R1       copy N for subtraction
          DIV     R1,R2       compute greatest multiple
          MUL     R1,R2       ...of M <= N
          SUB     R0,R1       remainder is N - this result
RMD.OUT   RTN     R7,         return rmdr in R0
```

8.3.3 In-line Transmission

Recovering parameters transmitted in line is quite a bit easier on this machine than on the previous one. Here is an example of the remainder procedure with the two parameters passed by value. We use the form that places a branch around the parameters as the first statement following the CALL:

```
        ...
     CALL     R7,RMDR          push rtn addr on R7 stk
     BR       *+3              branch around parameters
     DATA     7,41             values of M and N
        ...

** RMDR   -   RETURNS THE WHOLE REMAINDER OF A QUOTIENT
*             (DEFINED AS 0 IF DIVISOR IS 0)
*
*         INPUT (VALUE, IN-LINE)
*             <RETURN>+1   -   DIVISOR (M)
*             <RETURN>+2   -   DIVIDEND (N)
*
*         OUTPUT
*             R0   -   WHOLE REMAINDER OF QUOTIENT
*
RMDR      LOAD    R0,@R7        points to parameters
          LOAD    R1,2(R0)      fetch value of N
          LOAD    R0,1(R0)      fetch value of M
          BREQ    RMD.OUT

          LOAD    R2,R0         copy M to free R0
          LOAD    R0,R1         copy N for subtraction
          DIV     R1,R2         compute greatest multiple
          MUL     R1,R2         ... of M <= N
          SUB     R0,R1         remainder is N - this result
RMD.OUT   RTN     R7,           return rmdr in R0
```

The return address is brought into R0 from the location pointed to by the stack pointer. This is the address of the instruction

```
        BR        *+3                     branch around parameters
```

If the CALL instruction is at location 600B, then R0 holds the address 601B. The effect of the instruction

```
        LOAD      R1,2(R0)                fetch value of N
```

is

```
                  R1  <--  M[1 + R0]
```

Substituting for the contents of R0, we are left with

```
                  R1  <--  M[603B]
```

which is the location where the value of N was assembled in line.

We can also make good use of our new address modes if we consider passing reference rather than value parameters:

```
             ...
        CALL      R7,RMDR                 push rtn addr on R7 stk
        BR        *+3                     branch around parameters
        DATA      M,N                     addresses of M and N
             ...

** RMDR   -   RETURNS THE WHOLE REMAINDER OF A QUOTIENT
*             (DEFINED AS 0 IF DIVISOR IS 0)
*
*          INPUT (REFERENCE, IN-LINE)
*              <RETURN>+1   -   DIVISOR (M)
*              <RETURN>+2   -   DIVIDEND (N)
*
*          OUTPUT
*              R0   -   WHOLE REMAINDER OF QUOTIENT
*
RMDR       LOAD    R0,@R7          points to parameters
           LOAD    R1,@2(R0)       fetch value of N
           LOAD    R0,@1(R0)       fetch value of M
           BREQ    RMD.OUT

           LOAD    R2,R0           copy M to free R0
           LOAD    R0,R1           copy N for subtraction
           DIV     R1,R2           compute greatest multiple
           MUL     R1,R2           ... of M <= N
           SUB     R0,R1           remainder is N - this result
RMD.OUT    RTN     R7,             return rmdr in R0
```

Look at how the values of *M* and *N* were recovered. Using *indexed indirect* addressing, we can recover the value of a reference parameter in a single instruction. The effect of the instruction

```
        LOAD    R1,@2(R0)       fetch value of N
```

is

```
        R1  <--  M[ M[ 2 + R0] ]
```

If, as we assumed a moment ago, the CALL instruction is at location 600B so that R0 contains the address 601B, then the expression simplifies by substituting for the contents of R0 to

```
        R1  <--  M[ M[ 601B ] ]
```

Location 603B contains the address N, so the expression simplifies once again to

```
        R0  <--  M[ N ]
```

The value finally brought into R0 is the value stored at memory location N. We can apply the same reasoning to the instruction

```
        LOAD    R0,@1(R3)       fetch value of M
```

to show that its effect is simply

```
        R0  <--  M[ M ]
```

In-line parameter transmission is still a valuable method on this new machine. It is all the more attractive when passing reference parameters because the indexed indirect address mode allows us to recover parameter values in just one instruction.

8.3.4 Parameter List Transmission

Transmitting parameters by means of a parameter list, as we noted earlier, shares many features with in-line transmission. This similarity is especially clear as we use the RMDR procedure to illustrate the parameter list method with this new machine. A pointer to the list of reference parameters through R0:

```
        ...

        LOAD    R0,=PARAM       address of parameter list
        CALL    RMDR            push rtn addr on R7 stk

        ...
```

```
PARAM    DATA    M,N             parameter list

         ...

** RMDR  -  RETURNS THE WHOLE REMAINDER OF A QUOTIENT
*           (DEFINED AS 0 IF DIVISOR IS 0)
*
*        INPUT (REFERENCE, PARAMETER LIST THROUGH R0)
*           <PARAM>+0   -   DIVISOR  (M)
*           <PARAM>+1   -   DIVIDEND (N)
*
*        OUTPUT
*           R0   -   WHOLE REMAINDER OF QUOTIENT
*
RMDR     LOAD    R1,@1(R0)    fetch value of N
         LOAD    R0,@0(R0)    fetch value of M
         BREQ    RMD.OUT

         LOAD    R2,R0        copy M to free R0
         LOAD    R0,R1        copy N for subtraction
         DIV     R1,R2        compute greatest multiple
         MUL     R1,R2        ... of M <= N
         SUB     R0,R1        remainder is N - this result
RMD.OUT  RTN     R7,          return rmdr in R0
```

8.4 PASSING PARAMETERS BY STACK

A stack is also a good way to pass parameters. After looking at the other two stack manipulation instructions available on this machine, we will examine two strategies for passing parameters by stack.

8.4.1 The PUSH and POP Instructions

The instructions CALL and RTN push and pop return addresses, but they are not useful for pushing and popping an arbitrary number. Instead, we can use two new instructions.

The PUSH instruction pushes a value onto a stack. Here is how PUSH works:

```
PUSH       {MBR   ←—   M[MAR]}
            Ri   ←—   Ri - 1
            M[Ri]   ←—   MBR
```

PUSH brings the value to be pushed into the MBR, decrements the stack pointer, and stores the MBR in memory at that location. For example,

```
PUSH    R7,=3
```

pushes the number 3 onto the R7 stack. If the value being pushed is in memory, PUSH reads it into the MBR as its first step.

The POP instruction pops a value from the stack. Here is how POP works:

```
POP          MBR    ←   M[Ri]
             M[MAR] ←   MBR
             Ri     ←   Ri + 1
```

POP copies the top stack value into the MBR, stores it in memory at the effective address, and increments the stack pointer. For example,

```
POP     R7,SAVE.IT
```

pops the value from the top of the R7 stack and stores it at memory location SAVE.IT. The instruction

```
POP     R7,R3
```

saves the value popped in R3.

8.4.2 Passing Parameters on a Parameter Stack

The first method requires setting up a separate stack for passing parameters. For example,

```
PAR.STK    BSS     100
              ...
           LOAD    R6,=PARSTK+100            init param stk
```

reserves memory for a parameter stack and initializes R6 with its stack pointer.

Suppose that storage for a stack has been established and that R6 serves as the parameter stack pointer. We will pass *M* and *N* to our RMDR procedure by value on the R6 stack. Although the result could be returned through R0 as usual, we will write this version of the RMDR procedure to return its value on the R6 stack instead. The R7 stack is still used as a return stack. Here is the procedure call:

```
PUSH    R6,M
PUSH    R6,N
CALL    R7,RMDR
POP     R6,RESULT
```

Figure 8-4 shows what the parameter stack looks like at this point. Here is the procedure itself:

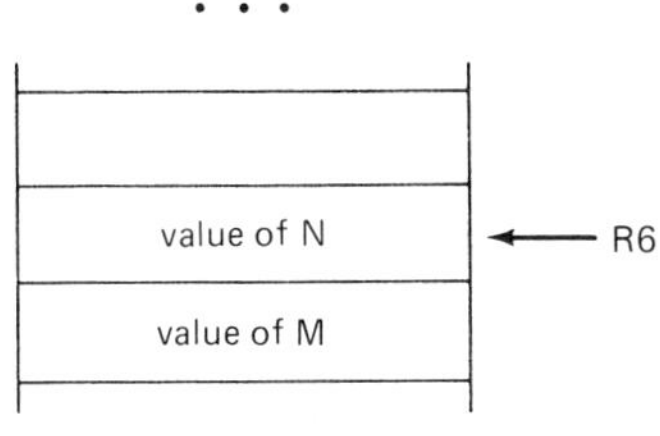

Figure 8-4 Two values pushed onto a parameter stack

```
** RMDR   --   RETURNS THE WHOLE REMAINDER OF A QUOTIENT
*              (DEFINED AS 0 IF DIVISOR IS 0)
*
*            INPUT (VALUE)
*               R6 STACK - DIVIDEND (N)  (TOP)
*                          DIVISOR  (M)
*
*            OUTPUT
*               R6 STACK - WHOLE REMAINDER OF QUOTIENT
*
RMDR         POP     R6,R1        fetch value of N
             POP     R6,R0        fetch value of M
             BREQ    RMD.OUT

             LOAD    R2,R0        copy M to free R0
             LOAD    R0,R1        copy N for subtraction
             DIV     R1,R2        compute greatest multiple
             MUL     R1,R2        ... of M <= N
             SUB     R0,R1        remainder is N - this result

RMD.OUT      PUSH    R6,R0        push result back on the stack
             RTN     R7,          ... and return
```

The value of *N* was the last to be pushed onto the stack and is also the first popped from the stack. We can no longer simply return if the value of *M* is 0. The result must be pushed onto the stack before returning from the procedure.

Notice that the procedure popped the parameters from the stack. This procedure follows the discipline that *makes the called procedure responsible* for removing its parameters from the stack before returning. The other approach *makes the caller responsible* for removing the parameters as well as the result upon return:

```
PUSH   R6,M
PUSH   R6,N
CALL   R7,RMDR
POP    R6,RESULT
```

```
        ADD     R6,=2           remove input parameters
```

```
** RMDR   --  RETURNS THE WHOLE REMAINDER OF A QUOTIENT
*             (DEFINED AS 0 IF DIVISOR IS 0)
*
*           INPUT (VALUE)
*             R6 STACK - DIVIDEND (N)  (TOP)
*                        DIVISOR  (M)
*
*           OUTPUT
*             R6 STACK - WHOLE REMAINDER OF QUOTIENT
*
RMDR        LOAD    R1,0(R6)     fetch value of N
            LOAD    R0,1(R6)     fetch value of M
            BREQ    RMD.OUT

            LOAD    R2,R0        copy M to free R0
            LOAD    R0,R1        copy N for subtraction
            DIV     R1,R2        compute greatest multiple
            MUL     R1,R2        ... of M <= N
            SUB     R0,R1        remainder is N - this result

RMD.OUT     PUSH    R6,R0        push result back on the stack
            RTN     R7,          ... and return
```

Rather than popping the two input values, this version uses indexed LOADs. The value of N is pointed to by the stack pointer in R6, and the value of M is one location beyond that.

There are advantages to both these methods. Having the calling routine clean up the stack on return allows a procedure to be called with a variable number of parameters. Depending on the value of the first few parameters, the procedure may not require any of the ones that follow. If the calling routine knows this, it is unnecessary for it to push the extra ones that are never used.

On the other hand, having the called procedure clean up its parameters is often more convenient. It may also save code because the extra instruction for each call to clean up the stack can be eliminated. Although both methods are widely used, we will follow the discipline of having the called procedure clean up the stack before returning in the following examples.

8.4.3 Passing Parameters on the Return Stack

So far, we have used a stack as a parameter stack and as a return stack but not as both at the same time. One argument for combining the two is that it provides a more

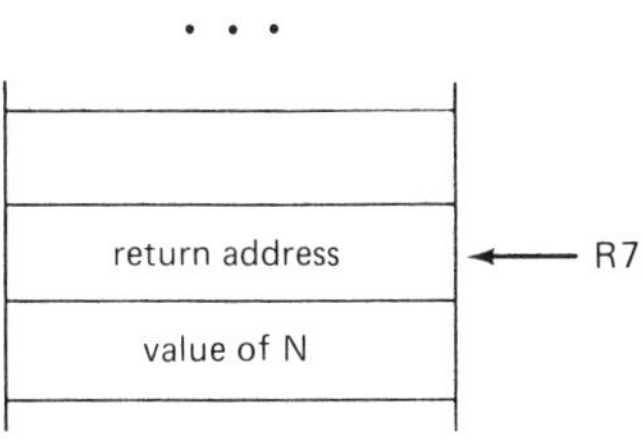

Figure 8-5 Return stack upon entering procedure NFACT.

flexible use of storage. If separate stacks are allocated, one may become full while there is still plenty of room in the other. If they are combined, this will not happen unless there really is no more room for either. On the other hand, using the return stack for parameters takes a bit more care, as we shall see.

To see how it is done, we will write a procedure NFACT that computes the *factorial* of a number. Represented by the notation $N!$, the factorial of N is defined by the formula:

$$N! = N * (N - 1) * (N - 2) * \ldots * 3 * 2 * 1$$

or, in mathematical notation,

$$N! = \prod_{i=1}^{N} i$$

For example,

$$\begin{aligned} 1! &= 1 \\ 2! &= 2 = 2 * 1 \\ 3! &= 6 = 3 * 2 * 1 \\ 4! &= 24 = 4 * 3 * 2 * 1 \end{aligned}$$

The special case of 0! is defined as 1.

Here is a version of NFACT that passes the value of N and returns its result on the return stack. We will continue to use R7 for this purpose. The calling sequence would look like this:

```
PUSH    R7,N
CALL    R7,NFACT
```

Upon entry to NFACT, the stack contains the return address as the top item, and the parameter N just under it, as shown in Figure 8-5.

In the previous example, we could have simply popped the value of N off the stack. We can no longer do that, because the return address is in the way. Instead, we must LOAD the value of N, indexing off R7. The procedure can achieve the effect of removing its parameter from the stack by storing its result back to this location just before returning. Here is a version of NFACT that does this:

```
** NFACT -- RETURNS THE FACTORIAL OF A NUMBER
*
*        INPUT (VALUE)
*           R7 STACK  -  NUMBER (N)
*
*        OUTPUT
*           R7 STACK  -  FACTORIAL OF N
*
NFACT    LOAD     R1,=1              initialize result
         LOAD     R0,1(R7)           fetch value of N
         BRLE     NFOUT              exit if out of range

NFLOOP   MUL      R1,R0              mult. next term
         SUB      R0,=1              decrement N
         BRGT     NFLOOP             repeat if N>0

NFOUT    STORE    R1,1(R7)           replace N by N!
         RTN      R7,                return from CALL
```

The situation is a little trickier if there are more or fewer parameters than values returned. Consider the case of a procedure that returns a value on the stack but is not passed any parameters. Instead it relies strictly on *global data*.

Suppose, for example, that two global values, UPPERLIM and LOWERLIM, represent the upper and lower bounds along some line. A procedure MIDPOINT computes the midpoint between these two and returns it on the stack.

One way to handle this is to make the caller responsible for allocating a location on the stack before invoking MIDPOINT:

```
SUB      R7,=1              reserve result loc
CALL     R7,MIDPOINT
```

Decrementing the stack pointer simply reserves a location on the stack, without initializing it to a specific value. Figure 8-6 shows the stack upon entry into MIDPOINT. We could just as well have pushed a dummy value on the stack, but that would have cost an extra memory reference to store it.

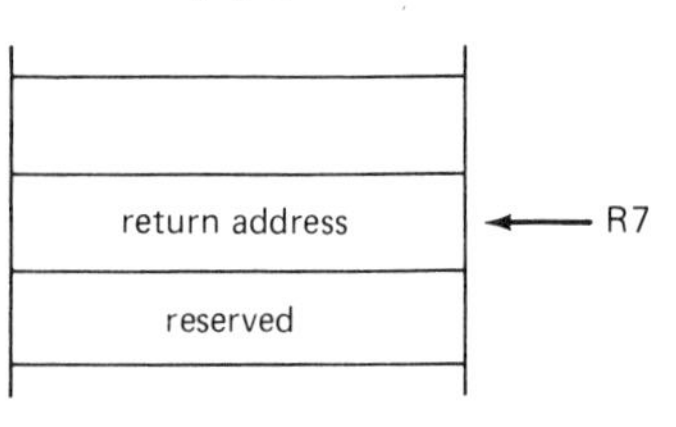

Figure 8-6 Stack with space reserved for result

Here is procedure MIDPOINT. The result is returned on the stack in the reserved location:

```
** MIDPOINT -- RETURNS A NUMBER HALF WAY BETWEEN
*              LOWERLIM AND UPPERLIM
*
*          INPUT (GLOBAL)
*             UPPERLIM   -   UPPER LIMIT
*             LOWERLIM   -   LOWER LIMIT
*
*          OUTPUT
*             R7 STACK   -   MIDPOINT
*
MIDPOINT   LOAD     R0,UPPERLIM
           ADD      R0,LOWERLIM
           DIV      R0,=2              truncates to integer
           STORE    R0,1(R7)           return result on stk
           RTN      R7,
```

A somewhat better solution is to make the procedure responsible for allocating a storage location. All that is required is to move the return address (and the stack pointer) up one position, to leave a slot for the result (Figure 8-7). An easy way to carry this off is simply to push another copy of the return address onto the stack. The old return address location will be overwritten by the result. Here is a version of MIDPOINT that does this:

```
** MIDPOINT -- RETURNS A NUMBER HALF WAY BETWEEN
*              LOWERLIM AND UPPERLIM
*
*          INPUT (GLOBAL)
*             UPPERLIM   -   UPPER LIMIT
*             LOWERLIM   -   LOWER LIMIT
*
*          OUTPUT
*             R7 STACK   -   MIDPOINT
*
MIDPOINT   PUSH     R7,0(R7)           move return address
           LOAD     R0,UPPERLIM
           ADD      R0,LOWERLIM
           DIV      R0,=2              truncates to integer
           STORE    R0,1(R7)           return result on stk
           RTN      R7,
```

The other problem is how to clean up the stack if there are more parameters than results returned. Suppose that MIDPOINT is passed the upper and lower limits by value on the stack and returns the midpoint on the stack as well. Figure 8-8 shows

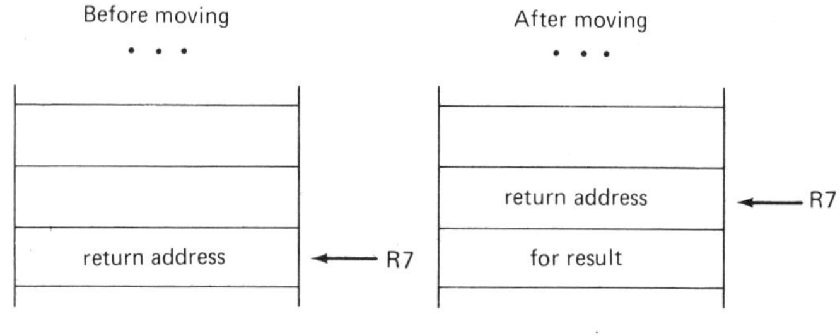

Figure 8-7 Return address moved to reserve space for result

the stack just at entry to MIDPOINT and how we would like the stack to look just before executing the RTN instruction. There are several ways of getting the stack into its final configuration; here is one of the more compact methods:

```
** MIDPOINT -- RETURNS A NUMBER HALF WAY BETWEEN
*              LOWERLIM AND UPPERLIM
*
*            INPUT (VALUE)
*               R7 STACK    -   UPPER LIMIT (TOP)
*                               LOWER LIMIT
*
*            OUTPUT
*               R7 STACK    -   MIDPOINT
*
MIDPOINT     LOAD     R0,1(R7)         value UPPERLIM
             ADD      R0,2(R7)         value LOWERLIM
             DIV      R0,=2            truncates to integer
             STORE    R0,2(R7)         return result on stk
```

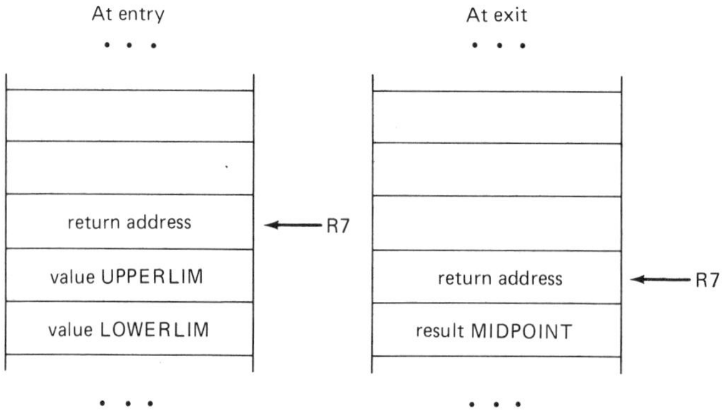

At entry

return address ← R7

value UPPERLIM

value LOWERLIM

At exit

return address ← R7

result MIDPOINT

Figure 8-8 Return address moved to overwrite second parameter

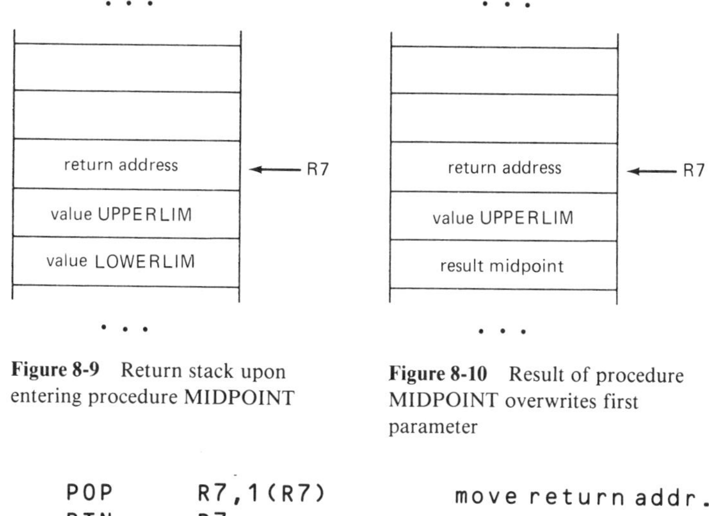

Figure 8-9 Return stack upon entering procedure MIDPOINT

Figure 8-10 Result of procedure MIDPOINT overwrites first parameter

```
POP     R7,1(R7)        move return addr.
RTN     R7,
```

Figure 8-9 shows the R7 stack upon procedure entry. The values of UPPERLIM and LOWERLIM are at M[R7 + 1] and M[R7 + 2], respectively. Once the midpoint is computed, it is stored back in the stack, replacing the value of LOWERLIM.

Figure 8-10 shows how the stack looks after all of this. Since the return address is now on the top of the stack, it can be moved down one location by simply popping it into M[R7 + 1]. The return address overwrites the value of UPPERLIM stored there. In the process, the stack pointer is also adjusted, so that it still points to the return address (Figure 8-11). This is just the condition we were looking for.

As we have discovered, it is possible to use the same stack as both a parameter stack and a return stack. However, some extra overhead may be associated with using it this way. It is important to make sure that the stack is cleaned up before returning to the calling routine. If the number of parameters passed in by stack does not match the number of words returned as the result, some extra steps must be taken to ensure that this happens.

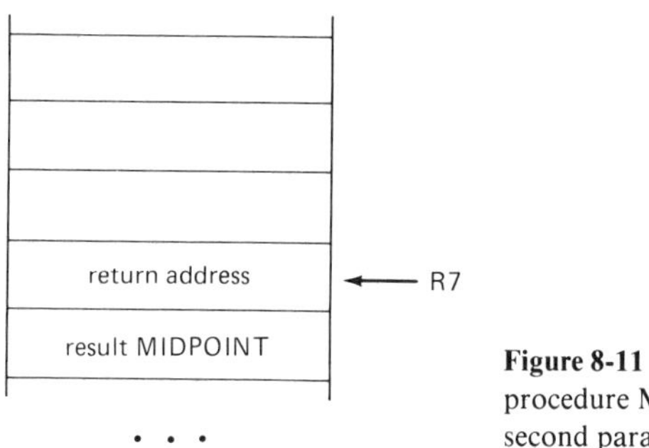

Figure 8-11 Return address of procedure MIDPOINT overwrites second parameter

8.5 REGISTER MANAGEMENT

The number of combinations of N things taken K at a time is defined by the formula

$$\binom{N}{K} = \frac{N!}{K! * (N - K)!}$$

For example, the number of ways to photograph seven people in groups of three is

$$\binom{7}{3} = \frac{7!}{3! * (7 - 3)!} = 35$$

In writing a procedure to compute combinations, we can use the factorial procedure NFACT developed earlier. COMB takes two value parameters N and K, passed to procedure COMB by value on the R7 stack:

```
PUSH     R7,N
PUSH     R7,K
CALL     R7,COMB
```

Here is procedure COMB:

```
** COMB -- RETURNS NUMBER OF COMBINATIONS OF N THINGS
*           TAKEN K AT A TIME.
*
*        INPUT
*           R7 STACK - VALUE OF K (TOP)
*                      VALUE OF N
*
*        OUTPUT
*           R7 STACK - NUMBER OF COMBINATIONS
*
COMB     LOAD      R0,2(R7)         N
         SUB       R0,1(R7)         N-K
         PUSH      R7,R0
         CALL      R7,NFACT
         POP       R7,R0            (N-K)!

         PUSH      R7,1(R7)         K
         CALL      R7,NFACT
         POP       R7,R1            K!

         PUSH      R7,2(R7)
         CALL      R7,NFACT
         POP       R7,R2            N!

         DIV       R2,R1            N!/K!
```

```
DIV      R2,R0          N!/(K! * (N-K)!)
STORE    R2,2(R7)
POP      R7,1(R7)       move return addr.
RTN      R7,
```

Figure 8-12 shows the stack upon entering COMB. The first step is to compute $(N - K)$ and push it onto the stack. The value K is at M[1 + R7], and the value N is at M[2 + R7]. After computing and pushing the difference $(N-K)$, the stack now looks like Figure 8-13. Procedure NFACT is now called, and returns $(N-K)!$ on the stack in place of $(N-K)$ (Figure 8-14). The rest is straightforward. The quantities $(N-K)!$, $K!$, and $N!$ are computed and popped from the stack in turn. Then the result is assembled from these individual terms.

There is, however, a hitch in this solution. Notice that $(N-K)!$ is popped from the stack into R0. NFACT then reuses R0 as a temporary register when it is called again to compute $K!$. $K!$ is popped into R1 and is in turn overwritten when NFACT is called to compute $N!$.

The issue here is how to manage registers when procedures call other procedures, perhaps several levels deep. This problem occurs no matter how parameters are passed to a procedure. It is convenient to use existing code only if this problem can be solved. There are two possible solutions.

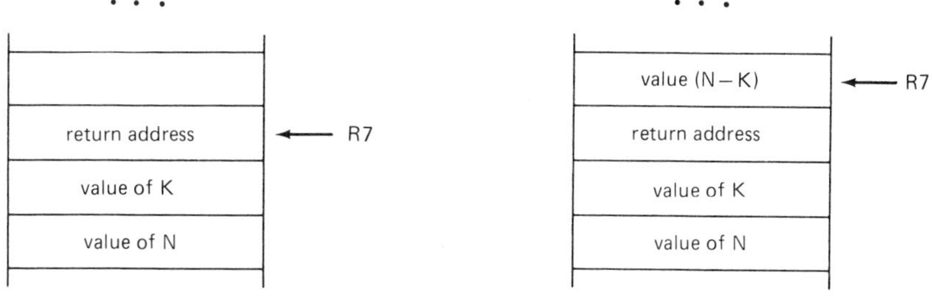

Figure 8-12 Return stack upon entering procedure COMB

Figure 8-13 *N-K* pushed onto return stack before call to procedure NFACT

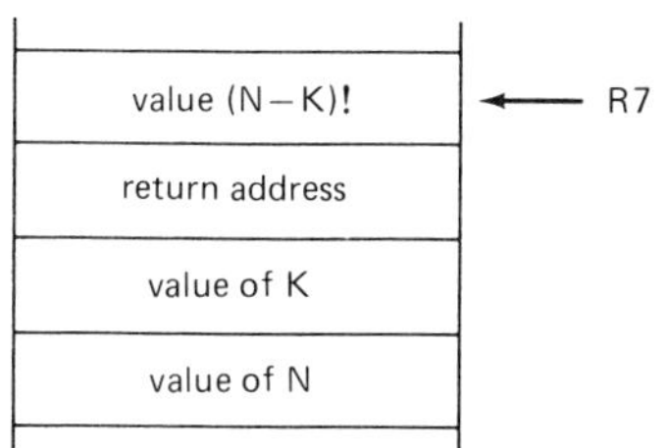

Figure 8-14 *(N-K)*! returned on return stack after call to procedure NFACT

The first is the *make the calling routine responsible* for ensuring that values in registers do not get overwritten by other procedures. If the number of levels is not too deep, this can be done by using alternate registers. Realizing that R0 and R1 are used by NFACT, we could have written COMB to pop the values into R2, R3, and R4 instead. This would have avoided the register collision:

```
** COMB  -- RETURNS NUMBER OF COMBINATIONS OF N THINGS
*           TAKEN K AT A TIME.
*
*        INPUT
*           R7 STACK  -  VALUE OF K  (TOP)
*                        VALUE OF N
*
*        OUTPUT
*           R7 STACK  -  NUMBER OF COMBINATIONS
*
*        REGISTERS USED
*           R0 - R4
*
COMB     LOAD      R2,2(R7)        N
         SUB       R2,1(R7)        N-K
         PUSH      R7,R2
         CALL      R7,NFACT
         POP       R7,R2           computed (N-K)!

         PUSH      R7,1(R7)        fetch K
         CALL      R7,NFACT
         POP       R7,R3           computed K!

         PUSH      R7,2(R7)        fetch N
         CALL      R7,NFACT
         POP       R7,R4           computed N!

         DIV       R4,R3           N!/K!
         DIV       R4,R2           N!/(K!  *  (N-K)!)
         STORE     R4,2(R7)
         POP       R7,1(R7)        move return addr.
         RTN       R7,
```

With this method, each procedure must carefully document which registers may be modified. Included are any register modified by procedures called by this one. Here, NFACT would document the use of R0 and R1. COMB would document the use of R2, R3, and R4, plus R0 and R1, because COMB uses NFACT. A procedure that uses COMB could then decide which of its registers to save.

The advantage of this method is that only registers that *must* be saved will be saved. This minimizes the amount of extra code and overhead associated with procedure calls. The disadvantage is having to take much more care in writing a routine to be sure that the contents of registers are not destroyed while still needed. Errors of this kind are easy to introduce and difficult to find later.

The second method is to *make each called procedure responsible* for saving any registers used and restoring them before returning. Here is NFACT written in this way:

```
** NFACT -- RETURNS NUMBER OF COMBINATIONS OF N THINGS
*            TAKEN K AT A TIME.
*
*         INPUT (VALUE)
*            R7 STACK - VALUE OF K (TOP)
*                       VALUE OF N
*
*         OUTPUT
*            R7 STACK - NUMBER OF COMBINATIONS
*

NFACT     PUSH     R7,R1          save R1
          PUSH     R7,R0          save R0

          LOAD     R1,=1          initialize result
          LOAD     R0,3(R7)       fetch value of N
          BRLE     NFOUT          exit if out or range

NFLOOP    MUL      R1,R0          mult. next term
          SUB      R0,=1          decrement N
          BRGT     NFLOOP         repeat if N>0

NFOUT     STORE    R0,3(R7)       replace N by N!

          POP      R7,R0          restore R0
          POP      R7,R1          restore R1

          RTN      R7,
```

It is convenient to save any of the registers used immediately and restore them just before returning. The return stack itself is a good place to use as a temporary storage area. Since the space is reclaimed on return, no extra storage is wasted by allocating extra locations to each procedure for this purpose.

Notice that references to the parameter must be adjusted to compensate for the registers saved. Figure 8-15 shows what the stack looks like just after saving R1 and R0 on the R7 stack. COMB should also be modified to save its registers if this technique is used.

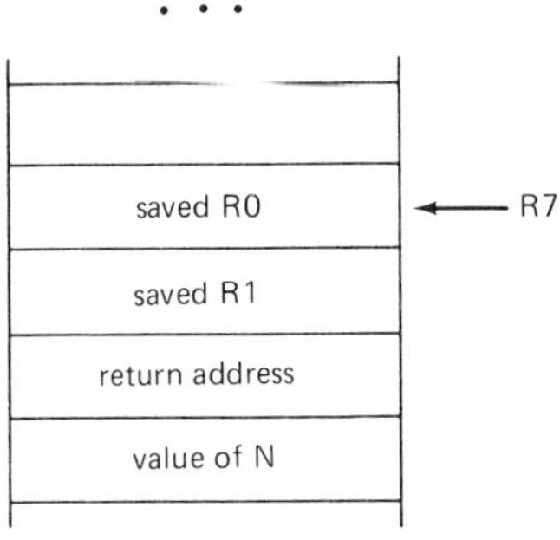

Figure 8-15 Registers saved on return stack upon entry to procedure NFACT

The advantage to this method is that it is not as prone to error. Each procedure may safely assume that calling another procedure does not alter the contents of the registers. The disadvantage is that some registers may be saved unnecessarily. The overhead of each procedure goes up based on the number of registers it uses. This may be a small price to pay for the added security. On the other hand, it may degrade overall performance to an unacceptable degree.

In practice, the needs of a particular application must be analyzed carefully before deciding between these methods. The trade-off is usually between more efficient execution on the one hand and increased security on the other. In fact, a proper mix of the two methods in the same application sometimes proves to be the best compromise.

One policy sometimes followed is to treat the first few registers as scratch storage. These would not have to be saved and restored on entry and exit. This policy works well in many instances.

8.6 RECURSION

Among the more useful techniques available in many higher-level languages is the concept of *recursion*. Although not very much use is made of recursive procedures at the machine level, studying them here can help give insight into how they are implemented in higher-level languages.

A recursive procedure implements an operation by making one or more calls on *itself* to solve a smaller part of the problem. When the problem is "small enough," the procedure can solve it directly, with no further calls to itself.

It will help to look at a specific example. We mentioned earlier that the *factorial* of a number N can be defined as

$$N! = N * (N - 1) * (N - 2) * \ldots * 3 * 2 * 1$$

But there is another definition for factorial that follows the form described:

$$\begin{array}{lll} \text{Base:} & 0! = 1 & \\ \text{Recursion:} & N! = N * (N - 1)! & N>0 \end{array}$$

For example,

$$\begin{aligned} 4! &= 4 * 3! \\ &= 4 * (3 * 2!) \\ &= 4 * (3 * (2 * 1!)) \\ &= 4 * (3 * (2 * (1 * 0!))) \\ &= 4 * (3 * (2 * (1 * (1)))) \end{aligned}$$

The expansion of lesser factorials stops with 0!, since it is defined as a simple constant and cannot be expanded further.

A language like Pascal can express an algorithm of this form directly:

```
FUNCTION NFACT (N : INTEGER) : INTEGER;
 BEGIN
     IF N =0 THEN
       NFACT:= 1
     ELSE
       NFACT:= NFACT (N-1) * N
  END;
```

The important part is to test for the base case *before* resorting to recursion. The base case is what eventually stops the process and causes the procedure to return.

The code generated by translating this recursive procedure into machine language instructions requires the use of a stack for both parameter and return address. To see why, suppose instead that a single location for each return address was allocated, as with the previous machine.

When NFACT is called, the return address would be stored at location NFACT. For an input parameter greater than zero, NFACT is called once again *before having even returned from the first call*. The first return address has now been overwritten by the second one, so there is no way to return to the correct location when the procedure is through.

Using a stack, the second return address is pushed after the first one, rather than overwriting it. After returning from the second call with NFACT (N – 1), we form the product with N and return to the first return address. An argument similar to this one can be made for stacking N as well.

If we just blindly translate the procedure for our machine, using a stack for both parameter and return address, this is what we get:

```
** NFACT -- RETURNS THE FACTORIAL OF A NUMBER
*           (RECURSIVE VERSION)
*
*        INPUT (VALUE)
*           R7 STACK - NUMBER (N)
```

```
*
*        OUTPUT
*           R7 STACK - FACTORIAL
*
*        REGISTERS USED:
*           R0
*
NFACT    LOAD      R0,1(R7)          fetch N
         BRGT      NFRECUR
NFBASE   LOAD      R0,=1             define 0! = 1
         BR        NFOUT

NFRECUR  SUB       R0,=1             compute (N-1)!
         PUSH      R7,R0
         CALL      R7,NFACT
         POP       R7,R0             fetch (N-1)!
         MUL       R0,1(R7)          N! = (N-1)! * N

NFOUT    STORE     R0,1(R7)          return result
         RTN       R7,
```

To assure ourselves that it is correct, we will try it for several different cases.

Case 1:

```
         PUSH      R7,=0
         CALL      R7,NFACT
```

The base case is correct by inspection. In this case, the 0 is replaced by a 1 on the stack, and the procedure returns.

Case 2:

```
         PUSH      R7,=3
         CALL      R7,NFACT
```

We will refer to the return address for the initial call as ⟨RA0⟩ and the return address

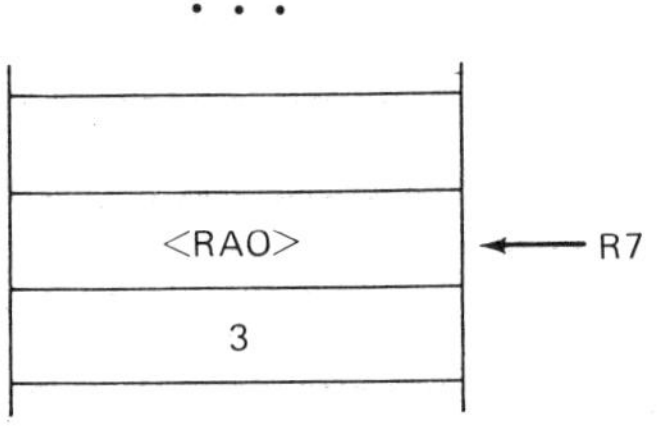

Figure 8-16 Stack upon initial call of NFACT with n = 3

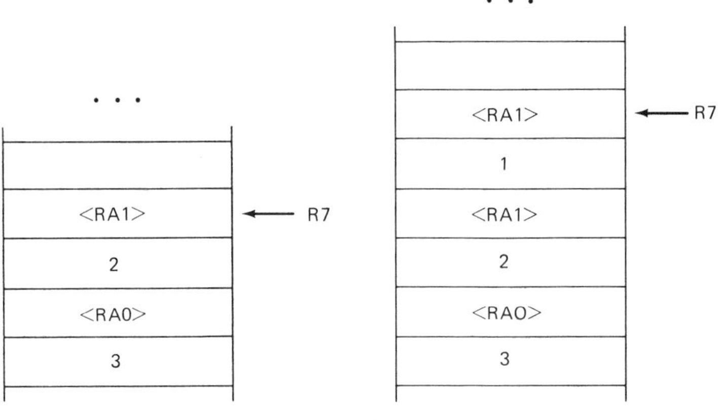

Figure 8-17 Stack upon recursive call of NFACT with $n = 2$

Figure 8-18 Stack upon recursive call of NFACT with $n = 1$

for the call within NFACT itself as ⟨RA1⟩. Figure 8-16 shows the initial status of the stack. Since 3 is greater than 0, we must first compute 2! by pushing 2 onto the stack and calling NFACT (Figure 8-17). Again, 2 is greater than 0, so we first compute 1! (Figure 8-18). Finally, 1 is also greater than 0, so we compute 0! (Figure 8-19).

We know that the procedure correctly returns 1 in this case. The stack now looks like Figure 8-20. The return was to RA1 in NFACT. The next instructions pop 0! from

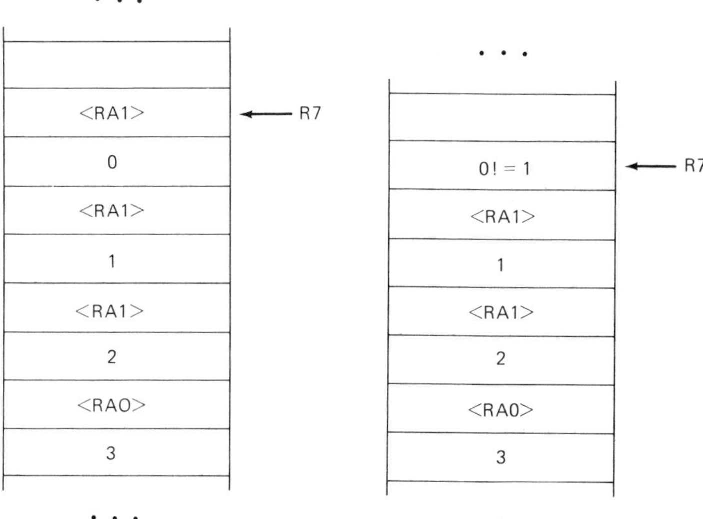

Figure 8-19 Stack upon recursive call of NFACT with $n = 0$

Figure 8-20 Stack upon return from NFACT with $0! = 1$

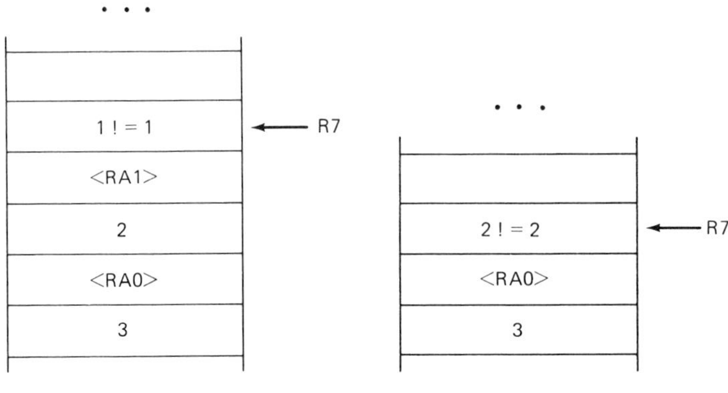

Figure 8-21 Stack upon return from NFACT with 1! = 1

Figure 8-22 Stack upon return from NFACT with 2! = 2

the stack and multiply it by 1, the current value of *N*, to get 1!. After storing this on the stack, the procedure returns. The stack now looks like Figure 8-21.

Again control returns to return address RA1. The result, 1!, is popped from the stack and multiplied by 2, the current value of *N*, to get 2!. The result is again stored on the stack, and the procedure returns (Figure 8-22).

Control returns one last time to return address RA1. The result, 2!, is popped from the stack and multiplied by 3, the current value of *N*, to get 3!. The result is stored back on the stack. This time, the procedure returns to return address RA0 at the original point of call. Figure 8-23 shows the final state of the stack.

As a final example, we will write another recursive procedure. Recall that the Fibonacci numbers are also defined by a formula that can be applied recursively:

```
FIB  (1) = 1
FIB  (2) = 1
FIB  (N) = FIB (N-2) + FIB(N-1)     N>2
```

Here is a straightforward encoding of this algorithm for our machine. The only thing to remember about this function is that the intermediate result FIB(N − 2) must

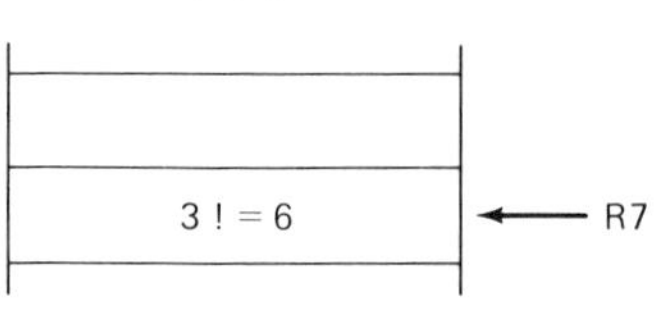

Figure 8-23 Stack upon return from NFACT with 3! = 6

be held on the stack while FIB(N – 1) is being computed. Verify that the following procedure computes the *n*th Fibonacci number:

```
** FIB -- RETURNS THE N-th FIBONACCI NUMBER
*          (RECURSIVE VERSION)
*
*         INPUT (VALUE)
*            R7 STACK - NUMBER (N)
*
*         OUTPUT
*            R7 STACK - N-TH FIBONACCI NUMBER
*         REGISTERS USED:
*            R0
*
FIB       LOAD    R0,1(R7)        fetch N
          SUB     R0,=2
          BRGT    FRECUR
FBASE     LOAD    R0,=1           N<=2
          STORE   R0,1(R7)
          RTN     R7,

FRECUR    PUSH    R7,R0
          CALL    R7,FIB          compute FIB(N-2)
*                                 ... leave it on stk
          LOAD    R0,2(R7)        fetch N (one higher now)
          SUB     R0,=1
          PUSH    R7,R0
          CALL    R7,FIB          compute FIB(N-1)
          POP     R7,R0           fetch FIB(N-1)
          ADD     R0,0(R7)        add FIB(N-2)
          STORE   R0,2(R7)        return result
          ADD     R7,=1           delete FIB(N-2) from stk
          RTN     R7,
```

As can be seen from these few examples, there is nothing difficult about implementing a recursive algorithm. The stack provides a natural way of representing a recursive computation. Each new *activation* of the procedure is allocated space on the stack for its return address, parameters, and local storage. Since the procedure always refers to storage on the stack relative to the current stack pointer, there is no conflict when a recursive call is made.

8.7 SUMMARY

In this chapter we have studied how to implement procedures on our new machine. Many of the techniques presented in connection with the previous machine carry over directly or with little modification. Register transmission of parameters has become more practical because more registers are available. Along with this, however, comes the problem of register management between procedures.

The new parameter passing method introduced on this machine is the *stack*. The main advantage to a stack is that there is little need to allocate specific storage for each procedure to save parameters. This can become important in larger programs. Even though the number of procedures increases, the nesting depth increases very little, if at all, in the limiting case. We also saw how the stack can be used to save return addresses during procedure invocation. This can also result in a space savings because of limited nesting depth.

To support the stack data structure, four new instructions were introduced. Two of them make it easier to run a parameter stack, by allowing values to be pushed onto and popped from the stack. The other two provide a new way to transfer to and return from a procedure, using a stack to hold the return address.

We will make use of the stack a number of times in the following chapters, both for parameters and for return addresses.

PROBLEMS

8-1. Which of these terms best describes the behavior of data on a stack?
   (a) Top item is the last to be removed.
   (b) First item pushed is the last item popped.
   (c) First item pushed is the first item popped.
   (d) Items are popped in the order they are pushed.
   (e) Top item can never be popped.

8-2. What is meant by *return stack*? What is pushed onto a return stack?

8-3. What role does a stack pointer play in the implementation of a stack?

8-4. Describe the behavior of the stack pointer in a decreasing stack. How would it behave in an increasing stack? Does the CALL instruction implement a decreasing or an increasing stack?

8-5. Figure 8-24 is a picture of a stack whose stack pointer is in R7. Draw a picture of the stack that shows its condition after executing the instruction

```
HERE            CALL      R7,PROC
```

8-6. Figure 8-25 is a picture of a stack whose stack pointer is in R7. Draw a picture of the stack that shows its condition after executing the instruction

```
RTN      R7,
```

8-7. What is the address of the corresponding CALL instruction in Problem 8-6?

8-8. What is the address of the next instruction executed after the RTN instruction in Problem 8-6?

8-9. Into which field is R7 assembled in the following instruction?

```
RTN      R7
```

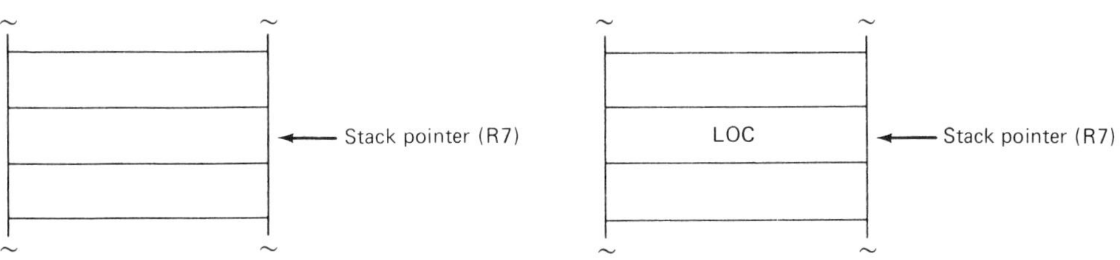

Figure 8-24 **Figure 8-25**

8-10. Into which field would R7 be assembled if we had instead written

```
RTN     R7
```

8-11. Write a procedure GCD that computes the greatest common divisor of two numbers. The greatest common divisor is the largest integer that evenly divides both numbers. Call one of the numbers *M* and the other *N*. The algorithm can be expressed as follows:

1. `[Find Remainder] Divide M by N and let R be the remainder.`
2. `[Test Remainder] If R is 0, then the algorithm terminates and N is the answer.`
3. `[Interchange] Set M←N, N←R and repeat at step 1.`

Transmit *M* and *N* to GCD by value in registers R0 and R1, and return the result in R0.

8-12. Rewrite GCD to expect reference parameters, transmitted in line. Here is a sample invocation:

```
CALL    R7,GCD
BR      *+3
DATA    M,N
```

8-13. Rewrite GCD to expect reference parameters, transmitted by a parameter list. The parameter list address is passed through R0. Here is a sample invocation:

```
        LOAD    R0,=PARLIST
        CALL    R7,GCD
          ...
PARLIST DATA    M,N
```

8-14. Figure 8-26 is a picture of a stack whose stack pointer is in R7. Draw a picture of the stack that shows its condition after executing the instruction

```
PUSH    R7,=3
```

8-15. Figure 8-27 is a picture of a stack whose stack pointer is in R7. Draw a picture of the stack that shows its condition after executing the instruction

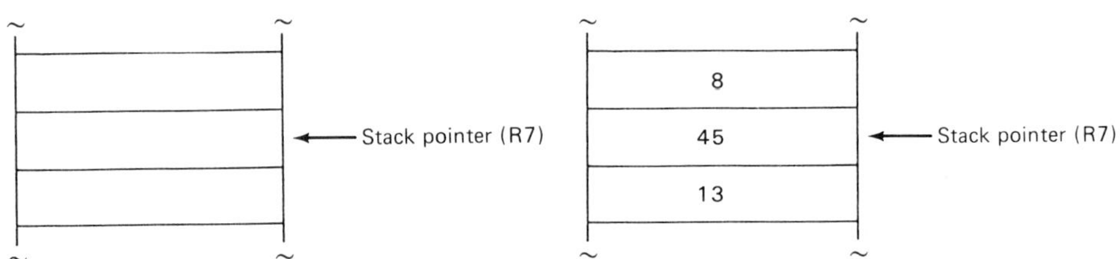

Figure 8-26

Figure 8-27

```
POP     R7,LOC
```

8-16. Show the content of M[LOC] after executing the POP instruction in Problem 8-15.

8-17. What is a *parameter stack*? How is it different from a *return stack*?

8-18. Rewrite GCD to expect value parameters, transmitted on a separate parameter stack. The procedure should return its results on the parameter stack. Assume that R6 is a pointer to the parameter stack. Show a sample call, along with the procedure itself. (Be sure that the two input parameters have been removed from the parameter stack before returning.)

8-19. What is the advantage of using the return stack as a parameter stack as well? Why is it more difficult to combine the two stacks?

8-20. Write a procedure MAX that finds the maximum value from among its parameters. Pass the parameters to MAX by reference using a sentinel-delimited parameter list. The parameter list address is sent to the procedure on the return stack. MAX should return its result on the return stack. (Be sure that the result is top of stack after returning and that the parameter list address is no longer on the stack.

8-21. Why is it a better solution to make the procedure responsible for adjusting the stack if more or fewer values are returned than were originally transmitted?

8-22. Write a procedure MINMAX that finds both the minimum and the maximum value from among its parameters. Pass the parameters to MINMAX by reference using a sentinel-delimited parameter list. The parameter list address is sent to the procedure on the return stack. MINMAX should return both values on the return stack. (Be sure that the results are top of stack after returning and that the parameter list address is no longer on the stack.

8-23. When returning more values than were originally passed on the stack, is it easier to allocate the extra stack storage upon procedure entry or exit? Explain why.

8-24. Write a procedure PWR that takes two numbers, M and N, and computes M raised to the nth power for any nonnegative value of N. Pass the parameters to PWR by value on the return stack. PWR should return its result on the return stack. If N is zero or negative, return the value 1 as its result. (Be sure that the result is on the top of stack after returning and that the parameter list address is no longer on the stack.

8-25. When returning fewer values than were originally passed on the stack, is it easier to release the extra stack storage upon procedure entry or exit? Explain why.

8-26. Describe the problem of register collision that can arise when one procedure calls another one.

8-27. Why is trying to avoid using overlapping registers between procedures not a practical solution in most cases?

8-28. What advantages are there to making the *calling procedure* responsible for saving the contents of any registers? What are its drawbacks?

8-29. Rewrite GCD to call the RMDR procedure described in this chapter, rather than computing the remainder in line. Make GCD responsible for saving any registers that must be preserved past the call to RMDR. Both GCD and RMDR should accept value parameters transmitted on the return stack and return their results on the return stack.

8-30. What advantages are there to making the *called procedure* responsible for saving the contents of any registers? What are its drawbacks?

8-31. Modify the version of GCD and RMDR from Problem 8-29 so that each is responsible for saving any registers upon entry that will be modified in the procedure and restoring the registers before returning. Both GCD and RMDR should accept value parameters transmitted on the return stack and return their results on the return stack.

8-32. Ackerman's function has the following definition:

$$\begin{aligned} a(0,y) &= y + 1 && y > 0 \\ a(x,0) &= a(x - 1,1) && x > 0 \\ a(x,y) &= a(x - 1,a(x,y - 1)) && x > 0,\ y > 0 \end{aligned}$$

Although Ackerman's function is of more theoretical than practical interest, it does make a good exercise. Write a procedure ACK that computes Ackerman's function. ACK expects two value parameters transmitted on the return stack and returns its result on the return stack. Test ACK by computing the first four diagonal values:

$$\begin{aligned} a(0,0) &= 1 \\ a(1,1) &= 3 \\ a(2,2) &= 7 \\ a(3,3) &= 61 \end{aligned}$$

(*Warning*: This function grows *very* quickly: $a(4,4)$ is much too large to represent even with our 32-bit word size!)

9

Bit Manipulation

In many cases we would like to store information more compactly than one item per word of memory. Consider, for example, the problem of encoding the results of a survey that has 32 yes/no questions. The results of each questionnaire could be compactly encoded in a single word of our machine, using one bit per response. This is a very different view than we have taken so far, in which a word is the smallest unit of storage.

In this chapter we will discuss a number of techniques that can be used to perform *bit manipulation*—that is, being able to change and rearrange individual bits or *fields* of bits within a word of memory. Also introduced are two new kinds of operations that make bit manipulation relatively easy to perform.

9.1 LOGICAL OPERATIONS

If we think of bits as representing true/false states, we can apply several functions derived from mathematical logic to operate on bits in a word. Both the domain and the range for these functions are the values true and false. We will let 1 stand for true and 0 stand for false.

9.1.1 The AND Operation

The first logical operation is AND. It is often denoted by the symbol "(*)" because it is analogous to arithmetic multiplication. Like multiplication, AND takes two logical (true/false) values and produces a third logical value as a result. The result is true only if both input values are true. Otherwise, the result is false. It is convenient to summarize this in the form of a *truth table*. Here is the truth table for AND:

AND (*)

\	0	1
0	0	0
1	0	1

9.1.2 The Inclusive OR Operation

The second logical operation is OR, denoted by the symbol "(+)". OR also takes two logical values and produces a logical result. The result of OR is true if either (or both) input value is true. Otherwise, the result is false. Here is the truth table for OR:

OR (+)

\	0	1
0	0	1
1	1	1

OR is sometimes referred to as *inclusive OR* because it includes the case in which both inputs are true.

9.1.3 The Exclusive OR Operation

The next logical operation is XOR, denoted by the symbol "(−)". Like AND and OR, XOR takes two logical values and produces a logical result. The result of XOR is true if either (but not both) input value is true. Otherwise, the result is false. Here is the truth table for XOR:

XOR (-)

\	0	1
0	0	1
1	1	0

XOR is referred to as *exclusive OR* because it excludes the case in which both inputs are true.

9.1.4 The NOT Operation

The last logical operation is NOT. NOT is denoted by "(~)" to distinguish it from XOR. Unlike the other operations, NOT is a *unary* operator. That is, it operates on one value instead of two. NOT takes a single logical value and produces a logical result. The result of NOT is true if its input is false and false if its input is true. Here is the truth table for NOT:

NOT (~)

	0
0	1
1	0

9.1.5 Word-Length Logical Operations

Each of these logical operations takes one or two logical values and produces a single logical result. These operations can be applied to each bit in a word or pair of words to produce a single-word result. For example, the logical negation of the word

```
00 001 010 011 100 101 110 111 110 101 100
```

is the word

```
11 110 101 100 011 010 001 000 001 010 011
```

Each occurrence of a 1 is replaced by a 0, and each occurrence of a 0 is replaced by a 1, according to the truth table for NOT.

Suppose that we have two words:

```
10 010 011 110 010 101 111 100 110 001 110
11 011 111 000 000 000 110 110 010 011 111
```

The OR of these two words is the result of applying the OR operation to each pair of bits, one from each word:

```
    10 010 011 110 010 101 111 100 110 001 110
(+) 11 011 111 000 000 000 110 110 010 011 111
    ------------------------------------------
    11 011 111 110 010 101 111 110 110 011 111
```

Wherever there is a 1 in either or both words, the corresponding position in the result contains a 1 as well. The two words are effectively merged together to form the result. We will find the ability to merge the contents of two words to be a very useful operation.

The AND of these same two words is the result of applying the AND operation to each pair of bits:

```
      10 010 011 110 010 101 111 100 110 001 110

(*)   11 011 111 000 000 000 110 110 010 011 111
      -------------------------------------------
      10 010 011 000 000 000 110 100 010 001 110
```

Wherever there is a 1 in *both* words, the corresponding position in the result contains a 1 as well. Notice especially how there is a "hole" in the middle 9 bits of the result that corresponds to a "hole" in the second operand:

```
10 010 011 000 000 000 110 100 010 001 110
           --- --- ---
```

The hole in the second operand effectively *masks* the corresponding positions in the first operand. A mask is a word used with a logical operation to change one or more fields in some other word. This method of selectively changing fields of bits in word will prove useful shortly.

Finally, the XOR of these two words is the result of applying the XOR operation to each pair of bits:

```
      10 010 011 110 010 101 111 100 110 001 110

(-)   11 011 111 000 000 000 110 110 010 011 111
      -------------------------------------------
      01 001 100 110 010 101 001 010 100 010 001
```

Wherever there is a 1 in either *but not both* words, the corresponding position in the result contains a 1 as well. Some good uses for this operation will be presented later.

9.1.6 Logical Instructions

Here are the instructions on our machine that correspond to these logical operations:

```
AND       {MBR  <--  M[MAR]}
           Ri   <--  Ri (*) MBR
           CMPR <--  Ri ? 0

OR        {MBR  <--  M[MAR]}
           Ri   <--  Ri (+) MBR
           CMPR <--  Ri ? 0
```

```
XOR        {MBR  <--  M[MAR]}
           Ri  <--  Ri (-) MBR
           CMPR  <--  Ri ? 0

NOT        {MBR  <--  M[MAR]}
           Ri  <--  (~) MBR
           CMPR  <--  Ri ? 0
```

The first three instructions have the same form as their arithmetic counterparts. The last one looks much like the form of a LOAD instruction.

9.1.7 Operations on a Single-Bit Field

We now return to the problem of compactly storing data from a questionnaire that has 32 yes/no questions. We noted that an entire questionnaire can be encoded in a single word of memory. The response to each question is represented by a single bit. We will look at two aspects of this problem:

1. how to get the data into this encoded form
2. how to extract information once encoded

Changing single bits in a word. Our first concern is how to get data into an encoded form. The problem is one of being able to turn on or off any bit in a word. Turning on a given bit is simple enough, if we have the appropriate mask handy. For example, we can turn on bit 30 in the word

```
10 010 011 110 010 101 111 100 110 001 110
```

by ORing (merging) it with another word in which *only* bit 30 is set:

```
00 100 000 000 000 000 000 000 000 000 000
```

As we saw earlier, we can also turn off a given bit if we AND it with the correct mask. First, the mask should have the bit position set to 0. But to preserve the rest of the word, all other bits must be set to 1. We can turn off bit 29 in the previous example by ANDing it with the mask

```
11 101 111 111 111 111 111 111 111 111 111
```

Since being able to turn on or off a given bit is generally useful, we will write a procedure to do it. Procedure BIT takes three parameters by value in R0, R1, and R2. These parameters are

R0 Word to set
R1 Bit position in word
R2 Setting (1 = on, 0 = off)

We will use R7 again as the return stack pointer. Assume that the stack has already been set up. Here is procedure BIT along with a sample invocation:

```
        LOAD    R0,MYWORD       word to set
        LOAD    R1,=15          bit position
        LOAD    R2,=1           turn bit on
        CALL    R7,BIT
            ...

** BIT - Replace an individual bit in a word
*
*       input:
*         R0: Word to set
*         R1: Bit position in word
*         R2: Setting (1=on, 0=off)
*       output:
*         R0: Word with bit replaced
*
BIT         PUSH    R7,R1           save R1
            CMPR    R2,=0           check for setting
            BREQ    BITOFF          branch to turn bit off
            OR      R0,MSK(R1)      turn bit on
            BR      BITEND

BITOFF      NOT     R1,MSK(R1)      get NOT of mask
            AND     R0,R1           turn bit off

BITEND      POP     R7,R1           restore R1
            RTN     R7,

** this is an array of masks, one for each of the 32 bits
*
MSK         DATA    00000000001B,  00000000002B,  00000000004B
            DATA    00000000010B,  00000000020B,  00000000040B
            DATA    00000000100B,  00000000200B,  00000000400B
            DATA    00000001000B,  00000002000B,  00000004000B
            DATA    00000010000B,  00000020000B,  00000040000B
            DATA    00000100000B,  00000200000B,  00000400000B
            DATA    00001000000B,  00002000000B,  00004000000B
            DATA    00010000000B,  00020000000B,  00040000000B
            DATA    00100000000B,  00200000000B,  00400000000B
            DATA    01000000000B,  02000000000B,  04000000000B
            DATA    10000000000B,  20000000000B
```

The array MSK holds masks for each of the 32 bit positions in the word. Each word in MSK has a single bit set. Thus, MSK(0) has only bit 0 turned on, while MSK(31) has only bit 31 turned on.*

To make sure that the procedure works, we will run through a few examples:

```
LOAD    R0,TSTWORD      word to set
LOAD    R1,=14          bit position
LOAD    R2,=1           set bit
CALL    R7,BIT
```

The first step is to save R1, since it may be modified by this procedure. It will be restored before returning. Since R2 indicated that the bit is to be set, control falls through to the instruction

```
OR      R0,MSK(R1)          turn bit on
```

The contents of R1 is ORed with the contents of M[MSK + 14], the mask for bit 14:

```
00 000 000 000 000 000 100 000 000 000 000
```

All bits in R0 except bit 14 remain the same because, according to the truth table for OR,

$$0 + x \longrightarrow x$$

no matter what the value of x. By the same argument, bit 14 is always set to 1 because the truth table for OR says that

$$1 + x \longrightarrow 1$$

no matter what the value of x. Thus, BIT leaves all bits but bit 14 as they were and sets bit 14 to 1 no matter what its previous value.

We must now show that it also works correctly to clear bit 14:

```
LOAD    R0,TSTWORD      word to set
LOAD    R1,=14          bit position
LOAD    R2,=0           clear bit
CALL    R7,BIT
```

After saving R1, control transfers to the instruction labeled BITOFF, since R2 indicated that the bit is to be turned off.

*Recall that we designate bit positions by the power of 2 the position represents. Bit 0 is the least significant bit and is the rightmost bit in the word. Bit 31 is in the leftmost bit position.

```
BITOFF      NOT     R1,MSK(R1)          get NOT of mask
            AND     R0,R1               turn bit off
```

In this case, the object is to preserve all bits *except* bit 14. The contents of R0 is ANDed with the complement of M[MSK + 14]:

```
11  111  111  111  111  111  011  111  111  111  111
```

All bits in R0 except bit 14 remain the same because, according to the truth table for AND,

$$1 * x \longrightarrow x$$

no matter what the value of x. By the same argument, bit 14 is always set to 0 because the truth table for AND says that

$$0 * x \longrightarrow 0$$

no matter what the value of x. Thus, BIT leaves all bits but bit 14 as they were and sets bit 14 to 0 no matter what its previous value.

We have now shown that BIT correctly sets or clears a bit position, no matter what its previous value. The last thing to point out is that BIT also preserves all registers except R0, which serves as the return register. The only other register modified by BIT is R1. This register is saved on the R7 stack immediately upon entering the procedure and is restored just before returning. Both cases flow through this code.

There is another way to implement BIT that is several words shorter. We have a mask with only bit 29 set. This can be used directly, without forming a complementary mask first. Look again at the truth table for exclusive OR (XOR). If we could be sure that bit 29 in the subject word was already on, it could be turned off by XORing it with the mask we have. Here is a shorter version of procedure BIT:

```
BIT         OR      R0,MSK(R1)      force bit on
            CMPR    R2,=1           check for setting
            BREQ    *+2             branch if 'on'
            XOR     R0,MSK(R1)      else force bit off
            RTN     R7,
```

We can be sure bit 29 is already on by forcing it on immediately. If the setting in R2 is on, we are done. Otherwise, the bit is forced off by the XOR instruction. This implementation saved four instructions from the previous version, a savings of almost 50 percent. Although this implementation is not as obvious, the savings are more than worthwhile. Careful documentation makes a difference here.

Extracting single bits from a word. The second part of the problem is how to extract information once encoded in this form. Assume that we have all questionnaires encoded in an array of N words. We would now like to ask certain questions that may be useful in tabulating our results. Some of the fields of the questionnaire might have been:

Bit	Data		Bit	Data	
0	Are you:	single	15	Diploma:	None
1		married	16		Grade school
2		divorced	17		High school
3		widowed	18		College
	...			...	
7	Are you:	under 21	22	Are you:	conservative
8		21-35	23		moderate
9		36-55	24		liberal
10		Over 55	25		radical

One thing we might like to know is whether a respondent is between 21 and 35. To find out, we must isolate bit 8 and see if it is set. A simple way to do this is to clear all bits except bit 8 and see if the result is nonzero. We can do this by ANDing the word with M[MSK + 8], which has only bit 8 set:

```
    01  101  100  101  001  000  111  100  100  000  001
(*) 00  000  000  000  000  000  000  000  100  000  000
    ---------------------------------------------------
    00  000  000  000  000  000  000  000  100  000  000
```

Since the result is nonzero, we conclude that this questionnaire was answered by someone between 21 and 35.

We could also ask whether a respondent is a moderate with a college education. Here the mask has two bits set: bit 18 for "college" and bit 23 for "moderate." If we apply this mask by ANDing, we find that this individual is also a moderate with a college education:

```
    01  101  100  101  001  000  111  100  100  000  001
(*) 00  000  000  100  001  000  000  000  000  000  000
    ---------------------------------------------------
    00  000  000  100  001  000  000  000  000  000  000
```

Does a nonzero result in this case indicate both moderate *and* college degree? Clearly not, because a radical with a college degree would also produce a nonzero result.

Rather than compare the result with zero, we must instead compare it with the mask, to ensure that both conditions are met. The result is the same as the mask only if exactly the conditions indicated by the mask are true.

From this discussion, we can state the following conclusions:

1. To test for one or more of several conditions, AND with a mask that includes all of them. The test succeeds if the result is nonzero.
2. To test for an exact set of conditions, AND with a mask that includes all of them. The test succeeds only if the result and the mask are identical.

9.2 SHIFT OPERATIONS

Operations on single bits in a word can easily be generalized to *fields* of bits as well. Two steps are involved, whether inserting or extracting information. The first is to isolate the bits in the field. As we saw earlier, this can be done by forming a mask corresponding to the field, then applying the AND operation between the mask and the word. For example, to isolate bits 10 through 20, AND the word with the mask

00 000 000 000 111 111 111 110 000 000 000

Once the field has been isolated, it may not be positioned where we want it within the word. If the field represents a number, for example, it should be moved to the lower-order bits of the word.

This could be done using division in some cases, but there are several problems with the method. First, many ALUs do not include division (or multiplication) among their operators. While many newer machines do have these instructions, we cannot rely on this as a general method.

The second problem is speed. Moving bits within a word is a much simpler operation than division. A division algorithm is designed to handle the full range of divisors and dividends. Our needs require only division by powers of 2. The extra overhead makes using division less attractive.

Another kind of operation specifically designed to move fields of bits within a word is known as *shift*. We can use a shift operation to move bits 10 through 20 from the previous example:

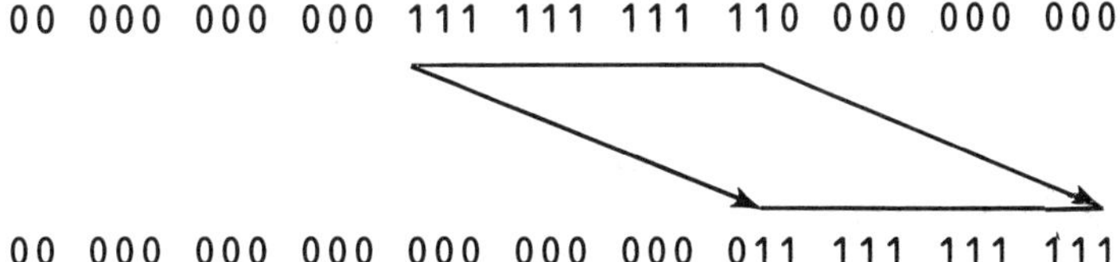

There are three types of shift operations. The main difference between them is in what happens at either end of the word. A shift operation also has a direction. If the shift is toward the lower-order end, it is called a *right shift*. A shift toward the high-order end is called a *left shift*.

9.2.1 The Logical Shift

The first kind of shift is called a *logical shift*. It is sometimes referred to as an *end-off shift* because the bits that are shifted past the end of the word are lost. Zeros fill in at the other end of the word. A shorter, 8-bit word is used to simplify these illustrations. Here is a 1-bit logical right shift:

```
     1 0   0 1 1   1 0 1
  —→ 0 1   0 0 1   1 1 0
```

With a logical left shift, the 1 is lost from the left end of the word, and a 0 fills in from the right:

```
  1  0   0 1 1   1 0 1
   0 0   1 1 1   0 1 0 ←—
```

The result of shifting by more than one bit at a time is the same as shifting by one bit several times. For example, here is a 2-bit logical left shift:

```
  1 0   0 1 1   1 0 1
  0 1   1 1 0   1 0 0 <<—
```

9.2.2 The Circular Shift

The second type of shift is called a *circular shift* or *rotate*. It differs from the logical shift in that bits pushed off one end of the word appear at the other end to fill in the void. Here is a 1-bit right circular shift:

```
     1 0   0 1 1   1 0 1
                       ^
  —→ 1 1   0 0 1   1 1 0
     ^
```

A 1-bit left circular shift rotates the bit off the left end into the least significant bit position:

```
1 0   0 1 1   1 0 1
^

0 0   1 1 1   0 1 1  ←
                  ^
```

Notice that unlike the logical shift, the circular shift does not destroy information. A left circular shift followed by a right circular shift of the same number restores the word to its initial value. A left logical shift followed by a right logical shift of the same number leaves bits in the left part of the word set to 0.

9.2.3 The Arithmetic Shift

The third type of shift is called an *arithmetic shift*. The arithmetic shift treats the word as a signed number. It is meant to be equivalent to multiplying or dividing the word by a power of 2. Thus the sign bit never changes as a result of an arithmetic shift.

First, we will look the effect of an arithmetic shift on positive numbers. In the case of a right arithmetic shift, bits are lost from the right end of the word, and copies of the sign bit (0) fill in the void from the left. Here is a 1-bit arithmetic right shift applied to a positive number:

```
0 0   1 1 0   1 1 1
^

0 0   0 1 1   0 1 1
^ ^
```

This is equivalent to integer division. Since the number is odd, the number loses precision because the rightmost 1 is lost from the right end of the word.

Next, here is a 1-bit left arithmetic shift of a positive number:

```
0 0   1 1 0   1 1 1
^

0 1   1 0 1   1 1 0
^                 ^
```

The bit to the right of the sign bit is lost, and the position to the right is filled in with 0. This is equivalent to multiplication by 2. Notice that the result represents an even number.

How the arithmetic shift is handled for negative numbers depends on how negative numbers are represented by the ALU. As discussed in Appendix A, there are three common representations of negative numbers:

- One's complement
- Two's complement
- Signed magnitude

The rules for arithmetic shifts of negative numbers can be discovered because the result must be the same as integer multiplication and division by a power of 2. Consider the 8-bit signed representation of −32 in Table 9-1.

TABLE 9-1 ARITHMETIC SHIFTS OF A NEGATIVE NUMBER (−32)

	−32	−32 * 2 (left 1)	−32 / 2 (right 1)
One's complement:	11 011 111	10 111 111	11 101 111
Two's complement:	11 100 000	11 000 000	11 110 000
Signed magnitude:	10 100 000	11 000 000	10 010 000

If the ALU uses one's complement, positions are filled in from either side with copies of the *sign bit*, as shown in Table 9-2. For two's complement, positions are filled in from the left with copies of the *sign bit* and from the right with zeros, as shown in Table 9-3. Finally, signed magnitude fills in bits from either end with *zeros*, as shown in Table 9-4.

TABLE 9-2 ONE'S COMPLEMENT

```
Arithmetic left shift:
1 1   0 1 1   1 1 1
^     ___________
1 0   1 1 1   1 1 1
^  ____________   ^

Arithmetic right shift:
1 1   0 1 1   1 1 1
^  ____________
1 1   1 0 1   1 1 1
^ ^   ___________
```

Table 9-5 is a summary of how bits are filled in for arithmetic shift. The method depends on how the ALU represents negative numbers. The table entries hold for both negative and positive numbers.

TABLE 9-3 TWO'S COMPLEMENT

Arithmetic left shift:

```
(-32)   1 1   1 0 0   0 0 0
        ^

(-64)   1 1   0 0 0   0 0 0  <--
        ^
```

Arithmetic right shift:

```
(-32)   1 1   1 0 0   0 0 0
        ^

(-16)   1 1   1 1 0   0 0 0
        ^ ^
```

TABLE 9-4. SIGNED MAGNITUDE

Arithmetic left shift:

```
(-32)   1 0   1 0 0   0 0 0
        ^

(-64)   1 1   0 0 0   0 0 0  <--
        ^
```

Arithmetic right shift:

```
(-32)   1 0   1 0 0   0 0 0
        ^
(-16)   1 0   0 1 0   0 0 0
        ^
```

TABLE 9-5 SUMMARY OF ARITHMETIC SHIFT OPERATIONS

Form of Negative	Shift Left	Shift Right
One's complement	Sign bit	Sign bit
Two's complement	0	Sign bit
Signed magnitude	0	0

9.2.4 Shift Instructions

Our ALU can perform logical, circular, and arithmetic shifts. The corresponding CPU instructions for these shifts are:

Mnemonic	Description	Example
LSH	Logical shift	LSH R0, − 1
CSH	Circular shift	CSH R3,NBITS
ASH	Arithmetic shift	ASH R2, = − 4

The word to be shifted is in the data register. The shift count (number of bits to shift) and direction are indicated by the operand. A *positive* count causes a *left* shift by that many positions. A *negative* count causes a *right* shift by the absolute value of the number.

We could use shifts to write another version of BIT. Instead of looking up the mask in a table, it can be built during execution:

```
** BIT - Replace an individual bit in a word
*
*       input:
*          R0: Word to set
*          R1: Bit position in word
*          R2: Setting (1=on, 0=off)
*       output:
*          R0: Word with bit replaced
*
BIT        PUSH    R7,R3          save R3
           LOAD    R3,=1          build mask
           LSH     R3,R1
           OR      R0,R3          force bit on
           CMPR    R2,=1          check setting
           BREQ    *+2            branch if 'on'
           XOR     R0,R3          else force bit off
           POP     R7,R3          restore R3
           RTN     R7,
```

The mask is built by turning the lower-order bit, then rotating it up to the correct position.

9.2.5 Operating on Variable Fields in a Word

To insert and extract any multibit field from a word, we will write two procedures, INSERT and EXTRACT. Procedure INSERT stores data into a field of a word. The field width can be anything from one bit to a full word. EXTRACT performs the opposite function of returning the contents of a particular field in a word.

Several pieces of data are needed by both procedures:

1. The word to insert into or extract from
2. The position of the field
3. The size of the field

Procedure INSERT also requires the new information to be placed in the field.

Extracting a field from a word. An algorithm for EXTRACT involves three steps. The first is to build a mask the same size as the field to be EXTRACTed (Figure 9-1). The next step is to shift the field to the right end of the word, so that it lines up with the mask (Figure 9-2). Finally, AND the word and mask to eliminate information in the word outside the mask (Figure 9-3).

There are several ways to build a mask of a given size. If the ALU performs one's or two's complement arithmetic, we can use the fact that the arithmetic shift fills in with 1's if the sign bit is set. For example, if we need a mask of 5 bits, simply turn on the sign bit, then arithmetically shift right by four places:

```
LOAD    R0,=1       turn on bit
CSH     R0,=-1      ... and move to sign
ASH     R0,=-4      extend sign downward
CSH     R0,=5       rotate to bottom
```

If masks are built like this often, it would be worthwhile to initialize a word, SIGNBIT, with only the sign bit turned on:

```
SIGNBIT    DATA    20000000000B
```

Notice that we *cannot* simply say

```
LOAD    R0,=20000000000B
```

because the address field is only 18 bits wide. The cost of the extra word can be spread out if it is used in several places, and the resulting code is easier to read:

```
LOAD    R0,SIGNBIT    turn on bit
ASH     R0,=-4        extend sign downward
CSH     R0,=5         rotate to bottom
```

This method works as long as the field width is a constant. However, we are probably given the field width as a positive number in some register, say R1. To make this solution work requires computing the shift count (1 – R1) first.

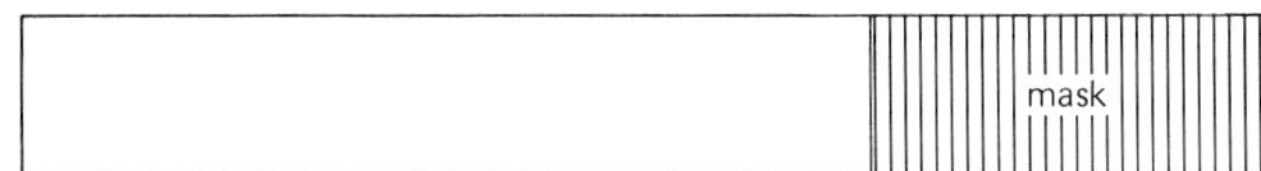

Figure 9-1 Mask built in lower part of word

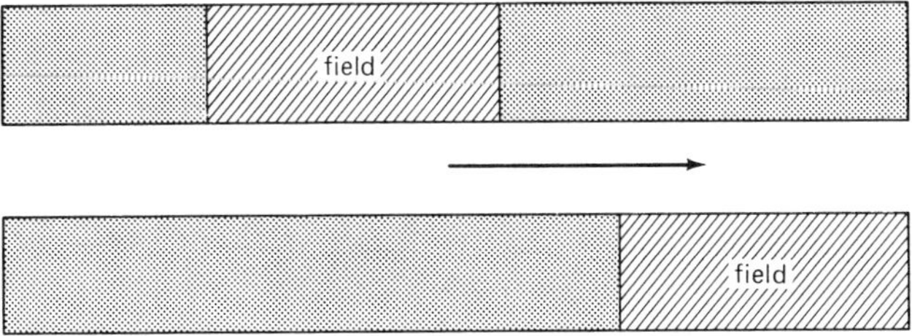

Figure 9-2 Field shifted to lower part of word

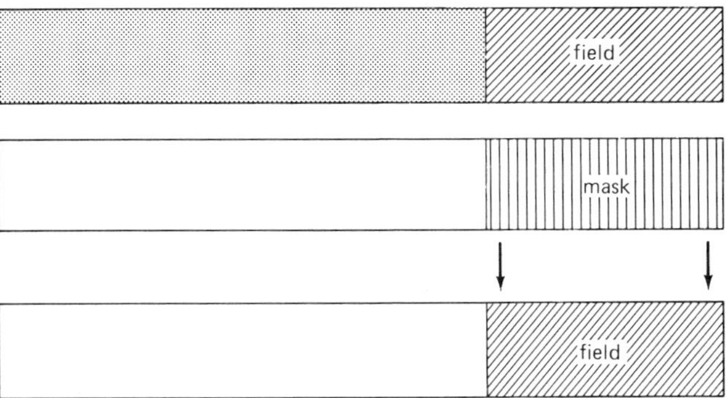

Figure 9-3 Field isolated by applying mask

Another method can be used only if the ALU performs one's complement arithmetic. It still uses SIGNBIT but arithmetically shifts left instead of right. This takes advantage of the fact that arithmetic left shift fills in to the right with copies of the sign bit on a one's complement machine. Assume that the field width is given in R1:

```
LOAD    R0,SIGNBIT     turn on bit
ASH     R0,=-1(R1)     extend sign around
CSH     R0,=1          rotate sign bit
```

Indexed immediate addressing is used in the second instruction to compute the shift count (R1 − 1). This method is handy for adding or subtracting a constant from a register whenever the result fits in 18 bits or less. The advantage to performing an arithmetic left shift is that we are given a positive number to start with. Notice that this method does *not* work if the ALU represents numbers in either two's complement or signed magnitude form.

A problem with both of these methods is that they do not work correctly if the field width is zero. Although this case does not normally come up, it would be a good idea to do something reasonable if it does. What does it mean to build a mask of width zero? If a mask of width 5 has 5 bits set and the rest zero, then a mask of width zero should have no bits set and all bits zero.

There is a method that behaves correctly when the field width is zero. It uses the logical left shift on a word with all bits set. Complementing the result leaves the correct mask. We will need a word, MSKALL, with all bits set:

```
MSKALL     DATA   37777777777B   masks all bits

                  ...

           LOAD   R0,=MSKALL     mask all bits
           LSH    R0,R1          shift in 0's right
           NOT    R0,R0          flip mask
```

We are now ready to write procedure EXTRACT. The procedure expects three parameters:

- Word to extract from
- Start bit of field
- Field width

The first one is a reference parameter, and the other two are passed by value. Parameters will be passed by means of a parameter list, whose address is pushed onto the R7 stack. The content of the field is returned on the R7 stack. Here is EXTRACT, along with a sample invocation:

```
           PUSH   R7,=PARLIST
           CALL   R7,EXTRACT
                  ...

** parameter list for EXTRACT
*
PARLIST    DATA   MYWORD         word to extract from
           DATA   25             start bit
           DATA   7              field width
                  ...

** EXTRACT - Extract a field of bits from a word
*
*          input: (parameter list on R7 stack)
*            address of word to extract from
*            start bit of field
*            field width
*
*          output: (on R7 stack)
*            contents of specified field
*
```

```
EXTRACT   PUSH   R7,R2          save registers
          PUSH   R7,R1
          PUSH   R7,R0
          LOAD   R0,4(R7)       fetch param list

          LOAD   R2,2(R0)       fetch field width
          LOAD   R1,MSKALL      mask all bits
          LSH    R1,R2          shift in 0's right
          NOT    R1,R1          flip mask
          SUB    R2,1(R0)       compute shift count
          LOAD   R0,@0(R0)      fetch subject word
          LSH    R0,=-1(R2)     shift field right
          AND    R0,R1          extract field

          STORE  R0,4(R7)       return field
          POP    R7,R0          restore registers
          POP    R7,R1
          POP    R7,R2
          RTN    R7,
```

The amount to shift in order to move the field to the bottom of the word is a function of both the field width and the start bit. If the start bit is 31 and the field width is 1, then the amount to shift is (31 − 1) + 1, or 31 bits. If the start bit is 31 and the field width is 32, then the amount to shift is (31 − 32) + 1, or 0 bits. Since the sign of the shift count for right shifts is negative, the correct computation is

$$(\text{Field width} - \text{start bit}) - 1$$

The field width is already in R2, so we simply subtract the start bit number. Subtracting the constant 1 can be done in the effective address computation of the shift itself.

Inserting a field into a word. Procedure INSERT takes information and inserts it in a specified field of the subject word. An algorithm for insertion might be

1. Clear field in subject word.
2. Rotate new information to align with field in subject word.
3. Insert new information into field.

The first step requires a complementary mask that preserves all information in the subject word except in the specified field. The method of building a mask presented earlier involved building a complementary mask as a first step. Once the complementary mask is built, it can be shifted left to align with the field in the subject word. The amount to shift the mask is the same distance as in EXTRACT. This time, though, the shift count must be positive for a left shift.

The second step is to shift the information left to align with the field in the subject word. We computed the shift count in the previous step.

The last step inserts the new information into the field. One thing to consider is what happens if the information inserted is wider than the specified field. If something is not done, other parts of the word may be destroyed. Here is another instance where anticipating an error and doing something reasonable could avert trouble later. In this case, it would be reasonable to truncate the information to the width of the field. A complementary mask is already in position. It is a simple matter to form the positive mask and apply it to the information before insertion into the field.

The parameters are again transmitted by means of a parameter list whose address is on the R7 stack. The parameter list includes a fourth parameter, the information to be inserted. This parameter is transmitted by reference. INSERT returns a copy of the subject word on the R7 stack, with the specified field replaced by new information. Here is INSERT, along with a sample call:

```
            PUSH   R7,=PARLIST
            CALL   R7,INSERT
                   ...

** parameter list for INSERT
*
PARLIST     DATA   MYWORD              word to insert into
            DATA   25                  start bit
            DATA   7                   field width
            DATA   MYINFO              info to insert
                   ...

** INSERT - Insert a field of bits into a word
*
*           input: (parameter list on R7 stack)
*             address of word to extract from
*             start bit of field
*             field width
*             new information
*
*           output: (on R7 stack)
*             contents of specified field
*
INSERT      PUSH   R7,R3               save registers
            PUSH   R7,R2
            PUSH   R7,R1
            PUSH   R7,R0
            LOAD   R0,5(R7)            fetch param list

            LOAD   R1,MSKALL           mask all bits
            LSH    R1,2(R0)            shift in 0's right
```

```
LOAD   R2,1(R0)      compute shift count
SUB    R2,2(R0)
LSH    R1,=1(R2)     shift mask to field
LOAD   R3,@0(R0)     fetch subject word
AND    R3,R1         clear out field in word
LOAD   R0,@3(R0)     fetch new info
LSH    R0,=1(R2)     shift info to field
NOT    R1,R1         flip mask
AND    R0,R1         mask info
OR     R2,R0         insert info into word
STORE  R3,5(R7)      return new word
POP    R7,R0         restore registers
POP    R7,R1
POP    R7,R2
POP    R7,R3
RTN    R7,
```

9.3 SUMMARY

This chapter introduced the concept of manipulating quantities smaller than a word. Two kinds of instructions were presented that are invaluable in performing these manipulations. The first group is the logical or Boolean instructions. Using the AND, OR, XOR, and NOT operations taken from Boolean algebra, these instructions are good for deleting, replacing, or adding to information in fields of a word. The notion of a mask was also first introduced in connection with this group of intructions. Masks correspond to specific bits or fields of bits in a word and are an important tool for bit manipulation.

The other group of operations is the shift instructions. These instructions allow us to reposition and rearrange bits or fields of bits within a word. We saw that there are three kinds of shift operations: logical, circular, and arithmetic. Logical shifts push information off one end of the word and fill in at the other end with zeros. Circular shifts simply rotate the information off one end of the word around to the other end. No information is lost in the process. The arithmetic shift is equivalent to multiplication and division by powers of 2. Since the method of representing negative numbers varies with one's or two's complement, or signed magnitude ALUs, the rules for arithmetic shifts also depend on which of the three methods is used. Fortunately, given a method of representing negatives, a simple set of rules apply for both positive and negative numbers.

Using these instructions, we explored several applications. The first allowed us to set and clear individual bits within a word selectively. Single bits are useful for storing information whose character is essentially binary. Examples include answers to yes/no questions. There are several other interesting uses for bit-wide fields that are suggested in the exercises at the end of the chapter. Included among these are the implementation of "set" operations like those provided by the Pascal language.

The second application dealt with extracting and inserting arbitrary-sized fields of information in a word. The challenge here was to build a mask of any size during execution and move it into position. This application made use of the newly introduced shift operations to do both.

We will get more practice with logical and shift operations as we turn in the next chapter to the topic of representing and calculating with floating-point numbers.

PROBLEMS

9-1. Show the result of applying each of the three binary logical operations, AND, OR, and XOR, between these two fields:

```
1  0  1  1  1  1  0  1  1  0  0  0
1  1  1  0  0  1  0  1  1  0  1  1
```

9-2. Show the result of applying the unary NOToperation to each of the answers from Problem 9-1.

9-3. Apply the unary NOToperation to the two fields from Problem 9-1. Repeat Problem 9-1 using these two fields. How are the results related to the answers to Problems 9-1 and 9-2?

9-4. Why is the OR function sometimes referred to as "inclusive OR"? How is it different from the "exclusive OR" function?

9-5. Give a mask that can be used either to turn on or to turn off indicated bits in another word. Also, name the logical operation that should be used.

(a) to turn on bit 30
(b) to turn off bit 0
(c) to turn on the lower 18 bits
(d) to turn off all but bits 6 and 19
(e) to turn on all odd bits
(f) to turn off all even bits
(g) to turn on all bits that were off *and* to turn off all bits that were on

9-6. Give a mask to be used, the logical operation, and what the result should be compared with to determine whether the indicated bits in another word are turned on.

(a) only bit 15
(b) either bit 6 *or* bit 29
(c) all even bits
(d) both bit 21 *and* bit 31
(e) any of the lower 10 bits

9-7. Why is using a shift operation preferable to multiplication or division for moving bits within a word?

9-8. What happens to bits that are shifted off the end of a word during a logical shift? What fills in at the other end of the word?

9-9. What is another name for the logical shift?

9-10. Show the result of performing the indicated logical shift on these fields of bits:

(a) left 1: 0 0 0 0 0 0 0 1
(b) right 1: 0 0 0 0 0 0 0 1
(c) left 3: 0 0 0 0 0 0 0 1
(d) right 3: 1 0 0 0 0 0 0 0
(e) left 7: 0 0 0 0 0 0 0 1
(f) right 8: 1 0 0 0 0 0 0 0
(g) left 4: 1 1 1 1 1 1 1 1
(h) right 4: 1 1 1 1 1 1 1 1
(i) left 1: 1 0 1 0 1 0 1 0
(j) right 1: 1 0 1 0 1 0 1 0

9-11. What happens to bits that are shifted off the end of a word during a circular shift? What fills in at the other end of the word?

9-12. What is another name for the circular shift?

9-13. Show the result of performing the indicated circular shift on these fields of bits:

(a) left 1: 0 0 0 0 0 0 0 1
(b) right 1: 0 0 0 0 0 0 0 1
(c) left 3: 1 1 1 0 0 0 0 1
(d) right 3: 1 1 1 0 0 0 0 1
(e) left 7: 1 1 1 0 0 0 0 1
(f) right 8: 1 1 1 0 0 0 0 1
(g) left 4: 1 1 1 1 1 0 1 1
(h) right 4: 1 1 1 1 1 0 1 1
(i) left 1: 1 0 1 0 1 0 1 0
(j) right 1: 1 0 1 0 1 0 1 0

9-14. What arithmetic operation is equivalent to a 1-bit arithmetic left shift? To a 1-bit arithmetic right shift?

9-15. Why is the sign bit not shifted during an arithmetic shift?

9-16. Show the result of performing the indicated arithmetic shift on these *signed, positive fields* of bits:

(a) left 1: 0 0 0 0 0 0 0 1
(b) right 1: 0 0 0 0 0 0 0 1
(c) left 2: 0 1 1 0 0 0 0 1
(d) right 7: 0 1 1 0 0 0 0 1
(e) left 8: 0 1 1 0 0 0 0 1

9-17. Which of the operations in Problem 9-16 could be interpreted to have caused arithmetic overflow?

9-18. Why does the effect of the arithmetic shift on a negative number depend on the representation used by the ALU? Why is this not the case for positive numbers?

9-19. Show the result of performing the indicated arithmetic shift on these *signed, negative fields* of bits, assuming *one's complement* representation:

(a) left 1: 1 1 1 1 0 1 0 1
(b) right 1: 1 1 1 0 1 0 0 1
(c) left 2: 1 0 1 0 1 0 0 1
(d) right 7: 1 1 1 0 0 0 0 1
(e) left 8: 1 0 1 0 0 0 0 1

9-20. Which of the operations in Problem 9-19 could be interpreted to have caused arithmetic overflow?

9-21. Repeat Problem 9-19 assuming *two's complement* representation.

9-22. Which of the operations in Problem 9-21 could be interpreted to have caused arithmetic overflow?

9-23. Repeat Problem 9-19 assuming *signed magnitude* representation.

9-24. Which of the operations in Problem 9-23 could be interpreted to have caused arithmetic overflow?

9-25. The following sequence of code does something useful. What does it do? What is the advantage of this method over the more obvious implementation?

```
XOR     R0,R1
XOR     R1,R0
XOR     R0,R1
```

9-26. The following sequence of code does something useful, assuming one's complement representation. What does it do? Why does it not work for the other two representations?

```
LOAD    R1,R0
ASH     R1,-31
XOR     R1,R0
```

9-27. Taking the square root of a number can be done efficiently using the following algorithm, published by Peter K. Bice in the May 1981 edition of *Electronic Design*. Given a 32-bit number SQUARE, the algorithm produces the 16-bit result ROOT:

```
1. [initialization]: LOOPCOUNT ⟵ 16 (number of bits
   in the result); SQUARE1,TRY,ROOT ⟵ 0.
2. [extract next 2 bits]: Shift upper two bits of SQUARE
   left into the lower two bits of SQUARE1. Shift ROOT left
   one bit.
3. [compute trial dividend]: TRY ⟵ ROOT. Shift TRY
   left 1 bit and add 1. If TRY > SQUARE1, then continue at
   step 5.
4. [update root and remainder]: SQUARE1 ⟵ SQUARE1-
   TRY; ROOT ⟵ ROOT+1
5. [test for termination]: LOOPCOUNT ⟵ LOOPCOUNT-1.
   If LOOPCOUNT=0 then terminate, else repeat at step 2.
```

Write a procedure SQRT that expects a positive number passed by value on the return stack. SQRT returns its square root on the return stack. (*Hint:* Try using a circular shift when shifting the upper 2 bits of SQUARE left into the lower 2 bits of SQUARE1. When the algorithm terminates, SQUARE will have been restored to its original condition.)

9-28. The Pascal language supports the notion of a *packed array.* Depending on the kind of information, a packed array can be stored in less space than an array that is not packed.

The programmer can, for example, declare that the information in the array lies between 0 and 31:

```
TYPE SmallNumber = 0..31;
        ...
VAR A: PACKED ARRAY [10..25] OF SmallNumber;
```

Each element of this packed array requires only 5 bits of storage. Space for the array would be allocated as shown in Figure 9-4. While a packed array requires less space, an element of the array is more expensive to read or write because it must be either unpacked from or packed into a field that may even cross a word boundary. Code generated by a Pascal compiler for a statement like

```
X:= A[I];
```

usually includes a call on a run-time routine that unpacks and returns an element from the array. Assume that the code generated for the assignment statement is

```
CALL    R7,PKGET        get packed array element
DATA    A                  address of packed array
DATA    10                 lower bound
DATA    5                  no. bits/element
DATA    I                  index of element
POP     R7,X            pop result into X
```

Write the run-time routine PKGET. PKGET takes four parameters, as indicated. The array and the index are passed by reference. The lower bound and number of bits per element are known to the compiler and so can be passed by value. These parameters are transmitted in line, and the procedure is responsible for returning past the parameters. The result is returned on the return stack (in this case, R7).

9-29. Assuming the same packed array described in Problem 9-28, code generated by a Pascal compiler for the statement

```
A[I]:= X;
```

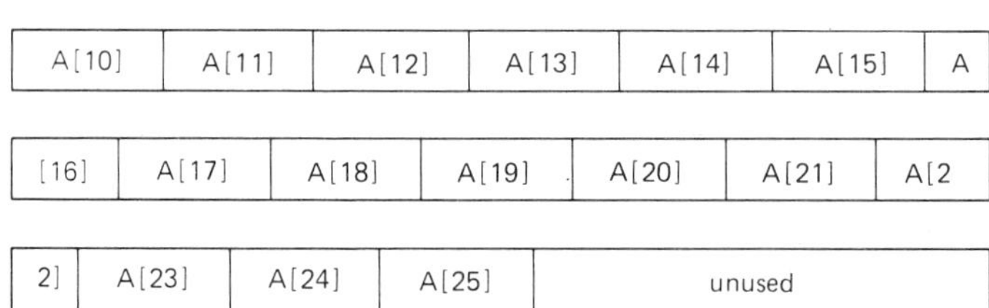

Figure 9-4

might look like this:

```
PUSH     R7,X          push value to be stored
CALL     R7,PKPUT      put packed array element
DATA     A                address of packed array
DATA     10               lower bound
DATA     5                no. bits/element
DATA     I                index of element
```

Write the run-time routine PKPUT. PKPUT takes four parameters, as indicated. The array and the index are passed by reference. The lower bound and number of bits per element are known to the compiler and so can be passed by value. These parameters are passed in line, and the procedure is responsible for returning past the parameters. The value to be stored is transmitted by value on the return stack (in this case, R7).

9-30. Pascal provides a built-in procedure to unpack a packed array. Assume another array B:

```
TYPE  B= ARRAY [0..15] OF SmallNumber;
```

Here is how UNPACK is defined:

```
UNPACK (A,B,I)           means  FOR J:= 10 TO 25 DO
                                    B[J-10+I]:= A[J];
```

A call on this routine might produce the following code:

```
CALL     R7,UNPACK     unpack elements of an array
DATA     A                address of packed array A
DATA     25-10+1          number of elements to unpack
DATA     5                no. bits/element
DATA     B                address of array B
DATA     0                lower bound of B
DATA     I                starting index in B
```

Arrays A and B and the starting index I are passed by reference. The number of elements to unpack, the number of bits per element, and the lower bound of array B are passed by value. The parameters are passed in line, and the procedure is responsible for returning past the parameters. (*Hint:* For best performance, take advantage of the sequential nature of the problem.)

9-31. Pascal also provides a built-in procedure to pack an array. Assuming the packed array A and the array B from Problems 9-29 and 9-30, here is how PACK is defined:

```
PACK (A,I,B)             means  FOR J:= 10 TO 25 DO
                                    A[J]:= B[J-10+I];
```

A call on this routine might produce the following code:

```
CALL     R7,PACK          pack elements into an array
DATA     A                   address of packed array A
DATA     25-10+1             number of elements to unpack
DATA     5                   no. bits/element
DATA     I                   starting index in B
DATA     B                   address of array B
DATA     0                   lower bound of B
```

Arrays A and B and the starting index I are passed by reference. The number of elements to unpack, the number of bits per element, and the lower bound of array B are passed by value. The parameters are passed in line, and the procedure is responsible for returning past the parameters. (*Hint:* For best performance, take advantage of the sequential nature of the problem.)

10

Floating-Point Numbers

An important application in which logical and shift operations play a prominent role is in the manipulation of *real* or *floating-point* numbers. Numbers on our machine are in what is known as *integer* format. An integer is a *fixed-point* number whose fraction point is "fixed" just to the right of the right-hand bit. Unlike integers, floating-point numbers can represent both whole numbers and fractions, and the fraction point can lie between any two digits. The fraction point seems to "float" within the number.

Before going further, a brief note is in order. The issues involved with representing and operating on floating-point numbers are fairly complex. Thorough coverage of the many details required is beyond the scope of an introductory text. The purpose in this chapter is to introduce the idea of floating-point representation and to design a set of routines that perform floating-point arithmetic. A number of issues have been simplified or skipped over entirely in this chapter to facilitate the presentation.

10.1 REPRESENTING FLOATING-POINT NUMBERS

A convenient way of representing floating-point numbers is provided by a form known as *scientific notation*. For instance, the distance from the earth to the sun is about 93 million miles. Expressed in scientific notation, this is

$$0.93 \times 10^8 \text{ miles}$$

A number is represented by a *fraction* or *mantissa* and an *exponent*. The fraction is scaled to be a number in the open interval $(-1, +1)$. That is,

$$-1 < \text{fraction} < +1$$

The exponent indicates the number of places that the decimal point has been shifted to get it in this form. As with our shift operations, positive numbers indicate that the decimal place has been shifted left. Negative numbers indicate a shift to the right. In this case, the decimal point has been shifted to the left by eight places to bring it into this form:

93 000 000
↑ 8 places

A number in scientific notation is said to be *normalized* or in *normal form* if the number to the right of the decimal place contains a digit other than 0. For example,

$$0.93 \times 10^8 \text{ miles}$$

is a normalized number, while

$$0.093 \times 10^7 \text{ miles}$$

is not normalized. The number 0 is normalized by definition.

A decimal representation is based on powers of 10. Thus the places around the decimal point are

6	4	7	3	•	2	8	9
10^3	10^2	10^1	10^0		10^{-1}	10^{-2}	10^{-3}

The same idea will work in binary. A binary representation is based on powers of 2. The places around a *binary point* are

1	0	1	1	•	0	1	1
2^3	2^2	2^1	2^0		2^{-1}	2^{-2}	2^{-3}

Instead of tenths, hundredths, and thousandths, the binary number system uses halves, quarters, and eighths. The binary number shown here is represented in scientific notation as

$$0.1011011 \times 2^{100}$$

The binary point has been shifted four (100 base-2) places to get it into its normal form.

As we will see later, normalization is important. The algorithms for many floating-point operations rely on the fact that their operands are normalized. The result of using unnormalized operands may be less precision than necessary or a completely wrong answer altogether!

10.2 THE FLOATING-POINT FORMAT

The two important pieces of information about a number written in scientific notation are the mantissa and the exponent. In designing a *floating-point format*, we must allow space for both. On machines with a 32-bit word size, it is common to find both fields packed together in one or two words of storage. If one word is used, it is referred to as a *single-precision* floating-point format. Two contiguous words are required for a *double-precision* floating-point format and can represent a number with greater accuracy than the single-precision format. We will use a single-precision format in our discussion.

In deciding how to divide the space between the two fields, the size of the mantissa and the exponent must be carefully balanced. On the one hand, the mantissa must have enough bits to represent a number with reasonable precision. On the other, the exponent must have enough bits to represent a useful dynamic range. Many machines that provide 32 bits for floating-point numbers divide the word as shown in Figure 10-1. This format allows 23 bits for the mantissa, plus a sign bit. Twenty-three bits is sufficient to represent the equivalent of between six and seven decimal digits of accuracy. Negative mantissas are represented in the sign and mantissa fields using whatever form is supported by the ALU.

The exponent is 8 bits wide. The exponent can represent a dynamic range of

$$2^{-127} \text{ to } 2^{+127} \text{ (one's complement)}$$
$$2^{-128} \text{ to } 2^{+127} \text{ (two's complement)}$$

The exponent in this format is stored in *biased* form. This means that a constant called a bias is added to the true exponent to create a biased exponent. The bias is chosen so that all numbers in the exponent field become positive. With a bias of 200B, the most positive exponent is stored as 377B and the most negative as 0. Notice that on a one's complement machine, the exponent −1 is stored as 176B, not 177B.

By using a biased exponent, the numeric order of two normalized floating-point numbers is the same as their order if the bits were treated as simple integers.

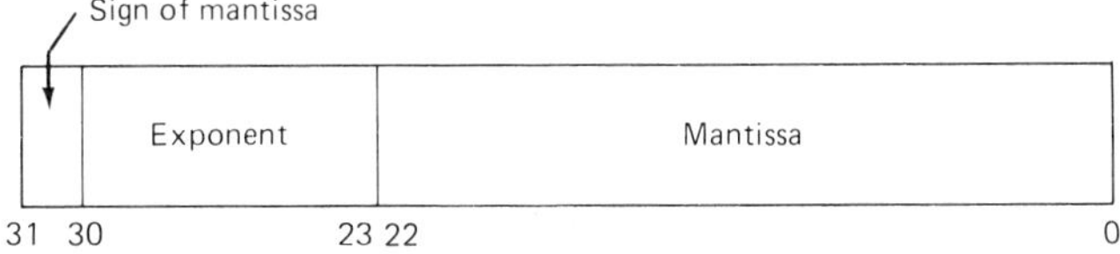

Figure 10-1 A typical floating-point format

This means that two normalized floating-point numbers can be compared without taking any special action.

Here are a few examples of numbers stored in our floating-point format:

1. *Number:*

$$67_{10} = 1\ 000\ 011.0_2 = 0.100\ 001\ 100 \times 2^{111}$$

Mantissa:

10000110000000000000000

Exponent:

$$10000000 + 111 = 100000111$$

Floating-point format:

0 10000111 10000110000000000000000

2. *Number:*

$$0.0859375_{10} = 0.0001011_2 = 0.1011 \times 2^{-11}$$

Mantissa:

10110000000000000000000

Exponent:

$$01111111 - 11 = 01111100 \text{ (one's complement)}$$
$$10000000 - 11 = 01111101 \text{ (two's complement)}$$

Floating-point format:

0 01111100 10110000000000000000000 (one's complement)
0 01111101 10110000000000000000000 (two's complement)

3. *Number:*

$$-453_{10} = -111\ 000\ 101.0_2 = -0.111\ 000\ 101 \times 2^{1001}$$

Mantissa:

1 00011101011111111111111 (one's complement)
1 00011101100000000000000 (two's complement)

Exponent:

$$10000000 + 1001 = 10001001$$

Floating-point format:

1 10001001 00011101011111111111111 (one's complement)
1 10001001 00011101100000000000000 (two's complement)

The second example shows a negative exponent in both one's and two's complement form. Notice that we use 177B instead of 200B in the one's complement form. 177B corresponds to an exponent of -0, while 200B corresponds to an exponent of $+0$. We bias negative one's complement exponents using 177B so that their range will begin with -1 at 176B. Adding 200B is correct in all other cases.

The third example shows a negative mantissa in both one's and two's complement form. Even though the leftmost bit of the mantissa is 0, the number is considered normalized because the positive form is normalized.

10.3 PACKING THE MANTISSA AND EXPONENT

To perform the four arithmetic functions, we must be able to create floating-point numbers. A procedure that does this is called PACK. PACK takes a mantissa and an exponent and packs them into our floating-point format. The mantissa is in the form of a whole number, with the binary point to the right of the rightmost bit. The exponent should be correctly adjusted for a binary point in this position. For example,

$$
\begin{aligned}
& 391.25_{10} \\
= {} & 110\ 000\ 111\ .\ 010 \times 2^{0} \\
= {} & 11\ 000\ 011\ 101.\quad \times 2^{-2}
\end{aligned}
$$

The mantissa has been multiplied by 4 to make it a whole number.

First, we can save some work if the mantissa is zero. We will define the normal floating-point form of 0.0 to have all bits set to 0. If the machine performs one's complement arithmetic, there are two forms of zero. The positive form, with all bits set to 0, is the one to return.

In packing a number, we must be sure that the mantissa is not given with more than 23 bits of precision. If it is, PACK should *scale the mantissa to 23-digit precision*. This involves shifting the mantissa right and incrementing the exponent until it has only 23 bits of precision. For example, the number

$$\underline{11000111000100011000011101} \times 2^{0}$$

is given to 26 bits of precision. By arithmetically shifting it right three times, the number retains only 23 bits of precision, and the exponent is increased by three, so that the number stays the same:

$$\underline{00011000111000100011000011} \times 2^{3}$$

It would be incorrect to throw away the most significant bits, because this changes the number itself. Discarding the least significant bits only makes the number less precise.

We must also *normalize the mantissa.* A one's or two's complement mantissa is normalized if the most significant bit of the mantissa is the opposite of the sign bit. If not, the mantissa is arithmetically shifted left and the exponent decremented to compensate. This step is repeated until the mantissa becomes normalized.

Once we have a normalized mantissa, the final step is to *adjust the binary point and bias the exponent.* Our floating-point format has the binary point to the left of the most significant bit. The mantissa given as input has the binary point to the right of the least significant bit. Adjusting the binary point is as simple as adding 23 to the exponent:

$$\underline{110001110001000110000011.} \times 2^{3}$$
$$\downarrow$$
$$= .110001110001000110000011 \times 2^{26}$$

We saw earlier that biasing the exponent by adding 200B is correct for all cases except negative exponents in one's complement form. In that case, we must add the bias corresponding to −0 (177B) instead of +0 (200B).

There is a simple way to do this that works correctly for both one's and two's complement exponents that are in range. First, we extract the lower 8 bits of the exponent by ANDing with the mask 377B. Then, we perform the XOR operation between this result and the mask 200B. Here is how this technique is applied to the exponent −3, in both one's and two's complement form:

One's complement form

```
    11 111 111 111 111 111 111 111 111 111 100
(*) 00 000 000 000 000 000 000 000 011 111 111
    -------------------------------------------
                                     11 111 100
                                 (−) 10 000 000
                                 --------------
Biased exponent for −3  -->          01 111 100
```

Two's complement form

```
    11 111 111 111 111 111 111 111 111 111 101
(*) 00 000 000 000 000 000 000 000 011 111 111
    -------------------------------------------
                                     11 111 101
                                 (−) 10 000 000
                                 --------------
Biased exponent for −3  -->          01 111 101
```

Compare these with the values we found earlier. This treatment can also be applied to positive exponents, although it will have no effect.

Finally, we *pack the mantissa and exponent fields* together. This involves shifting the exponent into position and ORing the two fields together.

Here is an algorithm for packing a floating-point number:

1. [Check for 0 mantissa]: If the mantissa is 0, return the positive normalized form of floating-point 0.
2. [Normalize the mantissa]: Form a mask by arithmetically shifting the sign of the mantissa right one bit and isolating that bit (bit 30). While bit 30 of the mantissa and bit 30 of the mask are different, arithmetically left-shift the mantissa and increment the exponent to compensate.
3. [Scale the mantissa]: Scale the mantissa to 23-bit precision by arithmetically shifting it right eight places and adding 8 to the exponent to compensate.
4. [Adjust and bias the exponent]: Add 23 to the exponent to move the binary point to the left of the mantissa. Bias the exponent so that it lies in the range 0 to 377B.
5. [Pack the mantissa and exponent]: Shift the exponent up to the exponent field, clear the exponent field of the mantissa, and combine the two to give the packed result.

The two fields are passed to PACK by value in R0 and R1. The result is returned in R0, and the content of R1 is unchanged. Here is the code for PACK, along with a sample invocation:

```
            LOAD   R0,=-453          mantissa in R0
            LOAD   R1,=0             exponent in R1
            CALL   R7,PACK           floating point -453.0
                 ...

** PACK - Pack mantissa, exponent into floating point number
*
*           INPUT
*             R0 - mantissa, with binary point to right of 1sb
*             R1 - signed exponent corresponding to mantissa
*           OUTPUT
*             R0 - floating point number
*
PACK        PUSH   R7,R4             save registers
            PUSH   R7,R3
            PUSH   R7,R2
            PUSH   R7,R1
```

```
        LOAD   R2,R0              trap zero mantissa
        BRNE   PKNORM
        LOAD   R0,=0              (non-twos complement ALUs)
        BR     PKDONE

* normalize mantissa in 23-bit field
PKNORM  LOAD   R3,PKMSB           mask of mantissa MSB
        ASH    R2,=-1             mask to detect significant
        AND    R2,R3              ... bit in MSB position
PKLOOP  LOAD   R4,R0              see if mask and MSB
        AND    R4,R3              ... are different
        CMPR   R4,R2
        BRNE   PKSCALE            branch if different
        ASH    R0,=1              else shift out MSB
        SUB    R1,=1              decrement exponent
        BR     PKLOOP

* scale mantissa for 23-bit field
PKSCALE ASH    R0,=-8             move mantissa right
        AND    R0,PKNEXP          clear field in mantissa
        ADD    R1,=23+8           adjust binary pt
        AND    R1,=377B           truncate exponent
        XOR    R1,=200B           bias exponent
        ASH    R1,=23             position exponent
        OR     R0,R1              insert exponent

PKDONE  POP    R7,R1              restore registers
        POP    R7,R2
        POP    R7,R3
        POP    R7,R4
        RTN    R7,

PKNEXP  DATA   20037777777B       mask all but exponent
PKMSB   DATA   10000000000B       mask msb of word
```

10.4 UNPACKING A FLOATING-POINT NUMBER

The inverse operation is UNPACK. It takes a floating-point number and returns a mantissa and exponent. The mantissa and exponent are both returned as signed 32-bit quantities.

The first step is to extract the exponent field and unbias it. If we are working with one's complement numbers and the biased exponent is less than 200B, we subtract 177B; otherwise, we subtract 200B to unbias the exponent.

The exponent can also be unbias by using a method similar to the one presented earlier. First, we shift the exponent to the top of the word. Then, we XOR the result with a mask that has only the sign bit set. This reverses the top bit of the exponent. Finally, we extend the sign bit by arithmetically shifting the exponent to the bottom of the word. The result is the signed exponent. Here is how it would be done for a biased exponent representing the one's complement version of −3:

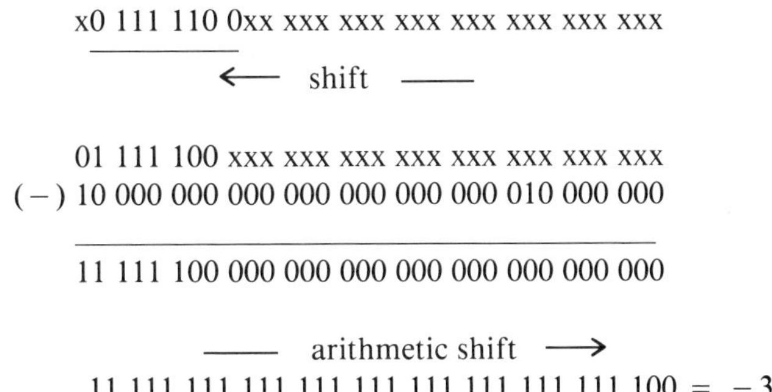

After unbiasing the exponent, the next step is to move the binary point to the right end of the mantissa field by subtracting 23. This puts the mantissa in the form of a whole number, with the exponent adjusted to compensate.

The third step is to extract the mantissa by extending the sign bit through the 8 bits that held the exponent. This can be done by arithmetically shifting the mantissa up next to the sign bit, then arithmetically shifting it back down, to extend the sign through the exponent field.

For example, here is what UNPACK would return for the floating-point form of 67.0 that we created earlier:

Floating-point number:

0 10000111 10000110000000000000000

Mantissa:

00 000 000 010 001 100 000 000 000 000 000

Exponent:

−16

The unpacked mantissa appears as a large positive integer. The implied binary point is to the right of the least significant bit. The exponent returned indicates that the true binary point lies 16 places to the left.

Here are the steps needed to unpack a floating-point number:

1. Extract and unbias the exponent.
2. Adjust the binary point to the right of the mantissa.
3. Extend the sign bit in the mantissa.

UNPACK expects a floating-point number by value in R0. It returns a signed mantissa in R0 and a signed exponent in R1 as a result. Here is the code for UNPACK, along with a sample invocation:

```
        LOAD R0,FLOATWD     floating point number
        CALL R7,UNPACK      unpack the word
           ...

** UNPACK - Unpack float number into mantissa, exponent
*
*       INPUT
*            R0 - floating point number
*       OUTPUT
*            R0 - mantissa, adjusted to be whole number
*            R1 - signed exponent corresponding to mantissa
*
UNPACK  LOAD R1,R0          copy for exponent
        LSH  R1,=1          ... move it to top of word
        XOR  R1,UPKSIGN     ... toggle sign bit
        LSH  R1,=-24        ... shift down and extend sign
        SUB  R1,=23         shift binary point

        ASH  R0,=8          shift mantissa up to sign bit
        ASH  R0,=-8         extend sign downward
        RTN  R7,

UPKSIGN DATA 20000000000B mask sign bit of word
```

10.5 FLOATING-POINT ADDITION

Now that we can get numbers into and out of floating-point format, we are ready to think about implementing the four arithmetic operations. The first operation we will try is addition. Consider the addition of two decimal numbers in scientific notation:

$$\begin{array}{r} .998 \times 10^5 \\ +\ .315 \times 10^3 \\ \hline \end{array}$$

This really represents the addition problem

$$\begin{array}{r} 99\,800. \\ +\quad 315. \\ \hline \end{array}$$

We know that to add two ordinary numbers, their decimal points must be aligned. For two numbers in scientific notation, this means making the exponents the same. For example, to perform the addition indicated above, we must rewrite the problem as

$$\begin{array}{r} .99800 \times 10^5 \\ + \ .00315 \times 10^5 \\ \hline \end{array}$$

The mantissa of the number with the smaller exponent has been shifted until the two exponents match. Now, we simply add the mantissas:

$$\begin{array}{r} .99800 \times 10^5 \\ + \ .00315 \times 10^5 \\ \hline 1.00115 \times 10^5 \end{array}$$

Notice that the result is no longer in normal form. This may happen if the sum is one digit longer than the addends, assuming that they are both of fixed length.

The same sort of thing happens in binary. First, the two numbers must be unpacked. Then, the mantissa of the number with the smaller exponent is shifted right so that the two mantissas have the same exponent. If the number is shifted so far that all significant bits are lost, the number with the larger exponent will be unchanged by the addition. Adding the mantissas may produce an unnormalized number that is one bit longer than the 23-bit mantissa. When we use our pack procedure, the result will be rescaled so that it fits in the mantissa again.

Here are the steps involved in adding two floating-point numbers:

1. Unpack both numbers.
2. Adjust the number with the smaller exponent.
3. Add the mantissas.
4. Repack the result.

Consider the floating-point sum 5678.0 + 42.0. Here is how the addition proceeds:

$$\begin{array}{rl} 5678.0 = & 0 \;\; 10001101 \;\; 10110001011100000000000 \\ 42.0 = & 0 \;\; 10000110 \;\; 01010000000000000000000 \end{array}$$

1. Unpack both numbers:

$$\begin{array}{l} 00\ 000\ 000\ 010\ 110\ 001\ 011\ 100\ 000\ 000\ 000. \times 2^{-10} \\ 00\ 000\ 000\ 010\ 101\ 000\ 000\ 000\ 000\ 000\ 000. \times 2^{-17} \end{array}$$

2. Adjust the number with the smaller exponent:

$$\begin{array}{l} 00\ 000\ 000\ 010\ 110\ 001\ 011\ 100\ 000\ 000\ 000. \times 2^{-10} \\ 00\ 000\ 000\ 000\ 000\ 001\ 010\ 100\ 000\ 000\ 000. \times 2^{-10} \end{array}$$

3. Add the mantissas:

$$
\begin{array}{r}
00\ 000\ 000\ 010\ 110\ 001\ 011\ 100\ 000\ 000\ 000. \times 2^{-10} \\
00\ 000\ 000\ 000\ 000\ 001\ 010\ 100\ 000\ 000\ 000. \times 2^{-10} \\
\hline
00\ 000\ 000\ 010\ 110\ 010\ 110\ 000\ 000\ 000\ 000. \times 2^{-10}
\end{array}
$$

4. Repack the result:

$$
\begin{array}{rcl}
5678.0 & = & 0\ 10001101\ 10110001011100000000000 \\
+42.0 & = & 0\ 10000110\ 10101000000000000000000 \\
\hline
5720.0 & = & 0\ 10001101\ 10110010110000000000000
\end{array}
$$

Our floating-point add procedure is FADD. The two floating-point operands are passed in by value through R0 and R1. The normalized floating-point sum is returned in R0. The content of R1 is not changed by the procedure. Here is procedure FADD, along with a sample call:

```
            LOAD    R0,OPND1        first floating operand
            LOAD    R1,OPND2        second floating operand
            CALL    R7,FADD         add two operands
                ...

** FADD - Add two floating point numbers
*
*           INPUT
*             R0 - first floating point operand
*             R1 - second floating point operand
*           OUTPUT
*             R0 - floating point sum
*
FADD        PUSH    R7,R3           save registers
            PUSH    R7,R2
            PUSH    R7,R1

            CALL    R7,UNPACK       unpack first operand
            LOAD    R2,R0           copy mantissa,
            LOAD    R3,R1           ... and exponent
            LOAD    R0,0(R7)        copy of second operand
            CALL    R7,UNPACK       unpack second operand

            CMPR    R3,R1           find smaller exponent
            BRGE    FAJOP2          branch if second one
            SUB     R3,R1           adjust first mantissa
            ASH     R2,R3
            BR      FADONE
FAJOP2      SUB     R1,R3           adjust second mantissa
            ASH     R0,R1
```

```
        LOAD    R1,R3       and use first exponent
FADONE  ADD     R0,R2       add mantissas
        CALL    R7,PACK     repack result
        POP     R7,R1       restore registers
        POP     R7,R2
        POP     R7,R3
        RTN     R7,
```

Notice that in equalizing the exponents, we did not update the corresponding exponent to match. The exponent of the other mantissa already has the correct value. If the exponent is not already in R1, then it is a simple matter to move it there from R3.

10.6 FLOATING-POINT SUBTRACTION

We will leave the simple modification to get FSUB as an exercise. The changes to FADD involve very few lines of code.

10.7 FLOATING-POINT MULTIPLICATION

The procedure for carrying out floating-point multiplication is quite different from the one for either addition or subtraction. To see how it works, here is an example:

$$\begin{array}{r} 0.5432 \times 10^5 \\ * \; \underline{0.8760 \times 10^3} \end{array}$$

This is scientific notation for

$$\begin{array}{r} 54320. \\ * \quad \underline{876.} \end{array}$$

The rule for multiplication using scientific notation is to *multiply the mantissas and add the exponents*. Unlike addition, multiplication does not require that the two exponents be the same. In this sample, we get the result

$$\begin{array}{rr} 0.5432 & \times 10^5 \\ * \; 0.8760 & \times 10^3 \\ \hline 0.4758432 & \times 10^8 \end{array}$$

Although this algorithm seems simple enough, there is an implementation problem that must be addressed first. If two numbers have M and N digits, their product can have as many as $(M + N)$ digits. This means having to deal with the possibility of a 46-bit precision mantissa!

One way to fit the product into a 31-bit field is to adjust both operands to retain only 15 bits of precision before multiplying them. To see what this would do to the precision of the product, suppose we want thc square of the floating-point number 9999.0 but require that the result have only four digits of significance. We would have to approximate 9999.0 by 9900.0 and use this number to form the square:

$$\begin{array}{rl} 0.9999 & \times 10^4 \\ *0.9999 & \times 10^4 \\ \hline 0.9998001 & \times 10^4 \end{array} \qquad \begin{array}{rl} 0.99 & \times 10^4 \\ *\ 0.99 & \times 10^4 \\ \hline 0.9801 & \times 10^4 \end{array}$$

This can introduce quite a bit of error in the product as a result of truncating the original operands before multiplying.

The method we will use instead is based on the idea of *partial products*. We use partial products whenever we perform ordinary multiplication:

```
   1234
 * 5678
 ------
   9872  |
  8638   |  partial
 7404    |  products
6170     |
-------
7006652
```

Each partial product is the result of multiplying the first operand by one digit of the second operand. Successive partial products are each shifted left one place before being added in.

The same thing is done in binary:

```
    1101
  * 1011
  ------
    1101  |
   1101   |  partial
  0000    |  products
 1101     |
--------
10001111
```

In binary, each partial product is either the first operand or zero, depending on the value of the corresponding digit in the second operand.

For a 23-bit mantissa, this method requires 23 iterations, one for each bit in the mantissa of the second operand. Rather than computing 23 partial products and adding them up all at once, it is more convenient to accumulate a *partial sum* of partial products computed so far.

Since we are working on a fixed-size word, the partial sum is limited to 31 bits of accuracy at each step. Partial products cannot simply be shifted left by one bit and added to the partial sum because the partial sum will eventually overflow the word. Instead, the partial sum is arithmetically shifted to the right one bit and the exponent of the product increased to compensate before the next partial product is added in.

Here is the multiplication from the previous example. This time, assume that we can retain only 5 bits of significance in the partial sum and 4 in the final product:

Initial problem	1101×2^0
	$* \ 1011 \times 2^0$
First partial sum	1101×2^0
Shift partial sum	110×2^1
Add in partial product	1101
Second partial sum	10011×2^1
Shift partial sum	1001×2^2
Add in partial product	0000
Third partial sum	1001×2^2
Shift partial sum	0100×2^3
Add in partial product	1101
Fourth partial sum	10001×2^3
Shift for final product	1000×2^4

There are three further points to note. The first is that the algorithm presented works as long as the second operand is positive. To preserve the sign of the final product, it is necessary to reverse the sign of both operands if the second one is negative.

Second, if either mantissa is zero, there is no point in continuing. It is easy to add tests while unpacking the two operands to see if either mantissa is zero. If so, we can immediately return zero as a result.

The last point is that both operands must be normalized for all of this to work properly. If not, significant bits of the partial sum will be lost as it is shifted right to add in the next partial product. Consider the process applied to the product 1*3, if neither operand is normalized first:

1: 0 10010111 00000000000000000000001
3: 0 10010111 00000000000000000000011

First, we unpack the numbers into mantissas and exponents:

$$
\begin{array}{r}
00\ 000\ 000\ 000\ 000\ 000\ 000\ 000\ 000\ 000\ 001. \times 2^0 \\
\hline
00\ 000\ 000\ 000\ 000\ 000\ 000\ 000\ 000\ 000\ 011. \times 2^0 \\
\hline
\end{array}
$$

The first partial product is a copy of the first operand, since the low-order bit in the second operand is 1:

$$00\ 000\ 000\ 000\ 000\ 000\ 000\ 000\ 000\ 000\ 001. \times 2^0$$

This becomes the initial value of the partial sum. The second partial product is also a copy of the first operand, since the next bit in the second operand is 0. The partial sum is shifted right by one, and the first operand is added to form the second partial sum:

$$00\ 000\ 000\ 000\ 000\ 000\ 000\ 000\ 000\ 000\ 001 \times 2^1$$

The third and subsequent partial products are all zero, corresponding to zeros in the rest of the second operand. Even if we stopped now, the product 1∗3 would be given as 1 because a significant bit was lost during the shift. If all 23 partial products are added in, all significant bits of the product will be lost. The product 1∗3 is ultimately reported as 0. If both mantissas were normalized before multiplying, we would have gotten the correct answer. It is important, then, to use only normalized mantissas with this algorithm.

To review, the algorithm for multiplying two normalized floating-point numbers is

1. Unpack both numbers. If either is zero, the product is 0.
2. Add the exponents, plus 22 to adjust for shifts of the partial sum (23 less 1 for the first shift).
3. Change the signs of the mantissas if the second one is negative.
4. For each of 23 bits in the second mantissa, shift the partial sum and add in the first mantissa if the corresponding bit in the second mantissa is 1.
5. Repack the result.

Our floating-point multiplication procedure is FMUL. The two floating-point operands are passed in by value through R0 and R1. The normalized floating-point product is returned in R0. The content of R1 is not changed by the procedure. Here is procedure FMUL, along with a sample invocation:

```
        LOAD   R0,OPND1        first floating operand
        LOAD   R1,OPND2        second floating operand
        CALL   R7,FMUL         multiply two operands
          ...
```

```
** FMUL - Multiply two floating point numbers
*
*           INPUT
*             R0 - first floating point operand
*             R1 - second floating point operand
*           OUTPUT
*             R0 - floating point product
*                  <<returns 0 if either operand is 0>>
*
FMUL        PUSH   R7,R4          save registers
            PUSH   R7,R3
            PUSH   R7,R2
            PUSH   R7,R1

            CALL   R7,UNPACK      unpack 1st operand
            LOAD   R3,R1          save exponent
            LOAD   R2,R0          ... and mantissa
            BREQ   FMULOK         >>return 0 if 1st operand 0<<

            LOAD   R0,0(R7)       copy 2nd operand
            CALL   R7,UNPACK      unpack 2nd operand
            LOAD   R4,R0          save 2nd mantissa
            BREQ   FMULOK         >>return 0 if 2nd operand 0<<
            BRGT   FMULINIT       branch if mantissa positive
            LOAD   R4,=0          else change signs of 1st
            SUB    R4,R2
            LOAD   R2,R4
            LOAD   R4,=0          ... and 2nd mantissas
            SUB    R4,R0

FMULINIT    ADD    R1,=22(R3)     exponents + 22 shifts
            LOAD   R0,=0          init partial sum
            LOAD   R3,=23         init shift count

FMULOOP     ASH    R0,=-1         shift partial sum right
            CSH    R4,=-1         shift LSB to sign bit
            BRGE   *+2            branch if sign bit is zero
            ADD    R0,R2          else add in first operand
            SUB    R3,=1          decrement shift count
            BRGT   FMULOOP        branch for next bit

FMULOK      CALL   R7,PACK        repack result
            POP    R7,R1          restore registers
            POP    R7,R2
            POP    R7,R3
            POP    R7,R4
            RTN    R7,
```

Notice how the bits of the second operand are extracted and tested. Each iteration rotates the least significant bit up to the sign bit position. A simple test for negative determines whether the bit is on or off. This is much less expensive than making a copy of the mantissa each time and extracting the bit by masking the least significant bit's position.

10.8 FLOATING-POINT DIVISION

The last of the four arithmetic operations is floating-point division. This is the most difficult operation, so it would be a good idea to start by looking at a specific example.

In the traditional longhand method, division of 5472 by 12 begins by choosing which leading digits of the dividend to use in computing the first digit of the quotient. The first guess of 5 is wrong, because 12 is larger than 5. The second guess of 54 will work, because 12 is smaller than 54. To get the first digit of the quotient, we must guess the number of times 12 goes into 54. The answer is 4 with 6 left over. The 4 becomes the first digit of the quotient, and the next digit of the numerator is "brought down" and combined with the 6 to make 67:

```
          4
     ________
12  |  5 4 7 2
      -4 8 ↓
       ---
         6 7
```

This number will be divided by the divisor on the next iteration. The process repeats to form the final quotient:

```
          4 5 6
     ___________
12  |  5 4 7 2
      - 4 8 ↓  |
        ---    |
          6 7  |
        - 6 0  ↓
          ---
            7 2
          - 7 2
            ---
              0
```

In scientific notation, division is very similar to multiplication. Instead of adding exponents and multiplying mantissas, division *subtracts exponents* and *divides mantissas*:

$$\frac{5472 \times 2^{0}}{1200 \times 2^{-2}} = (5472/1200) \times 2^{0-(-2)}$$

The exponents are subtracted, and division is carried out on the mantissas. If the mantissa of the quotient is always to represent a whole number, we will need to decrement the exponent each time a zero is added to the right as division progresses:

```
              4 × 2^2
        ---------
1 2 0 0 | 5 4 7 2
          4 8 0 0
          -------
            6 7 2
```

```
              4 5 × 2^1
        -----------
1 2 0 0 | 5 4 7 2 0
          4 8 0 0 ↓
          -------
            6 7 2 0
            6 0 0 0
            -------
              7 2 0
```

```
              4 5 6 × 2^0
        -------------
1 2 0 0 | 5 4 7 2 0 0
          4 8 0 0   |
          -------   |
            6 7 2 0 |
            6 0 0 0 ↓
            -------
              7 2 0 0
              7 2 0 0
            ---------
                    0
```

The algorithm is even easier in binary. Since both operands are in normal form and to the same precision, there is no need to guess how many times the divisor goes into the dividend: Either it goes once or not at all. A simple comparison is sufficient to decide. If it goes once, a subtraction computes the remainder. If it does not go at all, the next bit of the dividend is brought down. Consider the problem of dividing 55 by 5:

$$\frac{0.110111 \times 2^{0}}{0.101000 \times 2^{-3}} = (0.110111/0.101000) \times 2^{0-(-3)}$$

Again, the exponent is decremented once for each zero added to the right of the dividend in order to keep the mantissa of the quotient a whole number:

```
                     1 0 1 1  × 2^0
           ___________________
1 0 1 0 0 0 | 1 1 0 1 1 1 0 0 0
              1 0 1 0 0 0 ↓ ↓
              -----------
                  1 1 1 1 0 0
                  1 0 1 0 0 0 ↓
                  -----------
                    1 0 1 0 0 0
                    1 0 1 0 0 0
                    -----------
                              0
```

To implement this algorithm, it is useful to think of building the mantissa of the quotient one bit at a time. For each iteration, the previous quotient is shifted left one place and the exponent decremented to compensate. If the dividend is smaller than the divisor, we shift the dividend left one place and repeat the process. Otherwise, set the least significant bit of the quotient to show that the divisor goes into the dividend once. The remainder becomes the dividend for the next iteration. The algorithm terminates when the dividend becomes zero. Here is the same problem implemented in this way:

```
(Dividend - divisor)      Quotient bit      Exponent
  110111                      1                 3
- 101000
  ------
  001111      <-┐
                
  011110      ──┐             0                 2
- 101000        │
  ------        │
  xxxxxx      <-┘
  
  111100                      1                 1
- 101000
  ------
  010100      <-┐

  101000                      1                 0
- 101000
  ------
       0
```

So far, we have only looked at cases where the divisor divides the dividend exactly. However, many quotients cannot be represented exactly within 23 bits. In fact, some quotients cannot be represented exactly no matter how many bits are used. For example, the fraction 1/10 is represented as the repeating binary fraction

$$0.00011001100110\ldots$$

If the quotient takes more than 23 bits to represent, the algorithm must be stopped after a 1 appears in the most significant bit of the mantissa. It is not sufficient to iterate 23 times. For example, the fraction 1/10 requires 24 iterations to bring a 1 into the most significant bit of the mantissa.

This algorithm has its restrictions too. First, both the dividend and the divisor must be nonnegative. We can satisfy this by taking the absolute value of both at the beginning of the algorithm, then setting the sign of the quotient, once it is complete, based on the sign of the divisor and dividend. The quotient is positive unless the signs of the two operands are *different*.

The second restriction is that a zero divisor is not allowed. If one just happened to get by, here is what would happen. For each iteration, 0 is always no bigger than the dividend, so a 1 is turned on in the mantissa of the quotient. Subtracting zero from the dividend leaves the same number as before. As a result, the dividend never becomes zero, so the loop terminates only when a 1 appears in the most significant bit of the mantissa. The answer returned would be meaningless.

Zero divisors can arise when working with floating-point numbers, for example, as the result of underflow from a previous operation. To guard against this, we should test for a zero divisor at the beginning of the algorithm. We will also test for a zero dividend as well and define the quotient when either the divisor or the dividend is zero as zero. Several exercises consider other alternatives.

To review, here is the algorithm for floating-point division:

1. Unpack the operands.
2. Take the absolute value of the operands.
3. If dividend or divisor is 0, return 0; go to step 7.
4. Arithmetically left-shift the quotient and decrement the exponent. If the divisor is less than the dividend, go to step 6.
5. Set the LSB of the mantissa and subtract the divisor from the dividend. If the dividend becomes 0, the number divides evenly; go to step 7.
6. If the quotient MSB has not been set yet, arithmetically left-shift the dividend to "bring down" the next 0; repeat at step 4.
7. Give the quotient the proper sign, based on the sign of the operands.
8. Pack the quotient mantissa and exponent.

Our floating-point division algorithm is FDIV. Both operands are passed by value. The dividend is in R0, and the divisor is in R1. FDIV returns its quotient in R0. Here is the code for FDIV, along with a sample invocation:

```
            LOAD    R0,OPND1        first floating operand
            LOAD    R1,OPND2        second floating operand
            CALL    R7,FDIV         divide two operands
                 ...

** FIDV - Divide two floating point numbers
*
*           INPUT
*             R0 - first floating point operand
*             R1 - second floating point operand
*           OUTPUT
*             R0 - floating point quotient
*                 <<returns 0 if either operand is 0>>
*
FDIV        PUSH    R7,R4           save registers
            PUSH    R7,R3
            PUSH    R7,R2
            PUSH    R7,R1
            PUSH    R7,R0           (save for sign)

            CALL    R7,UNPACK       unpack 1st operand
            LOAD    R3,R1           save exponent
            LOAD    R2,R0           ... and mantissa
            BREQ    FDIVOK          >>return 0 if 1st operand is 0<<
            BRGT    *+3             branch if mantissa positive
            LOAD    R2,=0           else make it positive
            SUB     R2,R0

            LOAD    R0,1(R7)        copy 2nd operand
            CALL    R7,UNPACK       unpack 2nd operand
            LOAD    R4,R0           save 2nd mantissa
            BREQ    FDIVOK          >>return 0 if 2nd operand is 0<<
            BRGT    *+3             branch if mantissa positive
            LOAD    R4,=0           else make it positive
            SUB     R4,R0

            SUB     R3,R1           init exponent of quotient
            LOAD    R1,=1(R3)       ... plus one for loop start
            LOAD    R0,=0           init mantissa of quotient
            LOAD    R3,FDIVMSB      mask for MSB of mantissa

FDIVLOOP    LSH     R0,=1           shift in next quotient bit
            SUB     R1,=1           decrement exponent
            CMPR    R2,R4           divisor divides dividend?
            BRLT    FDIVNEXT        no -- branch for next division
            OR      R0,=1           turn on LSB of quotient
            SUB     R2,R4           decrease dividend
            BREQ    FDIVOK          branch if divides evenly
```

```
FDIVNEXT  ASH    R2,=1        "bring down" next 0 in dividend
          CMPR   R0,R3        mantissa MSB set?
          BRLT   FDIVLOOP     repeat loop if false

FDIVOK    POP    R7,R4        compute sign of result
          XOR    R4,0(R7)
          LSH    R4,=-31      move sign bit to bottom of word
          BREQ   *+3          branch if sign bit is positive
          LOAD   R4,R0        else make result negative
          LOAD   R0,=0
          SUB    R0,R4

          CALL   R7,PACK      repack result
          POP    R7,R1        restore registers
          POP    R7,R2
          POP    R7,R3
          POP    R7,R4
          RTN    R7,

FDIVMSB   DATA   20000000B    mask for MSB of mantissa
```

Notice how the procedure computes the sign of the result. Upon entry to FDIV, a copy of the first operand in R0 is pushed onto the stack after the other registers are saved. The second operand in R1 is already saved on the stack. If both operands have the same sign, the quotient will be positive. A negative quotient can occur only when the sign of the two operands is different.

The XOR operation is ideal for checking this case. The result of XOR is true only if the two operands are different. By XORing the two operands, the sign bit is set if the two operands are different and is clear otherwise. The only thing to watch out for is the possibility of generating negative zero on a one's complement machine. For example:

	1 010101	first operand
(−)	0 101010	second operand
	1 111111	−0 (one's complement)

Instead, we perform a logical left shift to move the sign bit to the bottom and fill the rest of the word with zeros. The result is 0 if the quotient should be positive and 1 if it should be negative. One a two's complement machine, the result of XOR could be tested for negative directly.

10.9 ABOUT BOUNDARY CONDITIONS AND ACCURACY

As noted at the beginning of the chapter, a number of issues have been simplified or skipped over entirely in this chapter to facilitate the presentation. In this section we will touch briefly on some of them.* Readers with no further interest in floating-point arithmetic may wish to skip this section.

10.9.1 Boundary Conditions

The routines presented in this chapter, while adequate, did very little sophisticated boundary testing. As long as they were presented with "average" inputs, the routines would usually perform correctly. However, a number of exceptional conditions were not covered.

One thing that the routines did not check for was the *overflow condition*. Overflow occurs when the exponent of a normalized floating-point number is too large to fit in the exponent field. PACK simply truncates the exponent, leading to a meaningless result.

Perhaps a better treatment would be to return the special value *infinity.* We might reserve the largest biased exponent, 377B, to use as a flag for an infinite result.

What happens if infinity is given as a parameter to a floating-point operation? The answer depends on which operation and the values of the other parameters. For example, infinity divided by a number is still infinity. On the other hand, a number divided by infinity is zero. Finally, a number divided by zero is infinity. In FDIV, we simply returned 0 as the result in this case.

Another condition to check for is underflow. Underflow occurs if the exponent of a normalized floating-point number is too small to fit in the exponent field. Again, PACK simply truncates the exponent.

A better solution would be to *denormalize* the mantissa to bring the exponent back in range. This involves right-shifting the normalized mantissa until the exponent reaches the smallest biased value, 0. This exponent must also be reserved so that the condition can be recognized. UNPACK would have to unpack the mantissa correctly, renormalize it, and adjust the exponent to match.

Finally, some operations have no meaningful numeric result. There is no "good" answer for an attempt to take the square root of a negative number. It may be useful to reserve a special value that marks the result of an invalid operation. This value is sometimes referred to as *not a number (NaN).* We could, for example, use an exponent of 377B with a zero mantissa to indicate infinity and an exponent of 377B with a nonzero mantissa to indicate NaN. Each of the operations must recognize NaN. The result of using NaN with any operation should be NaN.

It should be clear from this discussion that handling boundary conditions for floating-point operations properly is very complicated indeed. The number of conditions times the number of procedures leads to quite an increase in code size over the simple routines presented in this chapter.

*Much of the following discussion is based on a proposed standard floating-point format that has become widely accepted in the last several years. For more details, see the discussion preceding Problem 10-33 at the end of this chapter.

10.9.2 Accuracy

Another thing that our routines did not control very well is numeric accuracy. While adjusting the mantissa with the smaller exponent during addition, for example, we simply shifted the least significant bits off the right end of the word. The problem is that the resulting mantissa may have the wrong least significant bit. If the mantissa was positive and the last bit shifted off the end was a 1,

```
. . . |1 0 1 0| 1  1 ⟶
```

then the original number would be more accurately represented by rounding the mantissa to

```
               1 0
. . .  1 0 1 X X |  1 ⟶
```

The same sort of thing happens in several other places. One is during floating-point multiplication when the partial sum is shifted right. Another is during normalization. While a bit or two of accuracy may not seem like much, it can seriously change the results if the scale represents millions of miles. As inaccurate numbers are generated and used in other calculations, these errors can pile up until the final answer is meaningless.

One way to control error is to keep a couple of extra bits at the least significant end of the result during a floating-point operation. These bits are used both for rounding and for recording the fact that other bits have been shifted off the end. Three bits are generally used, as shown in Figure 10-2. As the mantissa is shifted right, the least significant bits of the mantissa are shifted into the *guard bit* and *round bit* positions. The purpose of the *sticky bit* is to record the fact that other bits have been shifted off the end. As bits are shifted out of the round bit, they are ORed into the sticky bit, which never shifts. The three bits together are sufficient to round the result properly.

All these measures to control accuracy are meant to produce the best possible approximation to the true answer. The added overhead also greatly increases the complexity of floating-point operations. Implementing a full floating-point package can be quite complex and requires quite a bit of care and thought.

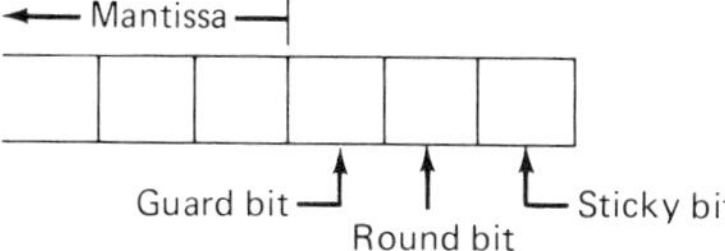

Figure 10-2 Mantissa with guard, round, and sticky bits

10.10 SUMMARY

In this chapter we looked at how floating-point numbers can be represented and manipulated. The basis for this discussion is scientific notation. This system treats a number as a small magnitude and an exponent that serves as a scale factor for the mantissa. These two fields are encoded in a word of memory to form a single-precision floating-point format for our machine. This format uses a signed mantissa and a biased exponent.

Using this floating-point format, we designed a set of simple floating-point math routines. Included were two routines that convert a number into and out of this format. Floating-point multiplication and division presented special problems because they may produce a mantissa that is larger than a single word of storage.

The final section presented a discussion of boundary conditions and numeric accuracy for floating-point routines. As we saw, writing a floating-point package that properly handles boundary conditions such as overflow, underflow, and invalid input to the operations is not easy. We also discovered that errors due to approximating a floating-point result in a fixed number of bits are important to control. This is especially true when the result of one operation is used as input to other operations.

The intent of this chapter was to present the design of a typical floating-point format and algorithms for the four floating-point arithmetic operations. Many simplifications were made in the algorithms to facilitate this presentation. The exercises suggest some improvements to the existing routines, as well as extensions to our modest start at a full floating-point library.

PROBLEMS

10-1. Reexpress these numbers in normalized scientific notation:

(a) 123.4	**(b)** 0.086
(c) -4	**(d)** 346789.0123
(e) 72.0	**(f)** 0
(g) 0.0000000149	**(h)** 1000000
(i) 42	**(j)** 0.94

10-2. Reexpress these numbers in regular decimal notation:

(a) 0.314×10^3	**(b)** 456.3×10^{-6}
(c) -4.1×10^0	**(d)** 0.0143×10^2
(e) 1×10^{-4}	**(f)** -0.895×10^{-2}
(g) -0.100×10^6	**(h)** 0×10^{-5}
(i) 14×10^0	**(j)** 0.00001×10^5

10-3. For each of the numbers given in Problem 10-2, indicate which are already normalized. For those that are not, rewrite them in normalized form.

10-4. A 23-bit mantissa can represent between six and seven decimal digits of precision. Why can seven digits not always be represented? Give the smallest seven-digit number that cannot be represented in 23 bits.

10-5. How many decimal digits of precision can be expressed with the indicated number of bits in the mantissa?

(a) 2 bits **(b)** 8 bits **(c)** 16 bits
(d) 24 bits **(e)** 31 bits

10-6. What is meant by the "dynamic range of the exponent"? Why is this range different depending on whether numbers are represented in one's complement or two's complement form?

10-7. Explain the principle of a "biased exponent." Why is the exponent biased instead of using one's or two's complement representation? What is the bias in our floating-point format? How is the correct bias chosen?

10-8. If the machine represents in one's complement form, why is the biased exponent 177B not used? What does this exponent mean? What is used instead?

10-9. Show the normalized floating-point representation of these numbers in one's complement form:

(a) 0 **(b)** 129
(c) 0.125 **(d)** 346.75
(e) −39 **(f)** 14.1
(g) −123.875 **(h)** −0.375
(i) −0.00391 **(j)** −0.1

10-10. Repeat Problem 10-9 with the two's complement form.

10-11. What is the advantage of having all floating-point operations return a word with all bits off as the standard form of 0.0? Suggest an alternative and discuss its advantages and disadvantages.

10-12. When packing a floating-point number, what is the effect of scaling the mantissa by discarding the least significant bits? What would happen if the most significant bits were discarded instead?

10-13. Show the following exponents in their biased form, assuming one's complement representation:

(a) 127 **(b)** 3
(c) 0 **(d)** −1
(e) −13 **(f)** −127

10-14. Repeat Problem 10-13 assuming two's complement representation.

10-15. Show the following biased exponents in signed form, assuming one's complement representation:

(a) 221B **(b)** 0B
(c) 176B **(d)** 100B
(e) 377B **(f)** 300B

10-16. Repeat Problem 10-15 assuming two's complement representation.

10-17. In performing floating-point addition, why is it important to equalize the exponents before adding the mantissas? What happens to the mantissa corresponding to the smaller exponent when the exponents are equalized?

10-18. How much bigger can the sum of the mantissas be, compared to the mantissas themselves?

10-19. One way to retain more accuracy in FADD is first to shift both mantissas left by 7 bits, adjusting the exponents to correspond. How could this help? When will this method not work.

10-20. Implement the subtraction procedure FSUB, which corresponds to FADD presented in this chapter.

10-21. How much bigger can the product of the mantissas be, compared to the mantissas themselves? Why does this make the implementation of floating-point multiplication more complicated on our machine? Why is adjusting the mantissas not a good solution to the problem?

10-22. What is partial product? Why is forming a partial product particularly simple in base 2?

10-23. Why is it important that the second operand be made positive before using the multiplication algorithm given in this chapter? What has to be done if it is negative? What would happen if the second operand was not made positive first?

10-24. Why is it important that both operands be in normal form? What is the effect on the product if either or both operands are not in normal form?

10-25. The algorithm for performing floating-point multiplication can be improved by taking advantage of the integer multiplication instruction available on our machine. Instead of single digits, we can form partial products from *groups of digits*. As partial products are formed, each is shifted the same number of places as there are digits in the group. If we multiply 1,234 by 5,678 and choose a group size of two digits, there would be only two partial products. The second one would be shifted two places from the first:

```
     1234
   * 5678
   ------
    96252   <--   1234 * 78
   69104    <--   1234 * 56
  -------
  7006652
```

The number of bits in each group is determined by the number of places available for the partial product. A mantissa takes up 23 bits, not including the sign bit. Products could be allowed to grow as large as 31 bits before overflowing the word. Since a 23-bit number multiplied by an 8-bit number can produce up to a 31-bit sum, 8 is the largest group size that we can use for any partial product. A 23-bit operand must be broken up into three 8-bit groups to produce three partial sums.

One way to extract 8-bit chunks eliminates the need to ensure that the sign of the second operand is positive. Each chunk must be sign-extended to a full 32-bit number before multiplying it with the first operand. This requires nothing more than arithmetically shifting the chunk up next to the sign bit, then back down to the bottom end of the word. We used this technique earlier for UNPACK.

To review, a modified algorithm for multiplying two normalized floating-point numbers is

1. Unpack both numbers.
2. Add the exponents, plus 16 to adjust for two 8-bit shifts of the partial sum.
3. Extract and sign-extend each 8-bit group of the second operand.
4. Multiply the first operand by the 8-bit group.

5. Shift the partial sum right 8 bits and add each partial product.
6. Repack the result.

Write a version of FMUL to take advantage of our built-in multiply instruction. The two floating-point operands are passed in by value through R0 and R1. The normalized floating-point product is returned in R0. The content of R1 is not changed by the procedure.

10-26. Give an analysis of the two floating-point multiplication procedures, in terms of both the size of each procedure and the number of instructions executed by each. Which takes up less room? Which executes fewer instructions?

10-27. A difficulty with division in decimal is the need to "guess" how many times divisor goes into the dividend. Why is this easier in binary?

10-28. The algorithms presented in this chapter work correctly for both one's and two's complement form. Verify that they are also correct assuming that our machine represented negative numbers in *signed magnitude* form.

10-29. Floating point square root is computed by taking the square root of the mantissa and dividing the exponent by 2. One requirement is that the exponent be even, so that dividing the exponent by 2 will cause no loss of information. If the exponent is odd, the mantissa can be shifted left one place and the exponent decremented by 1. Here are two examples:

Even exponent	Odd exponent
$\sqrt{4 \times 10^2}$	$\sqrt{4 \times 10^3}$
	$= \sqrt{40 \times 10^2}$
$= \sqrt{4} \times 10^1$	$= \sqrt{40} \times 10^1$
$= 2 \times 10^1$	$= 6.325 \times 10^1$

An algorithm for taking an integer square root was given in the problem section of Chapter 9. This algorithm can be applied here by treating the mantissa as an integer. Implement the floating-point square root procedure FSQRT. FSQRT expects a non-negative floating-point number to be passed by value in R0 and returns the normalized floating-point square root in R0.

10-30. Write a procedure FABS that returns the absolute value of a floating-point number. FABS expects a floating-point number passed by value in R0 and returns its normalized result in R0.

10-31. Write two procedures, FLOAT and INT. FLOAT converts an integer into a floating-point number. INT converts a floating-point number to the largest integer that is less than or equal to the floating-point number. Both procedures expect their input by value in R0 and also return their result in R0. How should INT handle input that is too large to be represented by the 32-bit integer format?

10-32. Write a procedure FCMPR that compares two floating-point numbers. FCMPR expects two floating-point numbers in R0 and R1 and returns its results in R0. FCMPR returns an integer that indicates how the contents of R0 and R1 are related:

-1	if	$R0 < R1$
0	if	$R0 = R1$
1	if	$R0 > R1$

The remainder of the problems are based on the following information. Some related material is also presented in section 10.9.*

Another floating-point format has been proposed as a standard by the Institute of Electrical and Electronics Engineers (IEEE). This floating-point format uses a signed magnitude representation for the mantissa and a biased representation for the exponent, as depicted in Figure 10-3.

One of the interesting features of the standard is that a normalized mantissa can represent one extra bit of precision. To do this, the mantissa is first scaled and normalized to 24 bits; then, the most significant bit is discarded to make a 23-bit mantissa. For example, we would represent the constant π (~ 3.141593) in our floating-point format as

0 10000000 11001001000011111101101

The IEEE format, on the other hand, discards the 1 in the most significant position of the mantissa, shifts the mantissa one position left, and fills in the least significant position with an extra bit of the number:

0 10000000 10010010000111111011011 $\longleftarrow$ 1

Any operations on floating-point numbers would have to take this "implied" high-order bit into account.

In addition to the normal range of numbers, several patterns are reserved to indicate negative and positive infinity and undefined. An arithmetic operation would return the appropriate form of infinity in the case where the result is too big to represent in the floating-point format. Here is how a floating-point number is interpreted (s = the sign field, e = the biased exponent field, and f = the fraction or mantissa field):

1. If $e = 255$ and $f \neq 0$, then v = <NaN> (*not a number*).
2. If $e = 255$ and $f = 0$, then $v = (-1)^s \infty$.
3. If $0 < e < 255$, then $v = (-1)^s\, 2^{e-127}\quad (1.f)$
4. If $e = 0$ and $f \neq 0$, then $v = (-1)^s\, 2^{-126}\quad (0.f)$ (this is called the *denormalized* form).
5. If $e = 0$ and $f = 0$, then $v = (-1)^s\, 0$.

10-33. Modify PACK, UNPACK, FADD, FSUB, FMUL, and FDIV to deal with the new

*This is only a very brief sketch of the proposed IEEE floating-point standard. Section 10.9 also discusses some related material on boundary conditions and accuracy. Readers who are seriously interested in attempting the following problems should consult any available standards descriptions, including:

Jerome T. Coonen, "An Implementation Guide to a Proposed Standard for Floating Point Arithmetic," *IEEE Computer*, 13, no. 1 (January 1980), pp. 68–79.

"A Proposed Standard for Floating Point Arithmetic," *IEEE Computer*, 14, no. 3 (March 1981), pp. 51–62.

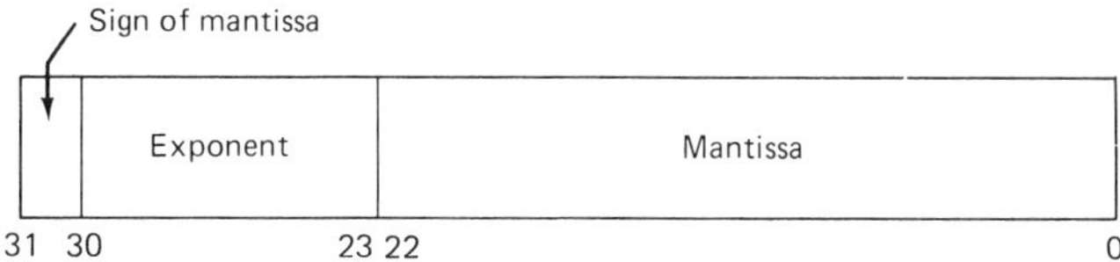

Figure 10-3

floating-point format. Consider the following questions and indicate how they have been dealt with:

(a) Would it be more useful for UNPACK to return the mantissa in signed magnitude or either one's or two's complement form?

(b) Can any of the procedures be simplified because the mantissa is in signed magnitude form?

(c) Where is the appropriate place to deal with the "implied" high-order bit in the mantissa?

(d) How will the procedures deal with an input number that is either "not a number" or negative or positive infinity?

(e) Where is the appropriate place to detect and signal floating-point overflow?

10-34. Modify FSQRT to deal with the IEEE floating-point format. What should the procedure return in case of a negative input? What should the procedure do in the case of either infinity or "not a number"?

10-35. Write a version of FABS to deal with the IEEE floating-point format. What advantage does this format have in taking absolute values?

10-36. Write a version of FCMPR to deal with the IEEE floating-point format.

11

Character and String Manipulation

Up to now, we have used our machine to manipulate numeric data. With the addition of input/output hardware, we will also need to manipulate alphabetic as well as numeric characters. Character and string manipulation is a very interesting topic by itself, and it is the topic of this chapter. In the next chapter we will apply this understanding as we consider the subject of input/output programming techniques.

11.1 CHARACTER REPRESENTATIONS

We turn first to the problem of how to represent letters, digits, and punctuation on a machine that is geared to manipulate only numeric quantities. The only sensible representation assigns a small positive number called a *character code* to each letter, digit, and punctuation mark. The problem of character representation, then, is largely a matter of assigning a meaning to the codes.

Character representations vary according to the number of characters available and the specific codes assigned. The representation chosen depends on the nature of the application, as well as on the amount of room available for each character. We will look at several character representations in the following sections.

11.1.1 Simple Numeric Codes

Simple numeric codes are capable of representing only numeric data. Codes of this kind are referred to as *binary coded decimal (BCD)*. BCD is called a *4-bit code* because each digit of the number is encoded in a 4-bit-wide field. The 6 extra bit configurations are called "forbidden codes" and remain unused. There are several BCD codes. Perhaps the simplest is called *natural BCD (NBCD)*. The NBCD character code used for each digit is just its own 4-bit binary representation:

Digit	BCD code
0	0000
1	0001
2	0010
3	0011
4	0100
5	0101
6	0110
7	0111
8	1000
9	1001

As an example, the number 349 has the NBCD representation

0011 0100 1001

BCD representations are in limited use as a character code because they cannot represent letters and other special symbols. It is interesting that BCD is sometimes also used as an internal numeric representation. There are some good algorithms for performing arithmetic directly on the BCD numeric representations. BCD is especially desirable when performing high-precision floating-point arithmetic calculations. Many calculators use a BCD representation for both internal calculations and displaying results. A number of full-scale computers have recently adopted it as well.

11.1.2 Limited Alphanumeric Codes

Codes of this kind are primarily for specialized applications or for situations in which storage space is at a premium. Numbers can be represented, along with a single case of characters and some special symbols. An interesting example is a 5-bit code standardized by the International Communications Union, called Alphabet CCITT No. 2, shown in Table 11-1.

Five bits is enough to represent only 32 characters. The letters and numbers already take up 36 codes. To get around this problem, 2 characters are assigned to each code. Which of the 2 characters is correct depends on which of two "shifts" is in effect. Here is how the message "IT IS 8:50 P.M." would be encoded:

Character	Code
<letter shift>	11111
"I"	01100
"T"	00001
<space>	00100
"I"	01100
"S"	10100
<space>	00100
<figure shift>	11011
"8"	01100
":"	01110
"5"	00001
"0"	01101
<space>	00100
<letter shift>	11111
"P"	01101
<figure shift>	11011
"."	00111
<letter shift>	11111
"M"	00111
<figure shift>	11011
"."	00111

Frequently used characters appear in both sets to minimize the number of shift changes required. Once a particular shift is in effect, all codes that follow are interpreted as characters from that shift. Shift changes are only necessary to use characters from the other shift.

Limited alphanumeric codes are still used for some specialized applications that do not require a full range of letters and special symbols. The code just illustrated was developed for use with early mechanical paper-tape readers and punches. Each character was represented by a row of punched holes across a narrow strip of paper. Since mechanical punches and readers were expensive to build, it was very important to limit the number of punches.

11.1.3 Full Alphanumeric Codes

Full alphanumeric codes can represent both uppercase and lowercase characters, as well as numbers and a reasonable set of special symbols. This requires at least 90 characters. In practice, full alphanumeric codes are usually stored in an 8-bit field. This quantity of storage is referred to as a *byte* or character of storage. There are two full alphanumeric codes whose usage dominates. These are EBCDIC and ASCII.

The EBCDIC character code. EBCDIC (Extended Binary Coded Decimal Interchange Code) is an 8-bit code developed by International Business Machines (IBM) Corporation for their line of Model 360/370 computers. It is also used by

TABLE 11-1 ALPHABET CCITT NO. 2

Letters	Figures	Code
A	–	11000
B	?	10011
C	:	01110
D		10010
E	3	10000
F		10110
G		01011
H		00101
I	8	01100
J		11010
K	(	11110
L	)	01001
M	.	00111
N	,	00110
O	9	11100
P	0	01101
Q	1	11100
R	4	01010
S	,	10100
T	5	00001
U	7	11100
V	=	01111
W	2	11001
X	/	10111
Y	6	10101
Z	+	10001
Blank		00000
Letter shift		11111
Figure shift		11011
Space		00100
Carriage return		00010
Line feed		01000

input/output devices designed to be compatible with those machines. Table 11-2 is a partial listing of the character codes and their assignments. Codes 00000000 through 00111111 are *control codes* used as special commands to certain devices. These codes have been omitted from the table for the sake of brevity. Notice especially the large gaps between certain ranges of codes. In fact, gaps within the uppercase and lowercase alphabets themselves sometimes add an extra level of complexity to certain kinds of operations on characters.

The ASCII character code. ASCII (American Standard Code for Information Interchange) is a 7-bit character code comparable to EBCDIC. Table 11-3 is a partial listing of ASCII character codes. Codes 0000000 through 0011111 are

TABLE 11-2 PARTIAL TABLE OF EBCDIC CHARACTER CODES

bits 3–0	bits 7–4 0100	0101	0110	0111	1000	1001	1010	1011	1100	1101	1110	1111
0000	SP	&	–									0
0001			/		a	j			A	J		1
0010					b	k	s		B	K	S	2
0011					c	l	t		C	L	T	3
0100					d	m	u		D	M	U	4
0101					e	n	v		E	N	V	5
0110					f	o	w		F	O	W	6
0111					g	p	x		G	P	X	7
1000					h	q	y		H	Q	Y	8
1001					i	r	z		I	R	Z	9
1010		!		:								
1011		$	‘	#								
1100	⟨	*	%	@								
1101	(	)	–	’								
1110	+	;	>	=								
1111	:	~	?	”								

control codes whose use is specific to certain input/output applications. These codes have been omitted from the table for the sake of brevity. Unlike EBCDIC, ASCII contains no gaps in its character code assignment. An extra leading 0 can be added to turn 7-bit ASCII into an 8-bit code. There is also an 8-bit ASCII code called ASCII-8. The corresponding ASCII-8 codes are shown along the bottom row in Table 11-3. Most devices now available understand only 7-bit ASCII.

Seven-bit ASCII is the most widely accepted full alphanumeric character code, and we will use it in our examples throughout the rest of the book. This does not automatically rule out using some other code like EBCDIC. However, some of the algorithms presented later may be slightly different if another code is used. We will be as careful as possible to isolate character code dependencies in all examples presented.

11.2 STRING REPRESENTATIONS

Once we have decided on a character representation, we still face the problem of performing operations on characters. A useful concept is that of a *string* of characters. The word derives from the notion of a sequence of characters that are "strung" together. Since most operations on characters involve groups or strings of characters, we will consider the issues involved with string representations.

The simplest form of a string is as an *array of characters*. Each character is adjusted right in the lower end of a word, with the remaining bits set to zeros. Thus the string "the string" requires ten words of storage:

```
000000000000000000000000 01110100   t
000000000000000000000000 01101000   h
000000000000000000000000 01100101   e
000000000000000000000000 01000000
000000000000000000000000 01110011   s
000000000000000000000000 01110100   t
000000000000000000000000 01110010   r
000000000000000000000000 01101001   i
000000000000000000000000 01101110   n
000000000000000000000000 01100111   g
```

As an alternative, we could *pack* as many characters as possible into each word. Our 32-bit word holds up to four 7-bit ASCII characters. Each character is adjusted right in an 8-bit field with the upper bit set to 0. Characters fill the word from left to right, with lower bytes of the last word padded with zeros. The character whose code is zero is called ⟨NUL⟩ in many character representations, including ASCII and EBCDIC. It is used mainly as a padding character. This string representation is called a *packed array of characters*. The string "the string" requires only three words when stored as a packed array:

```
01110100 01101000 01100101 01000000   "the "
01110011 01110100 01110010 01101001   "stri"
01101110 01100111 00000000 00000000   "ng"
```

TABLE 11-3 PARTIAL TABLE OF ASCII CHARACTER CODES

bits 3–0	bits 6–4 (7-bit ASCII) 010	011	100	101	110	111
0000	SP	0	@	P	‘	p
0001	!	1	A	Q	a	q
0010	”	2	B	R	b	r
0011	#	3	C	S	c	s
0100	$	4	D	T	d	t
0101	%	5	E	U	e	u
0110	&	6	F	V	f	v
0111	’	7	G	W	g	w
1000	(	8	H	X	h	x
1001	)	9	I	Y	i	y
1010	*	:	J	Z	j	z
1011	+	;	K	[	k	{
1100	,	<	L	\	l	:
1101	—	=	M	]	m	}
1110	.	>	N	∧	n	~
1111	/	?	O	-	o	DEL
	0100	0101	1010	1011	1110	1111

bits 3–0 7–4 (ASCII-8)

Each of these representations has its good points. It is easier to work with a string as a simple array of characters. Any character can be accessed in only a few instructions. The packed array representation makes more efficient use of storage. It is also quicker to move strings in this form, because four times the information is transferred per word copied. We will examine this trade-off in more detail shortly.*

The other issue is how to delimit a string. As with parameter lists, there are two methods: either keep a count that gives the string length or place a sentinel at the end of the string.

If the length of the string is kept explicitly, we must decide what that length means. For a string stored as a simple array of characters, the length is just the number of characters in the string. The length of a packed array of characters, however, could refer to either the number of characters in the string or the number of words taken up by those characters. The better interpretation here is still the number of characters, not words. The exact number of words can easily be computed from the number of characters, but the opposite is usually not true. Recall that strings in this form are padded with enough trailing ⟨NUL⟩ characters to make up whole numbers of words. The number characters could be computed only to the nearest multiple of 4 if the length was in words.

We could store the length of the string at the beginning of the string storage space itself. The string "the string" would be represented in packed array form as

```
0    00000000000000000000000000001010      10 (length)
01110100 01101000 01100101 01000000       "the "
01110011 01110100 01110010 01101001       "stri"
01101110 01100111 00000000 00000000       "ng"
```

The advantage of this method is simplicity. Everything can be known about a string, given its starting address. For certain kinds of operations, though, this method does have a weak point. We may sometimes want to work with only a portion or *substring* of a larger string. To create a substring using this method, we would first have to copy the substring to a new location, with the correct length information in the first word. For example, the substring "ring" in the previous example can be represented only by copying it into a new string and giving it the length 4:

```
0    00000000000000000000000000000100       4 (length)
01110010 01101001 01101110 01100111       "ring"
```

If substrings do not play an important part in an application, the simplicity of this method may outweigh this consideration.

One way to overcome this problem is to keep the information about a string in a separate *string descriptor*. For a string stored as a simple array of characters, the

*Of course, for machines with byte-addressable memory, there is no need even to consider the problem of packed string representation.

string descriptor contains the length and starting address of the string. Suppose that the string "the string" is stored in memory starting at MYSTRING:

```
*                         "t"   "h"   "e"   " "
MYSTRING      DATA      164B, 150B, 145B, 100B
*                         "s"   "t"   "r"   "i"   "n"   "g"
*             DATA      163B, 164B, 162B, 151B, 156B, 147B
```

The string descriptor that represents the entire string might be stored in two consecutive words:

```
STRING10    DATA    MYSTRING      start address of string
            DATA    10            length of string (chars)
```

We can now refer to the substring "ring" by simply creating another string descriptor:

```
STRING4     DATA    MYSTRING+6    start address of string
            DATA    4             length of string (chars)
```

The situation is a little more complicated for the packed array representation. Since several characters are packed into a single word, the descriptor must also indicate the position of the starting character in the string. This is necessary because a substring might begin with a character other than the first one in the word. Here again is the packed representation of the string "the string":

```
*                          "the "       "stri"       "ng"
MYSTRING    DATA     16432062500B,16335071151B,15631600000B
```

The starting address used in the descriptor is the address of the word that contains the first character. The starting position is the character number in the string. The leftmost character is 0, and the rightmost character is 3. Here is a descriptor that represents the entire string:

```
STRING10    DATA    MYSTRING      start address of string
            DATA    10            length of string (chars)
            DATA    0             start char in word
```

The substring "ring" is represented by the string descriptor

```
STRING4     DATA    MYSTRING+1    start address of string
            DATA    4             length of string (chars)
            DATA    2             start char in word
```

Notice that the substring actually begins at the third character (character position 2)

of MYSTRING + 1 and extends to the second character (character position 1) of MYSTRING + 2.

Rather than keep an explicit length, the second method delimits the string by a sentinel. One commonly used sentinel value is the character ⟨NUL⟩. An upacked representation of "the string" would look like this:

```
000000000000000000000000 01110100        t
000000000000000000000000 01101000        h
000000000000000000000000 01100101        e
000000000000000000000000 01000000
000000000000000000000000 01110011        s
000000000000000000000000 01110100        t
000000000000000000000000 01110010        r
000000000000000000000000 01101001        i
000000000000000000000000 01101110        n
000000000000000000000000 01100111        g
000000000000000000000000 00000000      <NUL> (sentinel)
```

Since a packed string is padded with ⟨NUL⟩s to the nearest whole word, there is already a terminating ⟨NUL⟩ character in three out of four cases:

```
01110100 01101000 01100101 01000000 "the"
01110011 01110100 01110010 01101001 "stri"
01101110 01100111 00000000 00000000 "ng" <NUL>
                  --------
```

The only time something special must be done is when the string is a multiple of four characters, such as the substring "ring". In this case, an extra word is allocated and padded with ⟨NUL⟩ characters:

```
01110010 01101001 01101110 01100111 "ring"
00000000 00000000 00000000 00000000 <NUL>
--------
```

11.3 STRING OPERATIONS

In the remainder of the chapter, we will develop a library of procedures that operate on strings. Many of the simpler routines presented earlier will be called by the ones presented later in the chapter. These string procedures will also be used again in the next chapter.

Throughout the rest of the book, we will represent strings as unpacked arrays of characters, terminated by ⟨NUL⟩. When it is sufficient, we can refer to a string by its starting address. Where necessary, we will use a string descriptor that includes both a pointer to the string and the string length.

11.3.1 Measuring the Length of a String

The simplest routine is one that measures the length of a string. Given a pointer to the start of the string, this routine simply counts characters until it encounters ⟨NUL⟩. At this point it returns the number of characters it counted, not including ⟨NUL⟩. We will pass the pointer by value and return the length on the R7 stack:

```
** STRLEN - RETURN THE LENGTH OF A STRING
*
*         INPUT
*              R7 STACK - POINTER TO STRING (VALUE)
*
*         OUTPUT
*              R7 STACK - LENGTH OF STRING
*
*         CONSTANTS
*              NUL      - CHARACTER CODE 0
*                         -- USED AS END OF STRING MARKER
*
STRLEN    PUSH      R7,R1          save registers
          PUSH      R7,R0
          LOAD      R0,3(R7)       get pointer to string

STLCHR    POP       R0,R1          get next character from string
          CMPR      R1,=NUL        end of string?
          BRNE      STLCHR         no -- try next character

          SUB       R0,3(R7)       subtract base of string
          SUB       R0,=1          less one for last POP
          STORE     R0,3(R7)       return length
          POP       R7,R0          restore registers
          POP       R7,R1
          RTN       R7,
```

Notice how the POP instruction was used to recover successive values from the string and increment the pointer. We could also have used a LOAD instruction to fetch the character and an ADD instruction to increment the pointer.

11.3.2 The Index of a Character in a String

Another simple routine finds the *index* of a character in a string. The index is the position at which the character is found in the string. Consider the string "string". The index of the character "s" in this string is 1, while the index of the character "g" is 6. If the character is not found in the string, its index is 0. We will define the index of a character that appears twice in the string to be the index of its first occurrence. For example, the index of "t" in "test" is defined as 1.

Procedure STRINDX is passed two parameters on the R7 stack: a pointer to the start of the string and the character whose index we seek. The index is returned on the R7 stack.

```
** STRINDX - RETURN THE INDEX OF A CHARACTER IN A STRING
*            (0 IF NOT FOUND, 1 IF FIRST ONE, ETC.)
*
*         INPUT (VALUE)
*             R7 STACK - CHARACTER TO INDEX (TOP)
*                      - POINTER TO STRING
*         OUTPUT
*             R7 STACK - INDEX OF CHARACTER
*
*         CONSTANTS
*             NUL      - CHARACTER CODE 0
*                        -- USED AS END OF STRING MARKER
*
STRINDX   PUSH    R7,R2        save registers
          PUSH    R7,R1
          PUSH    R7,R0
          LOAD    R0,5(R7)     get pointer to string
          LOAD    R2,4(R7)     character to index

STXCHR    POP     R0,R1        get next char from string
          CMPR    R1,=NUL      end of string?
          BREQ    STXNUL       yes -- break from loop
          CMPR    R1,R2        character found?
          BRNE    STXCHR       no -- try next character

          SUB     R0,5(R7)     index of char found
          BR      STXOUT

STXNUL    LOAD    R0,=0        char not found
STXOUT    STORE   R0,5(R7)     return index
          POP     R7,R0        restore registers
          POP     R7,R1
          POP     R7,R2
          POP     R7,1(R7)     move rtn address
          RTN     R7,
```

Notice that STRINDX has one more input than output parameter. Before returning, we must clean up the stack by removing this extra input parameter. As we discussed earlier, the easiest way is to pop the return address back onto the stack just before returning (Figure 11-1).

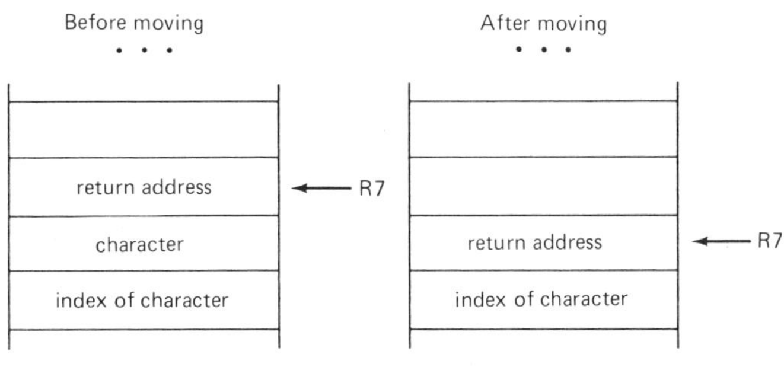

Figure 11-1 Return address adjusted prior to returning from STRINDX

11.3.3 Skipping Blanks

For many string applications, blanks simply serve as separators between items. We will need a routine that skips over any leading blanks in a string. Our routine takes a string pointer as input and returns an updated string pointer to the first nonblank character that follows. For example, given the string and string pointer in Figure 11-2, the routine advances the pointer to the first nonblank character in the string, as shown in Figure 11-3.

Procedure SKIPSP expects a string pointer on the R7 stack and returns an updated string pointer on the R7 stack:

```
** SKIPSP - SKIP OVER SPACES IN CHARACTER STRING
*
*         INPUT (VALUE)
*              R7 STACK - POINTER TO STRING
*
*         OUTPUT
*              R7 STACK - UPDATED STRING POINTER
*
*         CONSTANTS
*              NUL      - CHARACTER CODE 0
*                         -- USED AS END OF STRING MARKER
*              SP       - CHARACTER CODE FOR SPACE
*
```

" "	" "	"a"	"b"	<NUL>	
↑					

Figure 11-2 String with pointer ahead of leading blanks

" "	" "	"a"	"b"	<NUL>	
		↑			

Figure 11-3 String with pointer advanced past leading blanks

```
SKIPSP  PUSH   R7,R1      save registers
        PUSH   R7,R0
        LOAD   R0,3(R7)   get pointer to string

SKSCHR  POP    R0,R1      get next char from string
        CMPR   R1,=NUL    end of string?
        BREQ   SKSOUT     yes -- break from loop
        CMPR   R1,=SP     character found?
        BREQ   SKSCHR     no -- try next character

SKSOUT  SUB    R0,=1      back up one pos
        STORE  R0,3(R7)   return index
        POP    R7,R0      restore registers
        POP    R7,R1
        TRN    R7,
```

11.3.4 Copying a String

A number of applications require the ability to copy strings from one location to another. This algorithm simply copies characters from a source string to a destination string up to and including ⟨NUL⟩.

Our version is STRCOPY. It takes pointers to source and destination arrays on the R7 stack and returns a pointer to ⟨NUL⟩ in the destination array as a result:

```
** STRCOPY - COPY A STRING FROM SOURCE TO DESTINATION
*
*        INPUT (VALUE)
*            R7 STACK - POINTER TO SOURCE STRING (TOP)
*                       POINTER TO DESTINATION STRING
*
*        OUTPUT
*            R7 STACK - POINTER TO <NUL> IN DESTINATION
*                       STRING
*
*        CONSTANTS
*            NUL      - CHARACTER CODE 0
*                       -- USED AS END OF STRING MARKER
*
STRCOPY  PUSH     R7,R2         save registers
         PUSH     R7,R1
         PUSH     R7,R0

         LOAD     R0,5(R7)      pointer to dest str
         LOAD     R1,4(R7)      pointer to src str

STYCHR   POP      R1,R2         next char from src str
         STORE    R2,@R0        copy to dest str
         CMPR     R2,=NUL       end of src str?
```

```
            BREQ     STYOUT        yes -- break out of loop
            ADD      R0,=1         else increment dest ptr
            BR       STYCHR        repeat for next char

STYOUT      STORE    R0,5(R7)      return dest ptr
            POP      R7,R0         restore registers
            POP      R7,R1
            POP      R7,R2
            POP      R7,1(R7)      adjust return address
            RTN      R7,
```

The rationale behind returning a pointer is that we might want to copy several source strings to a single destination string, one after another. To copy another string to the destination array, we simply push a new source string pointer onto the stack and call STRCOPY once again (Figure 11-4).

11.3.5 String Comparison

Another useful operation is the comparison of two strings. Two strings are related in the same three basic ways as numeric values. One string is either less than, equal to, or greater than the other. String comparison is usually based on the position of the characters in the character set.

The relationship between two strings is established by scanning along both strings and comparing corresponding characters. The strings are equal as long as corresponding characters are equal. If two characters are different, the comparison is based on their relative order in the character set. The character whose code is less belongs to the lesser string. Thus,

"abcd" < "abcz"

If the two strings are of different length but identical up to the end of the shorter one, then the shorter string is the lesser of the two:

"abc" < "abcd"

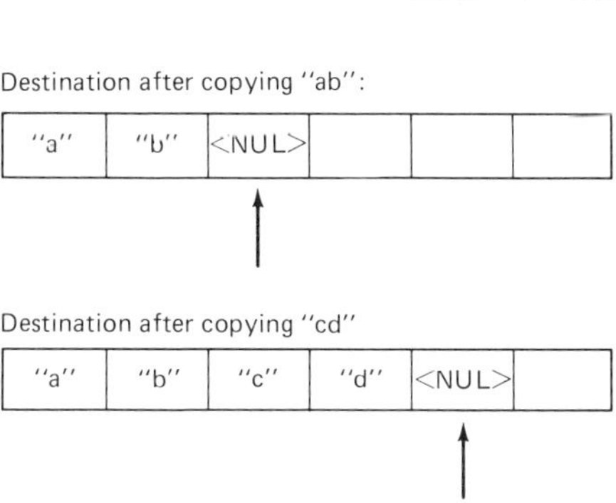

Figure 11-4 String pointer used as starting point for second copy operation

The algorithm for comparing two ⟨NUL⟩-delimited strings is really very simple:

1. Scan along the two strings until encountering a pair of characters that are different or until the end of either string is reached.
2. If the current pair of characters are equal, we can conclude that the two characters must both be ⟨NUL⟩ and that the strings are equal.
3. If the two characters are not equal, then the lesser string is the one with the character code that is less. We can exploit the fact that the character code for ⟨NUL⟩ is less than the code for any of the other characters when making this comparison. This gets us past the case of being at the end of one string but not the other.

Our string comparison procedure is STRCMPR. It expects pointers to two strings by value on the R7 stack. STRCMPR returns a flag on the R7 stack, based on the relation between the two strings. A positive number indicates that the first string was greater than the second. A negative number means that the first string was less than the second. The value 0 means that the two strings were equal.

```
** STRCMPR - COMPARE TWO STRINGS FOR EQUALITY
*
*           INPUT
*                R7 STACK - POINTER TO 2ND STRING (TOP)
*                         - POINTER TO 1ST STRING
*
*           OUTPUT
*                R7 STACK - (-) IF 1ST < 2ND
*                            0  IF 1ST = 2ND
*                           (+) IF 1ST > 2ND
*
*           CONSTANTS
*                NUL      - CHARACTER CODE 0
*                         -- USED AS END OF STRING MARKER
*
STRCMPR     PUSH     R7,R2           save registers
            PUSH     R7,R1
            PUSH     R7,R0

            LOAD     R0,5(R7)        pointer to 1st str
            LOAD     R1,4(R7)        pointer to 2nd str

STCNEXT     POP      R0,R2           char from 1st str
            CMPR     R2,@R1          different than 2nd str?
            BRNE     STCOUT          yes -- break out of loop
```

```
        CMPR    R2,=NUL         at end of str?
        BREQ    STROUT          yes -- break out of loop
        ADD     R1,=1           increment 2nd str ptr
        BR      STCNEXT         repeat for next chr

STCOUT  SUB     R2,@R1          result is sign
        STORE   R2,5(R7)

        POP     R7,R0           restore registers
        POP     R7,R1
        POP     R7,R2
        POP     R7,1(R7)        adjust return address
        RTN     R7,
```

It may seem wrong at first that only characters from the first string are tested against ⟨NUL⟩ as part of the loop condition. However, we can show that this test is sufficient. The other part tests for inequality and catches three of the four possible conditions:

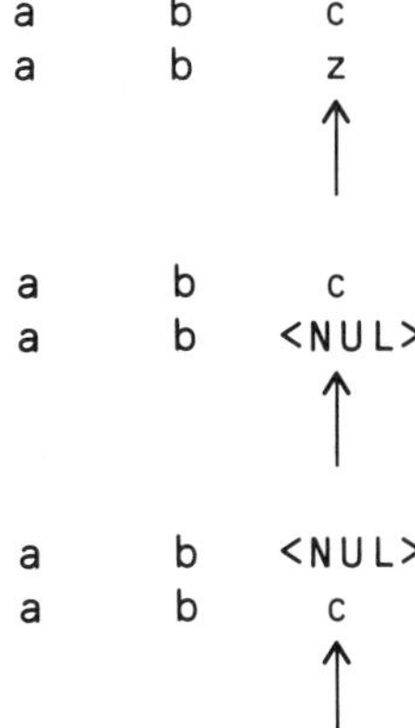

All three cases have character pairs that are unequal. In fact, the only case *not* caught by the inequality test is that of two identical strings!

```
a   b   <NUL>
a   b   <NUL>
          ↑
```

To detect this, we need only check one of the two characters. The other possibilities are already taken care of.

11.3.6 Converting a String to a Number

Information comes into our machine from a device like a keyboard in the form of characters. To interpret a string of characters as a number requires a routine that can scan the string and convert it to an equivalent representation in our internal binary format. For example, we would like to convert the string "497" into binary format as

```
00 000 000 000 000 000 000 000 111 110 001
```

The problem is really not as difficult as it first appears. Consider the simpler problem of converting a single character digit "6" into its equivalent binary form. The ASCII code for the digit "6" is 54 in decimal. The code for "0" is 48. To convert "6" to binary, simply subtract "0". That is,

$$\text{"6"} - \text{"0"} = 54 - 48 = 6$$

This same idea can be applied repeatedly by keeping a partial sum in much the same way as we did earlier with floating-point numbers. This time, though, we multiply the partial sum by 10 to make room for the next *decimal* digit. Here is how "497" would be converted to the number 497:

Partial sum	Operation
0	initial partial sum
4	(0 * 10) + 10 ("4" – "0")
49	(4 * 10) + ("9" – "0")
497	(49 * 10) + ("7" – "0")

We would also like to convert strings that represent negative numbers. This can be done by remembering the sign, converting the magnitude, then changing the sign if the input string represents a negative number.

A routine that converts a string of characters to a number could be used to help interpret a line of input that contains both text and numbers. When a compiler reads an assignment statement like

```
X := 497;
```

it begins by taking the statement apart into its component parts. First, it recognizes the variable name *X*, then the assignment operator :=, and finally encounters the digit 4. At this point, the routine that converts a string to a number is called. The routine performs the conversion just described and returns the number 497 as a result.

In addition to returning the number, it would be convenient if the routine gave some indication of where in the string it stopped scanning for a number. We will design our string-to-number converter to return *two* results. The first is the number itself. The second is a new pointer to the first character following the last digit in the number. We are guaranteed that there is at least one ⟨NUL⟩ following the last digit, so there is never a chance of stepping past the end of the string.

As a final item, we will find it useful to have the routine skip over any leading spaces it may encounter. We can use SKIPSP to handle this part. Here is an algorithm for converting a string of digits to a number:

1. [Initialization]: Set the partial sum to 0 and skip over any leading spaces.
2. [Record sign]: Save a flag for the sign of the result. If the string has a leading sign, skip to the next character before starting conversion.
3. [Convert next digit]: If the character is a digit, multiply the partial sum by 10 and add in the numeric value of the digit; get the next character and repeat this step.
4. [Apply sign]: If the sign was negative, make the result negative.

We will pass a pointer to the string by value on the R7 stack. The result and the updated pointer are returned on the R7 stack. On the top of the stack is the result, with the new pointer directly beneath it. Our string-to-number conversion routine is CVTNUM:

```
** CVTNUM - CONVERT A STRING OF DIGITS TO A NUMBER
*
*         INPUT
*              R7 STACK - POINTER TO STRING (VALUE)
*
*         OUTPUT
*              R7 STACK - NUMBER (TOP)
*                         UPDATED POINTER
*         PROCEDURES
*              SKIPSP     - SKIPS OVER LEADING BLANKS
*
*         CONSTANTS
*              DIGO       - CHARACTER CODE FOR "0"
*              MINUS      - CHARACTER CODE FOR "-"
*              NUL        - CHARACTER CODE 0
*                           -- USED AS END OF STRING MARKER
*              PLUS       - CHARACTER CODE FOR "+"
*              SP         - CHARACTER CODE FOR SPACE
*
CVTNUM    PUSH      R7,0(R7)       make room for 2nd result
          PUSH      R7,R2          save registers
          PUSH      R7,R1
          PUSH      R7,R0

* initialize sum and skip leading spaces
          LOAD      R1,=0          set partial sum to 0
          LOAD      R0,5(R7)       fetch string ptr
```

```
            PUSH     R7,R0          push as parameter
            CALL     R7,SKIPSP      skip over leading spaces
            POP      R7,R0          init ptr to string
            POP      R0,R2          fetch next char in string
* handle sign of number
            PUSH     R7,R2          save as sign flag
            CMPR     R2,=PLUS       if char is "+"
            BREQ     CVNNXT         -- skip to next char
            CMPR     R2,=MINUS      if char is "-"
            BREQ     CVNNXT         -- skip to next char

* convert each digit in number
CVNDIG      SUB      R2,=DIG0       convert digit to number
            BRLT     CVNOUT         break from loop if too small
            CMPR     R2,=9
            BRGT     CVNOUT         break from loop if too big
            MUL      R1,=10         shift left one decimal place
            ADD      R1,R2          ... and add in next digit

CVNNXT      POP      R0,R2          fetch next digit in string
            BR       CVNDIG         repeat for next digit

* adjust sign of result
CVNOUT      POP      R7,R2          get sign flag
            CMPR     R2,=MINUS      if not negative
            BRNE     *+2            ... then value ok
            MUL      R1,=-1         else change sign first

            STORE    R1,4(R7)       return converted number
            SUB      R0,=1          back up one pos
            STORE    R0,5(R7)       return updated pointer
            POP      R7,R0          restore registers
            POP      R7,R1
            POP      R7,R2
            RTN      R7,
```

Since we must reserve an extra location on the R7 stack, a second copy of the return address is pushed upon entry. The location occupied by the old copy is overwritten by the converted number on return, as shown in Figure 11-5.

The simplest indication of whether the first character is a minus sign is to save a copy of the character itself. It is used at the end to make the result negative if necessary. If there is either a positive or a negative sign at the beginning of the number, the string pointer is advanced to the next character before entering the conversion loop.

Returning the new pointer on the stack just below the result has an added benefit. After the number is popped from the stack on return, the new pointer is at the top of the stack, ready for another call to CVTNUM. This is especially handy if the string

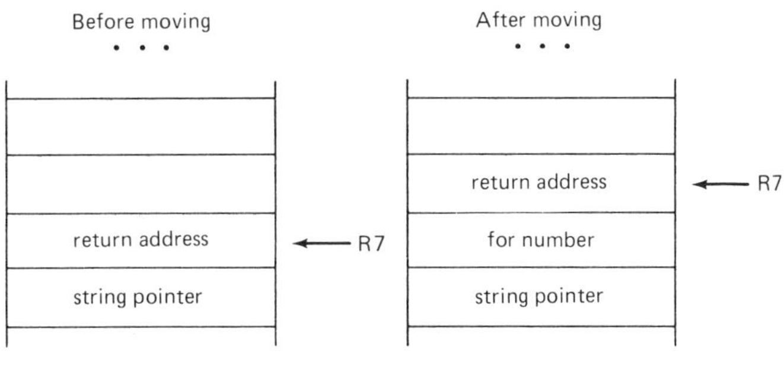

Figure 11-5 Return address adjusted upon entry to CVTNUM

represents a list of numbers separated by one or more spaces. If we knew that a string contained three numbers, we could convert all three very easily:

```
PUSH    R7,=STRING          push string pointer
CALL    R7,CVTNUM           convert first number
POP     R7,NUM1             ... and save result
CALL    R7,CVTNUM           convert second number
POP     R7,NUM2             ... and save result
CALL    R7,CVTNUM           convert third number
POP     R7,NUM3             ... and save result
```

11.3.7 Converting a Number to a String

To display our results, we must also be able to convert numbers from their internal binary form into strings. The process is pretty much the reverse of converting a string to a number. At each step, we extract the least significant decimal digit from the number. The digit is converted to character form, and the number is shifted right by a decimal place. Here is how the number 497 from the previous section would be converted back to a character string:

String	Operation
""	initial string
"7"	(497 mod 10) + "0"
"97"	(49 mod 10) + "0"
"497"	(4 mod 10) + "0"

The process stops when the number becomes zero after shifting it by a decimal place.

We have used the "mod" or remainder function in various examples throughout the text. It is defined as

$$a \bmod b = a - (a \operatorname{div} b) * b \quad (b > 0)$$

where "div" indicates integer division. The function is used here to extract the lower decimal digit from a partial difference.

One drawback to this algorithm is that the digits are generated in reverse order from the way we would like to have them in the string array. A simple way to solve this problem is to push the characters onto the R7 stack as they are generated. When the number finally reaches 0, we can pop them off the stack in forward order into the string array. It is convenient to push ⟨NUL⟩ onto the stack before starting the conversion. To convert a negative number, we simply process its absolute value and store a minus sign as the first character in the string array.

Here is the algorithm for converting a number into a character string:

1. [Initialization]: Push ⟨NUL⟩ onto the R7 stack. If the number is negative, store a minus sign into the string array and take the absolute value of the number.
2. [Extract digit]: Extract the lower decimal digit from the number. Convert it to a character and push it onto the stack.
3. [Shift number]: Shift the number right one decimal place. If it is nonzero, repeat at step 2.
4. [Copy string]: Pop the characters from the R7 stack into the string array, up to and including the ⟨NUL⟩ character.

Our procedure is CVTSTR. It expects a number and a pointer to a string array by value on the R7 stack. The number is converted to a string and stored in the string array. The procedure returns a pointer on R7 that points to the ⟨NUL⟩ character in the array. This is the same way we handled the destination pointer in STRCOPY. Here is an implementation of CVTSTR:

```
** CVTSTR - CONVERT A NUMBER TO A STRING OF DIGITS
*
*         INPUT (VALUE)
*              R7 STACK - NUMBER TO CONVERT (TOP)
*                         POINTER TO SPACE FOR RESULT STRING
*
*         OUTPUT
*              R7 STACK - UPDATED POINTER TO <NUL> CHARACTER
*                         IN RESULT STRING
*
*         CONSTANTS
*              DIGO   - CHARACTER CODE FOR "0"
*              MINUS  - CHARACTER CODE FOR "-"
*              NUL    - CHARACTER CODE 0
*                     -- USED AS END OF STRING MARKER
*
CVTSTR    PUSH    R7,R3          save registers
          PUSH    R7,R2
          PUSH    R7,R1
```

```
          PUSH    R7,R0

          LOAD    R0,6(R7)      pointer to result string
          LOAD    R1,5(R7)      number to convert
          PUSH    R7,=NUL       mark end of string on stk

* handle negative number
          CMPR    R1,=0         is number non-negative?
          BRGE    CVSDIG        yes -- branch to convert
          MUL     R1,=-1        else change sign of number
          LOAD    R2,=MINUS     put "-" in result string
          STORE   R2,@R0
          ADD     R0,=1


* convert each digit in number
CVSDIG    LOAD    R2,R1         copy number
          LOAD    R3,R1         get lower digit of number
          DIV     R3,=10
          MUL     R3,=10
          SUB     R2,R3
          ADD     R2,=DIG0      convert digit to char
          PUSH    R7,R2         ... and stack it
          DIV     R1,=10        update number
          BRGT    CVSDIG        repeat if more digits

* copy chars to output buffer
CVSCPY    POP     R7,R1         copy next char to string
          STORE   R1,@R0
          CMPR    R1,=NUL       end of string?
          BREQ    CVSOUT        yes -- break out of loop
          ADD     R0,=1         else increment string ptr
          BR      CVSCPY        repeat for next char

CVSOUT    STORE   R0,6(R7)      return new ptr.
          POP     R7,R0         restore registers
          POP     R7,R1
          POP     R7,R2
          POP     R7,R3
          POP     R7,1(R7)      adjust return address
          RTN     R7,
```

11.3.8 Packing a String

We discussed earlier the idea of using packed strings as a means of saving space. A packed string of characters on this machine is four times as compact as our normal unpacked string. This section presents a procedure that copies an unpacked string into a packed one. Recall that a packed string has characters adjusted left in the word, with excess character positions in the final word filled with zeros (⟨NUL⟩).

The algorithm for packing a string is really very simple:

1. [Get next character]: Fetch the next character from the unpacked string.
2. [Insert in word]: Insert the new character in its correct position in the current packed word.
3. [Check for string end]: If at the end of the unpacked string, exit the algorithm.
4. [Check for full]: If the current packed word is full, start a new packed word. In any case, repeat at step 1.

A shift count can be used to shift the current character left into its position in the current packed word. The initial value of the count should be 24, the difference between the word size and the number of bytes in a character. This shift count can also be used to determine whether there is any more room left in the current packed word. Here is an implementation of STRPAK. It expects two string pointers on the R7 stack. STRPAK does not return a result.

```
** STRPAK - COPY AN UNPACKED STRING INTO A PACKED STRING
*
*         INPUT (VALUE)
*             R7 STACK - POINTER TO SOURCE STRING (TOP)
*                        POINTER TO SPACE FOR DEST. STRING
*
*         OUTPUT
*             NONE
*
*         CONSTANTS
*             NUL     - CHARACTER CODE 0
*                       -- USED AS END OF STRING MARKER
*
STRPAK   PUSH    R7,R4        save registers
         PUSH    R7,R3
         PUSH    R7,R2
         PUSH    R7,R1
         PUSH    R7,R0
         LOAD    R0,6(R7)     ptr to source str
         LOAD    R1,7(R7)     ptr to dest str

STPNXT   LOAD    R3,=24       shift count
         LOAD    R2,=0        temp for packing

STPCHR   POP     R0,R4        fetch next char
         LSH     R4,R3        shift left to position
         OR      R2,R4        insert char in word
         CMPR    R4,=NUL      end of string?
```

```
         BREQ    STPOUT       yes -- break out of loop
         SUB     R3,=8        else decrement shift count
         BRGE    STPCHR       repeat if more room in word

         STORE   R2,@R1       save packed word
         ADD     R1,=1        increment result ptr.
         BR      STPNXT       repeat for next word

STPOUT   STORE   R2,@R1       save last packed word
         POP     R7,R0        restore registers
         POP     R7,R1
         POP     R7,R2
         POP     R7,R3
         POP     R7,R4
         POP     R7,2(R7)     discard both params
         ADD     R7,=1        adjust stack ptr one more
         RTN     R7,
```

11.3.9 Unpacking a String

The inverse function copies a packed string into an unpacked string, with one character in the lower end of each word and zero filled from the left. Here is an algorithm for unpacking a packed string:

1. [Get next word]: Fetch the next word from the packed string.
2. [Extract next character]: Extract the next character from the packed word and store it in the unpacked string.
3. [Check for string end]: If at the end of the packed string, exit the algorithm.
4. [Check for empty word]: If the current packed word is empty, repeat for next word at step 1. Otherwise, repeat for next character at step 2.

A shift count can again be used to shift the current character. This time, though, the packed word is shifted right so that the current character is in the bottom of the word. The character is then masked and inserted in the unpacked string. Here is an implementation of STRUPK. It expects two string pointers on the R7 stack. STRUPK does not return a result.

```
** STRUPK - COPY A PACKED STRING INTO AN UNPACKED STRING
*
*        INPUT (VALUE)
*             R7 STACK - POINTER TO SOURCE STRING (TOP)
*                      - POINTER TO SPACE FOR DEST. STRING
*
*        OUTPUT
*             NONE
*
```

```
*          CONSTANTS
*              NUL     - CHARACTER CODE 0
*                        -- USED AS END OF STRING MARKER
*
STRUPK     PUSH    R7,R4         save registers
           PUSH    R7,R3
           PUSH    R7,R2
           PUSH    R7,R1
           PUSH    R7,R0
           LOAD    R0,6(R7)      ptr to source str
           LOAD    R1,7(R7)      ptr to dest str

STUNXT     LOAD    R3,=-24       shift count
           POP     R0,R2         packed word

STUCHR     LOAD    R4,R2         copy of word
           LSH     R4,R3         move char to bottom of word
           AND     R4,=377B      mask all but char in word.
           STORE   R4,@R1        save unpacked char
           CMPR    R4,=NUL       end of string?
           BREQ    STUOUT        yes -- break out of loop
           ADD     R1,=1         else increment unpacked ptr
           ADD     R3,=8         decrement shift count
           BRLE    STUCHR        repeat if more chars in word
           BR      STUNXT        else repeat for next word

STUOUT     POP     R7,R0         restore registers
           POP     R7,R1
           POP     R7,R2
           POP     R7,R3
           POP     R7,R4
           POP     R7,2(R7)      discard both params
           ADD     R7,=1         adjust stack ptr one more
           RTN     R7,
```

11.4 SUMMARY

In this chapter we have explored the idea of representing alphanumeric information on our machine. A number of character representations are available, depending on the application. These range from simple numeric character encodings to full alphanumeric codes.

Characters are usually manipulated in groups called strings. We considered several representations. The first was as an unpacked array of characters, with only one character per word. The other was as a packed array of characters, with up to four characters packed into each word of the array. The trade-off in deciding which representation to use must consider the ease of accessing the unpacked form against the storage efficiency of the packed representation. Two methods were also presented for delimiting the string. The first kept separate size information to indicate how many characters are in the string. The other placed a sentinel at the end of the string.

The final part of the chapter presented a number of useful string manipulation routines. They were written assuming an unpacked string, delimited by character ⟨NUL⟩ as a sentinel. We will make use of many of these string routines as we turn our attention to the subject of input/output programming in Chapter 12.

PROBLEMS

11-1. What does BCD mean? What kind of characters can be represented using a BCD encoding. What is special about the form called NBCD?

11-2. Show how the number 4938 would be represented in NBCD.

11-3. What is the meaning of the NBCD code

```
1000 0001 1001 0111 0101
```

11-4. What is wrong with the NBCD code

```
0010 1110 0110 1001 0011
```

11-5. What is the purpose of limited alphanumeric codes? What can these kinds of codes usually represent that cannot be represented using a BCD code?

11-6. Using the CCITT No. 2 code shown in the chapter, show how to represent the message

```
VOL. 8, NO. 5 (MAY 1976)
```

11-7. The CCITT No. 2 code can represent many more characters than the 32 allowed for by its 5 bits. How is this done? How are very frequently used symbols handled to minimize the number of characters in a message?

11-8. What kind of characters can be represented by full alphanumeric codes that could not be expressed in either limited alphanumeric or BCD codes?

11-9. How many bits are usually used to store a full alphanumeric character code? What is this unit of storage called?

11-10. What is the meaning of the acronym EBCDIC? By whom was the EBCDIC code developed, and for what purpose?

11-11. Give the EBCDIC encoding of the message

```
The EBCDIC (8-bit) code
```

11-12. Who developed the ASCII character code?

11-13. Give the 7-bit ASCII encoding of the message

```
The ASCII (7-bit) code
```

11-14. Give the ASCII-8 encoding of the message

```
The ASCII (8-bit) code
```

11-15. What is a string? How did the name evolve?

11-16. Show the representation of the following string as an array of ASCII characters. The quotes merely delimit the string and are not part of it.

```
"an array of characters"
```

11-17. Show the representation of the following strings as *packed* arrays of characters:

(a) "x" **(b)** "house"
(c) "Mississippi" **(d)** "It is 10:15 p.m."
(e) "5-4-3-2-1 liftoff!"

11-18. What is the advantage of representing a string as an array of characters? What is the drawback?

11-19. What is the advantage of representing a string as a packed array of characters? What is the drawback?

11-20. If a string represented as a packed array of characters is delimited by its length, why is it better to let the length represent the number of *characters* in the string rather than the number of *words* taken up by the string?

11-21. Assume a string represented by an array of characters, with the length of the string as the first word of the array. Write a procedure SUBSTR that extracts a substring of the input string. SUBSTR has four parameters, passed by reference in a parameter list. The first is the input string, the second is a result parameter for the substring, the third is the starting character position in the string, and the fourth is the final character position. The first character position in the string, not including the length, is position 1. If the starting position is less than 1, use 1 instead. If the ending position is greater than the length of the input string, use the length of the input string instead. If the ending position is less than the starting position, the result is the null string (a string of length 0).

11-22. Repeat Problem 11-21 with a *packed* array of characters.

11-23. What is the advantage of keeping a separate string descriptor instead of embedding the length information in the string?

11-24. Repeat Problem 11-17 with the strings represented as sentinel-delimited arrays of characters.

11-25. Repeat Problem 11-17 with the strings represented as sentinel-delimited *packed* arrays of characters.

11-26. It would be useful to generalize the string index routine STRINDX to find the index of a string instead of just a character within another string. for example, the index of "sip" in the string "Mississippi" is 7. Finding this would be difficult using the simple version of STRINDX described in this chapter. This new version of STRINDX expects the subject string and pattern string by reference on the return stack and returns the index of the pattern string in the subject string on the return stack. STRINDX returns the value 0 if the pattern string was not found in the subject string.

11-27. A more general version of SKIPBL is provided in languages that support operations on strings. The SNOBOL4 language provides a facility called SPAN, which skips over all leading characters in a subject string that are found in a pattern string. Here is an example in a more conventional syntax:

```
SPAN ("hello there", "abcdefghijklmnopqrstuvwxyz")
```

The string pointer would be advanced to the blank after the word "hello". Write a version of SPAN that expects the subject string and pattern string by reference on the return stack. SPAN returns a pointer on the return stack to the first character in the subject string that is not in the pattern string.

11-28. SNOBOL4 also provides a facility called BREAK, which skips over all leading characters in a subject string that are not found in a pattern string. Here is an example in a more conventional syntax:

```
BREAK ("The time is 2:00 p.m.", "0123456789")
```

The string pointer would be advanced to the "2". Write a version of BREAK that expects the subject string and pattern string by reference on the return stack. BREAK returns a pointer on the return stack to the first character in the subject string that is in the pattern string. Given the null string as the pattern, where in the subject string should the pointer returned by BREAK point?

11-29. Write a procedure STRCAT that concatenates two strings. For example, given the two strings "Bah, " and "humbug!", STRCAT would return the string "Bah, humbug!". STRCAT expects three parameters. The first is a pointer to space for the result. The other two are pointers to the two strings being concatenated. STRCAT returns a pointer to the first character in the result string.

11-30. As written, STRCOPY works correctly as long as the destination pointer is less than the source pointer. This is because characters are copied starting at the beginning of the string. However, STRCOPY does not always work correctly if the destination pointer is greater than the source pointer. Suppose that S is the 5-character-long string "abcde". What would happen if the following call were made on STRCOPY?

```
PUSH    R7,=S+1       destination string
PUSH    R7,=S         source string
CALL    R7,STRCOPY
```

11-31. Modify STRCOPY to work correctly, no matter whether the source pointer is greater or less than the destination pointer.

11-32. The version of CVTNUM in this chapter does not check to see whether the string it is converting represents a number that is too large for the word size. Modify CVTNUM to check for overflow. What should it do if overflow is detected?

11-33. The assemblers for the two machines presented in this book accept numbers in either base 10 or base 8. A number in base 8 is followed by the letter *B* and of course cannot contain the digits 8 and 9. Modify CVTNUM to accept either a decimal or an octal number in this form.

11-34. Write a routine CVTSTRB that converts a number to a string that represents the number in base 8. For example, the number 489 would result in the string "751B". The routine has the same parameters as CVTSTR.

11-35. A difficulty with the method we use to represent octal constants is that the *B* is at the end of the string and must be sought out before starting the conversion. Another common representation precedes the number with a character that represents its base. For example,

B111101001	binary	(base 2)
O771	octal	(base 8)
D489	decimal	(base 10)

Write a version of CVTNUM that accepts a string representing either a normal number or one preceded by a radix or base indicator as shown.

11-36. Base 16 is often more convenient to use than base 8. The digits in the *hexadecimal* number system go from 0 to 15. The letters *A* through *F* stand for 10 through 15, respectively. Hexadecimal is convenient because each hexadecimal digit corresponds to 4 bits. Thus a word can be represented with only 8 hexadecimal digits instead of 11 octal digits. Modify the version of CVTNUM described in Problem 11-35 to accept hexadecimal constants as well. The hexadecimal constant corresponding to the ones shown in that problem is H1E9.

11-37. A routine to convert a string to a floating-point number would be useful in conjunction with the floating-point routines described in Chapter 10. A floating-point number has the general form

```
[+]                            [+]
[-] <number >[. [<number>]] [E [-] <number>]
```

The general form corresponds to a number in scientific notation. The items in brackets indicate optional parts, and ⟨number⟩ is one or more digits. Here is an algorithm to convert a string to a floating-point number:

1. [Initialization]: Record the sign of the mantissa. Set the mantissa and exponent to 0.
2. [Convert the whole part]: Begin building the mantissa by converting the whole part of the number. If the mantissa exceeds 23 bits of precision, stop with that character; step past the characters following up to either the decimal point or *E*, whichever comes first, and increment the exponent once for each character skipped.
3. [Convert the fractional part]: If the next character is a decimal point then while the mantissa does not exceed 23 digits of precision, continue converting digits for the

mantissa, decrementing the exponent once for each digit converted after the decimal point. Finally, apply the sign of the mantissa to the mantissa.

4. [Convert the exponent part]: Step past any digits remaining. If the next character is *E*, convert the number following and add it to the exponent.
5. [Pack the number]: Call PACK with the mantissa and exponent from the preceding steps.

Write the routine CVTFLOAT to convert a string to a floating-point number. The procedure expects a string pointer on the return stack and returns the floating-point number on the return stack.

12

Input and Output

The addition of input/output hardware to this new machine allows it to communicate in ways other than through the switch register on the front panel display. In this chapter we will look at the input/output hardware in some detail, as well as the new CPU instructions that control it. We will also design a set of procedures that make I/O operations easier to perform.

12.1 INPUT/OUTPUT HARDWARE

In the following sections we examine the various components of the input/output hardware, to learn how they function separately and how they work together.

12.1.1 How Input/Output Devices Represent Data

Input/output devices read or write data in one of two ways. Data are either in the same form as their internal representation or in the form of characters. The form depends to a great extent on the type of device involved.

Data that correspond to their internal representation are called *binary* data. Devices that represent data in binary form are usually involved in archival storage of information taken directly from memory. An example might be a program saved on a magnetic tape or disk for later execution.

The other form handled by an I/O device is *character* data. Numeric data that is encoded as characters can be manipulated without special knowledge of a particular machine's internal data representations. For this reason, numeric data meant to be transferred from one machine to another is usually encoded in character form. The penalty is that character-encoded data usually take up more space than the equivalent binary or internal form.

For a printer to print the number 345, it must be sent the characters 3, 4, and 5 in turn. Each character code causes a print mechanism to print the corresponding character. The problem, then, is to encode information as characters and transmit those characters to the printer or other output device. For an input device like a keyboard, the problem is just the opposite. The device must generate a character code that corresponds to the key just pressed and transmit the code back to the CPU for processing. We will look at this process next.

12.1.2 Device Controllers

Our machine can have many kinds of input/output devices attached to it, including keyboards, printers, video displays, and disks. Each requires its own specialized connections, commands, and signals to make it operate correctly. Connecting devices with so many different requirements directly to our machine would be difficult. Instead, each device comes with its own separate interface called a *device controller.*

The purpose of a device controller is to provide a more uniform way of controlling different pieces of equipment connected to the machine. A device controller accepts a set of commands appropriate to its device type and translates them to the specialized signals for a particular piece of hardware.

In addition to translating commands, the device controller includes some memory of its own. This memory is used to accumulate or *buffer* a quantity of information read from or written to the device. Many kinds of equipment are capable of transferring only a fixed block of information. A card reader, for example, may be able to transfer no less than a card's worth of data at a time. The smallest block of data that a device can transfer at one time is called a *record*. The size of the record is characteristic of that device. Memory in a device controller buffers records while they are being transferred to or from the device. Figure 12-1 illustrates a device controller.

A device controller sends and receives information over three lines. Two of these are the command and data lines. Together, they specify what action a controller takes. There are four possible device controller commands:

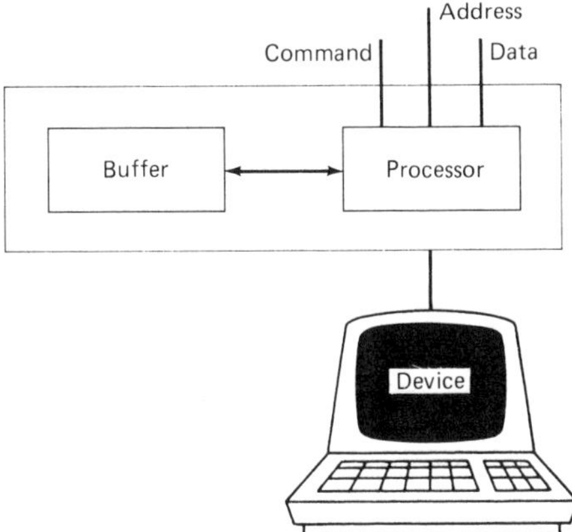

Figure 12-1 Block diagram of a device controller

- Input data
- Output data
- Return I/O status
- Execute I/O command

The first command causes the device controller to return the next item from its buffer over the data line. There may be some delay in responding to this command if the buffer is empty, because the controller must first read the next record from its device before it can return the next piece of information.

The second command does just the opposite. It tells the controller to place the information on the data line into its buffer. If the buffer is full, there may again be a delay while the controller writes a record to its device.

As a result of an I/O status request, the controller returns information about the device state over the data line. This includes whether the device is currently busy or idle. There may be other status information, depending on the nature of the device. A printer may signal an error if it runs out of paper. This error could be included in the status.

A particular piece of equipment may require certain commands in addition to reading or writing data. For example, a tape drive must be able to rewind and to space forward or backward some number of records. The purpose of the I/O command is to provide a way of issuing special commands to a device controller. The actual command is sent over the data line.

The third line into a device controller is the address line. As we shall see, this line determines whether or not the controller executes a command. Each device controller is identified by a unique *device address*. If the address on the address line matches the address of the device controller, the controller executes the command. Otherwise, the command is ignored. The reason for this line will become clear shortly.

12.1.3 I/O Bus

Device controllers are connected together along what is known as an *I/O bus*. It is similar to the memory bus used to interconnect the MU and CPU. Devices connected to the I/O bus have their own unique device address in the same way that each location in memory has a unique memory address. Figure 12-2 provides an illustration of devices connected to the I/O bus.

To communicate with one of the controllers, the appropriate information is put on the command and data lines of the I/O bus, and the address of the controller is sent along on the address line. Even though the command is broadcast to all devices connected along the bus, only the controller referred to by the address executes the command. The other controllers ignore the command because their addresses do not match the one on the address line.

A command has four possible values. A 2-bit-wide command line allows for just this many. The data line is 8 bits wide and can accommodate up to an 8-bit alpha-

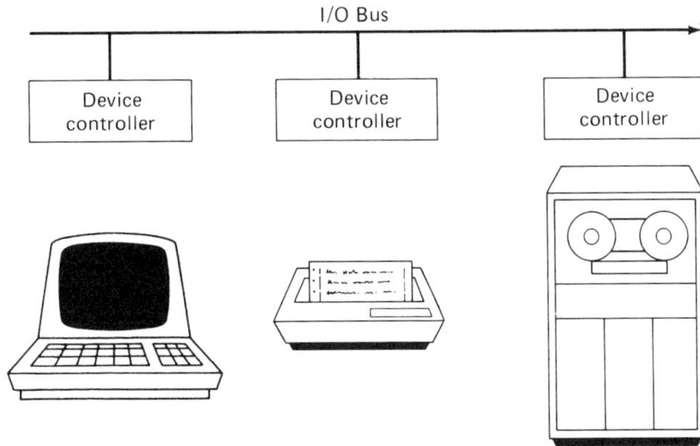

Figure 12-2 Devices connected to the I/O bus

numeric character code. If we want to transmit words of data over the data line, each word must be broken up into 4 bytes and sent serially, one byte after another. The address line must be wide enough to address as many devices as we care to connect to the I/O bus. An 8-bit address line allows us to reference up to 256 I/O devices.

12.1.4 Input/Output Unit (IOU)

Communicating with a device on the I/O bus requires a number of extra steps to actually establish and maintain contact with a device controller. Also, exceptional conditions that require special treatment can arise. Among these is the need to detect when the device addressed is either not connected or cannot respond to a command.

The *input/output unit (IOU)* interfaces the CPU and the device controllers connected along the I/O bus. The IOU serves as the *bus controller*, taking care of the extra overhead needed to establish and maintain communication with device controllers on the I/O bus. The IOU also handles exceptional conditions. Figure 12-3 provides a diagram of how the IOU interfaces the I/O bus to the CPU.

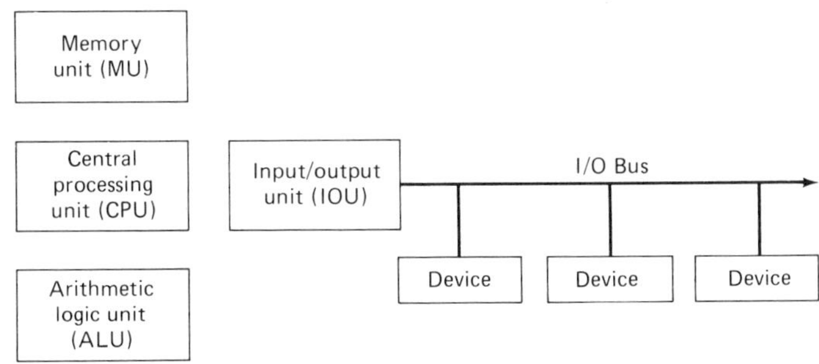

Figure 12-3 The input/output unit interfaces to the I/O bus to the CPU

12.2 I/O INSTRUCTIONS

The IOU is connected to the MBR and MAR in the same way as the MU. The IOU connects the address lines of the I/O bus to MAR⟨7:0⟩, the lower 8 bits of the MAR. The I/O bus data lines are connected to MBR⟨7:0⟩, the lower byte of the MBR. Four new internal operations can now take place:

```
MBR  ←  I/O_Data[ MAR ]          (bits 31-8 are set to 0)
I/O_Data[ MAR ]  ←  MBR<7:0>
MBR  ←  I/O_Stat[ MAR ]          (bits 31-8 are set to 0)
I/O_Cmd[ MAR ]  ←  MBR<0:7>
```

These operations correspond to the four commands understood by the device controllers:

- Input data
- Output data
- Return I/O status
- Execute I/O command

When either a character or I/O status is input by the CPU, it is placed in the lower 8 bits of the MBR. The upper 24 bits are set to zero. A character or I/O command output to the IOU is taken from the lower 8 bits of the MBR. Characters in the upper 24 bits are ignored, because the data line is only 8 bits wide. In the same way, I/O device address are taken from the lower 8 bits of the MAR in all cases.

Our machine has four I/O instructions that use these four new internal operations.

12.2.1 Input Character (INCHR)

This instruction places the next input character into the lower byte (8 bits) of a CPU register. The upper 24 bits of the register are set to zero. As an example,

```
INCHR    R0,=3            input char from device 3
```

has the following effect:

```
{MBR  ←  M[MAR]; MAR  ←  MBR}
MBR  ←  I/O_Data[MAR]
Ri  ←  MBR
CMPR  ←  Ri ? 0
```

or simply

```
Ri  ⟵  I/O_Data[ MAR ]
```

If the device number was stored in memory at location DEVNUM, we would instead write

```
INCHR   R0,DEVNUM
```

12.2.2 Output Character (OUTCHR)

This instruction outputs the lower byte (8 bits) of a CPU register. The upper 24 bits of the register are ignored. As an example,

```
OUTCHR   R0,=3                output char to device 3
```

has the following effect:

```
{MBR  ⟵  M[MAR]; MAR  ⟵  MBR}
MBR  ⟵  Ri
I/O_Data[MAR]  ⟵  MBR<7:0>
```

or simply

```
I/O_Data[ MAR ]  ⟵  Ri<7:0>
```

12.2.3 Input/Output Status (IOSTAT)

This instruction places device status information into the lower byte (8 bits) of a CPU register. The upper 24 bits of the register are set to zero. As an example,

```
IOSTAT  R0,=3                check status of device 3
```

has the following effect:

```
{MBR  ⟵  M[MAR]; MAR  ⟵  MBR}
MBR  ⟵  I/O_Stat[MAR]
Ri  ⟵  MBR
CMPR  ⟵  Ri ? 0
```

or simply

```
Ri  ⟵  I/O_Stat[MAR]
```

Status information is encoded in one or more bits of the status byte returned. The specific meaning of this information depends somewhat on the particular device.

12.2.4 Input/Output Command (IOCMD)

This instruction outputs a command in the lower byte (8 bits) of a CPU register to the device indicated. The upper 24 bits of the register are ignored. As an example,

```
IOCMD    R0,=3      output command to device 3
```

has the following effect:

```
{MBR  ←  M[MAR]; MAR  ←  MBR}
MBR  ←  Ri
I/O_Cmd[MAR]  ←  MBR<7:0>
```

or simply

```
I/O_Cmd[ MAR ]  ←  Ri<7:0>
```

Command information is encoded in one or more bits of the byte output. The specific meaning of this information depends somewhat on the particular device.

12.2.5 Using Input/Output Instructions

We will agree to reserve the first three I/O address for a keyboard, a video display, and a printer. Each of these is a separate I/O device, even though they are often found packaged together as a display or printing terminal. To distinguish the three devices from other keyboards, displays, or printers that may be connected, we will refer to them as the *system* I/O devices. The system keyboard is at device code 0, the display is at device code 1, and the printer is at device code 2. For the sake of convenience, we will agree to use mnemonic names for these three devices:

```
SYSKBD    EQU    0    device code of system keyboard
SYSDPY    EQU    1    device code of system display
SYSPRT    EQU    2    device code of system printer
```

All three are not necessarily connected on a particular machine. We simply agree that no other devices will be identified by these I/O addresses.

An input device like a keyboard is said to be *idle* if there are no characters in its device controller's buffer ready to be read. If we issue a read command to the device now, the CPU is forced to wait until a key on the keyboard is pressed. No processing can be done in the meantime. If we do not care to wait, we can request the status of the keyboard ahead of time. The lower bit in this word tells us whether or not there are keys waiting in the keyboard controller's buffer. If that bit is 0, the keyboard is idle, and no characters are waiting. We are free to do something else for a while.

Once a key is pressed, the character code for the key is placed in the keyboard controller's buffer. The keyboard is now said to be *busy.* If we request the status now, we will find that the lower bit is set to 1, indicating that a character is ready to be input. At this point, we can issue an INCHR instruction. The character is removed from the keyboard controller's buffer and sent over the I/O bus to the lower 8 bits of the MBR. The upper 24 bits are set to 0.

Processing input from a keyboard, then, can be characterized in the following way:

1. {Wait for keyboard status to become busy.}
2. Read character from the keyboard controller.
3. Process character.
4. Repeat for next character at step 1.

An output device like a video display is busy when it can no longer accept characters to place in its buffer. If we issue a write command to the device now, the CPU is forced to wait until the device controller is ready to accept another character for output. This usually means waiting until there is room in the display controller's buffer to place another character for output. No processing can be done in the meantime. If we would rather not wait, we can request the status of the display first. The lower bit in this word tells us whether or not the display controller can accept another character. If that bit is 1, the display controller is busy and cannot accept another output character.

Whenever the display is ready, its device controller removes the next character from its buffer and sends it to the display. If we request the display status now, we will find that the display is idle and that the lower bit of the status is set to 0. At this point, we can execute an OUTCHR instruction. The character is sent over the I/O bus to the video display controller and placed in its output buffer. Only the lower 8 bits of the MBR are sent over the data line. The upper 24 bits are ignored.

Output to a device like a video display can be characterized in the following way:

1. Prepare character for output.
2. {Wait for display status to become idle.}
3. Write character to display controller.
4. Repeat for next character at step 1.

12.3 A SIMPLE EXAMPLE

Here is a simple program that reads keys from the keyboard and *echoes* them to the system display. Echoing characters from the keyboard is not done automatically in hardware. This must be done by a program interacting with the two devices. Since there is nothing else to do while waiting for the keyboard and display, there is no need to check the status before executing an INCHR or OUTCHR instruction. The CPU will wait if a device lags behind. This program runs forever, so it must be stopped by pressing the HALT button on the front panel:

```
NEXTCHR  INCHR    R0,=SYSKBD   get key from the keyboard
         OUTCHR   R0,=SYSDPY   echo it to the display
         BR       NEXTCHR
```

The display device controller can continue writing characters from its buffer to the display, even if the CPU is waiting for a key from the keyboard. Both controllers are independent of the CPU and are delayed only when there is nothing else to do.

What happens if we make a mistake while typing characters at the keyboard? Most keyboards include a BACKSPACE key. Pressing this key generates character code 8 in the ASCII character set. This is one of the first 31 ASCII characters that are referred to as *control characters*. Control characters have a special meaning to some output devices, including displays and printers. The control characters are given mnemonic names for easier identification. Table 12-1 gives some of the more useful ones.

TABLE 12-1 SAMPLE CONTROL CHARACTERS

Mnemonic	Code	Purpose
BEL	7	rings bell or buzzer
BS	8	causes print head or cursor to move left one space
LF	10	advances paper one line on printer; moves display cursor to next line, same column
FF	12	causes printer to advance enough paper to place print head at top of new page
CR	13	moves print head or cursor to first column, same line
ESC	27	taken together with a character that follows, may signal a command to device

If the BACKSPACE key is pressed, INCHR reads the ⟨BS⟩ character from the keyboard controller. When it is echoed to the display, its controller moves the cursor left to position it over the previous character in the display. That character will be replaced in the display when the next character is sent:

```
□            cursor on screen

A □          output "A"
```

```
A  B  □        output "B"

A [B]          output <BS>

A  T  □        output "T"
```

We might want actually to erase the character that the cursor rests on when backspacing. To do this, we must issue a ⟨BS⟩, then ⟨SP⟩, then another ⟨BS⟩:

```
A  B  □        output "B"

A [B]          output <BS>

A     □        output <SP>

A  □           output <BS>

A  T  □        output "T"
```

Moving the cursor to the beginning of a new line in the display requires sending two control characters: character codes 13 (⟨CR⟩, for "carriage return") and 10 (⟨LF⟩, for "line feed"):

```
 A  B  C  □        cursor at end of line

[A] B  C           output <CR>

 A  B  C           output <LF>
 □
```

These codes are generated from the keyboard by pressing RETURN followed by LINEFEED. It is inconvenient to require both of these keystrokes. Instead, we will accept either RETURN or LINEFEED as signaling end of line and echo both ⟨CR⟩ and ⟨LF⟩ to the display.

We can modify our simple loop to handle both backspace and end of line in the manner just described. In addition, we will prevent the cursor from backspacing further once it reaches column 1 of the display. If this happens, we will ring the bell on the display and ignore the character.

Here is a modified version of our keyboard echoing loop:

```
BEL     EQU     7       bell
BS      EQU     8       backspace
LF      EQU     10      line feed
CR      EQU     13      carriage return
```

```
NEXTLIN   LOAD    R0,=0        init. line length
NEXTCHR   INCHR   R1,=SYSKBD   input char
          CMPR    R1,=BS       backspace key?
          BREQ    DOBKSP       yes -- backspace cursor
          CMPR    R1,=CR       carriage return key?
          BREQ    DOCRLF       yes -- issue <CR> and <LF>
          CMPR    R1,=LF       line feed key?
          BREQ    DOCRLF       yes -- issue <CR> and <LF>

* type a character
          OUTCHR  R1,=SYSDPY   else echo character
          ADD     R1,=1        increment line length
          BR      NEXTCHR      repeat for next char

* backspace over last character
DOBKSP    CMPR    R0,=0        any chars on line?
          BRGT    OUTBKSP      yes - bksp last one
          LOAD    R1,=BEL      else igore <BS> and
          OUTCHR  R1,=SYSDPY   ... ring bell
          BR      NEXTCHR      repeat for next char

OUTBKSP   OUTCHR  R1,=SYSDPY   bksp cursor
          LOAD    R2,=SP       erase char with <SP>
          OUTCHR  R2,=SYSDPY
          OUTCHR  R1,=SYSDPY   bksp cursor again
          SUB     R0,=1        decrement line length
          BR      NEXTCHR      repeat for next char

* end line with <CR> and <LF>
DOCRLF    LOAD    R1,=CR       echo <CR>
          OUTCHR  R1,=SYSDPY
          LOAD    R1,=LF       echo <LF>
          OUTCHR  R1,=SYSDPY
          BR      NEXTLIN      repeat for next line
```

12.4 LINE INPUT AND OUTPUT

There are times when we would like to wait until some amount of information has been input before processing it. If the input device is a keyboard, it makes sense to accumulate characters until either the RETURN or LINEFEED key is pressed. In many cases, it is also convenient to send an entire string to an output device like a printer rather than sending each character as it becomes available. In this section, we will look at two routines to perform these functions.

12.4.1 Input Line Buffering

As we saw earlier, there is more to making the keyboard a usable input device than simply reading characters. We must also allow corrections to the information and echo the information to the display. We will reuse quite a bit of the program presented earlier, along with some modifications to handle buffering the information.

To detect end of line, we accepted either the RETURN or the LINEFEED key and echoed both ⟨CR⟩ and ⟨LF⟩ to the display. To make internal storage easier, we will use a single character code in the input buffer to signify "end of line." This code must be detected and converted back to ⟨CR⟩ and ⟨LF⟩ upon output. We will follow the convention of using ⟨LF⟩ for this purpose.

One thing that we should address is the possibility that the input buffer may become full before the entire line is read. To handle this case, we need to know how many characters the result string can hold. This will be passed to our line input procedure, along with a pointer to the result string.

If the buffer becomes full, we will automatically insert ⟨LF⟩, just as though one was typed from the keyboard. To ensure that there is enough room in the buffer for both ⟨LF⟩ and ⟨NUL⟩, we can only read two characters less than the maximum string length before forcing an end of line.

Here is a revised version of the algorithm presented earlier:

1. [Input character]: Read a character from the keyboard.
2. [Check for backspace]: If the character is not ⟨BS⟩, continue at step 5.
3. [Check for empty buffer]: See if the input buffer is empty. If so, ignore backspace and repeat at step 1.
4. [Perform backspace]: Decrement the buffer pointer, erase the last character in the display, and repeat at step 1.
5. [Accept character]: If the character is ⟨CR⟩ or ⟨LF⟩, break out of the loop at step 7. Otherwise, enter the character into the buffer and echo it to the display.
6. [Check buffer full]: If the buffer is not full, repeat the loop at step 1.
7. [Process end of line]: Echo ⟨CR⟩ and ⟨LF⟩ to the display, and enter ⟨LF⟩ and ⟨NUL⟩ into the buffer.

Our procedure GETLIN expects a pointer to the result string buffer and a buffer length by value on the R7 stack. It returns a pointer to the ⟨NUL⟩ character in the string buffer on the R7 stack as its result:

```
** GETLIN - GET A LINE OF INPUT FROM THE KEYBOARD INTO A
*           STRING, TERMINATED BY <LF><NUL>. FORCES <LF>
*           IF BUFFER FULL.
*
*          INPUT (VALUE)
*              R7 STACK - MAX. STRING LENGTH (TOP)
*                       - POINTER TO RESULT STRING
```

```
*
*         OUTPUT
*              R7 STACK - UPDATED POINTER TO <NUL> CHARACTER
*                         IN RESULT STRING
*
*         CONSTANTS
*              BS       - CHARACTER CODE FOR BACKSPACE
*              CR       - CHARACTER CODE FOR CARRIAGE RETURN
*              LF       - CHARACTER CODE FOR LINE FEED
*                         -- USED AS END OF LINE MARKER
*              NUL      - CHARACTER CODE 0
*                         -- USED AS END OF STRING MARKER
*              SYSDPY   - DEVICE ADDRESS OF SYSTEM DISPLAY
*              SYSKBD   - DEVICE ADDRESS OF SYSTEM KEYBOARD
*
GETLIN    PUSH      R7,R2          save registers
          PUSH      R7,R1
          PUSH      R7,R0
          LOAD      R0,5(R7)       pointer to string buffer
          LOAD      R2,4(R7)       compute ptr to buffer end
          ADD       R2,=-2(R0)     ... less 2 for <CR><NUL>

GTLCHR    INCHR     R1,=SYSKBD     input char
          CMPR      R1,=BS         backspace key?
          BRNE      GTLOUT         no - put char in buffer


* backspace over last character
GTLBKS    CMPR      R0,5(R7)       any chars on line?
          BRLE      GTLCHR         no - ignore bksp
          OUTCHR    R1,=SYSDPY     else bksp cursor
          LOAD      R1,=SP         erase char with <SP>
          OUTCHR    R1,=SYSDPY
          LOAD      R1,=BS         bksp cursor again
          OUTCHR    R1,=SYSDPY
          SUB       R0,=1          decrement buf ptr
          BR        GTLCHR         repeat for next char


* handle non-bksp char
GTLOUT    CMPR      R1,=CR         carriage return?
          BREQ      GTLEOL         yes - end of input line
          CMPR      R1,=LF         line feed?
          BREQ      GTLEOL         yes - end of input line
          STORE     R1,@R0         else put char in buffer
          ADD       R1,=1          increment buffer ptr
          OUTCHR    R1,=SYSDPY     echo char
          CMPR      R2,R0          buffer full?
```

```
         BRGE    GTLCHR        no - repeat for next char
* end of line
GTLEOL   LOAD    R1,=CR        echo <CR>
         OUTCHR  R1,=SYSDPY
         LOAD    R1,=LF        echo <LF>
         OUTCHR  R1,=SYSDPY
         STORE   R1,@R0        put <LF> in buffer
         ADD     R1,=1         increment buffer ptr
         LOAD    R1,=NUL       end string with <NUL>
         STORE   R1,@R0

         STORE   R1,5(R7)      return new ptr.
         POP     R7,R0         restore registers
         POP     R7,R1
         POP     R7,R2
         POP     R7,1(R7)      move return addr.
         RTN     R7,
```

12.4.2 String Output

The other procedure outputs a string to the system printer. Whenever ⟨LF⟩ is encountered in the string, it is taken to mean an end of line, and both ⟨CR⟩ and ⟨LF⟩ are output. The algorithm is very straightforward:

1. [Fetch character]: Fetch the next character from the string.
2. [Check for end of string]: If the character is ⟨NUL⟩, the entire string has been processed; exit algorithm.
3. [Output character]: Output the character to the system printer.
4. [Check for ⟨LF⟩]: If the character is ⟨LF⟩, output both ⟨CR⟩ and ⟨LF⟩ to the printer. In any case, repeat at step 1.

Here is the code for PUTSTR:

```
** PUTSTR - OUTPUT A STRING TO THE SYSTEM PRINTER. INTERPRETS
*           <LF> AS END OF LINE AND OUTPUTS BOTH <CR> AND <LF>.
*
*        INPUT (VALUE)
*            R7 STACK - POINTER TO STRING.
*
*        OUTPUT
*            NONE.
*
*        CONSTANTS
*            CR          - CHARACTER CODE FOR CARRIAGE RETURN
*            LF          - CHARACTER CODE FOR LINE FEED
*                          -- USED AS END OF LINE MARKER
```

```
*            NUL        - CHARACTER CODE 0
*                         -- USED AS END OF STRING MARKER
*            SYSPRT     - DEVICE ADDRESS OF SYSTEM PRINTER
*
PUTSTR   PUSH     R7,R1           save registers
         PUSH     R7,R0
         LOAD     R0,3(R7)        pointer to string buffer

PTSCHR   POP      R0,R1           fetch next char
         CMPR     R1,=NUL         end of string?
         BREQ     PTSOUT          yes -- break out of loop
         CMPR     R1,=LF          end of line?
         BRNE     PTSPRT          no -- branch to print char
         LOAD     R1,=CR          else print <CR>
         OUTCHR   R1,=SYSPRT
         LOAD     R1,=LF          reload <LF>

PTSPRT   OUTCHR   R1,=SYSPRT      print character
         BR       PTSCHR          repeat for next char


PTSOUT   POP      R7,R0           restore registers
         POP      R7,R1
         POP      R7,1(R7)        move return address
         RTN      R7,
```

12.5 A SIMPLE FOUR-FUNCTION CALCULATOR

In this section we will develop an application that uses many of the routines presented so far. It simulates the actions of a simple four-function calculator. Only integer addition, subtraction, multiplication, and division are provided. For simplicity, all four operators will have the same precedence, and there are no parentheses.

We should first examine the kind of arithmetic expression just described. Minimally, it is a number like 7, +512, or −93. Otherwise, it has the general form

```
num    OP    num    OP    . . .    OP    num
```

Consider, for example, the expression

$$133 + 17 * -14 / 5$$

This expression is evaluated from left to right. The sum 133 + 17 is multiplied by −14 and the product is then divided by 5. The result is −420. A partial result is accumulated during the course of evaluation. At each step, the partial result comes from applying some operation to the partial result from the previous step and a new operand:

```
133 + 17 * -14 / 5        133
  ^
133 + 17 * -14 / 5        133+17 = 150
       ^
133 + 17 * -14 / 5        150*(-14) = -2,100
              ^
133 + 17 * -14 / 5        (-2,100)/5 = -420
                 ^
```

We will write our expression evaluator as a function. The input parameter is a pointer to a string representing the expression. Evaluation continues until a character is encountered that is not an operator. At this point the result and an updated pointer to the first character past the end of the expression are returned. This is the same way we handled detecting end of number for CVTNUM, the character-to-number conversion routine.

Here is the algorithm for our expression evaluator:

1. [Initialization]: Initialize a partial result by converting the first operand to a number.
2. [Find operator]: Scan for the next operator in the string. If none is found, the partial result is the final result; exit algorithm.
3. [Find operand]: Convert the next portion of the string to a number for the second operand.
4. [Perform operation]: Evaluate the next term of the expression according to the type of operator to form a new partial result. Repeat for the next term at step 2.

To test out EVAL, we will write a simple program that reads a line from the keyboard and echoes it to the printer, then evaluates the expression and prints the result. Notice that the test program keeps looping for more input lines, so it must be halted from the switch register. Here is EVAL together with this test program:

```
** sample routine to test EVAL
*
ENDLIN   DATA   LF,NUL        end of line for printer
MAXBUF   EQU    80+2          line width plus LF, NUL
IOBUF    BSS    MAXBUF        input/output buffer

* input and echo next expression
NEXTLIN  PUSH   R7,=IOBUF     read next expression
         PUSH   R7,=MAXBUF
         CALL   R7,GETLIN
         ADD    R7,=1         discard updated buf ptr
         PUSH   R7,=ENDLIN    eject line on printer
         CALL   R7,PUTSTR
         PUSH   R7,=IOBUF     echo line to printer
         CALL   R7,PUTSTR
```

```
          PUSH    R7,=IOBUF          init output ptr
          CALL    R7,EVAL            evaluate expression
          POP     R7,R1              result of evaluation
          ADD     R7,=1              discard updated buf ptr

* display result
          PUSH    R7,=IOBUF          convert result to str
          PUSH    R7,R1
          CALL    R7,CVTSTR
          ADD     R7,=1              discard updated ptr
          PUSH    R7,=IOBUF          output result
          CALL    R7,PUTSTR
          PUSH    R7,=ENDLIN         end output line
          CALL    R7,PUTSTR
          BR      NEXTLIN            repeat for next expr



** EVAL - EVALUATE A STRING EXPRESSION TO A NUMBER
*
*         INPUT
*              R7 STACK - POINTER TO STRING (VALUE)
*
*         OUTPUT
*              R7 STACK - NUMBER (TOP)
*                       - UPDATED POINTER
*
*         PROCEDURES
*              CVTNUM  - CONVERTS STRING TO NUMBER
*              SKIPSP  - SKIPS OVER LEADING SPACES
*              STRINDX - RETURNS INDEX OF CHAR IN STRING
*
*         CONSTANTS
*              MINUS        - CHARACTER CODE FOR ''-''
*              NUL          - CHARACTER CODE 0
*                             -- USED AS END OF STRING MARKER
*              PLUS         - CHARACTER CODE FOR ''+''
*              SLASH        - CHARACTER CODE FOR ''/''
*              STAR         - CHARACTER CODE FOR ''*''
*
EVOPTBL   DATA   PLUS,MINUS,STAR,SLASH,NUL   op char tbl
EVDSTBL   DATA   EVADD,EVSUB,EVMUL,EVDIV     distrib tbl
EVAL      PUSH   R7,0(R7)                    make room for result
          PUSH   R7,R3                       save registers
          PUSH   R7,R2
          PUSH   R7,R1
```

```
         PUSH   R7,R0

         PUSH   R7,6(R7)                copy initial buf ptr
         CALL   R7,CVTNUM               convert first number
         POP    R7,R2                   converted number

* find next operator
EVNEXT   CALL   R7,SKIPSP               skip leading spaces
         PUSH   R7,=EVOPTBL             op table string
         PUSH   R7,@1(R7)               op char (ptr on stk)
         CALL   R7,STRINDX              index op in op string
         POP    R7,R3
         CMPR   R3,=0                   found operator?
         BREQ   EVOUT                   no -- end evaluation
         POP    R7,R0                   else advance buf ptr
         PUSH   R7,=1(R0)

* convert second operand to number
         CALL   R7,CVTNUM
         POP    R7,R1                   converted number


* evaluate this term of expression
         BR     @EVDSTBL-1(R3)          distribute on op index


EVADD      ADD      R2,R1        code to add
           BR       EVNEXT

EVSUB      SUB      R2,R1        code to subtract
           BR       EVNEXT

EVMUL      MUL      R2,R1        code to multiply
           BR       EVNEXT

EVDIV      DIV      R2,R1        code to divide
           BR       EVNEXT


* end of evaluation
EVOUT      POP      R7,7(R7)     updated string ptr
           STORE    R2,5(R7)     result of evaluation
           POP      R7,R0        restore registers
           POP      R7,R1
           POP      R7,R2
           POP      R7,R3
           RTN      R7,
```

A lookup table is used to recognize the operator. The table is in the form of a string of all valid operators. If the current character appears in the string, its index is saved and used later to branch to the correct code. Otherwise, the character is not an operator, and evaluation terminates with R0 pointing to that character.

Once the second operand is converted, we can perform the operation indicated by the index found earlier. The method used is known as a *distribution table*. Each entry in the table corresponds to one of the operators in the operator string. Stored at each location in the table is a pointer to the code for the corresponding operation. By indexing into the table and branching indirectly, control can be transferred to any of the addresses in just one instruction.

It is important that the operation be recognized before trying to convert the next operand in the string. Consider a possible input to EVAL (Figure 12-4). When the first (and only) number is converted during initialization, CVTNUM advances the string pointer to the ⟨NUL⟩ character (Figure 12-5). At this point the procedure tries to interpret the next nonblank character as an operator. Since ⟨NUL⟩ is obviously not an operator, we expect the procedure to stop converting at this point.

A common mistake is to continue and convert the second operand before testing for a valid operator. The problem comes when R0 is incremented before calling CVTNUM for the second time. Since R0 is now past the end of string, there is no way to predict the behavior of CVTNUM. Even if the procedure returns, R0 is useless because it no longer points within the string. The problem may actually survive quite a bit of testing because most input strings are terminated by both ⟨LF⟩ and ⟨NUL⟩. Stepping R0 past ⟨LF⟩ before calling CVTNUM still leaves it pointing to ⟨NUL⟩ when CVTNUM returns. This kind of boundary condition is often difficult to test for and usually disastrous when finally hit upon.

Although we have made a number of simplifying assumptions in the design of EVAL, it does have some real applications. A routine very much like EVAL is used by most assemblers to perform address arithmetic. In fact, most assemblers only go so far as to allow addition and subtraction of addresses and constants. In practice, little more is ever needed.

One thing that complicates performing address arithmetic is that an address expression may contain both numbers and symbols that are defined in a symbol table. One way to make EVAL handle this is to replace CVTNUM by a routine that either looks up the value of a symbol or converts a number, depending on the input string. The routine STRCMPR from Chapter 11 might be used to look up definitions in a symbol table.

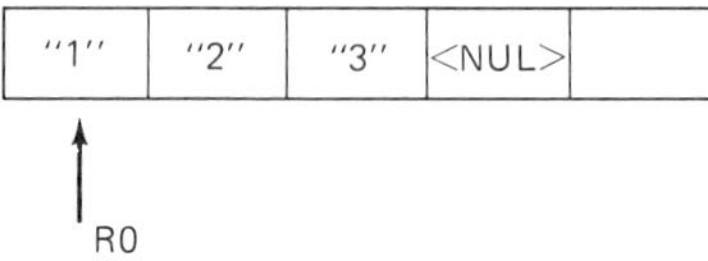

Figure 12-4 EVAL given a string representing a single number

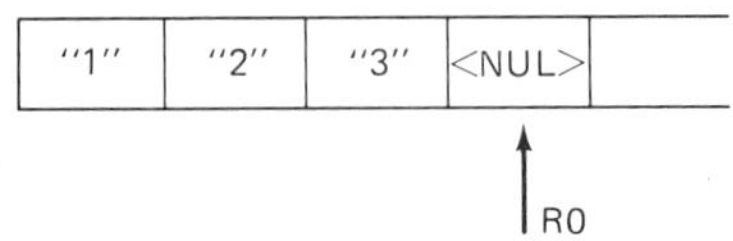

Figure 12-5 String pointer advanced to the end of the string by EVAL

12.6 MASS STORAGE DEVICES

So far, we have worked with the system keyboard as an input device and the display and printer as output devices. We would also like to be able to store and retrieve information for later use. In this final section, we will look at how to read and write information to a mass storage device called a *disk*. Disks are capable of storing and retrieving large amounts of information at relatively high speed.

A disk is a round plate of either metal or plastic, coated with a special magnetic recording surface. It has an appearance similar to that of a phonograph record with a coating like a magnetic tape. The recording surface is logically divided into a number of concentric rings called *tracks* and a number of wedges called *sectors*.

Some disk units mount several *platters* some distance apart on the same shaft. A line projected through all the platters from a given track and sector is called a *cylinder*. The word *sector* is also used when referring to the portion of a sector that lies within a single track and cylinder. Figure 12-6 is an illustration of a disk that shows the sectors, tracks, and cylinders. A magnetic recording head rides a very small distance above the surface of each platter and can be moved inward and outward, along a radial axis, from track to track. As the disk spins along its axis, each sector on a particular track moves under the recording head. A sector holds a fixed amount of information, which can only be read or written as a single record. Writing information to disk involves the following steps:

1. Move the data to a buffer in the disk controller.
2. Position the head to the proper track.
3. Wait for the correct sector to move under the head.
4. Write the data from the buffer onto the disk.

Reading information from a disk reverses this process:

1. Position the head to the proper track.

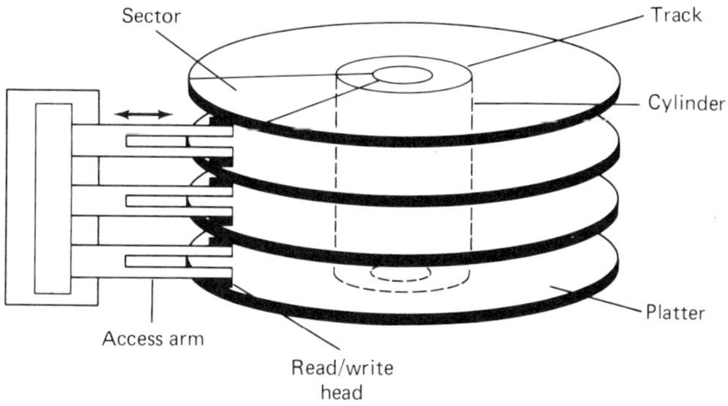

Figure 12-6 Disk showing sectors, tracks, and cyclinders

2. Wait for the correct sector to move under the head.
3. Read the data from the disk into the buffer.
4. Remove the data from a disk controller buffer.

Usually, moving the head inward or outward to the correct track is the most time-consuming operation. The average amount of time it takes to move the head to a given track position is called the *seek time*. The time spent waiting for the correct sector to move under the recording is called the *latency*.

Interaction between a program and the disk takes the form of commands to the disk controller. Here are a few of the commands available:

I/O command	Purpose
00000001	seek to position
00000010	read sector
00000011	write sector

A program must first tell the controller which sector and track to read. It takes some time for the head to move. Sending this information to the controller as soon as possible will allow it to operate more efficiently. The command to seek is followed by 3 bytes sent over the control line that give the new head position. The position is encoded in three fields within the bytes (Figure 12-7). Notice that the fields do not necessarily begin and end on byte boundaries.

By encoding the information in this way, we can think of the disk as having a large number of sectors without worrying about cylinders or tracks. If we really need to move to a particular cylinder or track, we must know how many sectors per track and tracks per platter there are for a particular disk drive.

Assume that the disk is at device address 10. Here is how to move the disk to a particular position:

```
SYSDSK   EQU    10          device code of system disk
DSKPOS   EQU    1           disk head position cmd
                ...

         LOAD   R0,=DSKPOS  position command
         IOCMD  R0,=SYSDSK
         LOAD   R0,POS      fetch position
         IOCMD  R0,=SYSDSK  send lower byte
         LSH    R0,=-8
         IOCMD  R0,=SYSDSK  send middle byte
         LSH    R0,=-8
         IOCMD  R0,=SYSDSK  send upper byte
```

Once the head is in position, we can command it to read the information from the sector into the controller's buffer:

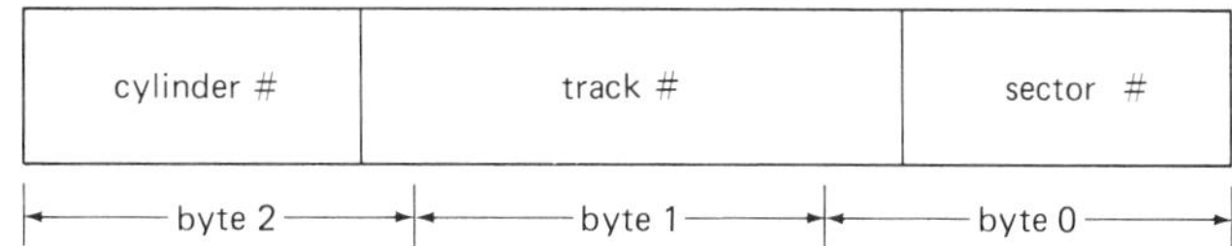

Figure 12-7 Encoded disk position information

```
DSKIN     EQU     2               disk read command
                ...

          LOAD    R0,=DSKIN
          IOCMD   R0,=SYSDSK
```

Inputting a sector from the disk does not alter the current position of the head. We can now read the information from the controller's buffer using INCHR instructions. Suppose that each sector contains 256 bytes of information:

```
SCTSIZ    EQU     256             number of bytes per sector
                ...

          LOAD    R1,=0

RDBYTE    INCHR   R0,=SYSDSK
          STORE   R0,BUF(R1)
          ADD     R1,=1
          CMPR    R1,=SCTSIZ
          BRLT    RDBYTE
```

After sending a character, the controller increments its own buffer pointer to the next character in the buffer. If the last character is read, the controller resets its pointer to the beginning of the buffer. The next INCHR instruction would read the first character in the buffer again. We can tell the controller to do this at any time by issuing the controller command

```
BUFRST    EQU     4               reset controller buf ptr
                ...

          LOAD    R0,=BUFRST
          IOCMD   R0,=SYSDSK
```

When writing to a sector, the process is just the opposite. After seeking the correct position, the information is first written to the controller's buffer. Before copying the information to the buffer, it is a good idea to reset the buffer pointer to the beginning. We could issue the controller command BUFRST, but we might want to erase the contents of the buffer first. Issuing the controller command

```
BUFCLR      EQU      5              clear controller buf
                ...

            LOAD     R0,=BUFCLR
            IOCMD    R0,=SYSDSK
```

clears all bits in the buffer to 0 and resets the buffer pointer to the beginning. The information can now be copied to the controller buffer:

```
            LOAD     R1,=0

WRBYTE      LOAD     R0,BUF(R1)
            OUTCHR   R0,=SYSDSK
            ADD      R1,=1
            CMPR     R1,=SCTSIZ
            BRLT     WRBYTE
```

Finally, the controller is commanded to output its buffer to the sector on disk that was specified by the last head position command:

```
DSKOUT      EQU      3                  disk write command
                ...

            LOAD     R0,=DSKOUT
            IOCMD    R0,=SYSDSK
```

Outputting a sector to the disk does not alter the current position of the head.

As a final set of utilities, we will write three routines that work with disk. The first is SEEK. This routine takes a single-value parameter representing the position. The parameter is passed on the R7 stack. SEEK returns no result:

```
** SEEK -- MOVES DISK HEAD TO POSITION
*
*          INPUT:
*               R7 STACK - SECTOR ADDRESS (VALUE)
*
*          OUTPUT:
*               NONE
*
*          CONSTANTS
*               DSKPOS  - POSITIONS DISK HEAD
*               SYSDSK  - ADDRESS OF DISK CONTROLLER
*
SEEK       PUSH      R7,R0          save registers
           LOAD      R0,=DSKPOS
           IOCMD     R0,=SYSDSK     move head to position
           LOAD      R0,2(R7)       sector address
```

```
          IOCMD    R0,=SYSDSK     send lower byte
          LSH      R0,=-8
          IOCMD    R0,=SYSDSK     send middle byte
          LSH      R0,=-8
          IOCMD    R0,=SYSDSK     send upper byte
          POP      R7,R0          restore register
          POP      R7,1(R7)       move rtn addr
          RTN      R7,
```

The second routine is GETSECT. This procedure reads up to a sector of information into a buffer, with one byte per word. The procedure takes three parameters. The first parameter is a disk address, the second the maximum number of bytes to read, and the third the buffer address. The buffer is passed by reference and the other two by value on the R7 stack. The procedure returns no result:

```
** GETSECT -- INPUT A SECTOR FROM DISK
*
*         INPUT:
*              R7 STACK - SECTOR ADDRESS (VALUE) (TOP)
*                       - MAX. NUMBER OF BYTES (VALUE)
*                       - INPUT BUFFER (REFERENCE)
*
*         OUTPUT:
*              NONE
*
*         PROCEDURES
*              SEEK     - MOVE DISK HEAD TO NEW POSITION
*
*         CONSTANTS
*              DSKIN    - INPUTS SECTOR INTO CONTROLLER BUF
*              SYSDSK   - ADDRESS OF DISK CONTROLLER
*
GETSECT   PUSH     R7,R2          save registers
          PUSH     R7,R1
          PUSH     R7,R0

          PUSH     R7,4(R7)       new head position
          CALL     R7,SEEK        move head to position
          LOAD     R1,6(R7)       ptr to first byte in input buf
          LOAD     R2,R1          ptr past last byte in input buf
          ADD      R2,5(R7)

          LOAD     R0,=DSKIN      input sector on disk
          IOCMD    R0,=SYSDSK     ... into controller buf

GTSBYT    CMPR     R1,R2          if input buffer full
          BRGE     GTSDONE        ... break out of loop
          INCHR    R0,=SYSDSK     else get next byte
```

```
          STORE   R0,@R1         save in input buf
          ADD     R1,=1          increment input buf ptr
          BR      GTSBYT         repeat for next byte

GTSDONE   POP     R7,R0          restore registers
          POP     R7,R1
          POP     R7,R2
          POP     R7,3(R7)       move rtn address
          ADD     R7,=2          adjust stk ptr
          RTN     R7,
```

Notice how the stack pointer was adjusted at the end of this procedure. There were three parameters to remove from the stack. After moving the return address, the stack pointer was incremented by an additional 2 because popping the return address only incremented the stack pointer by 1.

The third disk procedure is PUTSECT. This procedure writes information to a sector on disk. Its parameters are the same as for GETSECT. The buffer is an unpacked array of bytes passed by reference, and the sector address and number of bytes to write are passed by value on the R7 stack. This procedure also returns no result:

```
** PUTSECT -- OUTPUT A SECTOR TO DISK
*
*          INPUT:
*               R7 STACK - SECTOR ADDRESS (VALUE) (TOP)
*                        - NUMBER OF BYTES (VALUE)
*                        - INPUT BUFFER (REFERENCE)
*
*          OUTPUT:
*               NONE
*
*          PROCEDURES
*               SEEK     - MOVE DISK HEAD TO NEW POSITION
*
*          CONSTANTS
*               BUFCLR   - CLEARS CONTROLLER BUF AND PTR
*               DSKOUT   - OUTPUTS SECTOR FROM CONTROLLER BUF
*               SYSDSK   - ADDRESS OF DISK CONTROLLER
*
PUTSECT  PUSH    R7,R2          save registers
         PUSH    R7,R1
         PUSH    R7,R0

         PUSH    R7,4(R7)       sector address
         CALL    R7,SEEK        move head to position
         LOAD    R0,=BUFCLR     clear controller buf and ptr
         IOCMD   R0,=SYSDSK
```

```
        LOAD    R1,6(R7)    ptr to first byte in output buf
        LOAD    R2,R1       ptr past last byte in output buf
        ADD     R2,5(R7)

PTSBYT  CMPR    R1,R2       if all chars copied
        BRGE    PTSDONE     ... break out of loop
        LOAD    R0,@R1      else fetch byte from output buf
        OUTCHR  R0,=SYSDSK  and write it to controller buf
        ADD     R1,=1       increment output buf ptr
        BR      PTSBYT      repeat for next byte

PTSDONE LOAD    R0,=DSKOUT  output controller buf
        IOCMD   R0,=SYSDSK  ... to sector on disk
        POP     R7,R0       restore registers
        POP     R7,R1
        POP     R7,R2
        POP     R7,3(R7)    move rtn address
        ADD     R7,=2       adjust stk ptr
        RTN     R7,
```

12.7 DISCUSSION

A number of improvements can be made over the I/O architecture presented here. Perhaps one of the simplest is to give the IOU direct access to the memory. By doing this, we could send a command to, say, the disk controller to input or output an entire sector *directly* into memory. This would eliminate the need for a procedure like GETSECT or PUTSECT. Instead, we could simply command the operation to start and check the status periodically until an entire sector had been read and transferred to memory.

Another improvement is called an *interrupt*. This method eliminates having to check for transfer completion. When the transfer is complete, the IOU sets an *interrupt flag* in the CPU. A new step in the instruction cycle is to check this interrupt flag. If it is set, the CPU saves the PC and transfers control to a fixed address in memory. The programmer must write a special kind of procedure called an *interrupt routine* that deals with I/O completion, then returns to the address saved by the CPU. Although this seems a bit complicated, there are times when it is very useful. We eliminated the need for interrupts to some degree by making our device controllers more intelligent and capable of buffering a reasonable amount of data.

12.8 SUMMARY

In this chapter we looked at how computers perform input and output. We saw that an I/O device is not connected directly to the CPU. Instead, it is connected to a device controller. A device controller is a separate processor with a certain amount of its own storage. The storage is used to buffer information moving between the device and the CPU. The device controllers are all connected along an I/O bus. Each controller responds to a unique device address carried on the I/O bus. The bus also carries a command and some amount of data to the device. If a device recognizes its address, it executes the command on the bus. Otherwise, the controller ignores the command. The I/O bus is connected to the CPU through the input/output unit (IOU). This unit controls communications on the I/O bus and detects devices that are either disconnected or inoperative after a certain period of time.

Four CPU instructions are used to command the various devices. INCHR inputs a character or byte from a device into the MBR and from there into one of the registers. OUTCHR outputs a character or byte from the MBR to one of the devices. The byte was moved to the MBR from one of the registers. IOSTAT returns a byte-long status word for a particular device. The interpretation of the various bit fields within the status word is device-dependent. IOCMD is used to send control information to the device controllers. We saw how this was used in connection with disk input/output.

PROBLEMS

12-1. What is the difference between data output in binary form and data output in character form? Which is more compact? Which is meant for people to read?

12-2. Explain the purpose of a device controller.

12-3. Why is it necessary for some amount of buffering to be provided for some input and output devices? Why is the buffer some multiple of the device's record size?

12-4. There were only two commands to the memory controller, read and write. Explain the purpose of the other two commands to a device controller. Give an example where each might be used.

12-5. What is the purpose of the I/O bus? How is the address sent on the address line of the I/O bus used to direct information to a particular device controller?

12-6. What is the purpose of the IOU? What is meant by saying that the IOU serves as the bus controller?

12-7. How is the IOU connected to the CPU? How does the limited width of the I/O bus address and data paths affect these connections?

12-8. Write register transfer expressions that show the net effect of the following I/O instructions:

(a) `INCHR R7,=0`	**(b)** `OUTCHR R3,=2`
(c) `INCHR R2,KEYBD`	**(d)** `IOSTAT R2,=CRT`
(e) `IOCMD R4,=DISK`	**(f)** `OUTCHR R1,DEVTBL(R3)`
(g) `INCHR R1,@(R3)`	**(h)** `IOSTAT R2,@DEVPTR`
(i) `IOCMD R5,TAPE`	**(j)** `OUTCHR R1,PRINTER`

12-9. What does it mean for an input device to be *idle*? If an input device is idle, what happens if we issue a read command to that device?

12-10. What does it mean for an input device to be *busy*? If an input device is busy, what happens if we issue a read command to that device?

12-11. Why might we want to check the status of an input device before issuing a read command?

12-12. What does it mean for an output device to be *idle*? If an output device is idle, what happens if we issue a write command to that device?

12-13. What does it mean for an output device to be *busy*? If an output device is busy, what happens if we issue a write command to that device?

12-14. Why might we want to check the status of an output device before issuing a write command?

12-15. What is the purpose of *control codes*? Where are the control codes in the ASCII character set?

12-16. Write a program to ring the bell on the system printer ten times.

12-17. Some interesting characters can be created by *overprinting* one character with another. See what happens when the following strings are printed. (Some of these will look better than others, depending on the printer used.)

(a) = <BS> / **(b)** a <BS> ^
(c) u <BS> " **(d)** c <BS> ,
(e) 0 <BS> - **(f)** > <BS> _
(g) > <BS> < **(h)** e <BS> `
(i) + <BS> _ **(j)** c <BS> |

12-18. Characters can be underlined by printing the character, backspacing, then printing the underline character (_). Write a procedure UPUTSTR that expects a string by reference on the return stack. UPUTSTR prints the string underlined on the system printer.

12-19. The ASCII character set includes *horizontal tab* (⟨HT⟩) among its control characters. The character code for ⟨HT⟩ is 9. Many keyboards include a tab key that generates ⟨HT⟩. Modify GETLIN to recognize ⟨HT⟩ and to step the cursor to the next tab stop. Use fixed tab stops set every eight positions, starting at column 8. The buffer length should be extended to the cursor position, and the buffer should be padded with blanks to that point. If the next tab stop would go beyond column 80, set the buffer length to 80, pad the buffer with blanks through column 80, and proceed as though the buffer were full.

12-20. Having to stop a program that is waiting for input by pressing the HALT-button on the switch register is not a very good solution. By convention, most systems recognize a certain character from the keyboard as an end-of-input signal. Control-D, character code 4, is labeled end of transmission ⟨EOT⟩ and is frequently used for this purpose. Modify GETLIN to recognize ⟨EOT⟩. If the input line buffer has characters in it, GETLIN should return the current input buffer, ⟨NUL⟩ terminated but with *no* ⟨*LF*⟩. On the next call, GETLIN should return ⟨EOT⟩, ⟨NUL⟩ terminated, without reading any more characters from the keyboard. If ⟨EOT⟩ is detected and the input buffer is empty, return ⟨EOT⟩, ⟨NUL⟩ terminated immediately. What should be done about further calls to GETLIN after it detects ⟨EOT⟩?

12-21. The implementation of PUTSTR shown in this chapter expects a string represented as an array of characters. Modify PUTSTR to expect either an array of characters or a *packed* array of characters. (*Hint*: It is possible to tell from looking at the first word of the array which kind of string has been passed. Look at a few examples to see how.)

12-22. It is sometimes necessary to discard all characters buffered by the keyboard controller. This is known as *flushing* the keyboard buffer. Flushing the buffer is especially critical if the user must respond to an unexpected condition by typing a response. Write a procedure FLUSHKBD to flush the keyboard buffer. (*Hint*: be careful not to try reading any more characters than are actually in the buffer.)

12-23. Suppose that the keyboard controller responds to the command

```
BUFRST          EQU    4          reset keyboard buf ptr
```

Rewrite procedure FLUSHKBD to use this keyboard controller command.

12-24. A notation for an arithmetic expression called *reverse polish notation (RPN)* has the advantage of requiring no parentheses. For example, the expression

$$((12 + 9)/(11 - 4) + 5) * (-14 + 5)$$

would be written like this in RPN:

$$12\ 9 + 11\ 4 - /\ 5 + -14\ 5 + *$$

Evaluation in RPN is based on a stack. When a number is encountered, it is pushed on the stack. In the case of an operator, its operands are popped from the stack and its result is pushed back onto the stack.

Write a function EVALRPN that evaluates a string representing an RPN calculation. The parameter and results are handled the same as with EVAL. The string is passed by reference on the return stack. The result is returned on the return stack along with an updated string pointer to the first character past the end of the expression. Use the return stack during calculations as the evaluation stack. At least one space separates each number and operator in the string, as shown in the preceding paragraph. Numbers may be positive or negative.

Certain error conditions must be handled carefully. First, an operation requires at least two numbers on the stack. If there are too few, delete any numbers pushed onto the stack during evaluation, return the current string pointer in place of the result, and return the constant TOOFEW in place of the updated string pointer. Second, only one number should be on the stack after evaluation is completed. If there is more than one number, delete any numbers pushed onto the stack during evaluation, return the current string pointer in place of the result, and return the constant TOOMANY in place of the updated string pointer. Define the symbolic constants TOOFEW and TOOMANY so that they can easily be distinguished from valid pointers by the calling routine.

12-25. Describe how information is laid out on a disk unit. Why is it necessary for the disk to rotate? Why is it necessary for the read/write head to move?

12-26. What is the smallest unit of information that can be read from or written to a disk?

12-27. What is meant by *seek time* and *latency*? Why are these delays necessary? Which is the greater of the two delays?

12-28. Using the position encoding technique described, what is the total number of sectors possible on a disk unit? Assuming 256 bytes per sector, how many characters of information does this represent?

12-29. Why is it usually unnecessary to know the number of tracks per cylinder or sectors per track with the position encoding technique described? When would it be necessary to have this information?

12-30. Write a procedure CPYSECT that copies N sectors starting at sector X to sectors starting at Y. Pass input parameters by value on the R7 stack. The procedure returns no result. (*Hint*: CPYSECT should not allocate memory for a copy buffer. Why is one not needed?)

12-31. Write a program that stores *itself* on disk starting at sector 0.

12-32. Write a procedure STOPROG that stores a program at a specified location on disk. STOPROG requires four parameters:

1. address of first word in program
2. number of words in program
3. start address of program
4. start sector address on disk

STOPROG writes the information from the first three parameters on disk, followed by the program itself. This extra information will allow the program to be reloaded into memory and run later on. Pass the parameters to STOPROG by value through a parameter list, whose address is in R0.

12-33. Write a procedure LDPROG that loads a program that was stored on disk by STOPROG. The parameter to LDPROG is the start sector address on disk. The sector address is passed to LDPROG by value in R0. LDPROG loads the program into memory based on the information at the beginning of the first sector and returns the program start address in R0 as its result. Typically, the calling program would then transfer control to the newly loaded program using the start address returned by LDPROG. *Caution*: There is a potential for the program being loaded to overwrite part of LDPROG or the program that called it. Suggest and evaluate several ways to prevent this from happening.

Appendix A

The Binary Number System

In this appendix we review the basics of the binary number system, the representation of negative numbers, binary arithmetic, and the conversion of numbers to and from binary. This review is primarily intended for readers who have not yet been introduced to the binary number system. It is also suitable as a review for readers who have not worked with it for a while.

A.1 NUMBER REPRESENTATION

The familiar decimal number system we work with every day is a *positional* number system. Each position represents a successively higher power of ten. Consider the number 3,549:

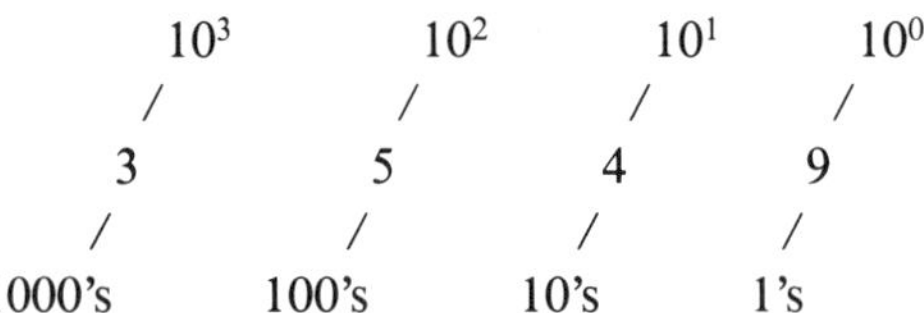

The number in each position is multiplied by the power of 10 assigned to that position. In this example, 10 is the *base* of the number system. Digits in the *decimal* or *base-10* number system go from 0 through 9.

The *binary* or *base-2* number system follows the same rules except that instead of powers of 10, each position represents a higher power of 2. The base-2 number system has only two digits, 0 and 1. A *b*inary dig*it* is commonly referred to as a *bit*. Consider the binary number 11010:

```
     2^4    2^3    2^2    2^1    2^0
    /      /      /      /      /
   1      1      0      1      0
  /      /      /      /      /
16's   8's    4's    2's    1's
```

The meaning of the binary number can be determined by simply evaluating the polynomial:

$$\begin{aligned} & 1 * 2^4 + 1 * 2^3 + 0 * 2^2 + 1 * 2^1 + 0 * 2^0 \\ = & 1 * 16 + 1 * 8 + 0 * 4 + 1 * 2 + 0 * 1 \\ = & 26 \end{aligned}$$

A.2 REPRESENTING NEGATIVE NUMBERS

There are three frequently used methods for representing negative numbers in a computer. Each has its advantages and disadvantages, as we shall discover shortly.

A.2.1 Signed Magnitude

The simplest method of representing a negative number is as a *signed magnitude*. An extra bit called a *sign bit* is placed in front of the number. If the bit is 0, the number is positive; if it is 1, the number is negative:

Signed magnitude		
0	1 1 0 1 0	+26
1	1 1 0 1 0	−26

Signed magnitude representation is also what we normally use to write numbers. Instead of a sign bit, the sign indicator + or − precedes the number.

Signed magnitude representation is said to be *symmetric*. That is, just as many positive numbers can be represented as negative numbers. For any negative number, simply change the sign bit to 0 to get its positive. To make a positive number negative, change the sign bit to 1.

One curious result of this symmetry is that there are two ways to represent zero. The first is 0 with a 0 for the sign bit. This is called *positive zero*. The second is a 0 with a 1 for the sign bit. This is called *negative zero*.

0	0 0 ... 0 0	+0
1	0 0 ... 0 0	−0

Both behave exactly the same when arithmetic is performed on them.

A.2.2. One's Complement

The two other ways of representing negative numbers are less obvious but have advantages for use with a computer. *One's complement* form also uses a sign bit, set to 0 for positive numbers and 1 for negative numbers. To form the negative of a positive number, replace all 0's by 1's and all 1's by 0's in both the number and the sign bit. This is called the one's complement or simply the complement of the number:

One's complement		
0	1 1 0 1 0	+26
1	0 0 1 0 1	−26

In general, the complement of a base-N digit is whatever must be added to the digit to yield the value $N-1$. For base 2, adding 1 to 0 yields $2-1$, or 1, so 1 is the complement of 0. Only 0 added to 1 yields 1, so 0 is the complement of 1. In base 10, 3 is the *nine's complement* of 6 because 3 added to 6 yields $10-1$, or 9.

Like the signed magnitude representation, one's complement representation is symmetric and has a negative form of zero that is the complement of the positive form:

One's complement		
0	0 0 ... 0 0	+0
1	1 1 ... 1 1	−0

A.2.3 Two's Complement

The third way of representing negative numbers, two's complement, is only slightly different from one's complement. After taking the complement of the positive number, simply add 1 to the result:

Two's complement		
0	1 1 0 1 0	+26
1	0 0 1 1 0	−26

The rule is easy to remember: *Two's* complement is *one's* complement *plus one.* Two's complement is the most popular form for representing numbers on a computer in spite of the difficulty most people have working with it. The reason has mostly to do with the fact that building a computer to work with two's complement numbers is much easier than building one to work with either of the other two forms. We will see why shortly.

Adding 1 after complementing makes two's complement representation asymmetric. In a given number of bits, one more negative than positive number can be represented.

As an example, 5 bits can represent a number as large as 31.

0 1 1 1 1 1 +31

By complementing the number and adding 1, we are left with the two's complement form of −31:

Two's complement		
0	1 1 1 1 1	+31
1	0 0 0 0 1	−31

Notice that there is still room to form one more negative number! By subtracting 1 from the two's complement representation of 31, we can form the two's complement representation of −32:

Two's complement		
1	0 0 0 0 0	−32

Where did we get room for the extra negative number? The two's complement form is asymmetric and has only one representation of zero. The entire negative range is "pushed" toward zero by adding 1 after complementing, leaving room for one more negative number.

A.3 BINARY ARITHMETIC

The steps for performing binary arithmetic are almost identical to those for using decimal numbers. In this section we look at how to perform the four basic arithmetic operations.

A.3.1 Binary Addition

The addition table for base 2 is much shorter than for base 10. Consider the following problem:

```
      1 1 1        <--  carries
    1 0 0 1 1          19
+   0 0 1 1 1           7
    ---------
    1 1 0 1 0          26
```

As with decimal arithmetic, each place in the sum is determined by the corresponding two digits in the addends, plus a possible carry from the previous place. The sum of 1 + 1 is 2, or 10 in binary. The 0 stands for that place in the sum, and the 1 is carried to the next place. The next place is the sum of the two digits, plus the carry from the previous place. Since 1 + 1 + 1 is 3, or 11 in binary, the 1 stands for that place in the sum, and the 1 is carried to the next place. The process is the same for the remaining digits.

When adding a negative number in signed magnitude form, it may be necessary to "borrow" from several places over:

```
sign bit                       Signed magnitude
  ↓
       0  1  1  1 10           ⟶ borrows
       ↑↗
  0    1  0  0  0  0              16
+ 1    0  0  0  0  1            −  1
  ----------------
  0    0  1  1  1  1              15
```

Since one number is positive and the other is negative, we subtract the smaller from the larger magnitude and use the sign of the larger magnitude. If both were positive or negative, the two magnitudes would be added and the result would have the same sign as the addends. The complexity of the rules makes it more difficult and expensive to build a computer that performs signed magnitude arithmetic.

The rules are simpler for one's complement arithmetic. Adding a negative number no longer requires borrowing. Here is the example just shown, this time using one's complement representation:

```
sign bit                       One's complement
    ↓
 1  1                          ⟵ carries
    0    1  0  0  0  0            16
+   1    1  1  1  1  0          −  1
    ----------------
 1  0    0  1  1  1  0
 └─>                   1
    ----------------
    0    0  1  1  1  1            15
```

Notice that the sign bit is involved in the computation too. The only complication comes if there is a carry out of the sign bit position. In that case, the 1 is "brought around" and added back into the sum. This is known as an *end-around carry.* A single addition using one's complement arithmetic may actually involve an extra addition if there is a carry out of the sign bit position. One's complement arithmetic is relatively easy for a computer to perform in spite of the end-around carry problem.

Two's complement representation eliminates the troublesome end-around carry. If there is a carry out of the sign position, it is simply ignored:

	sign bit						Two's complement
	↓						
1	1						← carries
	0	1	0	0	0	0	16
+	1	1	1	1	1	1	− 1
×	0	0	1	1	1	1	15

Two's complement is the most frequently used method for representing negative numbers on a computer because the rules for performing two's complement arithmetic are the simplest of the three.

A.3.2 Binary Subtraction

Subtraction is usually carried out as addition. Subtracting a number is really the same as adding a number of the opposite sign:

$$\begin{array}{rr} & +5 \\ + & -4 \\ \hline & +1 \end{array} \qquad \begin{array}{rr} & +5 \\ - & +4 \\ \hline & +1 \end{array}$$

We already know how to make +4 negative. The same method also works to make −4 positive:

1	0	0	1	0	0	complement sign	0	0	0	1	0	0
1	1	1	0	1	1	complement number	0	0	0	1	0	0
1	1	1	1	0	0	complement number and add 1	0	0	0	1	0	0

A.3.3 Binary Multiplication

The easiest way to deal with signed binary multiplication is to multiply the magnitudes, then apply the sign. The product is negative if either multiplier or multiplicand is negative. Here, for example, is how to multiply −6 * 5:

```
      1 1 0    +6
      1 0 1    +5
      -----
      1 1 0
    0 0 0
  1 1 0
  ---------
  1 1 1 1 0    +30

1 1 1 1 1 0    -30  (signed magnitude)
1 0 0 0 0 1    -30  (one's complement)
1 0 0 0 1 0    -30  (two's complement)
```

This algorithm is especially good for signed magnitude representation because it is so easy to extract the magnitudes.

There is a more efficient method if the numbers are in either one's or two's complement form. In many cases, it eliminates the extra work of changing the sign of the numbers before multiplication. This method works as long as the multiplier is positive, as is the case in the preceding example. If one number is positive and the other is negative, the positive one is used as the multiplier. Otherwise, the sign of both numbers must be reversed before multiplying. Here is the same example using the two's complement form of −6:

```
        ┌sign
        ↓
        1  0  1  0       −6  (two's complement)
        0  1  0  1       +5
  ----------------
  1  1  1  0  1  0
  0  0  0  0  0
  1  0  1  0
  ----------------
  1  0  0  0  1  0       −30
  ↑
  └ sign
```

Notice how the partial products are written. Each partial product is preceded by enough copies of its sign bit to match the length of the final product. The nonzero partial products in this example represent negative numbers. For addition to work correctly, each partial product must be the same length as the final product.

A.3.4 Binary Division

Division in binary is easier than in decimal because there is no need to "guess" how many times the divisor goes into the dividend at each step: Either it goes once or not at all. Here is how to divide 6 into 34:

```
                        1  0  1     ←— quotient
           ┌-------------------
  1  1  0  │   1  0  0  0  1  0
                  1  1  0
               --------
                     1  0  1  0
                        1  1  0
                        -------
                        1  0  0     ←— remainder
```

The answer is 5, with 4 left over. Only the magnitudes of both divisor and dividend are used for the division. If one of the operands is positive and the other is negative, the quotient is made negative at the end.

A.4 BASE CONVERSION

This section describes how to convert numbers to and from binary.

A.4.1 Binary to Decimal

To convert a binary number to decimal, multiply each digit by the corresponding power of 2 and add the products. Consider the binary number 11010:

$$
\begin{aligned}
& 1 * 2^4 + 1 * 2^3 + 0 * 2^2 + 1 * 2^1 + 0 * 2^0 \\
= {} & 1 * 16 + 1 * 8 + 0 * 4 + 1 * 2 + 0 * 1 \\
= {} & 26
\end{aligned}
$$

For a signed binary number, the correct sign is applied to the result after conversion.

A.4.2 Decimal to Binary

Converting a decimal number to binary is the reverse of the process just described. Each bit of the number is extracted by dividing the current number by the base, 2. The quotient is used as the dividend at the next step, and the remainder is the next bit of the binary number. The bits are generated from the least significant bit to the most significant bit. The process stops when the quotient becomes 0. Here is how to convert 26 back to binary:

```
     13
  2 ⟌26
     26
     --
      0  ──>  0

      6
  2 ⟌13
     12
     --
      1  ──>  1
                     ↑
      3
  2 ⟌ 6               r
      6               e
      -               a
      0  ──>  0       d
                     |
      1
  2 ⟌ 3
      2
      -
      1  ──>  1

      0
  2 ⟌ 1
      0
      -
      1  ──>  1
```

For a signed decimal number, the correct sign is applied after converting the magnitude.

A.4.3 Octal Notation

The *octal* or *base-8* number system is a useful shorthand notation for binary numbers. Instead of powers of 2, place values in octal represent powers of 8. Digits in base 8 are between 0 and 7. For example, the octal number 572 represents the decimal number

$$
\begin{aligned}
& 5 * 8^2 + 7 * 8^1 + 2 * 8^0 \\
= {} & 5 * 64 + 7 * 8 + 2 * 1 \\
= {} & 378
\end{aligned}
$$

A decimal number can be converted to octal using the same method described for converting a decimal number to binary. However, the divisor 8 is used this time because we want the octal representation.

The reason for considering base 8 is that an octal number is more compact than the same number in base 2. At the same time, converting between binary and octal is much easier than between binary and decimal.

To convert the binary number 101111010 (378 decimal) to octal, we first form groups of three bits, starting from the least significant bit of the number:

101 111 010

If the left-hand group had fewer than three bits, enough leading zeros would be added to make a group of three. Now we write the number represented by each group beneath the group:

```
101 111 010
 5   7   2
```

The result 572 is the octal equivalent of the binary number 101111010. Binary numbers are often written in groups of three to make conversion to octal easier. Converting an octal number back to binary is just the reverse of this process.

A.4.5 Hexadecimal Notation

The *hexadecimal* or *base-16* number system is another shorthand notation for binary numbers. Each place represents a power of 16. Obviously there are not enough digits to go from 0 through 15. Instead, the letters *A* through *F* are used to represent the numbers 10 through 15, respectively.

We can verify that the hexadecimal number 17A is equivalent to the decimal number 378:

$$\begin{aligned} & 1 * 16^2 + 7 * 16^1 + A * 16^0 \\ = & 1 * 16^2 + 7 * 16^1 + 10 * 16^0 \\ = & 1 * 256 + 7 * 16 + 10 * 1 \\ = & 378 \end{aligned}$$

A decimal number can be converted to hexadecimal using the same method described for converting a decimal number to binary. This time the divisor is 16 because we want the hexadecimal representation. Remainders greater than 9 must be converted to hexadecimal digits *A* through *F*.

Converting binary to hexadecimal requires forming groups of four bits, starting from the least significant bit of the number:

0001 0111 1010

Since the left-hand group has fewer than four bits, enough leading zeros are added to make a group of four. Now we write the corresponding number below each group of bits. Wherever the number is greater than 9, the corresponding letter is used instead:

```
0001 0111 1010
  1    7    A
```

To make conversion to hexadecimal easier, binary numbers are often written in groups of four. Converting a hexadecimal number back to binary is just the reverse of this process.

Working with hexadecimal notation takes quite a bit more practice than working with octal. We use octal rather than hexadecimal notation throughout the text to simplify the presentation. Be aware, however, that both hexadecimal and octal notation are in common use.

A.5 SUMMARY

In this appendix we have reviewed the basics of the binary number system. There are three ways to represent signed binary numbers in a computer:

- signed magnitude
- one's complement
- two's complement

Each representation has its advantages. Signed magnitude is the easiest for people to understand because we use this system ourselves. However, the complicated set of rules for performing arithmetic makes it difficult for a computer to use. One's complement form is a middle ground. It is fairly easy for people to read, and it is much easier for a computer to perform arithmetic on than signed magnitude. Two's complement, though not very easy for people to read, is the most efficient of the three for a computer to use.

We also looked at two ways to express numbers that are closely related to binary. Both the octal (base-8) and hexadecimal (base-16) number systems offer more compact ways to represent numbers than binary. It is also easier to convert between binary and octal or hexadecimal than it is between binary and decimal. Octal has the advantage of being more readily understandable than hexadecimal. Octal is used throughout the book as a compact substitute for binary where convenient.

PROBLEMS

A-1. Why is our everyday number system called a *positional* number system? What do the positions represent?

A-2. How do the positions in the binary number system differ from those in our decimal number system?

A-3. What is the meaning of *bit*? What values can a bit take on?

A-4. Convert the following binary numbers to decimal:

(a) 101	**(b)** 1001001
(c) 1000	**(d)** 10101
(e) 1001	**(f)** 110011001
(g) 1000001	**(h)** 1110111
(i) 11111	**(j)** 100000

A-5. What is the purpose of the extra bit added to a signed binary number? What do the values of that bit mean?

A-6. What is meant by saying that signed magnitude representation is symmetric?

A-7. How many ways are there to write 0 in signed magnitude representation?

A-8. Convert the following binary numbers in signed magnitude form to decimal:

(a) 1 000111	**(b)** 0 000000
(c) 0 110010	**(d)** 1 111111
(e) 0 100001	**(f)** 1 001110
(g) 1 000000	**(h)** 0 100000
(i) 1 001010	**(j)** 1 111000

A-9. Show the negative of each number in Problem A-8.

A-10. What is the complement of a base-*N* digit? Show the complement of each decimal digit.

A-11. Is one's complement symmetric or asymmetric? How many forms of zero does it have?

A-12. Convert the following binary numbers in one's complement form to decimal:

(a) 1 000111	**(b)** 0 000000
(c) 0 110010	**(d)** 1 111111
(e) 0 100001	**(f)** 1 001110
(g) 1 000000	**(h)** 0 100000
(i) 1 001010	**(j)** 1 111000

A-13. Show the negative of each number in Problem A-12.

A-14. State the rule that describes the difference between the one's and two's complement method.

A-15. Is two's complement symmetric or asymmetric? How many forms of zero does it have?

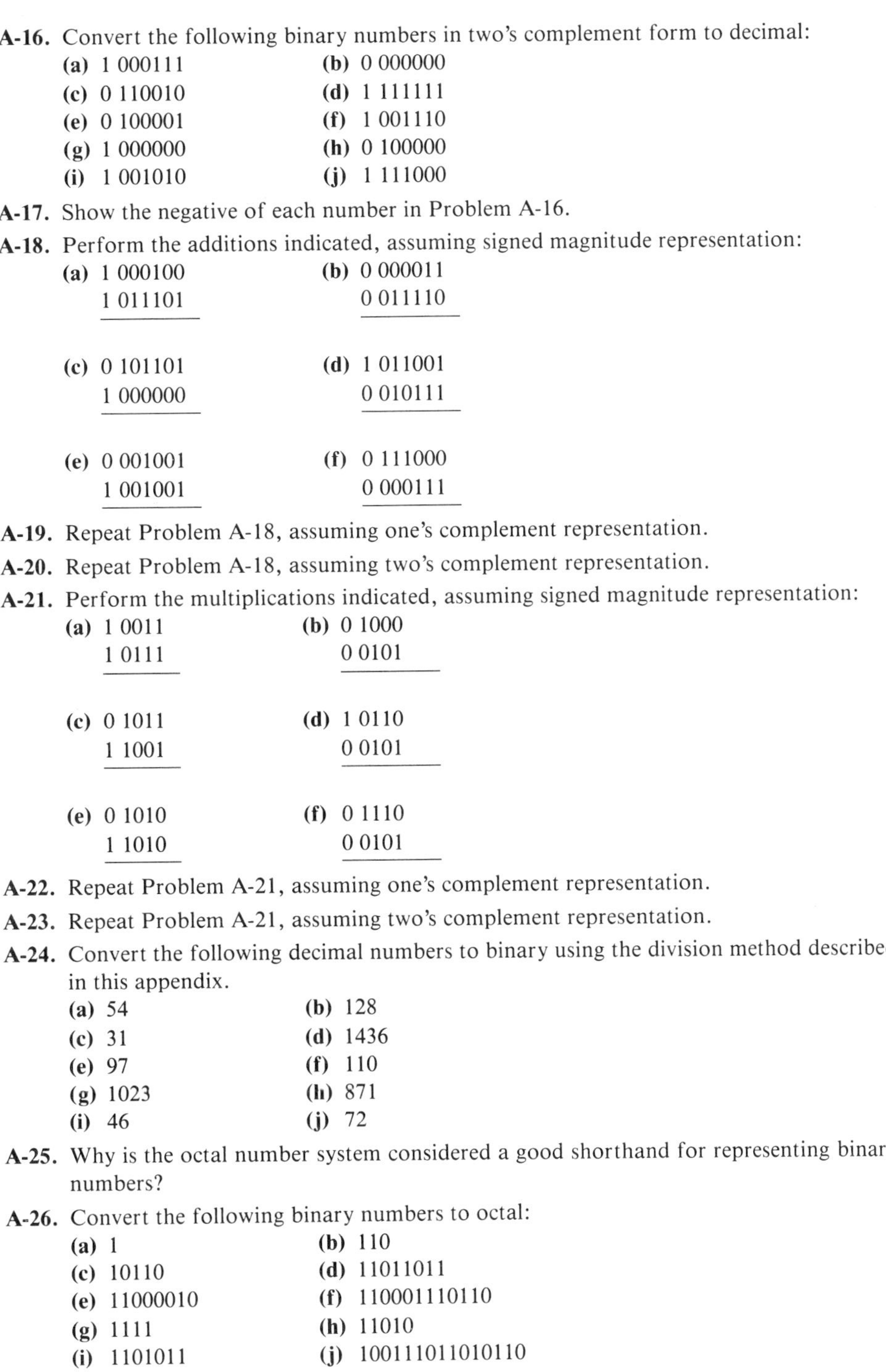

A-16. Convert the following binary numbers in two's complement form to decimal:

(a) 1 000111	**(b)** 0 000000
(c) 0 110010	**(d)** 1 111111
(e) 0 100001	**(f)** 1 001110
(g) 1 000000	**(h)** 0 100000
(i) 1 001010	**(j)** 1 111000

A-17. Show the negative of each number in Problem A-16.

A-18. Perform the additions indicated, assuming signed magnitude representation:

(a) 1 000100 1 011101	**(b)** 0 000011 0 011110
(c) 0 101101 1 000000	**(d)** 1 011001 0 010111
(e) 0 001001 1 001001	**(f)** 0 111000 0 000111

A-19. Repeat Problem A-18, assuming one's complement representation.

A-20. Repeat Problem A-18, assuming two's complement representation.

A-21. Perform the multiplications indicated, assuming signed magnitude representation:

(a) 1 0011 1 0111	**(b)** 0 1000 0 0101
(c) 0 1011 1 1001	**(d)** 1 0110 0 0101
(e) 0 1010 1 1010	**(f)** 0 1110 0 0101

A-22. Repeat Problem A-21, assuming one's complement representation.

A-23. Repeat Problem A-21, assuming two's complement representation.

A-24. Convert the following decimal numbers to binary using the division method described in this appendix.

(a) 54	**(b)** 128
(c) 31	**(d)** 1436
(e) 97	**(f)** 110
(g) 1023	**(h)** 871
(i) 46	**(j)** 72

A-25. Why is the octal number system considered a good shorthand for representing binary numbers?

A-26. Convert the following binary numbers to octal:

(a) 1	**(b)** 110
(c) 10110	**(d)** 11011011
(e) 11000010	**(f)** 110001110110
(g) 1111	**(h)** 11010
(i) 1101011	**(j)** 100111011010110

A-27. Convert the following octal numbers to binary:

(a) 5	**(b)** 61
(c) 37	**(d)** 700
(e) 235	**(f)** 14760
(g) 3615	**(h)** 22
(i) 1492	**(j)** 602

A-28. Why is the hexadecimal number system considered a good shorthand for a representing binary numbers? Why is it sometimes considered more difficult to work with than octal?

A-29. Convert the binary numbers from Problem A-26 into hexadecimal.

A-30. Convert the following hexadecimal numbers into binary:

(a) 19	**(b)** 1F3
(c) 7EDO	**(d)** ACE
(e) 5B9	**(f)** 22
(g) 101	**(h)** C1F
(i) A77	**(j)** 1F

Appendix B

Pascal Code for Assemblers and Emulators

This appendix presents Pascal code for "portable" versions of both the one- and two-address machine assemblers and emulators described in the text. The programs do not rely on any special host machine characteristics and should run directly on any machine that supports "standard" Pascal.

B.1 Installation Instructions

To achieve a level of portability, all machine-dependent data types and operations have been simulated directly in Pascal. For example, a word of memory is simulated by a packed array of bits (0..1). Corresponding machine operations on words, such as addition and logical shift, are implemented as Pascal procedures.

Although portable, this approach leads to quite a bit of inefficiency both in code space and in execution speed. While "standard" Pascal does not allow externally defined procedures, many Pascal implementations do. For those installations, it may be desirable to reimplement simulated operations and data type directly at the machine level, with Pascal-callable entry points.

For example, it would be a good idea to reimplement type word in terms of the host machine's word and operations. Many versions of Pascal also support string operations directly. The string module could be rewritten to use the built-in string type. The assemblers and emulators themselves have been written without depending on the specific implementation of these types and operations.

To facilitate this approach, and because so many data type and operations are common to all of the programs, their code is grouped into "modules," which are presented separately. Here is a summary of the modules:

One-address machine definitions: Definitions of constants and types specific to the one-address machine assembler and emulator.

Two-address machine definitions: Definitions of constants and types specific to the two-address machine assembler and emulator.

Word definitions and operations: Definitions and operations that simulate a word, as well as arithmetic/logical operations on words.

String definitions and operations: Definitions and operations that allow string manipulation in Pascal.

Symbol table definitions and operations: Definitions and operations to implement a symbol table for the one- and two-address machine assemblers.

Memory unit definitions and operations: Definitions and operations that simulate the memory unit for the one- and two-address machine emulators.

Input/output unit definitions and operations: Definitions and operations that simulate the input/output unit for the two-address machine emulator.

The assembler (Asm) and emulator (Sim) programs indicate where to include the appropriate parts of each module. The declarations and procedures for each module should be placed in their respective locations in the order specified. Some operations in the string module, for example, require the definitions and operations from the word module. Not all procedures from a module may be required in each program. Table B-1 provides a list of procedures that are not required by each of the programs.

A test program that implements a stack-based word calculator (Wordstack) has also been provided. This program should be helpful in testing new implementations of the word and string modules. It is also a useful tool for learning about the various arithmetic and logical operations and for verifying the results of a program. A list of procedures that are not required by this program can also be found in Table B-1.

TABLE B-1 PASCAL PROCEDURES NOT REQUIRED BY ALL PROGRAMS

Word	String	Symbol	Memory	I/O
Asm1				
andword	(all used)	(all used)	(none used)	(none used)
ashword				
cshword				
decrementword				
divword				
xorword				
Asm 2				
andword	(all used)	(all used)	(none used)	(none used)
ashword				
cshword				
decrementword				
divword				
xorword				
Sim1				
andword	makestr	(none used)	(all used)	(none used)
cshword	testeqstr			
xorword				
Sim2				
(all used)	makestr	(none used)	(all used)	(all used)
	testeqstr			
Wordstack				
(all used)	makestr	(none used)	(none used)	(none used)
	testeqstr			

B.2 LISTINGS OF PASCAL CODE

The following tables contain the complete listings for the one- and two-address machine assemblers, the one- and two-address machine emulators, the word-based stack test program, and the modules described earlier, which are common among them.

TABLE B-2 ONE-ADDRESS MACHINE DEFINITIONS

```
(* declarations for one-address machine
 *)
CONST
   hostsize = 32;                  (* no. bits in host machine integer *)
   wordsize = 16;                  (* no. bits per word *)
   wordlen  = 6;                   (* print length of word *)
   topbit   = 15;                  (* highest bit position *)

   addrsize = 10;                  (* no. bits in address *)
   addrlen  = 4;                   (* print length of address *)

   regsize  = 1;                   (* no. bits in reg. number (0 or 1) *)

   modesize  = 2;                  (* no. bits in mode field *)
   topmode   = 3;                  (* highest address mode *)
   maxmode   = 3;                  (* max. available mode *)
   direct    = 0;                  (* address mode table *)
   immediate = 1;
   indirect  = 2;
   indexed   = 3;

   opsize    = 4;                  (* no. bits in operation field *)
   topop     = 16;                 (* highest opcode *)
   maxop     = 11;                 (* max. available opcode *)
   haltop    =  0;                 (* op. table *)
   loadop    =  1;
   storeop   =  2;
   callop    =  3;
   brop      =  4;
   breqop    =  5;
   brgeop    =  6;
   brltop    =  7;
   addop     =  8;
   subop     =  9;
   mulop     = 10;
   divop     = 11;


TYPE
   addrmode = 0..topmode;
   opcode   = 0..topop;
```

TABLE B-3 TWO-ADDRESS MACHINE DEFINITIONS

```
(* declarations for two-address machine
 *)
CONST
   hostsize  = 32;                        (* no. bits in host machine integer *)
   wordsize  = 32;                        (* no. bits per word *)
   wordlen   = 11;                        (* print length of word *)
   topbit    = 31;                        (* highest bit position *)

   addrsize  = 18;                        (* no. bits in address *)
   addrlen   = 6;                         (* print length of address *)

   regsize   = 3;                         (* no. bits in register field *)
   reglen    = 1;                         (* print length of register field *)
   topreg    = 7;                         (* highest register number *)
   maxreg    = 7;                         (* max. available register number *)

   modesize  = 3;                         (* no. bits in mode field *)
   topmode   = 7;                         (* highest address mode *)
   maxmode   = 7;                         (* max. available mode *)
   direct    = 0;                         (* address mode table *)
   immediate = 1;
   indirect  = 2;
   indexed   = 4;

   opsize    =  5;                        (* no. bits in operation field *)
   topop     = 31;                        (* highest opcode *)
   maxop     = 29;                        (* max. available opcode *)
   haltop    =  0;   addop     = 15;      (* op. table *)
   loadop    =  1;   subop     = 16;
   storeop   =  2;   mulop     = 17;
   brop      =  3;   divop     = 18;
   cmprop    =  4;   andop     = 19;
   breqop    =  5;   orop      = 20;
   brneop    =  6;   xorop     = 21;
   brgtop    =  7;   notop     = 22;
   brltop    =  8;   ashop     = 23;
   brgeop    =  9;   cshop     = 24;
   brleop    = 10;   lshop     = 25;
   pushop    = 11;   inchrop   = 26;
   popop     = 12;   outchrop  = 27;
   callop    = 13;   iostatop  = 28;
   rtnop     = 14;   iocmdop   = 29;

TYPE
   regindex = 0..topreg;
   addrmode = 0..topmode;
   opcode   = 0..topop;
```

TABLE B-4 WORD DEFINITIONS AND OPERATIONS

```
(* Declarations for type word
 *    Notes:  Type word is implemented as an array of bits.  The least
 *            significant bit is 0, and the sign bit is defined as
 *            'topbit'.  The size of the array is defined as 'wordsize'.
 *
 *            type word:
 *
 *                  |<--------- wordsize --------->|
 *
 *              sign bit-.
 *                  ---V--------        -----------
 *                  |   |   |   ...    |   |   |
 *                  ------------        -----------
 *                 topbit                  1   0
 *
 *)
TYPE
   bit = 0..1;                               (* representation of bit *)
   bitindex = 0..topbit;                     (* range of bit indicies *)
   word  = PACKED ARRAY [bitindex] OF bit;   (* word of memory *)


VAR
   zeroword:  word;                          (* useful word of zeros *)


(*  Operations on type word
 *     Notes:  These operations are for a twos complement version.
 *             Only a few of the routines would need to be changed
 *             to implement ones complement or signed magnitude.
 *)


(* wordinit - initialization for type word
 *)
PROCEDURE wordinit;
VAR
   i: bitindex;
BEGIN
   FOR i:= 0 to topbit DO
   BEGIN
      zeroword[i]:= 0;
   END;
END;   (* wordinit *)


(* testltword - tests whether a word is less than zero
 *)
FUNCTION testltword (VAR operand: word): boolean;
BEGIN
   testltword:= (operand[topbit] = 1);
END;  (* testltword *)


(* testgeword - tests whether a word is greater than or equal to zero
 *)
```

TABLE B-4 WORD DEFINITIONS AND OPERATIONS (cont.)

```
FUNCTION testgeword (VAR operand: word): boolean;
BEGIN
   testgeword:= (operand[topbit] = 0);
END;  (* testgeword *)


(* testeqword - tests whether a word is equal to zero
 *)
FUNCTION testeqword (VAR operand: word): boolean;
LABEL
   1;
VAR
   i: bitindex;
BEGIN
   testeqword:= true;
   FOR i:= topbit DOWNTO 0 DO
   BEGIN
      IF operand[i] <> 0 THEN
      BEGIN
         testeqword:= false;
         GOTO 1;
      END;
   END;
1:
END;  (* testeqword *)


(* lshword - logical shift word by count (+n is left, -n is right)
 *)
PROCEDURE lshword (VAR result, operand: word; count: integer);
VAR
   i: bitindex;
   c: integer;
BEGIN
   IF abs(count) > wordsize THEN              (* put count is in range *)
   BEGIN
      count:= wordsize;
   END;
   c:= abs (count);
   IF count < 0 THEN                          (* logical right shift *)
   BEGIN
      FOR i:= c TO topbit DO                     (* shift word right *)
      BEGIN
         result[i-c]:= operand[i];
      END;
      FOR i:= topbit-c+1 TO topbit DO            (* zero upper bits *)
      BEGIN
         result[i]:= 0;
      END;
   END
   ELSE                                       (* logical left shift *)
   BEGIN
      FOR i:= topbit DOWNTO c DO                 (* shift word left *)
      BEGIN
         result[i]:= operand[i-c];
      END;
```

TABLE B-4 WORD DEFINITIONS AND OPERATIONS (cont.)

```
      FOR i:= c-1 DOWNTO 0 DO                    (* zero lower bits *)
      BEGIN
         result[i]:= 0;
      END;
   END;
END;   (* lshword *)


(* ashword - arithmetic shift word by count (+n is left, -n is right)
 *)
PROCEDURE ashword (VAR result, operand: word; count: integer);
VAR
   i, c: bitindex;
   t: bit;
BEGIN
   t:= operand[topbit];
   IF abs (count) >= wordsize THEN            (* put count in range *)
   BEGIN
      c:= wordsize-1;
   END
   ELSE
   BEGIN
      c:= abs (count);
   END;
   IF count < 0 THEN                          (* arithmetic right shift *)
   BEGIN
      FOR i:= c TO topbit-1 DO                   (* shift word right *)
      BEGIN
         result[i-c]:= operand[i];
      END;
      FOR i:= topbit-c TO topbit-1 DO            (* copy sign to upper bits *)
      BEGIN
         result[i]:= t;
      END;
   END
   ELSE                                       (* arithmetic left shift *)
   BEGIN
      FOR i:= topbit DOWNTO c DO                  (* shift word left *)
      BEGIN
         result[i]:= operand[i-c];
      END;
      FOR i:= c-1 DOWNTO 0 DO                     (* zero lower bits *)
      BEGIN
         result[i]:= 0;
      END;
   END;
   operand[topbit]:= t;
END;   (* ashword *)


(* cshword - circular shift word by count (+n is left, -n is right)
 *)
PROCEDURE cshword (VAR result: word; operand: word; count: integer);
VAR
   i, c: bitindex;
```

TABLE B-4 WORD DEFINITIONS AND OPERATIONS (cont.)

```
BEGIN
   c:= count MOD wordsize;                    (* put count in range *)
   IF c < 0 THEN
   BEGIN
      c:= wordsize + c;                          (* new count for right shift *)
   END;
   FOR i:= 0 TO topbit DO                     (* circular shift word *)
   BEGIN
      result[(i+c) MOD wordsize]:= operand[i];
   END;
END;   (* cshword *)


(* maskword - mask out all but lower bits of word
 *)
PROCEDURE maskword (VAR result,operand: word; nmask: integer);
VAR
   i: bitindex;
BEGIN
   result:= operand;
   IF nmask < 0 THEN                          (* put mask count in range *)
   BEGIN
      nmask:= 0;
   END;
   IF nmask < wordsize THEN
   BEGIN
      FOR i:= topbit DOWNTO nmask DO          (* clear lower bits of word *)
      BEGIN
         result[i]:= 0;
      END;
   END;
END;   (* maskword *)


(* andword - logical and of two words
 *)
PROCEDURE andword (VAR result,operand1,operand2: word);
VAR
   i: bitindex;
BEGIN
   FOR i:= 0 to topbit DO
   BEGIN
      IF (operand1[i] = 1) AND (operand2[i] = 1) THEN
      BEGIN
         result[i]:= 1;
      END
      ELSE
      BEGIN
         result[i]:= 0;
      END;
   END;
END;   (* andword *)


(* orword - logical inclusive or of two words
 *)
```

TABLE B-4 WORD DEFINITIONS AND OPERATIONS (cont.)

```
PROCEDURE orword (VAR result,operand1,operand2: word);
VAR
   i: bitindex;
BEGIN
   FOR i:= 0 to topbit DO
   BEGIN
      IF (operand1[i] = 1) OR (operand2[i] = 1) THEN
      BEGIN
         result[i]:= 1;
      END
      ELSE
      BEGIN
         result[i]:= 0;
      END;
   END;
END;   (* orword *)


(* xorword - logical exclusive or of two words
 *)
PROCEDURE xorword (VAR result,operand1,operand2: word);
VAR
   i: bitindex;
BEGIN
   FOR i:= 0 to topbit DO
   BEGIN
      IF operand1[i] = operand2[i] THEN
      BEGIN
         result[i]:= 0;
      END
      ELSE
      BEGIN
         result[i]:= 1;
      END;
   END;
END;   (* xorword *)


(* notword - logical complement of a word
 *)
PROCEDURE notword (VAR result,operand: word);
VAR
   i: bitindex;
BEGIN
   FOR i:= 0 to topbit DO
   BEGIN
      result[i]:= 1 - operand[i];
   END;
END;   (* notword *)


(* addword - arithmetic sum of two words
 *)
PROCEDURE addword (VAR result,operand1,operand2: word);
```

TABLE B-4 WORD DEFINITIONS AND OPERATIONS (cont.)

```
VAR
   i: bitindex;
   carry: bit;
   t: integer;
BEGIN
   carry:= 0;
   FOR i:= 0 to topbit DO
   BEGIN
      t:= operand1[i] + operand2[i] + carry;
      result[i]:= t MOD 2;
      carry:= t DIV 2;
   END;
END;   (* addword *)


(* subword - arithmetic difference of two words
 *)
PROCEDURE subword (VAR result, operand1,operand2: word);
VAR
   i: bitindex;
   carry: bit;
   t: integer;
BEGIN
   carry:= 1;
   FOR i:= 0 to topbit DO
   BEGIN
      t:= operand1[i] + 1 - operand2[i] + carry;
      result[i]:= t MOD 2;
      carry:= t DIV 2;
   END;
END;   (* subword *)


(* incrementword - arithmetic increment of a word
 *)
PROCEDURE incrementword (VAR result, operand: word);
VAR
   i: bitindex;
   carry: bit;
   t: integer;
BEGIN
   carry:= 1;
   FOR i:= 0 to topbit DO
   BEGIN
      t:= operand[i] + carry;
      result[i]:= t MOD 2;
      carry:= t DIV 2;
   END;
END;   (* incrementword *)


(* decrementword - arithmetic decrement of a word
 *)
PROCEDURE decrementword (VAR result, operand: word);
```

TABLE B-4 WORD DEFINITIONS AND OPERATIONS (cont.)

```
VAR
   i: bitindex;
   carry: bit;
   t: integer;
BEGIN
   carry:= 0;
   FOR i:= 0 to topbit DO
   BEGIN
      t:= 1 + operand[i] + carry;
      result[i]:= t MOD 2;
      carry:= t DIV 2;
   END;
END;   (* decrementword *)


(* negativeword - arithemtic negative of a word
 *)
PROCEDURE negativeword (VAR result, operand: word);
VAR
   i: bitindex;
   carry: bit;
   t: integer;
BEGIN
   carry:= 1;
   FOR i:= 0 to topbit DO
   BEGIN
      t:= 1 - operand[i] + carry;
      result[i]:= t MOD 2;
      carry:= t DIV 2;
   END;
END;   (* negativeword *)


(* mulword - arithemtic product of two words
 *)
PROCEDURE mulword (VAR result: word; operand1, operand2: word);
VAR
  i, nshift: bitindex;
BEGIN
   result:= zeroword;
   IF testltword (operand2) THEN            (* operand2 must be positive *)
   BEGIN
      negativeword (operand2,operand2);        (* exchange signs *)
      negativeword (operand1,operand1);
   END;
   nshift:= 0;
   FOR i:= 0 TO topbit-1 DO
   BEGIN
      IF operand2[i] = 1 THEN               (* add in non-zero term *)
      BEGIN
         lshword (operand1, operand1, nshift);
         addword (result, operand1, result);
         nshift:= 0;
      END;
      nshift:= nshift+1;
   END;
```

TABLE B-4 WORD DEFINITIONS AND OPERATIONS (cont.)

```
END;  (* mulword *)


(* divword - arithemtic integer quotient of two words
 *)
PROCEDURE divword (VAR result: word; operand1, operand2: word);
VAR
   i: bitindex;
   rmdr, test: word;
   rsltsign: boolean;
BEGIN
   result:= zeroword;
   rmdr:= zeroword;
   IF testeqword (operand2) THEN          (* attempt to divide by zero *)
   BEGIN
      result[topbit]:= 1;                   (* result is biggest number *)
      IF testgeword (operand1) THEN         (* set with correct sign *)
      BEGIN
         notword (result,result);
      END;
   END
   ELSE
   BEGIN
      rsltsign:= false;
      IF testltword (operand1) THEN         (* operands must be positive *)
      BEGIN
         negativeword (operand1,operand1);
         rsltsign:= NOT rsltsign;
      END;
      IF testltword (operand2) THEN
      BEGIN
         negativeword (operand2,operand2);
         rsltsign:= NOT rsltsign;
      END;
      FOR i:= topbit DOWNTO 0 DO
      BEGIN
         lshword (result,result,1);         (* position result *)
         lshword (rmdr,rmdr,1);             (* position remainder *)
         rmdr[0]:= operand1[i];             (* bring down next bit *)
         subword (test, rmdr, operand2);
         IF testgeword (test) THEN          (* test division succeeded *)
         BEGIN
            result[0]:=1;                     (* shift bit into result *)
            rmdr:= test;
         END;
      END;
      IF rsltsign THEN                      (* set correct sign of result *)
      BEGIN
         negativeword (result, result);
      END;
   END;
END;   (* divword *)


(* wordtonum - convert a word to the host internal number representation
 *             Note:  only works for word values that can be represented
```

TABLE B-4 WORD DEFINITIONS AND OPERATIONS (cont.)

```
 *                      in the precision of a host integer.
 *)
FUNCTION wordtonum (w: word): integer;
VAR
   i: bitindex;
   t,tincr: integer;
BEGIN
   t:= 0;
   IF testltword (w) THEN                     (* extract magnitude *)
   BEGIN
      tincr:= -1;
      negativeword (w,w);
   END
   ELSE
   BEGIN
      tincr:= 1;
   END;
   maskword (w,w,hostsize);                   (* truncate to host word size *)
   FOR i:= topbit DOWNTO 0 DO
   BEGIN
      t:= t*2;                                   (* 'shift' host word *)
      IF w[i] = 1 THEN
      BEGIN
         t:= t+tincr;                            (* add bit into host word *)
      END;
   END;
   wordtonum:= t;
END;   (* wordtonum *)


(* numtoword - convert host internal number representation to word
 *)
PROCEDURE numtoword (VAR result: word; n: integer);
VAR
   i: bitindex;
   t: integer;
BEGIN
   t:= abs (n);                               (* extract magnitude *)
   FOR i:= 0 TO topbit DO
   BEGIN
      result[i]:= abs(t MOD 2);                  (* add in bit of host word *)
      t:= t DIV 2;                               (* 'shift' host word *)
   END;
   IF n < 0 THEN                              (* set to correct sign *)
   BEGIN
      negativeword (result, result);
   END;
END;   (* numtoword *)


(* writeword - write octal representation of lower nbits of word to file f
 *)
PROCEDURE writeword (VAR f: text; VAR w: word; nbits: integer);
VAR
   bitsum,curbit,i,j,ndigits,nsum: integer;
```

TABLE B-4 WORD DEFINITIONS AND OPERATIONS (cont.)

```
BEGIN
   IF nbits > wordsize THEN                 (* bring nbits in range *)
   BEGIN
      nbits:= wordsize;
   END;
   ndigits:= (nbits+2) DIV 3;               (* number of digits in output *)
   nsum:= (nbits-1) MOD 3  + 1;             (* number of bits per digit *)
   curbit:= nbits;
   FOR i:= 1 TO ndigits DO                  (* for each digit *)
   BEGIN
      bitsum:= 0;
      FOR j:= 1 TO nsum DO                     (* for each bit in digit *)
      BEGIN
         curbit:= curbit-1;
         bitsum:= bitsum*2 + w[curbit];
      END;
      write (f,bitsum:1);
      nsum:= 3;                                (* reset bits per digit *)
   END;
END;   (* writeword *)
```

TABLE B-5 STRING DEFINITIONS AND OPERATIONS

```
(* Declarations for types string, shortstr and savestr
 *    Notes:  Type string is implemented as a character array.
 *            A linked list implementation would also be possible.
 *            An implementation-dependent string type could be used.
 *
 *            Type string:
 *
 *                      first        last
 *     char(len)-.    .-char         char-.    .----- unused ------.
 *            ---V----V--------       ---V----V---       ---------V--
 *            |   |   |   |   ...    |   |   |   ...   |   |   |
 *            ----------------        -----------        -----------
 *              0   1   2            len  len+1               maxstr
 *
 *            Type shortstr is an intermediate data type that allows a
 *            string to be initialized to a short literal.   No length
 *            information is stored.  A shortstr is only as long as the
 *            last non-blank character.  Implemented as character array.
 *
 *            Type shortstr:
 *
 *                 first        last
 *               .-char         char-.    .----- blanks ------.
 *            ---V-------       ---V----V---       ---------V--
 *            |   |   |  ...   |   |   |   ...   |   |   |
 *            -----------       -----------        -----------
 *              1   2           len  len+1              maxshortstr
 *
 *            Variable savestr is a string pool, addressed by an index.
 *            index.  A number of strings are stored end-to-end without
 *            the unused trailing characters present in type string. The
 *            first unused location in savestr is located by savestrptr.
 *
 *            Var savestr:
 *
 *            .-string(1)-..- string(2)      )-..---- unused -----.
 *            V            VV                VV                   V
 *            -----------------------        ----------        ------
 *            || len = i   || len = j   ...    |          ...      |
 *            -----------------------        ----------        ------
 *            ^            ^                   ^                  ^
 *            1            i+1                 |                  maxsavestr
 *                                   savestrptr-'
 *)
CONST
   null = 0;                                  (* null savestring index *)
   maxstr = 127;                              (* max. string index *)
   maxshortstr = 8;                           (* max. shortstring index *)
   maxsavestr = 3000;                         (* max. savestring index *)


TYPE
   savestrindex = 0..maxsavestr;              (* range of savestrs *)
   shortstrindex = 1..maxshortstr;            (* range of shortstrs *)
   strindex = 0..maxstr;                      (* range of strings *)
   shortstring =
```

TABLE B-5 STRING DEFINITIONS AND OPERATIONS (cont.)

```
         PACKED ARRAY [shortstrindex] OF char;  (* dfn. of shortstring *)
   string = PACKED ARRAY [strindex] OF char;    (* dfn. of string *)
   cset = SET OF char;                          (* for lexical scanning *)
   bases = (octal, decimal);                    (* bases for reading words *)


VAR
   savestr:
         PACKED ARRAY [savestrindex] of char;   (* save string space *)
   savestrptr: savestrindex;                    (* last used savestr char *)



(* operations for type string
 *)



(* strinit - initialize string index table
 *)
PROCEDURE strinit;
BEGIN
   savestr[0]:= chr (0);                      (* initialize string pool *)
   savestrptr:= 0;
END;   (* strinit *)


(* strlen - returns the length of a string
 *)
FUNCTION strlen (VAR s: string): strindex;
BEGIN
   strlen:= ord (s[0]);
END;   (* strlen *)


(* nextchar - returns character at given position in string
 *)
FUNCTION nextchar (VAR s: string; curpos: strindex): char;
BEGIN
   IF curpos <= strlen (s) THEN
   BEGIN
      nextchar:= s[curpos];
   END
   ELSE
   BEGIN
      nextchar:= ' ';
   END;
END;   (* nextchar *)


(* skipchar - advances string index past any chars in cset
 *)
PROCEDURE skipchar (VAR s: string; VAR curpos: strindex; pre: cset);
VAR
   slen: strindex;
   done: boolean;
```

TABLE B-5 STRING DEFINITIONS AND OPERATIONS (cont.)

```
BEGIN
   slen:= strlen (s);
   done:= false;
   WHILE (curpos <= slen) AND (NOT done) DO
   BEGIN
      IF s[curpos] IN pre THEN
      BEGIN
         curpos:= curpos+1;
      END
      ELSE
      BEGIN
         done:= true;
      END;
   END;
END;  (* skipchar *)


(* nexttoken - returns substring and advances index upto any char in cset
 *)
PROCEDURE nexttoken (VAR token, s: string; VAR curpos: strindex; post: cset);
VAR
   slen, toklen: strindex;
   done: boolean;
BEGIN
   slen:= strlen (s);
   toklen:= 0;
   done:= false;
   WHILE (curpos <= slen) AND (NOT done) DO
   BEGIN
      IF s[curpos] IN post THEN
      BEGIN
         done:= true;
      END
      ELSE
      BEGIN
         toklen:= toklen+1;
         token[toklen]:= s[curpos];
         curpos:= curpos+1;
      END;
   END;
   token[0]:= chr (toklen);
END;  (* nexttoken *)


(* strtoword - converts string representing base b number to a word
 *)
FUNCTION strtoword (VAR w: word; VAR s: string; b: bases): boolean;
VAR
   i,slen: strindex;
   ch: char;
   wbase, wdig: word;
BEGIN
   strtoword:= false;
   i:= 1;
   ch:= nextchar (s,i);
```

TABLE B-5 STRING DEFINITIONS AND OPERATIONS (cont.)

```
   IF ch IN ['0'..'9'] THEN                    (* valid number *)
   BEGIN
      slen:= strlen (s);
      IF nextchar (s,slen) IN ['b','B'] THEN    (* base is octal *)
      BEGIN
         b:= octal;
         slen:= slen-1;
      END;
      numtoword (w,0);
      IF b = octal THEN                        (* convert octal number *)
      BEGIN
         WHILE ch IN ['0'..'7'] DO
         BEGIN
            numtoword (wdig,ord (ch) - ord ('0'));
            lshword (w,w,3);
            orword (w,w,wdig);
            i:= i+1;
            ch:= nextchar (s,i);
         END;
      END
      ELSE                                     (* convert decimal number *)
      BEGIN
         numtoword (wbase,10);
         WHILE ch IN ['0'..'9'] DO
         BEGIN
            numtoword (wdig,ord (ch) - ord ('0'));
            mulword (w,w,wbase);
            addword (w,w,wdig);
            i:= i+1;
            ch:= nextchar (s,i);
         END;
      END;
      strtoword:= (i > slen);
   END;
END;   (* strtoword *)


(* testeqstr - compares two strings for equality
 *)
FUNCTION testeqstr (VAR s1,s2: string): boolean;
LABEL
   1;
VAR
   i: strindex;
BEGIN
   testeqstr:= true;
   FOR i:= 0 TO strlen (s1) DO
   BEGIN
      IF s1[i] <> s2[i] THEN
      BEGIN
         testeqstr:= false;
         GOTO 1;
      END;
   END;
   1:
END;   (* testeqstr *)
```

TABLE B-5 STRING DEFINITIONS AND OPERATIONS (cont.)

```
(* makestr - converts trimmed "short" string to a string
 *)
PROCEDURE makestr (VAR s: string; shorts: shortstring);
VAR
   i: shortstrindex;
   slen: strindex;
BEGIN
   slen:= 0;
   FOR i:= maxshortstr DOWNTO 1 DO
   BEGIN
      IF (shorts[i] <> ' ') AND (i > slen) THEN
      BEGIN
         slen:= i;
      END;
   END;
   FOR i:= 1 TO slen DO
   BEGIN
      s[i]:= shorts[i];
   END;
   s[0]:= chr (slen);
END;   (* makestr *)


(* readstr - read file f upto eoln and return line as a string
 *)
PROCEDURE readstr (VAR f: text; VAR s: string);
VAR
   i: strindex;
BEGIN
   i:= 0;
   WHILE NOT eoln (f) DO
   BEGIN
      i:= i+1;
      read (f,s[i]);
   END;
   s[0]:= chr (i);
END;   (* readstr *)


(* writestr - write string to file f
 *)
PROCEDURE writestr (VAR f: text; VAR s: string);
VAR
   i: strindex;
BEGIN
   FOR i:= 1 TO ord (s[0]) DO
   BEGIN
      write (f,s[i]);
   END;
END;   (* writestr *)


(* getstr - return a string from string pool
 *)
PROCEDURE getstr (VAR s: string; p: savestrindex);
VAR
```

TABLE B-5 STRING DEFINITIONS AND OPERATIONS (cont.)

```
   i: savestrindex;
BEGIN
   IF (p <> null) AND (p <= savestrptr) THEN
   BEGIN
      FOR i:= 0 TO ord (savestr[p]) DO
      BEGIN
         s[i]:= savestr[p+i];
      END;
   END
   ELSE
   BEGIN
      s[0]:= chr (0);
   END;
END;   (* getstr *)


(* putstr - place a string into string pool and return its index
 *)
FUNCTION putstr (VAR s: string): savestrindex;
VAR
   i, slen: strindex;
BEGIN
   slen:= ord (s[0]);
   IF savestrptr+1+slen <= maxsavestr THEN
   BEGIN
      FOR i:= slen DOWNTO 0 DO
      BEGIN
         savestr[savestrptr+1+i]:= s[i];
      END;
      putstr:= savestrptr + 1;
      savestrptr:= savestrptr+1+slen;
   END
   ELSE
   BEGIN
      putstr:= null;
   END;
END;   (* putstr *)
```

TABLE B-6 SYMBOL TABLE DEFINITIONS AND OPERATIONS

```
(* definiton of symbol table for words/strings
 *      Notes:  Uses first character of string as the primary
 *              hash key, with a linear secondary rehash.
 *
 *    hash table
 *       .----.        to save string table
 *     0 |    |
 *       |----|        ^                   ^
 *       ~    ~        |                   |
 *       |----|    --|-----------.     --|-----------.
 *     i |  ------>|    | word |  --->|  |   | word |  --->
 *       |----|    ---------------'    ---------------'
 *                   symbol record
 *)
CONST
   maxhash = 127;                              (* extent of hash table *)


TYPE
   symptr = ^symbol;
   symbol = RECORD
               symstr:  savestrindex;          (* name of symbol *)
               symword:  word;                 (* definition of symbol *)
               symnext: symptr                 (* ptr. to next symbol *)
            END;
   hashindex = 0..maxhash;


VAR
   hashtable:  ARRAY [hashindex] OF symptr;    (* hash index table *)


(* routines to manipulate symbol table
 *)


(* symtblinit - initialize symbol table
 *)
PROCEDURE symtblinit;
VAR
   i: hashindex;
BEGIN
   FOR i:= 0 TO maxhash DO
   BEGIN
      hashtable[i]:= nil;
   END;
END;   (* symtblinit *)


(* makekey - compute key for hash index table
 *)
FUNCTION makekey (VAR s: string): hashindex;
BEGIN
   makekey:= ord (nextchar (s,1));
```

TABLE B-6 SYMBOL TABLE DEFINITIONS AND OPERATIONS (cont.)

```
END;   (* makekey *)


(* lookup -  get definition of symbol from symbol table if defined
 *)
FUNCTION lookup (VAR defn: word; VAR name: string): boolean;
VAR
   cursym: symptr;
   curstr: string;
   done: boolean;
BEGIN
   lookup:= false;
   IF strlen (name) > 0 THEN
   BEGIN
      cursym:= hashtable [makekey (name)];   (* first entry for this key *)
      done:= (cursym = nil);
      WHILE NOT done DO                      (* more entries for this key *)
      BEGIN
         WITH cursym^ DO
         BEGIN
            getstr (curstr,symstr);             (* get label string *)
            IF testeqstr (name,curstr) THEN        (* string matches *)
            BEGIN
               defn:= symword;                        (* return definition *)
               done:= true;
               lookup:= true;
            END
            ELSE                                   (* no match *)
            BEGIN
               cursym:= symnext;                      (* try next entry *)
               done:= (cursym = nil);
            END;
         END;
      END;
   END;
END;   (* lookup *)


(* install -  enter a definition into the symbol table
 *)
FUNCTION install (VAR defn: word; VAR name: string): boolean;
VAR
   newsym: symptr;
   strloc: savestrindex;
   h: hashindex;
BEGIN
   install:= false;
   h:= makekey (name);                       (* hask key for string *)
   strloc:= putstr (name);                   (* enter string in pool *)
   IF strloc <> null THEN
   BEGIN
      new (newsym);                          (* new space for definition *)
      WITH newsym^ DO
      BEGIN
```

TABLE B-6 SYMBOL TABLE DEFINITIONS AND OPERATIONS (cont.)

```
        symstr:= strloc;                          (* label string index *)
        symword:= defn;                           (* definition *)
        symnext:= hashtable[h];                   (* link to next entry *)
     END;
     hashtable[h]:= newsym;                     (* intsall entry in table *)
     install:= true;
  END;
END;  (* install *)
```

TABLE B-7 MEMORY UNIT DEFINITIONS AND OPERATIONS

```
(* Definition of memory for one- and two-address machine emulators.
 *      Note: This implementation models memory as an array of
 *            words, and only allows as much memory as can be
 *            addressed with a host integer.
 *
 *            Trace information is stored in a string pool, which
 *            is pointed to by corresponding locations of a special
 *            trace memory.
 *
 *                 memory         trace memory
 *               ~        ~       ~        ~
 *               |--------|       |--------|
 *               |  word  |  ...  |    -----.
 *               |--------|       |--------| |
 *               ~        ~       ~        ~ |
 *                                           |
 *                                         --V--------------------
 *                                          | T | R | A | C | E |
 *                                       ------------------------
 *                                                 string pool
 *)

CONST
   maxaddr     = 1023;           (* highest address implemented; pwr of 2 *)
   maxaddrsize = 10;             (* no. bits for maxaddr *)

TYPE
   address = 0..maxaddr;

VAR
   tracememory                                    (* trace string pointers *)
      : PACKED ARRAY [address] OF savestrindex;
   memory: PACKED ARRAY [address] OF word;        (* word storage *)


(* meminit - initialize word and trace memories and first/last indicies
 *)
PROCEDURE meminit;
VAR
   i: address;
BEGIN
   FOR i:= 0 TO maxaddr DO
   BEGIN
      memory[i]:= zeroword;                    (* set memory to zeros *)
      tracememory[i]:= null;                   (* clear trace memory *)
   END;
END;   (* meminit *)

(* memindex - converts address to integer, or false if out of range
 *)
FUNCTION memindex (VAR i: integer;  w: word): boolean;
BEGIN
   maskword (w,w,addrsize);
   i:= wordtonum (w);
   memindex:= i <= maxaddr;
```

TABLE B-7 MEMORY UNIT DEFINITIONS AND OPERATIONS (cont.)

```
END;  (* memindex *)

(* writemem - writes contents to memory, or false if address out of range
 *)
FUNCTION writemem (VAR d,a: word; s: savestrindex): boolean;
VAR
   i: integer;
BEGIN
   writemem:= false;
   IF memindex (i,a) THEN
   BEGIN
      memory[i]:= d;
      tracememory[i]:= s;
      writemem:= true;
   END;
END;   (* writemem *)


(* readmem - returns contents of memory, or false if address out of range
 *)
FUNCTION readmem (VAR d,a: word; VAR s: savestrindex): boolean;
VAR
   i: integer;
BEGIN
   readmem:= false;
   IF memindex (i,a) THEN
   BEGIN
      d:= memory[i];
      s:= tracememory[i];
      readmem:= true;
   END;
END;   (* readmem *)
```

TABLE B-8 INPUT/OUTPUT UNIT DEFINITIONS AND OPERATIONS

```
(*  Input/output routines for two-address machine
 *      Notes:    1. Implementation assumes ASCII keyboard, printer
 *                   and display codes.  Build mapping routines if
 *                   host system uses some other code.
 *                2. Keyboard, printer and display are implemented
 *                   as text files 'keyboard', 'printer' and 'display'.
 *                   REWRITEing 'printer' and 'display' is deferred
 *                   until the first WRITE actually occurs.  RESETting
 *                   file 'keyboard'is deferred until the first READ
 *                   command actually occurs.
 *                3. The disk controller is implemented as an array of
 *                   sectors.  Each sector is an array of bytes.  The
 *                   controller also includes a sector buffer to hold
 *                   the current working sector.  The contents of disk
 *                   are archived on file 'disk'.  RESETting and reading
 *                   'disk' is deferred until the first disk read/write
 *                   occurs.  File 'disk' is written upon termination
 *                   only if the disk was actually used.
 *                4. Devices return the following status byte format.
 *                   Only the use of bit 0 is documented in the text.
 *                   Bit 7 tells whether a device is connected.
 *
 *                              status byte
 *        7       6       5       4       3       2       1       0
 *     +-------+-------+-------+-------+-------+-------+-------+-------+
 *     |1=nodev|                                               | 1=busy|
 *     |0=isdev|                                               | 0=idle|
 *     +-------+-------+-------+-------+-------+-------+-------+-------+
 *)
CONST
   syskbd     =  0;              (* system keyboard *)
   sysdpy     =  1;              (* system display  *)
   sysprt     =  2;              (* system printer  *)
   sysdsk     =  10;             (* system disk drive *)

   idle       =  0;              (* device idle bit *)
   busy       =  1;              (* device busy bit *)
   nodev      =  1;              (* device not present bit *)
   isdev      =  0;              (* device present bit *)

   maxsect    =  20;             (* last available sector on disk *)
   sectsize   = 256;             (* number of bytes/sector *)
   dskpos     =   1;             (* disk position command *)
   dskin      =   2;             (* disk input command *)
   dskout     =   3;             (* disk output command *)
   dskbufrst  =   4;             (* reset disk controller buffer ptr *)
   dskbufclr  =   5;             (* clear disk controller buffer *)

   nocode     =  -1;             (* non-valid ASCII character code *)
   asciieot   =   4;             (* ASCII code for end of file*)
   asciilf    =  10;             (* ASCII code for line feed *)
   asciicr    =  13;             (* ASCII code for carriage return *)

TYPE
   byte = 0..255;
```

TABLE B-8 INPUT/OUTPUT UNIT DEFINITIONS AND OPERATIONS (cont.)

```
   bufindex = 1..sectsize;
   sectindex = 0..maxsect;
   sector = PACKED ARRAY [bufindex] OF byte;
   diskstruct = ARRAY [sectindex] OF sector;
   diskinfo = RECORD                              (* disk controller info. *)
                 dsksect:      diskstruct;          (* disk storage *)
                 cursect:      sectindex;           (* current sector index *)
                 dskbuf:       sector;              (* disk controller buffer *)
                 curbuf:       bufindex;            (* current buffer position *)
                 pendingcmd:   byte;                (* pending controller cmd *)
                 nargbits,                          (* no. arg bits to collect *)
                 argbit:       bitindex;            (* next arg bit to collect *)
                 havearg:      boolean;             (* flags whole arg pending *)
                 pendingarg:   word;                (* storage for pending arg *)
                 dskfirst:     boolean;             (* first disk i/o *)
              END;
   diskarchive = FILE OF diskstruct;                 (* disk archive file *)


VAR
   disk:       diskarchive;                  (* system disk archive file *)
   keyboard,                                 (* system keyboard file *)
   display,                                  (* system display file *)
   printer:    text;                         (* system printer file *)
   diskdev:    diskinfo;                     (* system disk device *)
   kbdfirst,                                 (* first input from keyboard *)
   dpyfirst,                                 (* first output to dislay *)
   prtfirst:   boolean;                      (* first output to printer *)
   kbdlastch,                                (* code of last char read from kbd *)
   dpylastch,                                (* code of last char displayed *)
   prtlastch: integer;                       (* code of last char printed *)
(* clearsect - clear a sector to 0's
 *)
PROCEDURE clearsect (VAR s: sector);
VAR
   i: bufindex;
BEGIN
   FOR i:= 1 TO sectsize DO
   BEGIN
      s[i]:= 0;
   END;
END;  (* clearsect *)


(* ioinit - initialize input/output routines
 *)
PROCEDURE ioinit;
BEGIN
   kbdfirst:= true;                              (* setup system keyboard *)
   kbdlastch:= nocode;
   dpyfirst:= true;                              (* setup system display *)
   dpylastch:= nocode;
   prtfirst:= true;                              (* setup system printer *)
   prtlastch:= nocode;
   WITH diskdev DO                               (* setup system disk *)
```

TABLE B-8 INPUT/OUTPUT UNIT DEFINITIONS AND OPERATIONS (cont.)

```
   BEGIN
      clearsect (dskbuf);                  (* clear controller buffer *)
      cursect:= 0;                         (* init current sect index *)
      curbuf:= 1;                          (* init current buf index *)
      havearg:= false;                     (* no cmd arg pending *)
      nargbits:= 0;                        (* number of arg bits to read *)
      argbit:= 0;                          (* next arg bit to read *)
      dskfirst:= true;                     (* disk not yet accessed *)
   END;
END;   (* ioinit *)


(* ioflush - flush contents of buffered i/o devices
 *)
PROCEDURE ioflush;
BEGIN
   WITH diskdev DO
   BEGIN
      IF NOT dskfirst THEN              (* write disk to archive file *)
      BEGIN
         rewrite (disk);
         write (disk,dsksect);
      END;
   END;
END;   (* ioflush *)


(* bytecode - return lower eight bits of word as integer
 *)
FUNCTION bytecode (device: word): byte;
BEGIN
   maskword (device,device,8);
   bytecode:= wordtonum (device);
END;   (* bytecode *)


(* getio - reads data byte from selected device
 *         Note:  This version expands eoln (keyboard)
 *                to returns cr,lf on two successive calls.
 *                The procedure returns control-D  on the
 *                first call at eof (keyboard), and never
 *                thereafter.
 *)
PROCEDURE getio (VAR data: word;  device: word);
VAR
   dno:  byte;
   code: integer;
   ch:   char;
BEGIN
   dno:= bytecode (device);
   IF dno = syskbd THEN                 (* system keyboard device *)
   BEGIN
      IF kbdfirst THEN                    (* reset keyboard first time *)
      BEGIN
         reset (keyboard);
```

TABLE B-8 INPUT/OUTPUT UNIT DEFINITIONS AND OPERATIONS (cont.)

```
         kbdfirst:= false;
      END;
      IF eof (keyboard) THEN                        (* end of file processing *)
      BEGIN
         IF kbdlastch <> asciieot THEN              (* return eot first time *)
         BEGIN
            code:= asciieot;
         END
         ELSE
         BEGIN
            WHILE true DO;                          (* otherwise WAITS FOREVER! *)
         END;
      END
      ELSE
      BEGIN
         IF eoln (keyboard) THEN                    (* end of line processing *)
         BEGIN
            IF kbdlastch <> asciicr THEN            (* returned cr first time *)
            BEGIN
               code:= asciicr;
            END
            ELSE
            BEGIN                                   (* return lf second time *)
               code:= asciilf;
               readln (keyboard);
            END;
         END
         ELSE
         BEGIN
            read (keyboard,ch);                     (* return normal char *)
            code:= ord (ch);
         END;
      END;
      kbdlastch:= code;
      numtoword (data,code);
   END
   ELSE IF dno = sysdsk THEN                        (* system disk device *)
   BEGIN
      WITH diskdev DO
      BEGIN
         numtoword (data,dskbuf[curbuf]);           (* read byte from buffer *)
         curbuf:= (curbuf MOD sectsize) + 1;        (* incr buf ptr with wrap *)
      END;
   END;
END;  (* getio *)


(* putio - writes data byte to selected device
 *        Note:  To satisfy pascal i/o on character devices, this
 *               version buffers cr,lf or lf,cr and outputs both
 *               using writeln.  Single cr or lf is output by itself
 *               one character late.
 *)
PROCEDURE putio (data: word; device: word);
VAR
   code: integer;
```

TABLE B-8 INPUT/OUTPUT UNIT DEFINITIONS AND OPERATIONS (cont.)

```
  dno:  byte;


(* putchrdev - put to a character device like a printer or display
 *)
PROCEDURE putchrdev (VAR f: text; VAR lastcode: integer; VAR firstp: boolean);
BEGIN
   IF firstp THEN                                  (* rewrite dev first time *)
   BEGIN
      rewrite (f);
      firstp:= false;
   END;
   IF code IN [asciicr,asciilf] THEN               (* buffer cr,lf/lf,cr *)
   BEGIN
      IF ((lastcode = asciicr) AND (code = asciilf)) OR
         ((lastcode = asciilf) AND (code = asciicr)) THEN
      BEGIN
         writeln (f);                              (* prt both cr,lf *)
         code:= nocode;
      END
      ELSE IF lastcode IN [asciicr,asciilf] THEN   (* pending cr or lf *)
      BEGIN
         write (f,chr (lastcode));
      END;
   END
   ELSE
   BEGIN
      IF lastcode IN [asciicr,asciilf] THEN        (* pending cr or lf *)
      BEGIN
         write (f,chr (lastcode));
      END;
      write (f,chr (code));                        (* prt normal char *)
   END;
   lastcode:= code;
END;    (* putchrdev *)


BEGIN   (* putio *)
   code:= bytecode (data);
   dno:= bytecode (device);                     (* system display *)
   IF dno = sysdpy THEN
   BEGIN
      putchrdev (display,dpylastch,dpyfirst);
   END
   ELSE IF dno = sysprt THEN
   BEGIN                                        (* system printer *)
      putchrdev (printer,prtlastch,prtfirst);
   END
   ELSE IF dno = sysdsk THEN                    (* system disk *)
   BEGIN
      WITH diskdev DO
      BEGIN
         dskbuf[curbuf]:= code;                 (* write byte in buffer *)
         curbuf:= (curbuf MOD sectsize) + 1;    (* incr buf ptr with wrap *)
      END;
   END;
```

TABLE B-8 INPUT/OUTPUT UNIT DEFINITIONS AND OPERATIONS (cont.)

```
END;   (* putio *)


(* statio - reads status byte of selected device
 *         Note:  This version does very simple busy/idle processing.
 *)
PROCEDURE statio (VAR status: word; device: word);
VAR
   dno: integer;
BEGIN
   dno:= bytecode (device);
   IF dno = syskbd THEN                              (* system keyboard *)
   BEGIN
      IF kbdlastch = asciieot THEN
      BEGIN
         numtoword (status,idle);                     (* idle after eof *)
      END
      ELSE
      BEGIN
         numtoword (status,busy);                     (* say it is busy until eof *)
      END;
   END
   ELSE IF dno in [sysdpy,sysprt,sysdsk] THEN
   BEGIN
      numtoword (status,idle);                       (* say these are always idle *)
   END
   ELSE
   BEGIN
      numtoword (status,nodev);                      (* other devices not present *)
   END;
END;   (* statio *)


(* cmdio - writes command byte to selected device
 *         Note:  This version does nothing for printer, display and keyboard.
 *)
PROCEDURE cmdio (command, device: word);
VAR
   dno, cmd : byte;


(* getdisk - retrieve initial disk contents from archive file 'disk'
 *)
PROCEDURE getdisk;
VAR
   i: sectindex;
BEGIN
   WITH diskdev DO
   BEGIN
      reset (disk);
      IF NOT eof (disk) THEN                         (* read sectors if archived *)
      BEGIN
         read (disk,dsksect);
      END
      ELSE
      BEGIN                                          (* erase disk if new *)
```

TABLE B-8 INPUT/OUTPUT UNIT DEFINITIONS AND OPERATIONS (cont.)

```
         clearsect (dsksect[0]);
         FOR i:= 1 TO maxsect DO
         BEGIN
            dsksect[i]:= dsksect[0];
         END;
      END;
      dskfirst:= false;
   END;
END;   (* getdisk *)


BEGIN  (* cmdio *)
   dno:= bytecode (device);
   IF dno = sysdsk THEN                       (* system disk *)
   BEGIN
      WITH diskdev DO
      BEGIN
         IF argbit < nargbits THEN              (* build argument to command *)
         BEGIN
            maskword (command,command,8);
            lshword (command,command,argbit);
            orword (pendingarg,pendingarg,command);
            argbit:= argbit + 8;
            IF argbit >= nargbits THEN          (* last byte of arg. *)
            BEGIN
               cmd:= pendingcmd;                 (* restore command *)
               havearg:= true;
            END;
         END
         ELSE
         BEGIN
            cmd:= bytecode (command);
         END;
         IF argbit >= nargbits THEN             (* execute command *)
         BEGIN
            IF cmd = dskpos THEN                (* position disk head *)
            BEGIN
               IF havearg THEN                   (* already have arg. *)
               BEGIN
                  cursect:= wordtonum (pendingarg) MOD maxsect;
                  havearg:= false;
               END
               ELSE
               BEGIN                             (* need to collect arg. *)
                  pendingcmd:= dskpos;            (* save command *)
                  pendingarg:= zeroword;          (* init arg word *)
                  nargbits:= 24;                  (* 24 bit (3 byte)  arg. *)
                  argbit:= 0;                     (* init arg index *)
               END;
            END
            ELSE IF cmd = dskin THEN            (* input sector *)
            BEGIN
               IF dskfirst THEN                  (* read archive first time *)
               BEGIN
                  getdisk;
               END;
```

TABLE B-8 INPUT/OUTPUT UNIT DEFINITIONS AND OPERATIONS (cont.)

```
                dskbuf:= dsksect[cursect];
                curbuf:= 1;
             END
             ELSE IF cmd = dskout THEN            (* output sector *)
             BEGIN
                IF dskfirst THEN                    (* read archive first time *)
                BEGIN
                   getdisk;
                END;
                dsksect[cursect]:= dskbuf;
             END
             ELSE IF cmd = dskbufrst THEN         (* restore buf ptr *)
             BEGIN
                curbuf:= 1;
             END
             ELSE IF cmd = dskbufclr THEN         (* clear buf to 0 *)
             BEGIN
                clearsect (dskbuf);
                curbuf:= 1;
             END;
          END;
       END;
    END;
END;  (* cmdio *)
```

TABLE B-9 ONE-ADDRESS MACHINE ASSEMBLER

```
(* One-address machine assembler to accompany
 *    'Introduction to Machine and Assembly Language Programming'
 *     by Philip Gust,  published by Prentice-Hall Inc., 1985.
 *)
PROGRAM asm1 (source,object,output);

LABEL
   99;                                  (* for error exit *)


CONST
(*******************************************************************************
 *
 *   Include CONST declarations for "machine1", "word", "string" and "symbol"
 *
 *******************************************************************************
 *)

   maxerrno  = 8;                       (* highest error number *)

   bssps     = -1;                      (* ps-op defs *)
   dataps    = -2;
   endps     = -3;
   equps     = -4;
   listps    = -5;
   nolistps  = -6;
   notraceps = -7;
   orgps     = -8;
   pageps    = -9;
   traceps   = -10;


TYPE
(*******************************************************************************
 *
 *   Include TYPE declarations for "machine1", "word", "string" and "symbol"
 *
 *******************************************************************************
 *)

   lextype  = (instruction,comment);  (* statement type returned by lex *)

   errors   = 0..maxerrno;            (* range of error numbers *)


   errptr   = ^errinfo;
   errinfo  = RECORD                  (* records error information *)
                errnext: errptr;        (* next error record *)
                errline: integer;       (* source line number *)
                errno:   errors;        (* assembly error number *)
                errskip: boolean;       (* skip this line during code gen. *)
              END;

   dataptr  = ^datainfo;
   datainfo = RECORD                  (* records data block information *)
```

TABLE B-9 ONE-ADDRESS MACHINE ASSEMBLER (cont.)

```
              datanext: dataptr;      (* next data record *)
              dataword: word;         (* address of last word in block *)
            END;

VAR
(*****************************************************************************
 *
 *  Include VAR declarations for  "word", "string" and "symbol"
 *
 *****************************************************************************
 *)

   source,                        (* input source program *)
   object:    text;               (* object file of program *)
   ic,                            (* current assembly address *)
   startpc:   word;               (* execution start address of pc *)
   firstdata,                     (* first record of data list *)
   curdata:   dataptr;            (* current record of data list *)
   firsterr,                      (* first record of error list *)
   curerr:    errptr;             (* current record of error list *)
   line,                          (* working input line *)
   lblfld,                        (* label field of input line *)
   opfld,                         (* operation field of input line *)
   valfld:    string;             (* mode/address field of input line *)
   lbllen,                        (* length of label field string *)
   oplen,                         (* length of operation field string *)
   vallen,                        (* length of mode/address field string *)
   curline,                       (* current source line in assembly *)
   op:        integer;            (* code of current instruction or pseudo *)
   indatablk: boolean;            (* flags assembly within data/code block *)


(*****************************************************************************
 *
 *  Include procedures for "word", "string" and "symbol"
 *
 *****************************************************************************
 *)


(* exit - escape to outer level to print errors and quit
 *)
PROCEDURE exit;
BEGIN
   GOTO 99;
END;   (* exit *)


(* logerror - log errors in assembly
 *)
PROCEDURE logerror (errornum: errors; skipflag: boolean);
VAR
   newerr: errptr;
BEGIN
   new (newerr);
```

TABLE B-9 ONE-ADDRESS MACHINE ASSEMBLER (cont.)

```
   newerr^.errnext:= curerr^.errnext;   (* link record after curerr *)
   curerr^.errnext:= newerr;
   curerr:= newerr;
   curerr^.errline:= curline;           (* record new error info *)
   curerr^.errno:= errornum;
   curerr^.errskip:= skipflag;
END;   (* logerror *)


(*  asminit -  initializes assembler variables and tables
 *)
PROCEDURE asminit;


(* makeop - enter new opcode into symbol table
 *)
PROCEDURE makeop (opname: shortstring; n: integer);
VAR
   s: string;
   w: word;
BEGIN
   makestr (s,opname);
   numtoword (w,n);
   IF NOT install (w,s) THEN
   BEGIN
      logerror (1,false);
      exit;
   END;
END;   (* makeop *)


BEGIN  (* asminit *)
   wordinit;
   strinit;
   symtblinit;
   new (firstdata);                  (* starting dummy data record *)
   new (firsterr);                   (* starting dummy error record *)
   new (firsterr^.errnext);          (* ending dummy error record *)
   firsterr^.errnext^.errno:= 0;

   makeop ('ac      ',0);            makeop ('AC      ',0);
   makeop ('xr      ',1);            makeop ('XR      ',1);

   makeop ('halt    ',haltop);       makeop ('HALT    ',haltop);
   makeop ('load    ',loadop);       makeop ('LOAD    ',loadop);
   makeop ('store   ',storeop);      makeop ('STORE   ',storeop);
   makeop ('call    ',callop);       makeop ('CALL    ',callop);
   makeop ('br      ',brop);         makeop ('BR      ',brop);
   makeop ('breq    ',breqop);       makeop ('BREQ    ',breqop);
   makeop ('brge    ',brgeop);       makeop ('BRGE    ',brgeop);
   makeop ('brlt    ',brltop);       makeop ('BRLT    ',brltop);
   makeop ('add     ',addop);        makeop ('ADD     ',addop);
   makeop ('sub     ',subop);        makeop ('SUB     ',subop);
   makeop ('mul     ',mulop);        makeop ('MUL     ',mulop);
   makeop ('div     ',divop);        makeop ('DIV     ',divop);
```

TABLE B-9 ONE-ADDRESS MACHINE ASSEMBLER (cont.)

```
   makeop ('bss     ',bssps);         makeop ('BSS     ',bssps);
   makeop ('data    ',dataps);        makeop ('DATA    ',dataps);
   makeop ('end     ',endps);         makeop ('END     ',endps);
   makeop ('equ     ',equps);         makeop ('EQU     ',equps);
   makeop ('list    ',listps);        makeop ('LIST    ',listps);
   makeop ('nolist  ',nolistps);      makeop ('NOLIST  ',nolistps);
   makeop ('notrace ',notraceps);     makeop ('NOTRACE ',notraceps);
   makeop ('org     ',orgps);         makeop ('ORG     ',orgps);
   makeop ('page    ',pageps);        makeop ('PAGE    ',pageps);
   makeop ('trace   ',traceps);       makeop ('TRACE   ',traceps);
END;   (* asminit *)


(* lex -  break instruction up into fields
 *)
FUNCTION lex: lextype;
VAR
   i: strindex;
BEGIN
   IF strlen (line) = 0 THEN
   BEGIN
      lex:= comment;
   END
   ELSE IF nextchar (line,1) = '*' THEN   (* comment has '*' in column 1 *)
   BEGIN
      lex:= comment;
   END
   ELSE
   BEGIN
      i:= 1;
      IF nextchar (line,i) = ' ' THEN     (* label starts in column 1 *)
      BEGIN
         lbllen:= 0;
      END
      ELSE
      BEGIN
         nexttoken (lblfld,line,i,[' ']);
         lbllen:= strlen (lblfld);
      END;
      skipchar (line,i,[' ']);
      IF i >= 30 THEN                     (* ops begins before col 30 *)
      BEGIN
         i:= strlen (line)+1;
      END;
      nexttoken (opfld,line,i,[' ']);
      oplen:= strlen (opfld);
      skipchar (line,i,[' ']);
      IF i >= 30 THEN                     (* address begins before col 30 *)
      BEGIN
         i:= strlen (line)+1;
      END;
      nexttoken (valfld,line,i,[' ']);
      vallen:= strlen (valfld);
      IF lbllen+oplen+vallen = 0 THEN     (* comment if all three empty *)
      BEGIN
         lex:= comment;
```

TABLE B-9 ONE-ADDRESS MACHINE ASSEMBLER (cont.)

```
      END
      ELSE
      BEGIN
         lex:= instruction;
      END;
   END;
END;   (* lex *)


(* evalstr -  evaluate an address or constant expression
 *)
FUNCTION evalstr (VAR w: word; VAR s: string): boolean;
VAR
   evalok: boolean;
   pendop: char;
   term: string;
   i,slen: strindex;
   tw: word;
BEGIN
   w:= zeroword;
   pendop:= nextchar (s,1);
   i:= 2;
   IF NOT (pendop IN ['+','-']) THEN          (* check for leading sign *)
   BEGIN
      pendop:= '+';                               (* assume leading '+' *)
      i:= 1;
   END;
   evalok:= true;
   slen:= strlen (s);
   WHILE (i<= slen) AND evalok DO             (* for each term in expression *)
   BEGIN
      nexttoken (term,s,i,['+','-']);
      IF NOT strtoword (tw,term,decimal) THEN   (* next term not constant *)
      BEGIN
         IF (strlen (term) = 1)  AND  (nextchar (term,1) = '*') THEN
         BEGIN
            tw:= ic;                              (* use current ic *)
         END
         ELSE
         BEGIN
            evalok:= lookup (tw,term);            (* use definition *)
         END;
      END;
      IF evalok THEN                            (* factor in this term *)
      BEGIN
         IF pendop = '+' THEN
         BEGIN
            addword (w,w,tw);
         END
         ELSE
         BEGIN
            subword (w,w,tw);
         END;
         IF i <= slen THEN
         BEGIN
            pendop:= nextchar (s,i);                 (* get next operator *)
```

TABLE B-9 ONE-ADDRESS MACHINE ASSEMBLER (cont.)

```
            i:= i+1;
            evalok:= pendop IN ['+','-'];
         END;
      END;
   END;
   evalstr:= evalok;
END;  (* evalstr *)


(* pass1 - build symbol table and measure size of data blocks
 *)
PROCEDURE pass1;
VAR
   haveaddr: boolean;
   w: word;
   i: strindex;


(* makelbl - enter label into symbol table if not already defined
 *)
PROCEDURE makelbl (loc: word);
VAR
   junk: word;
BEGIN
   IF lbllen > 0 THEN
   BEGIN
      IF lookup (junk,lblfld) THEN
      BEGIN
         logerror (2,false);                (* duplicate label *)
      END
      ELSE IF NOT install (loc,lblfld) THEN
      BEGIN
         logerror (3,false);                (* install error *)
         exit;
      END;
   END;
END;  (* makelbl *)


BEGIN  (* pass1 *)
   reset (source);
   ic:= zeroword;
   curline:= 0;
   op:= haltop;
   indatablk:= false;
   curdata:= firstdata;
   curerr:= firsterr;

   WHILE NOT (eof (source) OR (op = endps)) DO
   BEGIN
      readstr (source,line);
      readln (source);
      curline:= curline+1;
      IF lex <> comment THEN
      BEGIN
```

TABLE B-9 ONE-ADDRESS MACHINE ASSEMBLER (cont.)

```
IF NOT lookup (w,opfld) THEN
BEGIN
   logerror (4,true);                    (* invalid op field *)
   makelbl (zeroword);
END
ELSE
BEGIN
   op:= wordtonum (w);
   IF op IN [haltop..topop,dataps] THEN
   BEGIN
      makelbl (ic);
      incrementword (ic,ic);
      IF op = dataps THEN
      BEGIN
         FOR i:= 1 TO vallen DO     (* count items in list *)
         BEGIN
            IF nextchar (valfld,i) = ',' THEN
            BEGIN
               incrementword (ic,ic);
            END;
         END;
      END;
      IF NOT indatablk THEN          (* start new data block *)
      BEGIN
         new (curdata^.datanext);
         curdata:= curdata^.datanext;
      END;
      curdata^.dataword:= ic;        (* new end of block addr *)
      indatablk:= true;
   END

   ELSE IF op IN [bssps,equps,endps,orgps] THEN
   BEGIN
      haveaddr:= evalstr (w,valfld);
      IF NOT haveaddr THEN           (* must be defined in pass1 *)
      BEGIN
         logerror (5,true);
         w:= zeroword;
      END;
      IF op IN [bssps,orgps] THEN
      BEGIN
         IF testltword (w) THEN
         BEGIN
            logerror (6,true);
            haveaddr:= false;
         END;
         IF NOT haveaddr THEN                (* ignore org/bss *)
         BEGIN
            makelbl (ic);
         END
         ELSE IF op = orgps THEN
         BEGIN
            indatablk:= false;
            maskword (ic,w,addrsize);
            makelbl (ic);
```

TABLE B-9 ONE-ADDRESS MACHINE ASSEMBLER (cont.)

```
                  END
                  ELSE
                  BEGIN
                     indatablk:= false;
                     makelbl (ic);
                     addword (ic,ic,w);
                     maskword (ic,ic,addrsize)
                  END;
               END
               ELSE IF op = equps THEN
               BEGIN
                  makelbl (w);
               END
               ELSE IF op = endps THEN
               BEGIN
                  startpc:= w;
               END;
            END

            ELSE IF op IN [traceps,notraceps,listps,nolistps,pageps] THEN
            BEGIN
               IF lbllen > 0 THEN                 (* can't label these *)
               BEGIN
                  logerror (7,false);
                  makelbl (zeroword);
               END;
            END

            ELSE
            BEGIN                                 (* unknown op/pseudo *)
               logerror (4,true);
               makelbl (zeroword);
            END;
         END;
      END;
   END;

   IF op <> endps THEN                            (* 'end' missing *)
   BEGIN
      curline:= curline+1;
      logerror (8,false);
      startpc:= zeroword;
   END;
END;   (* pass1 *)


(* pass2 -  assemble program and make listing
 *)
PROCEDURE pass2;
CONST
   errcol      = 2;          (* start col. for error mark *)
   iccol       = 4;          (* start col. for ic field *)
   objectcol   = 12;         (* start col. for object field *)
   sourcecol   = 25;         (* start col. for source line *)
   maxsource   = 45;         (* max. width of listed source line *)
   linenocol   = 75;         (* start col. for source line no. *)
```

TABLE B-9 ONE-ADDRESS MACHINE ASSEMBLER (cont.)

```
VAR
   addrfld: string;            (* address field mode *)
   tw,w: word;                 (* temps for decoding instruction *)
   mode: addrmode;             (* address mode number *)
   modech: char;               (* address mode symbol *)
   curcol,                     (* current list column *)
   i:     strindex;            (* token string index *)
   istrue,                     (* dummy flag *)
   errdone,                    (* break from error record loop *)
   errf,                       (* error assembling instruction *)
   skipf,                      (* skip source line *)
   dataf,                      (* first line in data pseudo list *)
   listf,                      (* list pseudo flag *)
   tracef: boolean;            (* trace pseudo flag *)


(* listcursor - move list cursor to column
 *)
PROCEDURE listcursor (colno: strindex);
VAR
   startcol,i: strindex;
BEGIN
   IF listf OR errf THEN
   BEGIN
      startcol:= curcol+1;
      FOR i:= startcol TO colno DO
      BEGIN
         write (output,' ');
         curcol:= curcol+1;
      END;
   END;
END;   (* listcursor *)


(* listerrmark - list error mark if assembly error
 *)
PROCEDURE listerrmark;
BEGIN
   IF listf AND errf THEN
   BEGIN
      listcursor (errcol);
      write (output,'+');
      curcol:= curcol+1;
   END;
END;   (* listerrmark *)


(* listsource - list source line
 *)
PROCEDURE listsource;
VAR
   i: strindex;
BEGIN
   IF listf OR errf THEN
   BEGIN
      listcursor (sourcecol);
```

TABLE B-9 ONE-ADDRESS MACHINE ASSEMBLER (cont.)

```
      FOR i:= 1 TO maxsource DO
      BEGIN
         write (output,nextchar(line,i));
      END;
      curcol:= curcol+maxsource;
      IF strlen (line) > maxsource THEN
      BEGIN
         write (output,'...');
         curcol:= curcol+3;
      END;
   END;
END;   (* listsource *)


(* listlineno - list source line number
 *)
PROCEDURE listlineno;
BEGIN
   IF listf OR errf THEN
   BEGIN
      listcursor (linenocol);
      write (output, curline:4);
      writeln (output);
   END;
   curcol:= 1;
END;   (* listlineno *)


(* listic - list instruction counter
 *)
PROCEDURE listic;
BEGIN
   IF listf OR errf THEN
   BEGIN
      listcursor (iccol);
      writeword (output,ic,addrsize);
      curcol:= curcol+addrlen;
   END;
END;   (* listic *)


(* listaddr - list short address field for bss/org
 *)
PROCEDURE listaddr;
BEGIN
   IF listf OR errf THEN
   BEGIN
      listcursor (objectcol+wordlen-addrlen);
      writeword (output,w,addrsize);
      curcol:= curcol+addrlen;
   END;
END;   (* listaddr *)


(* listdata - list data or instruction field
 *)
```

TABLE B-9 ONE-ADDRESS MACHINE ASSEMBLER (cont.)

```
PROCEDURE listdata;
BEGIN
   IF listf OR errf THEN
   BEGIN
      listcursor (objectcol);
      writeword (output,w,wordsize);
      curcol:= curcol+wordlen;
   END;
END;   (* listdata *)


(* writeobj - write word to object file
 *)
PROCEDURE writeobj;
VAR
   blksize: word;
BEGIN
   IF NOT indatablk THEN                        (* new data block *)
   BEGIN
      curdata:= curdata^.datanext;
      writeword (object,ic,addrsize);
      writeln (object);                          (* output start addr *)
      subword (blksize,curdata^.dataword,ic);
      writeword (object,blksize,addrsize);
      writeln (object);                          (* output block size *)
   END;
   writeword (object,w,wordsize);
END;   (* writeobj *)


BEGIN   (* pass2 *)
   reset (source);
   rewrite (object);
   writeword (object,startpc,addrsize);         (* write starting pc *)
   writeln (object);

   curerr:= firsterr;                           (* init. pass2 *)
   curdata:= firstdata;
   indatablk:= false;
   listf:= true;
   tracef:= false;
   ic:= zeroword;
   curline:= 0;
   curcol:= 1;
   op:= haltop;

   WHILE NOT (eof (source) OR (op = endps)) DO
   BEGIN
      readstr (source,line);
      readln (source);
      curline:= curline+1;
      skipf:= (lex = comment);
      errf:= false;
      REPEAT                                    (* scan errors on this line *)
         WITH curerr^.errnext^ DO
         BEGIN
```

TABLE B-9 ONE-ADDRESS MACHINE ASSEMBLER (cont.)

```
         errdone:= (errline <> curline);
         IF NOT errdone THEN
         BEGIN
            skipf:= skipf OR errskip;         (* treat as comment if set *)
            errf:= true;
            curerr:= curerr^.errnext;
         END;
      END;
   UNTIL errdone;
   IF skipf THEN                             (* skip if comment *)
   BEGIN
      listerrmark;
      listsource;
      listlineno;
   END
   ELSE
   BEGIN
      istrue:= lookup (w,opfld);
      op:= wordtonum (w);
      IF op IN [haltop..topop] THEN          (* machine instruction *)
      BEGIN
         lshword (w,w,modesize);              (* assemble mode field *)
         i:= 2;
         modech:= nextchar (valfld,1);
         IF modech = '=' THEN                   (* immediate mode *)
         BEGIN
            mode:= immediate;
         END
         ELSE IF modech = '$' THEN              (* indexed mode *)
         BEGIN
            mode:= indexed;
         END
         ELSE IF modech = '@' THEN              (* indirect mode *)
         BEGIN
            mode:= indirect;
         END
         ELSE
         BEGIN                                  (* direct mode *)
            mode:= direct;
            i:= 1;
         END;
         numtoword (tw,mode);                 (* install mode field *)
         orword (w,w,tw);
         lshword (w,w,addrsize);              (* assemble address field *)
         nexttoken (addrfld,valfld,i,[' ']);
         IF NOT evalstr (tw,addrfld) THEN
         BEGIN
            logerror (5,false);
            errf:= true;
         END
         ELSE
         BEGIN
            maskword (tw,tw,addrsize);        (* install address field *)
            orword (w,w,tw);
         END;
         writeobj;                           (* write instruction *)
```

TABLE B-9 ONE-ADDRESS MACHINE ASSEMBLER (cont.)

```
      indatablk:= true;
      IF tracef THEN                       (* write trace info *)
      BEGIN
         write (object,'  ');
         writestr (object,opfld);
         FOR i:= oplen+1 TO maxshortstr DO
         BEGIN
            write (object,' ');
         END;
         writestr (object,valfld);
      END;
      writeln (object);
      listerrmark;
      listic;
      listdata;
      listsource;
      listlineno;
      incrementword (ic,ic);
   END

   ELSE IF op = dataps THEN
   BEGIN
      i:= 0;
      dataf:= true;
      REPEAT
         i:= i+1;
         nexttoken (addrfld,valfld,i,[',',' ']);
         IF NOT evalstr (w,addrfld) THEN
         BEGIN
            logerror (5,false);
            errf:= true;
            w:= zeroword;
         END;
         writeobj;
         writeln (object);
         indatablk:= true;
         listerrmark;                    (* new list line for each item *)
         listic;
         listdata;
         IF dataf THEN
         BEGIN
            listsource;                  (* only on first list line *)
            dataf:= false;
         END;
         listlineno;
         errf:= false;
         incrementword (ic,ic);
      UNTIL nextchar (valfld,i) = ' '
   END


   ELSE
   BEGIN
      listerrmark;
      CASE op OF
         bssps:     BEGIN
```

TABLE B-9 ONE-ADDRESS MACHINE ASSEMBLER (cont.)

```
                                   indatablk:= false;
                                   istrue:= evalstr (w,valfld);
                                   listic;
                                   listaddr;
                                   addword (ic,ic,w);
                                END;
                 orgps:         BEGIN
                                   indatablk:= false;
                                   istrue:= evalstr (w,valfld);
                                   ic:= w;
                                   listic;
                                END;
                 traceps:       tracef:= true;
                 notraceps:     tracef:= false;
                 listps:        listf:= true;
                 nolistps:      listf:= false;
                 pageps:        page (output);
                 equps:         ;
                 endps:         ;
              END;
              listsource;
              listlineno;
           END;
        END;
   END;
END;   (* pass2 *)


(* pass3 - report errors accumulated during previous passes
 *)
PROCEDURE pass3;


(* reporterror - report error in assembly
 *)
PROCEDURE reporterror (lineno: integer; errno: errors);
BEGIN
   write (output,'   Line ');
   write (output,lineno:4);
   write (output,':  ');
   CASE errno OF
      1:  writeln (output,'Cannot install opcodes -- assembly terminated.');
      2:  writeln (output,'Duplicate label.');
      3:  writeln (output,'Symbol table overflow -- assembly terminated.');
      4:  writeln (output,'Unknown instruction.');
      5:  writeln (output,'Undefined symbol(s) in address field.');
      6:  writeln (output,'Negative number not allowed.');
      7:  writeln (output,'Cannot be labeled.');
      8:  writeln (output,'End line missing.');
   END;
END;   (* reporterror *)


BEGIN  (* pass3 *)
   curerr:= firsterr^.errnext;
```

TABLE B-9 ONE-ADDRESS MACHINE ASSEMBLER (cont.)

```
   IF curerr^.errno <> 0 THEN
   BEGIN
      page (output);
      writeln (output,' Errors in source program:');
      writeln (output);
      REPEAT
         reporterror (curerr^.errline,curerr^.errno);
         curerr:= curerr^.errnext;
      UNTIL curerr^.errno = 0;
   END;
END;   (* pass3 *)


BEGIN  (* asm1 *)
   asminit;
   pass1;
   pass2;
99:
   pass3;
END.   (* asm1 *)
```

TABLE B-10 TWO-ADDRESS MACHINE ASSEMBLER

```
(* Two-address machine assembler to accompany
 *    'Introduction to Machine and Assembly Language Programming'
 *     by Philip Gust,  published by Prentice-Hall Inc., 1985.
 *)
PROGRAM asm2 (source,object,output);

LABEL
   99;                                  (* for error exit *)


CONST
(*****************************************************************************
 *
 *   Include CONST declarations for "machine2", "word", "string" and "symbol"
 *
 *****************************************************************************
 *)

   maxerrno  = 8;                       (* highest error number *)

   bssps     = -1;                      (* ps-op defs *)
   dataps    = -2;
   endps     = -3;
   equps     = -4;
   listps    = -5;
   nolistps  = -6;
   notraceps = -7;
   orgps     = -8;
   pageps    = -9,
   traceps   = -10;


TYPE
(*****************************************************************************
 *
 *   Include TYPE declarations for "machine2", "word", "string" and "symbol"
 *
 *****************************************************************************
 *)

   lextype  = (instruction,comment);  (* statement type returned by lex *)

   errors   = 0..maxerrno;            (* range of error numbers *)
   errptr   = ^errinfo;
   errinfo  = RECORD                  (* records error information *)
                errnext: errptr;        (* next error record *)
                errline: integer;       (* source line number *)
                errno:   errors;        (* assembly error number *)
                errskip: boolean;       (* skip this line during code gen. *)
              END;

   dataptr  = ^datainfo;
   datainfo = RECORD                  (* records data block information *)
                datanext: dataptr;      (* next data record *)
                dataword: word;         (* address of last word in block *)
              END;
```

TABLE B-10 TWO-ADDRESS MACHINE ASSEMBLER (cont.)

```
VAR
(****************************************************************************
 *
 *   Include VAR declarations for  "word", "string" and "symbol"
 *
 ****************************************************************************
 *)

   source,                       (* input source program *)
   object:     text;             (* object file of program *)
   ic,                           (* current assembly address *)
   startpc:    word;             (* execution start address of pc *)
   firstdata,                    (* first record of data list *)
   curdata:    dataptr;          (* current record of data list *)
   firsterr,                     (* first record of error list *)
   curerr:     errptr;           (* current record of error list *)
   line,                         (* working input line *)
   lblfld,                       (* label field of input line *)
   opfld,                        (* operation field of input line *)
   valfld:     string;           (* mode/address field of input line *)
   lbllen,                       (* length of label field string *)
   oplen,                        (* length of operation field string *)
   vallen,                       (* length of mode/address field string *)
   curline,                      (* current source line in assembly *)
   op:         integer;          (* code of current instruction or pseudo *)
   indatablk: boolean;           (* flags assembly within data/code block *)


(****************************************************************************
 *
 *   Include procedures for "word", "string" and "symbol"
 *
 ****************************************************************************
 *)


(* exit - escape to outer level to print errors and quit
 *)
PROCEDURE exit;
BEGIN
   GOTO 99;
END;   (* exit *)


(* logerror - log errors in assembly
 *)
PROCEDURE logerror (errornum: errors; skipflag: boolean);
VAR
   newerr: errptr;
BEGIN
   new (newerr);
   newerr^.errnext:= curerr^.errnext;   (* link record after curerr *)
   curerr^.errnext:= newerr;
   curerr:= newerr;
   curerr^.errline:= curline;           (* record new error info *)
```

TABLE B-10 TWO-ADDRESS MACHINE ASSEMBLER (cont.)

```
   curerr^.errno:= errornum;
   curerr^.errskip:= skipflag;
END;   (* logerror *)


(*  asminit -  initializes assembler variables and tables
 *)
PROCEDURE asminit;


(* makeop - enter new opcode into symbol table
 *)
PROCEDURE makeop (opname: shortstring; n: integer);
VAR
   s: string;
   w: word;
BEGIN
   makestr (s,opname);
   numtoword (w,n);
   IF NOT install (w,s) THEN
   BEGIN
      logerror (1,false);
      exit;
   END;
END;   (* makeop *)


BEGIN  (* asminit *)
   wordinit;
   strinit;
   symtblinit;
   new (firstdata);                 (* starting dummy data record *)
   new (firsterr);                  (* starting dummy error record *)
   new (firsterr^.errnext);         (* ending dummy error record *)
   firsterr^.errnext^.errno:= 0;

   makeop ('r0      ',0);           makeop ('R0      ',0);
   makeop ('r1      ',1);           makeop ('R1      ',1);
   makeop ('r2      ',2);           makeop ('R2      ',2);
   makeop ('r3      ',3);           makeop ('R3      ',3);
   makeop ('r4      ',4);           makeop ('R4      ',4);
   makeop ('r5      ',5);           makeop ('R5      ',5);
   makeop ('r6      ',6);           makeop ('R6      ',6);
   makeop ('r7      ',7);           makeop ('R7      ',7);

   makeop ('halt    ',haltop);      makeop ('HALT    ',haltop);
   makeop ('load    ',loadop);      makeop ('LOAD    ',loadop);
   makeop ('store   ',storeop);     makeop ('STORE   ',storeop);
   makeop ('br      ',brop);        makeop ('BR      ',brop);
   makeop ('cmpr    ',cmprop);      makeop ('CMPR    ',cmprop);
   makeop ('breq    ',breqop);      makeop ('BREQ    ',breqop);
   makeop ('brne    ',brneop);      makeop ('BRNE    ',brneop);
   makeop ('brgt    ',brgtop);      makeop ('BRGT    ',brgtop);
   makeop ('brlt    ',brltop);      makeop ('BRLT    ',brltop);
   makeop ('brge    ',brgeop);      makeop ('BRGE    ',brgeop);
```

TABLE B-10 TWO-ADDRESS MACHINE ASSEMBLER (cont.)

```
   makeop ('brle    ',brleop);        makeop ('BRLE    ',brleop);
   makeop ('push    ',pushop);        makeop ('PUSH    ',pushop);
   makeop ('pop     ',popop);         makeop ('POP     ',popop);
   makeop ('call    ',callop);        makeop ('CALL    ',callop);
   makeop ('rtn     ',rtnop);         makeop ('RTN     ',rtnop);
   makeop ('add     ',addop);         makeop ('ADD     ',addop);
   makeop ('sub     ',subop);         makeop ('SUB     ',subop);
   makeop ('mul     ',mulop);         makeop ('MUL     ',mulop);
   makeop ('div     ',divop);         makeop ('DIV     ',divop);
   makeop ('and     ',andop);         makeop ('AND     ',andop);
   makeop ('or      ',orop);          makeop ('OR      ',orop);
   makeop ('xor     ',xorop);         makeop ('XOR     ',xorop);
   makeop ('not     ',notop);         makeop ('NOT     ',notop);
   makeop ('ash     ',ashop);         makeop ('ASH     ',ashop);
   makeop ('csh     ',cshop);         makeop ('CSH     ',cshop);
   makeop ('lsh     ',lshop);         makeop ('LSH     ',lshop);
   makeop ('inchr   ',inchrop);       makeop ('INCHR   ',inchrop);
   makeop ('outchr  ',outchrop);      makeop ('OUTCHR  ',outchrop);
   makeop ('iostat  ',iostatop);      makeop ('IOSTAT  ',iostatop);
   makeop ('iocmd   ',iocmdop);       makeop ('IOCMD   ',iocmdop);

   makeop ('bss     ',bssps);         makeop ('BSS     ',bssps);
   makeop ('data    ',dataps);        makeop ('DATA    ',dataps);
   makeop ('end     ',endps);         makeop ('END     ',endps);
   makeop ('equ     ',equps);         makeop ('EQU     ',equps);
   makeop ('list    ',listps);        makeop ('LIST    ',listps);
   makeop ('nolist  ',nolistps);      makeop ('NOLIST  ',nolistps);
   makeop ('notrace ',notraceps);     makeop ('NOTRACE ',notraceps);
   makeop ('org     ',orgps);         makeop ('ORG     ',orgps);
   makeop ('page    ',pageps);        makeop ('PAGE    ',pageps);
   makeop ('trace   ',traceps);       makeop ('TRACE   ',traceps);
END;   (* asminit *)


(* lex -  break instruction up into fields
 *)
FUNCTION lex: lextype;
VAR
   i: strindex;
BEGIN
   IF strlen (line) = 0 THEN
   BEGIN
      lex:= comment;
   END
   ELSE IF nextchar (line,1) = '*' THEN   (* comment has '*' in column 1 *)
   BEGIN
      lex:= comment;
   END
   ELSE
   BEGIN
      i:= 1;
      IF nextchar (line,i) = ' ' THEN     (* label starts in column 1 *)
      BEGIN
         lbllen:= 0;
      END
```

TABLE B-10 TWO-ADDRESS MACHINE ASSEMBLER (cont.)

```
      ELSE
      BEGIN
         nexttoken (lblfld,line,i,[' ']);
         lbllen:= strlen (lblfld);
      END;
      skipchar (line,i,[' ']);
      IF i >= 30 THEN                   (* ops begins before col 30 *)
      BEGIN
         i:= strlen (line)+1;
      END;
      nexttoken (opfld,line,i,[' ']);
      oplen:= strlen (opfld);
      skipchar (line,i,[' ']);
      IF i >= 30 THEN                   (* address begins before col 30 *)
      BEGIN
         i:= strlen (line)+1;
      END;
      nexttoken (valfld,line,i,[' ']);
      vallen:= strlen (valfld);
      IF lbllen+oplen+vallen = 0 THEN   (* comment if all three empty *)
      BEGIN
         lex:= comment;
      END
      ELSE
      BEGIN
         lex:= instruction;
      END;
   END;
END;   (* lex *)


(* evalstr -  evaluate an address or constant expression
 *)
FUNCTION evalstr (VAR w: word; VAR s: string): boolean;
VAR
   evalok: boolean;
   pendop: char;
   term: string;
   i,slen: strindex;
   tw: word;
BEGIN
   w:= zeroword;
   pendop:= nextchar (s,1);
   i:= 2;
   IF NOT (pendop IN ['+','-']) THEN          (* check for leading sign *)
   BEGIN
      pendop:= '+';                               (* assume leading '+' *)
      i:= 1;
   END;
   evalok:= true;
   slen:= strlen (s);
   WHILE (i<= slen) AND evalok DO             (* for each term in expression *)
   BEGIN
      nexttoken (term,s,i,['+','-']);
      IF NOT strtoword (tw,term,decimal) THEN   (* next term not constant *)
```

TABLE B-10 TWO-ADDRESS MACHINE ASSEMBLER (cont.)

```
      BEGIN
         IF (strlen (term) = 1)  AND  (nextchar (term,1) = '*') THEN
         BEGIN
            tw:= ic;                                 (* use current ic *)
         END
         ELSE
         BEGIN
            evalok:= lookup (tw,term);               (* use definition *)
         END;
      END;
      IF evalok THEN                              (* factor in this term *)
      BEGIN
         IF pendop = '+' THEN
         BEGIN
            addword (w,w,tw);
         END
         ELSE
         BEGIN
            subword (w,w,tw);
         END;
         IF i <= slen THEN
         BEGIN
            pendop:= nextchar (s,i);                    (* get next operator *)
            i:= i+1;
            evalok:= pendop IN ['+','-'];
         END;
      END;
   END;
   evalstr:= evalok;
END;   (* evalstr *)


(* pass1 - build symbol table and measure size of data blocks
 *)
PROCEDURE pass1;
VAR
   haveaddr: boolean;
   w: word;
   i: strindex;


(* makelbl - enter label into symbol table if not already defined
 *)
PROCEDURE makelbl (loc: word);
VAR
   junk: word;
BEGIN
   IF lbllen > 0 THEN
   BEGIN
      IF lookup (junk,lblfld) THEN
      BEGIN
         logerror (2,false);
      END
      ELSE IF NOT install (loc,lblfld) THEN
      BEGIN
```

TABLE B-10 TWO-ADDRESS MACHINE ASSEMBLER (cont.)

```
         logerror (3,false);
         exit;
      END;
   END;
END;   (* makelbl *)


BEGIN   (* pass1 *)
   reset (source);
   ic:= zeroword;
   curline:= 0;
   op:= haltop;
   indatablk:= false;
   curdata:= firstdata;
   curerr:= firsterr;

   WHILE NOT (eof (source) OR (op = endps)) DO
   BEGIN
      readstr (source,line);
      readln (source);
      curline:= curline+1;
      IF lex <> comment THEN
      BEGIN
         IF NOT lookup (w,opfld) THEN
         BEGIN
            logerror (4,true);
            makelbl (zeroword);
         END
         ELSE
         BEGIN
            op:= wordtonum (w);
            IF op IN [haltop..topop,dataps] THEN
            BEGIN
               makelbl (ic);
               incrementword (ic,ic);
               IF op = dataps THEN
               BEGIN
                  FOR i:= 1 TO vallen DO     (* count items in list *)
                  BEGIN
                     IF nextchar (valfld,i) = ',' THEN
                     BEGIN
                        incrementword (ic,ic);
                     END;
                  END;
               END;
               IF NOT indatablk THEN         (* start new data block *)
               BEGIN
                  new (curdata^.datanext);
                  curdata:= curdata^.datanext;
               END;
               curdata^.dataword:= ic;       (* new end of block addr *)
               indatablk:= true;
            END

            ELSE IF op IN [bssps,equps,endps,orgps] THEN
            BEGIN
```

TABLE B-10 TWO-ADDRESS MACHINE ASSEMBLER (cont.)

```
         haveaddr:= evalstr (w,valfld);
         IF NOT haveaddr THEN          (* must be defined in pass1 *)
         BEGIN
            logerror (5,true);
            w:= zeroword;
         END;
         IF op IN [bssps,orgps] THEN
         BEGIN
            IF testltword (w) THEN
            BEGIN
               logerror (6,true);
               haveaddr:= false;
            END;
            IF NOT haveaddr THEN                  (* ignore org/bss *)
            BEGIN
               makelbl (ic);
            END
            ELSE IF op = orgps THEN
            BEGIN
               indatablk:= false;
               maskword (ic,w,addrsize);
               makelbl (ic);
            END
            ELSE
            BEGIN
               indatablk:= false;
               makelbl (ic);
               addword (ic,ic,w);
               maskword (ic,ic,addrsize)
            END;
         END
         ELSE IF op = equps THEN
         BEGIN
            makelbl (w);
         END
         ELSE IF op = endps THEN
         BEGIN
            startpc:= w;
         END;
      END

      ELSE IF op IN [traceps,notraceps,listps,nolistps,pageps] THEN
      BEGIN
         IF lbllen > 0 THEN                  (* can't label these *)
         BEGIN
            logerror (7,false);
            makelbl (zeroword);
         END;
      END

      ELSE
      BEGIN                                  (* unknown op/pseudo *)
         logerror (4,true);
         makelbl (zeroword);
      END;
   END;
```

TABLE B-10 TWO-ADDRESS MACHINE ASSEMBLER (cont.)

```
   END;
END;
   IF op <> endps THEN                                   (* 'end' missing *)
   BEGIN
      curline:= curline+1;
      logerror (8,false);
      startpc:= zeroword;
   END;
END;  (* pass1 *)


(* pass2 -  assemble program and make listing
 *)
PROCEDURE pass2;
CONST
   errcol      = 2;           (* start col. for error mark *)
   iccol       = 4;           (* start col. for ic field *)
   objectcol   = 12;          (* start col. for object field *)
   sourcecol   = 25;          (* start col. for source line *)
   maxsource   = 45;          (* max. width of listed source line *)
   linenocol   = 75;          (* start col. for source line no. *)

VAR
   indxfld,                   (* index register field *)
   regfld,                    (* data register field *)
   addrfld: string;           (* address field mode *)
   tw,w: word;                (* temps for decoding instruction *)
   mode: addrmode;            (* address mode number *)
   modech: char;              (* address mode symbol *)
   curcol,                    (* current list column *)
   i,                         (* token string index *)
   isave: strindex;           (* suspended token string index *)
   istrue,                    (* dummy flag *)
   errdone,                   (* break from error record loop *)
   errf,                      (* error assembling instruction *)
   skipf,                     (* skip source line *)
   dataf,                     (* first line in data pseudo list *)
   listf,                     (* list pseudo flag *)
   tracef: boolean;           (* trace pseudo flag *)


(* listcursor - move list cursor to column
 *)
PROCEDURE listcursor (colno: strindex);
VAR
   startcol,i: strindex;
BEGIN
   IF listf OR errf THEN
   BEGIN
      startcol:= curcol+1;
      FOR i:= startcol TO colno DO
      BEGIN
         write (output,' ');
         curcol:= curcol+1;
      END;
```

TABLE B-10 TWO-ADDRESS MACHINE ASSEMBLER (cont.)

```
   END;
END;   (* listcursor *)


(* listerrmark - list error mark if assembly error
 *)
PROCEDURE listerrmark;
BEGIN
   IF listf AND errf THEN
   BEGIN
      listcursor (errcol);
      write (output,'+');
      curcol:= curcol+1;
   END;
END;   (* listerrmark *)


(* listsource - list source line
 *)
PROCEDURE listsource;
VAR
   i: strindex;
BEGIN
   IF listf OR errf THEN
   BEGIN
      listcursor (sourcecol);
      FOR i:= 1 TO maxsource DO
      BEGIN
         write (output,nextchar(line,i));
      END;
      curcol:= curcol+maxsource;
      IF strlen (line) > maxsource THEN
      BEGIN
         write (output,'...');
         curcol:= curcol+3;
      END;
   END;
END;   (* listsource *)


(* listlineno - list source line number
 *)
PROCEDURE listlineno;
BEGIN
   IF listf OR errf THEN
   BEGIN
      listcursor (linenocol);
      write (output, curline:4);
      writeln (output);
   END;
   curcol:= 1;
END;   (* listlineno *)


(* listic - list instruction counter
```

TABLE B-10 TWO-ADDRESS MACHINE ASSEMBLER (cont.)

```
 *)
PROCEDURE listic;
BEGIN
   IF listf OR errf THEN
   BEGIN
      listcursor (iccol);
      writeword (output,ic,addrsize);
      curcol:= curcol+addrlen;
   END;
END;   (* listic *)


(* listaddr - list short address field for bss/org
 *)
PROCEDURE listaddr;
BEGIN
   IF listf OR errf THEN
   BEGIN
      listcursor (objectcol+wordlen-addrlen);
      writeword (output,w,addrsize);
      curcol:= curcol+addrlen;
   END;
END;   (* listaddr *)


(* listdata - list data or instruction field
 *)
PROCEDURE listdata;
BEGIN
   IF listf OR errf THEN
   BEGIN
      listcursor (objectcol);
      writeword (output,w,wordsize);
      curcol:= curcol+wordlen;
   END;
END;   (* listdata *)


(* writeobj - write word to object file
 *)
PROCEDURE writeobj;
VAR
   blksize: word;
BEGIN
   IF NOT indatablk THEN                              (* new data block *)
   BEGIN
      curdata:= curdata^.datanext;
      writeword (object,ic,addrsize);
      writeln (object);                                 (* output start addr *)
      subword (blksize,curdata^.dataword,ic);
      writeword (object,blksize,addrsize);
      writeln (object);                                 (* output block size *)
   END;
   writeword (object,w,wordsize);
END;   (* writeobj *)
```

TABLE B-10 TWO-ADDRESS MACHINE ASSEMBLER (cont.)

```
BEGIN   (* pass2 *)
   reset (source);
   rewrite (object);
   writeword (object,startpc,addrsize);           (* write starting pc *)
   writeln (object);

   curerr:= firsterr;                             (* init. pass2 *)
   curdata:= firstdata;
   indatablk:= false;
   listf:= true;
   tracef:= false;
   ic:= zeroword;
   curline:= 0;
   curcol:= 1;
   op:= haltop;

   WHILE NOT (eof (source) OR (op = endps)) DO
   BEGIN
      readstr (source,line);
      readln (source);
      curline:= curline+1;
      skipf:= (lex = comment);
      errf:= false;
      REPEAT                                      (* scan errors on this line *)
         WITH curerr^.errnext^ DO
         BEGIN
            errdone:= (errline <> curline);
            IF NOT errdone THEN
            BEGIN
               skipf:= skipf OR errskip;           (* treat as comment if set *)
               errf:= true;
               curerr:= curerr^.errnext;
            END;
         END;
      UNTIL errdone;
      IF skipf THEN                               (* skip if comment *)
      BEGIN
         listerrmark;
         listsource;
         listlineno;
      END
      ELSE
      BEGIN
         istrue:= lookup (w,opfld);
         op:= wordtonum (w);
         IF op IN [haltop..topop] THEN            (* machine instruction *)
         BEGIN
            lshword (w,w,regsize);
            i:= 1;
            nexttoken (regfld,valfld,i,[',',' ']);
            IF nextchar (valfld,i) = ',' THEN        (* assemble data reg *)
            BEGIN
               IF NOT evalstr (tw,regfld) THEN
               BEGIN
                  logerror (5,false);
```

TABLE B-10 TWO-ADDRESS MACHINE ASSEMBLER (cont.)

```
            errf:= true;
         END
         ELSE
         BEGIN
            maskword (tw,tw,regsize);
            orword (w,w,tw);
         END;
         i:= i+1;
      END
      ELSE
      BEGIN
         i:= 1;
      END;
      mode:= direct;                               (* assemble mode field *)
      modech:= nextchar (valfld,i);
      IF modech = '=' THEN                          (* set immediate bit *)
      BEGIN
         mode:= immediate;
         i:= i+1;
      END
      ELSE IF modech = '@' THEN                     (* set indirect bit *)
      BEGIN
         mode:= indirect;
         i:= i+1;
      END;
      lshword (w,w,regsize);
      isave:= i;
      nexttoken (addrfld,valfld,i,['(',' ']);      (* check for indexed *)
      IF nextchar (valfld,i) = '(' THEN              (* found ')' *)
      BEGIN
         i:= i+1;
         nexttoken (indxfld,valfld,i,[')',' ']);
         IF nextchar (valfld,i) <> ')' THEN          (* ')' not found *)
         BEGIN
            i:= isave;                               (* '(' part of addr *)
            nexttoken (addrfld,valfld,i,[' ']);
         END
         ELSE
         BEGIN                                      (* set indexed bit *)
            i:= i+1;
            mode:= mode + indexed;
            IF NOT evalstr (tw,indxfld) THEN       (* assemble index reg *)
            BEGIN
               logerror (5,false);
               errf:= true;
            END
            ELSE
            BEGIN
               maskword (tw,tw,regsize);
               orword (w,w,tw);
            END;
         END;
      END;
      lshword (w,w,modesize);                      (* install mode field *)
      numtoword (tw,mode);
      orword (w,w,tw);
```

TABLE B-10 TWO-ADDRESS MACHINE ASSEMBLER (cont.)

```
            lshword (w,w,addrsize);                  (* assemble address field *)
            IF NOT evalstr (tw,addrfld) THEN
            BEGIN
               logerror (5,false);
               errf:= true;
            END
            ELSE
            BEGIN                                    (* install address field *)
               maskword (tw,tw,addrsize);
               orword (w,w,tw);
            END;
            writeobj;                            (* write instruction *)
            indatablk:= true;
            IF tracef THEN                       (* write trace info *)
            BEGIN
               write (object,'  ');
               writestr (object,opfld);
               FOR i:= oplen+1 TO maxshortstr DO
               BEGIN
                  write (object,' ');
               END;
               writestr (object,valfld);
            END;
            writeln (object);
            listerrmark;
            listic;
            listdata;
            listsource;
            listlineno;
            incrementword (ic,ic);
         END

         ELSE IF op = dataps THEN
         BEGIN
            i:= 0;
            dataf:= true;
            REPEAT
               i:= i+1;
               nexttoken (addrfld,valfld,i,[',',' ']);
               IF NOT evalstr (w,addrfld) THEN
               BEGIN
                  logerror (5,false);
                  errf:= true;
                  w:= zeroword;
               END;
               writeobj;
               writeln (object);
               indatablk:= true;
               listerrmark;                    (* new list line for each item *)
               listic;
               listdata;
               IF dataf THEN
               BEGIN
                  listsource;                    (* only on first list line *)
                  dataf:= false;
               END;
```

TABLE B-10 TWO-ADDRESS MACHINE ASSEMBLER (cont.)

```
               listlineno;
               errf:= false;
               incrementword (ic,ic);
            UNTIL nextchar (valfld,i) = ' '
         END

         ELSE
         BEGIN
            listerrmark;
            CASE op OF
               bssps:      BEGIN
                              indatablk:= false;
                              istrue:= evalstr (w,valfld);
                              listic;
                              listaddr;
                              addword (ic,ic,w);
                           END;
               orgps:      BEGIN
                              indatablk:= false;
                              istrue:= evalstr (w,valfld);
                              ic:= w;
                              listic;
                           END;
               traceps:    tracef:= true;
               notraceps:  tracef:= false;
               listps:     listf:= true;
               nolistps:   listf:= false;
               pageps:     page (output);
               equps:      ;
               endps:      ;
            END;
            listsource;
            listlineno;
         END;
      END;
   END;
END;   (* pass2 *)


(* pass3 - report errors accumulated during previous passes
 *)
PROCEDURE pass3;


(* reporterror - report error in assembly
 *)
PROCEDURE reporterror (lineno: integer; errno: errors);
BEGIN
   write (output,'   Line ');
   write (output,lineno:4);
   write (output,':  ');
   CASE errno OF
      1:  writeln (output,'Cannot install opcodes -- assembly terminated.');
      2:  writeln (output,'Duplicate label.');
      3:  writeln (output,'Symbol table overflow -- assembly terminated.');
```

TABLE B-10 TWO-ADDRESS MACHINE ASSEMBLER (cont.)

```
      4:  writeln (output,'Unknown instruction.');
      5:  writeln (output,'Undefined symbol(s) in address field.');
      6:  writeln (output,'Negative number not allowed.');
      7:  writeln (output,'Cannot be labeled.');
      8:  writeln (output,'End line missing.');
   END;
END;   (* reporterror *)


BEGIN  (* pass3 *)
   curerr:= firsterr^.errnext;
   IF curerr^.errno <> 0 THEN
   BEGIN
      page (output);
      writeln (output,' Errors in source program:');
      writeln (output);
      REPEAT
         reporterror (curerr^.errline,curerr^.errno);
         curerr:= curerr^.errnext;
      UNTIL curerr^.errno = 0;
   END;
END;   (* pass3 *)


BEGIN  (* asm2 *)
   asminit;
   pass1;
   pass2;
99:
   pass3;
END.   (* asm2 *)
```

TABLE B-11 ONE-ADDRESS MACHINE EMULATOR

```
(* One-address machine emulator to accompany
 *    'Introduction to Machine and Assembly Language Programming'
 *     by Philip Gust,  published by Prentice-Hall Inc., 1985.
 *)
PROGRAM sim1 (object,output);


LABEL
     99;                                          (* exit program *)


CONST
(*****************************************************************************
 *
 *   Include CONST declarations for "machine2", "word", "string" and "memory"
 *
 *****************************************************************************
 *)


TYPE
(*****************************************************************************
 *
 *   Include TYPE declarations for "machine2", "word", "string" and "memory"
 *
 *****************************************************************************
 *)


VAR
(*****************************************************************************
 *
 *   Include VAR declarations for "word", "string" and "symbol"
 *
 *****************************************************************************
 *)

  object:     text;                               (* object file *)
  tw,                                             (* temporary word *)
  firstmem,                                       (* addr of first used mem *)
  lastmem,                                        (* addr of last used mem *)
  pc,                                             (* program counter *)
  ir,                                             (* instruction register *)
  mar,                                            (* memory address register *)
  mbr,                                            (* memory buffer register *)
  xrregno,                                        (* mapped address of XR *)
  acregno:    word;                               (* mapped address of AC *)
  op,                                             (* instr. opcode *)
  mode:       integer;                            (* instr. address mode *)
  tracefirst: boolean;                            (* output trace header flag *)
  tracestr:   string;                             (* for trace string *)
  traceref:   savestrindex;                       (* trace save string index *)
```

TABLE B-11 ONE-ADDRESS MACHINE EMULATOR (cont.)

```
(*****************************************************************************
 *
 *   Include procedures for "word", "string" and "symbol"
 *
 *****************************************************************************
 *)


(* exit - exit from program
 *)
PROCEDURE exit;
BEGIN
   GOTO 99;
END;   (* exit *)


(* siminit - initialize simulation
 *)
PROCEDURE siminit;
BEGIN
   wordinit;
   meminit;
   strinit;
   pc:= zeroword;
   ir:= zeroword;
   mar:= zeroword;
   mbr:= zeroword;
   acregno:= zeroword;
   incrementword (xrregno,zeroword);
   notword (firstmem,zeroword);      (* build 2^(addrsize-1) - 1 *)
   maskword (firstmem,firstmem,addrsize-1);
   lastmem:= zeroword;
   tracefirst:= true;
END;   (* siminit *)


(* membounds - tracks first/last used memory addresses
 *)
PROCEDURE membounds (VAR addr: word);
VAR
  tw: word;
BEGIN
   tw:= addr;
   ashword (tw,tw,-regsize);
   IF NOT testeqword (tw) THEN         (* not a register *)
   BEGIN
      subword (tw,addr,firstmem);
      IF testltword (tw) THEN
      BEGIN
         firstmem:= addr;
      END;
      subword (tw,lastmem,addr);
      IF testltword (tw) THEN
      BEGIN
         lastmem:= addr;
```

TABLE B-11 ONE-ADDRESS MACHINE EMULATOR (cont.)

```
      END;
   END;
END;  (* membounds *)



(* simload - load memory from object file
 *)
PROCEDURE simload;
VAR
   addr,count,tw,w: word;


(* readobj - read next line of object file
 *)
PROCEDURE readobj (VAR objword: word);
VAR
   objline: string;
   i: strindex;
BEGIN
   IF eof (object) THEN
   BEGIN
      writeln (output,' LOAD: Unexpected EOF in object file.');
      exit;
   END;
   readstr (object,objline);
   readln (object);
   i:= 1;
   nexttoken (tracestr,objline,i,[' ']);
   IF NOT strtoword (objword,tracestr,octal) THEN
   BEGIN
      writeln (output,' LOAD: Bad line in object file.');
      exit;
   END;
   skipchar (objline,i,[' ']);
   nexttoken (tracestr,objline,i,[]);
END;  (* readobj *)


BEGIN  (* simload *)
   reset (object);
   IF eoln (object) THEN              (* empty file may have 1 empty line *)
   BEGIN
      readln (object);
   END;
   IF eof (object) THEN
   BEGIN
      writeln (output,' LOAD: Empty object file.');
      exit;
   END;
   readobj (pc);
   maskword (pc,pc,addrsize);
   WHILE NOT eof (object) DO
   BEGIN
      readobj (addr);
      maskword (addr,addr,addrsize);
```

TABLE B-11 ONE-ADDRESS MACHINE EMULATOR (cont.)

```
      readobj (count);
      decrementword (count,count);
      maskword (count,count,addrsize);
      membounds (addr);
      addword (tw,addr,count);
      membounds (tw);
      WHILE testgeword (count) DO
      BEGIN
         readobj (w);
         traceref:= null;
         IF strlen (tracestr) > 0 THEN
         BEGIN
            traceref:= putstr (tracestr);
            IF traceref = null THEN
            BEGIN
               writeln (output,' LOAD: Trace memory overflow.');
               exit;
            END;
         END;
         IF NOT writemem (w,addr,traceref) THEN
         BEGIN
            writeln (output,' LOAD: Address out of range.');
            exit;
         END;
         incrementword (addr,addr);
         decrementword (count,count);
      END;
   END;
END;   (* simload *)


(* dumpregs - dump the contents of PC, AC and XR to file f
 *)
PROCEDURE dumpregs (VAR f: text);
VAR
   readok: boolean;
   regval: word;
   junkref: savestrindex;
BEGIN
   write (f,'   PC: ');
   writeword (output,pc,addrsize);
   readok:= readmem (regval,acregno,junkref);
   write (f,'      AC: ');
   writeword (output,regval,wordsize);
   readok:= readmem (regval,xrregno,junkref);
   write (f,'   XR: ');
   writeword (output,regval,wordsize);
END;   (* dumpregs *)


(* simdump - dump contents of used portions of memory
 *)
PROCEDURE simdump;
VAR
   readok: boolean;
```

TABLE B-11 ONE-ADDRESS MACHINE EMULATOR (cont.)

```
   i: integer;
   w: word;
BEGIN
   subword (w,lastmem,firstmem);
   IF testgeword (w) THEN                   (* if memory has been loaded *)
   BEGIN
      page (output);
      write (output,' Program halted at');
      dumpregs (output);
      writeln (output);
      writeln (output);
      writeln (output);
      lshword (firstmem,firstmem,-3);       (* closest multiple of 8 words *)
      lshword (firstmem,firstmem,3);
      writeln (output);
      writeln (output);
      writeln (output,' Memory:');
      writeln (output);
      REPEAT
         write (output,'  ');
         writeword (output,firstmem,addrsize);
         write (output,':');
         FOR i:= 0 TO 7 DO                  (* print 8 words per row *)
         BEGIN
            write (output,'  ');
            readok:= readmem (w,firstmem,traceref);
            writeword (output,w,wordsize);
            incrementword (firstmem,firstmem);
         END;
         writeln (output);
         subword (w,lastmem,firstmem);
      UNTIL testltword (w);
   END;
END;   (* simdump *)


(* simrun - run program in memory, starting at current pc
 *)
PROCEDURE simrun;
VAR
   running: boolean;


(* simerror - report run-time error
 *)
PROCEDURE simerror;
BEGIN
   write (output,' RUN: Error at PC= ');
   writeword (output,pc,addrsize);
   write (output,'  ');
END;  (* simerror *)


(* getword - get word from memory; abort run if address out of range
```

TABLE B-11 ONE-ADDRESS MACHINE EMULATOR (cont.)

```
 *)
PROCEDURE getword (VAR data, addr: word);
BEGIN
   IF NOT readmem (data,addr,traceref) THEN
   BEGIN
      simerror;
      write (output,'Address reference out of range.');
      exit;
   END;
END;  (* getword *)


(* putword - put word to memory; abort run if address out of range
 *)
PROCEDURE putword (VAR data, addr: word);
BEGIN
   IF NOT writemem (data,addr,null) THEN
   BEGIN
      simerror;
      write (output,'Address reference out of range.');
      exit;
   END
   ELSE
   BEGIN
      membounds (addr);
   END;
END;   (* putword *)


(* getmbr - load mbr based on immediate address mode field
 *)
PROCEDURE getmbr;
BEGIN
   IF mode = immediate THEN
   BEGIN
      mbr:= mar;
   END
   ELSE
   BEGIN
      getword (mbr,mar);
   END;
END;   (* getmbr *)


(* simtrace - trace execution of instruction if trace flag is set
 *)
PROCEDURE simtrace;
BEGIN
   IF traceref <> null THEN
   BEGIN
      IF tracefirst THEN
      BEGIN
         tracefirst:= false;
         page (output);
         writeln (output,' Trace of program execution:');
```

TABLE B-11 ONE-ADDRESS MACHINE EMULATOR (cont.)

```
        writeln (output);
      END;
      dumpregs (output);
      write (output,'    IR: ');
      writeword (output,ir,wordsize);
      getstr (tracestr,traceref);
      write (output,'   ');
      writestr (output,tracestr);
      writeln(output);
   END;
END;   (* simtrace *)


BEGIN    (* simrun *)
   running:= true;
   WHILE running DO
   BEGIN
      getword (ir,pc);
      simtrace;
      maskword (mar,ir,addrsize);
      lshword (ir,ir,-addrsize);
      maskword (tw,ir,modesize);
      mode:= wordtonum (tw);
      lshword (ir,ir,-modesize);
      maskword (tw,ir,opsize);
      op:= wordtonum (tw);
      CASE mode OF
      immediate:
         BEGIN
         END;
      direct:
         BEGIN
         END;
      indexed:
         BEGIN
            getword (tw,xrregno);
            addword (mar,mar,tw);
            maskword (mar,mar,addrsize);
         END;
      indirect:
         BEGIN
            getword (mbr,mar);
            maskword (mar,mbr,addrsize);
         END;
      END;
      incrementword (pc,pc);
      maskword (pc,pc,addrsize);

      IF op > maxop THEN
      BEGIN
         simerror;
         writeln (output,'Op-code out of bounds.');
         exit;
      END;
      CASE op OF
      haltop:  BEGIN
```

TABLE B-11 ONE-ADDRESS MACHINE EMULATOR (cont.)

```
                 running:= false;
              END;
    loadop:   BEGIN
                 getmbr;
                 putword (mbr,acregno);
              END;
    storeop:  BEGIN
                 getword (tw,acregno);
                 putword (tw,mar);
              END;
    callop:   BEGIN
                 putword(pc,mar);
                 incrementword (pc,mar);
                 maskword (pc,pc,addrsize);
              END;
    brop:     BEGIN
                 pc:= mar;
              END;
    breqop:   BEGIN
                 getword (tw,acregno);
                 IF testeqword (tw) THEN
                 BEGIN
                    pc:= mar;
                 END;
              END;
    brgeop:   BEGIN
                 getword (tw,acregno);
                 IF testgeword (tw) THEN
                 BEGIN
                    pc:= mar;
                 END;
              END;
    brltop:   BEGIN
                 getword (tw,acregno);
                 IF testltword (tw) THEN
                 BEGIN
                    pc:= mar;
                 END;
              END;
    addop:    BEGIN
                 getmbr;
                 getword (tw,acregno);
                 addword (tw,tw,mbr);
                 putword (tw,acregno);
              END;
    subop:    BEGIN
                 getmbr;
                 getword (tw,acregno);
                 subword (tw,tw,mbr);
                 putword (tw,acregno);
              END;
    mulop:    BEGIN
                 getmbr;
                 getword (tw,acregno);
                 mulword (tw,tw,mbr);
                 putword (tw,acregno);
```

TABLE B-11 ONE-ADDRESS MACHINE EMULATOR (cont.)

```
                END;
      divop:    BEGIN
                   getmbr;
                   getword (tw,acregno);
                   divword (tw,tw,mbr);
                   putword (tw,acregno);
                END;
      END;
   END;
END;   (* simrun *)


BEGIN  (* sim1 *)
   siminit;
   simload;
   simrun;
99:
   simdump;
END.   (* sim1 *)
```

TABLE B-12 TWO-ADDRESS MACHINE EMULATOR

```
(* Two-address machine emulator to accompany
 *    'Introduction to Machine and Assembly Language Programming'
 *     by Philip Gust,  published by Prentice-Hall Inc., 1985.
 *)
PROGRAM sim2 (object,output,keyboard,display,printer,disk);

LABEL
     99;                                        (* exit program *)


CONST
(******************************************************************************
 *
 *   Include CONST declarations for "machine2", "word", "string",
 *                                  "memory" and "io"
 *
 ******************************************************************************
 *)


TYPE
(******************************************************************************
 *
 *   Include TYPE declarations for "machine2", "word", "string",
 *                                  "memory" and "io"
 *
 ******************************************************************************
 *)


VAR
(******************************************************************************
 *
 *   Include VAR declarations for "word", "string", "memory" and "io"
 *
 ******************************************************************************
 *)

   object:      text;                           (* object file *)
   tw,                                          (* temporary word *)
   firstmem,                                    (* addr of first used mem *)
   lastmem,                                     (* addr of last used mem *)
   datareg,                                     (* data register number *)
   cmpr,                                        (* compare register *)
   pc,                                          (* program counter *)
   ir,                                          (* instruction register *)
   mar,                                         (* memory address register *)
   mbr:         word;                           (* memory buffer register *)
   op:          opcode;                         (* instr. opcode *)
   mode:        addrmode;                       (* instr. address mode *)
   tracefirst: boolean;                         (* output trace header flag *)
   tracestr:    string;                         (* for trace string *)
   traceref:    savestrindex;                   (* trace save string index *)
```

TABLE B-12 TWO-ADDRESS MACHINE EMULATOR (cont.)

```
(*****************************************************************************
 *
 *   Include procedures for "word", "string", "memory" and "io"
 *
 *****************************************************************************
 *)


(* exit - exit from program
 *)
PROCEDURE exit;
BEGIN
   GOTO 99;
END;  (* exit *)


(* siminit - initialize simulation
 *)
PROCEDURE siminit;
BEGIN
   wordinit;
   meminit;
   strinit;
   ioinit;
   cmpr:= zeroword;
   pc:= zeroword;
   ir:= zeroword;
   mar:= zeroword;
   mbr:= zeroword;
   notword (firstmem,zeroword);      (* build 2^(addrsize-1) - 1 *)
   maskword (firstmem,firstmem,addrsize-1);
   lastmem:= zeroword;
   tracefirst:= true;
END;   (* siminit *)


(* membounds - tracks first/last used memory addresses
 *)
PROCEDURE membounds (VAR addr: word);
VAR
  tw: word;
BEGIN
   tw:= addr;
   ashword (tw,tw,-regsize);
   IF NOT testeqword (tw) THEN          (* not a register *)
   BEGIN
      subword (tw,addr,firstmem);
      IF testltword (tw) THEN
      BEGIN
         firstmem:= addr;
      END;
      subword (tw,lastmem,addr);
      IF testltword (tw) THEN
      BEGIN
         lastmem:= addr;
```

TABLE B-12 TWO-ADDRESS MACHINE EMULATOR (cont.)

```
      END;
   END;
END;   (* membounds *)


(* simload - load memory from object file
 *)
PROCEDURE simload;
VAR
   addr,count,tw,w: word;


(* readobj - read next line of object file
 *)
PROCEDURE readobj (VAR objword: word);
VAR
   objline: string;
   i: strindex;
BEGIN
   IF eof (object) THEN
   BEGIN
      writeln (output,' LOAD: Unexpected EOF in object file.');
      exit;
   END;
   readstr (object,objline);
   readln (object);
   i:= 1;
   nexttoken (tracestr,objline,i,[' ']);
   IF NOT strtoword (objword,tracestr,octal) THEN
   BEGIN
      writeln (output,' LOAD: Bad line in object file.');
      exit;
   END;
   skipchar (objline,i,[' ']);
   nexttoken (tracestr,objline,i,[]);
END;   (* readobj *)


BEGIN  (* simload *)
   reset (object);
   IF eoln (object) THEN              (* empty file may have 1 empty line *)
   BEGIN
      readln (object);
   END;
   IF eof (object) THEN
   BEGIN
      writeln (output,' LOAD: Empty object file.');
      exit;
   END;
   readobj (pc);
   maskword (pc,pc,addrsize);
   WHILE NOT eof (object) DO
   BEGIN
      readobj (addr);
```

TABLE B-12 TWO-ADDRESS MACHINE EMULATOR (cont.)

```
      maskword (addr,addr,addrsize);
      readobj (count);
      decrementword (count,count);
      maskword (count,count,addrsize);
      membounds (addr);
      addword (tw,addr,count);
      membounds (tw);
      WHILE testgeword (count) DO
      BEGIN
         readobj (w);
         traceref:= null;
         IF strlen (tracestr) > 0 THEN
         BEGIN
            traceref:= putstr (tracestr);
            IF traceref = null THEN
            BEGIN
               writeln (output,' LOAD: Trace memory overflow.');
               exit;
            END;
         END;
         IF NOT writemem (w,addr,traceref) THEN
         BEGIN
            writeln (output,' LOAD: Address out of range.');
            exit;
         END;
         incrementword (addr,addr);
         decrementword (count,count);
      END;
   END;
END;   (* simload *)


(* dumpregs - dump the contents of registers to file f
 *)
PROCEDURE dumpregs (VAR f: text);
VAR
   readok: boolean;
   i: regindex;
   regno,regval: word;
   junkref: savestrindex;
BEGIN
   regno:= zeroword;
   FOR i:= 0 TO maxreg DO
   BEGIN
      write (f,'    R');
      write (f,i:reglen);
      write (f,': ');
      readok:= readmem (regval,regno,junkref);
      writeword (f,regval,wordsize);
      IF (i MOD 4) = 3 THEN
      BEGIN
         writeln (f);
      END;
      incrementword (regno,regno);
   END;
```

TABLE B-12 TWO-ADDRESS MACHINE EMULATOR (cont.)

```
   IF (maxreg MOD 4) <> 3 THEN
   BEGIN
      writeln (f);
   END;
END;  (* dumpregs *)


(* simdump - dump contents of used portions of memory
 *)
PROCEDURE simdump;
VAR
   readok: boolean;
   i: integer;
   w: word;
BEGIN
   subword (w,lastmem,firstmem);
   IF testgeword (w) THEN                  (* if memory has been loaded *)
   BEGIN
      page (output);
      write (output,' Program halted at  PC: ');
      writeword (output,pc,addrsize);
      writeln (output);
      writeln (output);
      writeln (output);
      writeln (output,' Registers:');
      writeln (output);
      dumpregs (output);
      lshword (firstmem,firstmem,-2);      (* closest multiple of 4 words *)
      lshword (firstmem,firstmem,2);
      writeln (output);
      writeln (output);
      writeln (output,' Memory:');
      writeln (output);
      REPEAT
         write (output,'    ');
         writeword (output,firstmem,addrsize);
         write (output,':');
         FOR i:= 0 TO 3 DO                 (* print 4 words per row *)
         BEGIN
            write (output,'   ');
            readok:= readmem (w,firstmem,traceref);
            writeword (output,w,wordsize);
            incrementword (firstmem,firstmem);
         END;
         writeln (output);
         subword (w,lastmem,firstmem);
      UNTIL testltword (w);
   END;
END;  (* simdump *)


(* simrun - run program in memory, starting at current pc
 *)
PROCEDURE simrun;
```

TABLE B-12 TWO-ADDRESS MACHINE EMULATOR (cont.)

```
VAR
   running: boolean;


(* simerror - report run-time error
 *)
PROCEDURE simerror;
BEGIN
   write (output,' RUN: Error at PC= ');
   writeword (output,pc,addrsize);
   write (output,'  ');
END;  (* simerror *)


(* getword - get word from memory; abort run if address out of range
 *)
PROCEDURE getword (VAR data, addr: word);
BEGIN
   IF NOT readmem (data,addr,traceref) THEN
   BEGIN
      simerror;
      writeln (output,'Address reference out of range reading from memory.');
      exit;
   END;
END;  (* getword *)


(* putword - put word to memory; abort run if address out of range
 *)
PROCEDURE putword (VAR data, addr: word);
BEGIN
   IF NOT writemem (data,addr,null) THEN
   BEGIN
      simerror;
      writeln (output,'Address reference out of range writing to memory.');
      exit;
   END
   ELSE
   BEGIN
      membounds (addr);
   END;
END;   (* putword *)


(* signextend - extend address word to full signed word
 *)
PROCEDURE signextend (VAR result, operand: word);
BEGIN
   lshword (result,operand,addrsize);
   ashword (result,result,-addrsize);
END;   (* signextend *)


(* getmbr - load mbr based on immediate address mode field
 *)
```

TABLE B-12 TWO-ADDRESS MACHINE EMULATOR (cont.)

```
PROCEDURE getmbr;
BEGIN
   IF mode = immediate THEN
   BEGIN
      signextend (mbr,mar);
   END
   ELSE
   BEGIN
      getword (mbr,mar);
   END;
END;   (* getmbr *)


(* simtrace - trace execution of instruction if trace flag is set
 *)
PROCEDURE simtrace;
BEGIN
   IF traceref <> null THEN
   BEGIN
      IF tracefirst THEN
      BEGIN
         tracefirst:= false;
         page (output);
         writeln (output,' Trace of program execution:');
         writeln (output);
      END;
      dumpregs (output);
      write (output,'    PC: ');
      writeword (output,pc,addrsize);
      write (output,'         IR: ');
      writeword (output,ir,wordsize);
      getstr (tracestr,traceref);
      write (output,'    ');
      writestr (output,tracestr);
      writeln(output);
   END;
END;   (* simtrace *)


BEGIN  (* simrun *)
   running:= true;
   WHILE running DO
   BEGIN
      getword (ir,pc);
      simtrace;
      maskword (mar,ir,addrsize);
      lshword (ir,ir,-addrsize);
      maskword (tw,ir,modesize);
      mode:= wordtonum (tw);
      lshword (ir,ir,-modesize);
      IF mode >= indexed THEN                      (* assumes order of modes *)
      BEGIN
         maskword (tw,ir,regsize);
         getword (tw,tw);
         signextend (mar,mar);
```

TABLE B-12 TWO-ADDRESS MACHINE EMULATOR (cont.)

```
      addword (mar,mar,tw);
      maskword (mar,mar,addrsize);
      mode:= mode - indexed;
   END;
   IF mode >= indirect THEN                    (* assumes order of modes *)
   BEGIN
      getword (mar,mar);
      maskword (mar,mar,addrsize);
      mode:= mode - indirect;
   END;
   lshword (ir,ir,-regsize);
   maskword (tw,ir,regsize);
   datareg:= tw;
   lshword (ir,ir,-regsize);
   op:= wordtonum (ir);
   incrementword (pc,pc);
   maskword (pc,pc,addrsize);


   IF op > maxop THEN
   BEGIN
      simerror;
      writeln (output,'Op-code out of bounds.');
      exit;
   END;
   CASE op OF
   haltop:     BEGIN
                  running:= false;
               END;
   loadop:     BEGIN
                  getmbr;
                  putword (mbr,datareg);
                  cmpr:= mbr;
               END;
   storeop:    BEGIN
                  getword (mbr,datareg);
                  putword (mbr,mar);
               END;
   brop:       BEGIN
                  pc:= mar;
               END;
   cmprop:     BEGIN
                  getmbr;
                  getword (tw,datareg);
                  IF testltword (tw) <> testltword (mbr) THEN
                  BEGIN
                     cmpr:= tw;
                  END
                  ELSE
                  BEGIN
                     subword (cmpr,tw,mbr);
                  END;
               END;
   breqop:     BEGIN
                  IF testeqword (cmpr) THEN
                  BEGIN
```

TABLE B-12 TWO-ADDRESS MACHINE EMULATOR (cont.)

```
                    pc:= mar;
                 END;
              END;
   brneop:    BEGIN
                 IF NOT testeqword (cmpr) THEN
                 BEGIN
                    pc:= mar;
                 END;
              END;
   brgtop:    BEGIN
                 IF testgeword (cmpr) AND (NOT testeqword (cmpr))  THEN
                 BEGIN
                    pc:= mar;
                 END;
              END;
   brltop:    BEGIN
                 IF testltword (cmpr) THEN
                 BEGIN
                    pc:= mar;
                 END;
              END;
   brgeop:    BEGIN
                 IF testgeword (cmpr) THEN
                 BEGIN
                    pc:= mar;
                 END;
              END;
   brleop:    BEGIN
                 IF testltword (cmpr) OR testeqword (cmpr)  THEN
                 BEGIN
                    pc:= mar;
                 END;
              END;
   pushop:    BEGIN
                 getmbr;
                 getword (tw,datareg);
                 decrementword (tw,tw);
                 putword (tw,datareg);
                 putword (mbr,tw);
                 getword (cmpr,datareg);
              END;
   popop:     BEGIN
                 getword (tw,datareg);
                 getword (mbr,tw);
                 putword (mbr,mar);
                 getword (tw,datareg);
                 incrementword (tw,tw);
                 putword (tw,datareg);
                 cmpr:= tw;
              END;
   callop:    BEGIN
                 getword (tw,datareg);
                 decrementword (tw,tw);
                 putword (tw,datareg);
                 putword (pc,tw);
                 pc:= mar;
```

TABLE B-12 TWO-ADDRESS MACHINE EMULATOR (cont.)

```
                  getword (cmpr,datareg);
               END;
     rtnop:    BEGIN
                  getword (tw,datareg);
                  getword (pc,tw);
                  maskword (pc,pc,addrsize);
                  incrementword (tw,tw);
                  putword (tw,datareg);
                  cmpr:= tw;
               END;
     addop:    BEGIN
                  getmbr;
                  getword (tw,datareg);
                  addword (tw,tw,mbr);
                  putword (tw,datareg);
                  cmpr:= tw;
               END;
     subop:    BEGIN
                  getmbr;
                  getword (tw,datareg);
                  subword (tw,tw,mbr);
                  putword (tw,datareg);
                  cmpr:= tw;
               END;
     mulop:    BEGIN
                  getmbr;
                  getword (tw,datareg);
                  mulword (tw,tw,mbr);
                  putword (tw,datareg);
                  cmpr:= tw;
               END;
     divop:    BEGIN
                  getmbr;
                  getword (tw,datareg);
                  divword (tw,tw,mbr);
                  putword (tw,datareg);
                  cmpr:= tw;
               END;
     andop:    BEGIN
                  getmbr;
                  getword (tw,datareg);
                  andword (tw,tw,mbr);
                  putword (tw,datareg);
                  cmpr:= tw;
               END;
     orop:     BEGIN
                  getmbr;
                  getword (tw,datareg);
                  orword (tw,tw,mbr);
                  putword (tw,datareg);
                  cmpr:= tw;
               END;
     xorop:    BEGIN
                  getmbr;
```

TABLE B-12 TWO-ADDRESS MACHINE EMULATOR (cont.)

```
                    getword (tw,datareg);
                    xorword (tw,tw,mbr);
                    putword (tw,datareg);
                    cmpr:= tw;
                 END;
      notop:     BEGIN
                    getmbr;
                    notword (tw,mbr);
                    putword (tw,datareg);
                    cmpr:= tw;
                 END;
      ashop:     BEGIN
                    getmbr;
                    getword (tw,datareg);
                    ashword (tw,tw,wordtonum (mbr));
                    putword (tw,datareg);
                    cmpr:= tw;
                 END;
      cshop:     BEGIN
                    getmbr;
                    getword (tw,datareg);
                    cshword (tw,tw,wordtonum (mbr));
                    putword (tw,datareg);
                    cmpr:= tw;
                 END;
      lshop:     BEGIN
                    getmbr;
                    getword (tw,datareg);
                    lshword (tw,tw,wordtonum (mbr));
                    putword (tw,datareg);
                    cmpr:= tw;
                 END;
      inchrop:   BEGIN
                    getio (mbr,mar);
                    putword (mbr,datareg);
                    cmpr:= mbr;
                 END;
      outchrop:  BEGIN
                    getword (mbr,datareg);
                    putio (mbr,mar);
                 END;
      iostatop:  BEGIN
                    statio (mbr,mar);
                    putword (mbr,datareg);
                    cmpr:= mbr;
                 END;
      iocmdop:   BEGIN
                    getword (mbr,datareg);
                    cmdio (mbr,mar);
                 END;
      END;
   END;
END;   (* simrun *)
```

TABLE B-12 TWO-ADDRESS MACHINE EMULATOR (cont.)

```
BEGIN  (* sim2 *)
   siminit;
   simload;
   simrun;
99:
   simdump;
   ioflush;
END.   (* sim2 *)
```

TABLE B-13 STACK-BASED CALCULATOR TO TEST WORD AND STRING OPERATIONS

```
(* Stack-based calculator to test new implementations of word
 *  and string operations -- to accompany
 *    'Introduction to Machine and Assembly Language Programming '
 *     by Philip Gust, published by Prentice-Hall Inc., 1985.
 *)
PROGRAM wordstk (input,output);

CONST
(****************************************************************************
 *
 *   Include CONST declarations for "machine1"/"machine2", "word" and "string"
 *
 ****************************************************************************
 *)

   maxstack = 30;

TYPE
(****************************************************************************
 *
 *   Include TYPE declarations for "machine1"/"machine2", "word" and "string"
 *
 ****************************************************************************
 *)

   stkindex = 0..maxstack;
   wordstack = ARRAY [stkindex] OF word;

VAR
(****************************************************************************
 *
 *   Include VAR declarations for "word" and "string"
 *
 ****************************************************************************
 *)

   w1,w2: word;
   line: string;
   i: strindex;
   stack: wordstack;
   sp: stkindex;


(****************************************************************************
 *
 *   Include procedures for "word" and "string"
 *
 ****************************************************************************
 *)


(* initstack - initialize word stack
 *)
PROCEDURE initstack;
BEGIN
```

TABLE B-13 STACK-BASED CALCULATOR TO TEST WORK AND STRING OPERATIONS (cont.)

```
   strinit;
   wordinit;
   sp:= 0;
END;   (* initstack *)


(* pushword - push a word onto the stack
 *)
PROCEDURE pushword (VAR operand: word);
BEGIN
   IF sp > maxstack THEN
   BEGIN
      writeln ('*** stack is full -- word was not pushed.');
   END
   ELSE
   BEGIN
      stack[sp]:= operand;
      sp:= sp + 1;
   END;
END;   (* pushword *)


(* popword - pop and return the top word from the stack
 *)
PROCEDURE popword (VAR operand: word);
BEGIN
   IF sp <= 0 THEN
   BEGIN
      writeln ('*** stack is empty -- zero was returned.');
      numtoword (operand,0);
   END
   ELSE
   BEGIN
      sp:= sp - 1;
      operand:= stack[sp];
   END;
END;   (* popword *)


(* writestk - write contents of stack
 *)
PROCEDURE writestack;
VAR
   i: integer;
BEGIN
   write ('-->  ');
   IF sp <= 0 THEN
   BEGIN
      writeln ('*empty*');
   END
   ELSE
   BEGIN
      FOR i:= sp-1 DOWNTO 0 DO
      BEGIN
         writeword (output,stack[i],wordsize);
         write ('B');
```

TABLE B-13 STACK-BASED CALCULATOR TO TEST WORK AND STRING OPERATIONS (cont.)

```
         writeln;
         write ('     ');
      END;
   END;
   writeln;
END;   (* writestack *)

BEGIN   (* wordstk *)
   initstack;
   writeln ('Stack-based calculator for ',wordsize:1,'-bit word operations:');
   IF eoln THEN
   BEGIN
      readln;
   END;
   WHILE NOT eof DO
   BEGIN
      readstr (input,line); readln;
      i:= 1; skipchar (line, i, [' ']);
      nexttoken (line, line, i, [' ']);
      IF strtoword (w1,line,decimal) THEN
      BEGIN
         pushword (w1);
      END
      ELSE IF NOT (nextchar (line,1) IN  ['?','#','.','^',':','+','-',
                                          '*','/','%','_','~','&','|',
                                          '@','!','<','{','('])     THEN
      BEGIN
         writeln ('Please try again...');
      END
      ELSE
      BEGIN
         CASE nextchar (line,1) OF

         '?':  BEGIN
                  writeln;
                  write ('?   Help                              ');
                  write ('n   Push number n                     ');
                  writeln;
                  write ('#   Show contents of stack            ');
                  write ('.   Show and delete top word          ');
                  writeln;
                  write ('^   push copy of top stack word       ');
                  write (':   exchange top two words            ');
                  writeln;
                  write ('+   Add top two words                 ');
                  write ('-   Subtract top two words            ');
                  writeln;
                  write ('*   Multiplies top two words          ');
                  write ('/   Divides top two words             ');
                  writeln;
                  write ('%   Increments top word               ');
                  write ('_   Decrements top word               ');
                  writeln;
                  write ('~   Negative of top word              ');
                  write ('&   And top two words                 ');
                  writeln;
```

TABLE B-13 STACK-BASED CALCULATOR TO TEST WORK AND STRING OPERATIONS (cont.)

```
            write ('|   Or top two words                   ');
            write ('@   Xor top two words                  ');
            writeln;
            write ('!   Not of top word                    ');
            write ('<   Lsh 2nd word by top word           ');
            writeln;
            write ('{   Ash 2nd word by top word           ');
            write ('(   Csh 2nd word by top word           ');
            writeln;
         END;
   '.':  BEGIN
            popword (w1);
            write ('pop> ');
            writeword (output,w1,wordsize);
            write ('B');
            writeln;
         END;
   '#':  BEGIN
            writestack;
         END;
   '&':  BEGIN
            popword (w2);
            popword (w1);
            andword (w1,w1,w2);
            pushword (w1);
         END;
   '|':  BEGIN
            popword (w2);
            popword (w1);
            orword (w1,w1,w2);
            pushword (w1);
         END;
   '@':  BEGIN
            popword (w2);
            popword (w1);
            xorword (w1,w1,w2);
            pushword (w1);
         END;
   '%':  BEGIN
            popword (w1);
            incrementword (w1,w1);
            pushword (w1);
         END;
   '_':  BEGIN
            popword (w1);
            decrementword (w1,w1);
            pushword (w1);
         END;
   '!':  BEGIN
            popword (w1);
            notword (w1,w1);
            pushword (w1);
         END;
   '^':  BEGIN
```

TABLE B-13 STACK-BASED CALCULATOR TO TEST WORK AND STRING OPERATIONS (cont.)

```
          popword (w1);
          pushword (w1);
          pushword (w1);
       END;
  ':': BEGIN
          popword (w2);
          popword (w1);
          pushword (w2);
          pushword (w1);
       END;
  '+': BEGIN
          popword (w2);
          popword (w1);
          addword (w1,w1,w2);
          pushword (w1);
       END;
  '~': BEGIN
          popword (w1);
          negativeword(w1,w1);
          pushword (w1);
       END;
  '-': BEGIN
          popword (w2);
          popword (w1);
          subword (w1,w1,w2);
          pushword (w1);
       END;
  '*': BEGIN
          popword (w2);
          popword (w1);
          mulword (w1,w1,w2);
          pushword (w1);
       END;
  '/': BEGIN
          popword (w2);
          popword (w1);
          divword (w1,w2,w1);
          pushword (w1);
       END;
  '<': BEGIN
          popword (w2);
          popword (w1);
          lshword (w1,w1,wordtonum (w2));
          pushword (w1);
       END;
  '{': BEGIN
          popword (w2);
          popword (w1);
          ashword (w1,w1,wordtonum (w2));
          pushword (w1);
       END;
  '(': BEGIN
          popword (w2);
          popword (w1);
```

TABLE B-13 STACK-BASED CALCULATOR TO TEST WORK AND STRING OPERATIONS (cont.)

```
                  cshword (w1,w1,wordtonum (w2));
                  pushword (w1);
               END;
         END;
      END;
   END;
END.   (* wordstk *)
```

Index